OECD Reviews of Risk Management Policies

Boosting Resilience through Innovative Risk Governance

INSIGHTS FROM AUSTRIA, FRANCE AND SWITZERLAND

OECD
BETTER POLICIES FOR BETTER LIVES

This work is published under the responsibility of the Secretary-General of the OECD. The opinions expressed and arguments employed herein do not necessarily reflect the official views of OECD member countries.

This document, as well as any data and any map included herein, are without prejudice to the status of or sovereignty over any territory, to the delimitation of international frontiers and boundaries and to the name of any territory, city or area.

Please cite this publication as:
OECD (2017), *Boosting Resilience through Innovative Risk Governance: Insights from Austria, France and Switzerland*, OECD Reviews of Risk Management Policies, OECD Publishing, Paris.
http://dx.doi.org/10.1787/9789264281370-en

ISBN 978-92-64-28136-3 (print)
ISBN 978-92-64-28137-0 (PDF)

Series: OECD Reviews of Risk Management Policies
ISSN 1993-4092 (print)
ISSN 1993-4106 (online)

The statistical data for Israel are supplied by and under the responsibility of the relevant Israeli authorities. The use of such data by the OECD is without prejudice to the status of the Golan Heights, East Jerusalem and Israeli settlements in the West Bank under the terms of international law.

Photo credits: Cover © Vector Market/Shutterstock.com, © Shico/Shutterstock.com

Corrigenda to OECD publications may be found on line at: *www.oecd.org/about/publishing/corrigenda.htm*.

Foreword

Natural and human-induced disasters have disruptive impacts on societies and economies, especially at the local level. Repeated episodes of flooding can create significant economic stress, especially when countries' major urban areas are affected. Wildfires have proven challenging to contain in countries as diverse as Australia, Greece, France, Portugal, the US and Canada. Longer dry periods followed by extreme precipitation, such as California recently experienced, challenge governments' risk prevention capacities in many regions. Above all, disasters, such as the major earthquakes in Japan, New Zealand, Italy or Chile can probe countries' risk management abilities and create significant challenges for crafting appropriate prevention policy responses.

What can governments do to increase economic and social resilience in an interconnected world through disaster risk prevention and mitigation? This book provides concrete examples building upon the policy propositions put forward in the OECD report *Boosting Resilience through Innovative Risk Governance*, published in 2014. That report showed countries know quite well what can be done to strengthen disaster risk prevention and mitigation - the lack of knowledge or awareness is not the main stumbling block, but rather the "how to do it".

By looking at the country case studies of Austria, France and Switzerland the results of this report show that a number of promising country disaster risk prevention initiatives are emerging: countries have started bridging sectoral and geographical divides, bringing relevant actors together to focus on the functional area for disaster risk prevention, rather than one that is limited by administrative or line ministerial boundaries. To boost compliance with, and show their commitment to, the enforcement of existing prevention legislations, countries have followed unprecedented legal actions in the realm of hazard informed land use decisions. Although last resort measures, such as resettlement out of high risk areas, continue to face reluctance among policy makers, good practice cases emerge that can guide future policy decisions. Solidarity is the guiding principle for governments' engagements in disaster risk prevention. Nevertheless, countries recognise that their support needs to be designed in a way that fosters all actors' contributions, instead of crowding them out. Nevertheless, challenges remain and are omnipresent: risk awareness is one of them. Maintaining risk awareness at the levels sparked by major disasters is something policy makers across countries continue to look for guidance on. Many innovative communication efforts do not yield the expected results.

This report was prepared with the support of the Public Governance Directorate under the auspices of the OECD's High Level Risk Forum, which promotes an integrated, whole-of-government approach to risk management and governance. The Forum brings together policy makers from governments, practitioners from the private sector and civil society and experts from think tanks and academia to identify and share good practices and deepen their understanding of risk management. The work of the Forum is underpinned by the Recommendation of the OECD Council on the Governance of Critical Risks. The results will be of interest to international discussions on resilience at European and global level, including through the United Nations as part of the implementation of the Sendai Framework for Disaster Risk Reduction and the post-2015 Sustainable Development Goals.

Acknowledgements

This report was prepared under the auspices of the OECD High Level Risk Forum by the OECD Public Governance Directorate, led by Rolf Alter.

The report was co-ordinated and written by Cathérine Désirée Gamper. Stéphane Jacobzone, Deputy Head of the Reform of the Public Sector Division, and Jack Radisch, Senior Project Manager supervised the work. The authors would like to thank Pierre Alain Schieb and Walter Amman for valuable guidance and feedback throughout the project. The Secretariat is grateful for comments and suggestions received from colleagues at the OECD, including Charles Baubion (Public Governance Directorate), Michael Mullan (Environment Directorate), Leigh Wolfrom (Directorate for Financial and Enterprise Affairs). Highly valuable research assistance was provided by Melissa Li (Austria), Marien Pirot (France), and Teresa Deubelli (Switzerland), who also contributed to drafting the synthesis.

The study benefited from the many insights of country focal points: Maria Patek and Andreas Pichler (Austria); Christophe Ballet-Daz, Jessica Gentric, Elsa Laganier, Mathieu Morel, Bérangère Basin, and Marie-Pierre Meganck (France); Andreas Götz and Helen Gosteli (Switzerland). The Secretariat is also grateful for the contribution from the following individuals, for their active role during the missions or feedback during the process: *Austria:* Christoph Hackel, Franz Sinnabell, Sven Fuchs, Gerhard Mannsberger, Karl Schwaiger, Clemens Neuhold, Siegfried Jachs, Christian Rachoy, Thomas Hlatky, Helmut Habersack, Johannes Hübl, Elisabeth Stix, Leonhard Krimpelstätter, Helmut Mödlhammer, Michael Obermoser, Robert Loiyl, Michael Mitter, Josef Schwaiger, Siegfried Feiersigner, Astrid Rössler. *Switzerland:* Markus Wyss, Dr. Markus Zimmermann, Raymond Beutler, Stephan Zellmeyer, Matthias Künzler, Veronika Röthlisberger, Josef Hess, Gian Reto Bezzola, Philippe Arnold, Melanie Butterling, Markus Hohl, Christoph Werner, Hans-Peter Wyss, Martin Kamber, Christoph Hegg, Willy Eyer, Bruno Spicher, Prof. Margreth Keiler, Prof. Rolf Weingartner. *France:* Christophe Charrier, Gilles Rat, Michael Prevost, Daniel Marcovitch, Patrick Bidan, Antoine Quantin, Nancy Spinousa, Francis Poupel, Nicolas Bauduceau, Vincent Roque, Jen-Paul Bravard, Luc Levasseur, Gilbert Mergoud, Elodie Perrichon, Jean Luc Masson, Jean Pierre Gautier, Julien Langumier, Gilles Brocard, Alain Delaeuf, Celine Calpena, Stéphane Guérin, Claire Bernard, Guillaume Rousset, P. Vauterin, Yves Picoche, Christell Duc.

Liv Gaunt, Marie-Claude Gohier and Lynda Hawe prepared the report for publication. Kate Lancaster shared her editorial comments. The team is very grateful for assistance provided by Elisabeth Huggard and Susan Rantalainen throughout the project.

Acronyms and abbreviations

APSFR	Areas of Potentially Significant Flood Risk (Austria)
ARE	The Federal Office for Spatial Development (Switzerland)
ASA	Authorized unions (*associations syndicales autorisées)* (France)
BMF	Ministry of Finance (Austria)
BMI	Federal Ministry of Interior (Austria)
BMLFUW	Ministry of Agriculture, Forestry, Environment and Water Management (Austria)
BMLVS	Ministry of Defence and Sports (Austria)
BMVIT	Federal Ministry of Transport, Innovation and Technology Management (Austria)
BRGM	Bureau for Geological Research and Mining (France)
BWV	Federal Water Engineering Administration (Austria)
CATNAT	Natural catastrophes compensation scheme (France)
CBA	Cost-benefit analysis
CCR	Central Reinsurance Fund (*Caisse Centrale de Réassurance*) (France)
CDRNM	Departmental Commission of Major Natural Hazards (*Commission Départementale des Risques Naturels Majeurs)* (France)
CDRNM	Departmental Commission of Major Natural Hazards (*Commission Départementale des Risques Naturels Majeurs)* (France)
CEPRI	European Centre for Flood Risk Prevention (*Centre Européen de Prévention du risque d'inondation)* (France)
CI	critical infrastructure
CIB	Flood Commission of the Basin *(Comité Inondation de Bassin)* (France)
CMI	central-level Joint Flood Commission (*Commission Mixte Inondations)* (France)
CNR	National Company of the Rhone (*Compagnie Nationale du Rhône)* (France)
COGIC	Operational Centre for Interministerial Crisis Management (*Centre Opérationnel de Gestion Interministérielle des Crises)* (France)
CPER	State-Region Contracts (*Contrats de Plan État-Région)* (France)
DDT (M)	sub-national service arms of the MEDDE at the department level (*directions départementales des territoires (de la mer)* (France)
DDT(M)	Ministry of Ecology at departmental level (*directions départementale des Territoires)* (France)
DEAL	Directorate for Environment, Planning and Housing *(Direction de l'Environnement, de l'Aménagement et du Logement)* (France – overseas territories)

DETEC	Federal Department of the Environment, Transport, Energy and Communications (Switzerland)
DGPR	Directorate General for Risk Prevention (*Direction Générale de la Prévention des Risques*) (France)
DGSCGC	General Directorate for Civil Protection and Crisis Management (*Direction Générale de la Sécurité Civile et de la Gestion des Crises)* (France)
DHA	Daily Hazard Assessment (United Kingdom)
DICRIM	Local community information document about major prevailing risks (*Documents d'Information Communal sur les Risques Majeurs* (France)
DREAL	Regional Directorate for Environment, Planning and Housing (*Direction Régionale de l'Environnement, de l'Aménagement et du Logement)* (France)
EDF	Électricité de France
EFAS	European Flood Awareness System
EFD	Federal Department of Finance (Switzerland)
EPCI	public establishments for inter-communal co-operation (*Établissement Public de Coopération Intercommunale)* (France)
ERDF	European Regional Development Fund
ERP	European Recovery Fund
ETHZ	Swiss Federal Institute of Technology Zurich (*Eidgenössische Technische Hochschule Zürich*)
EU	European Union
EUSF	European Union Solidarity Fund
FAN	Natural Hazard Experts *(Fachleute Naturgefahren)* (Switzerland)
FEDRO	Federal Roads Office (Switzerland)
FINMA	Federal Financial Market Supervisory Authority (*Eidgenössische Finanzmarktaufsicht)* (Switzerland)
FOCP	Federal Office for Civil Protection (Switzerland)
FOEN	Federal Office for the Environment (Switzerland)
FPRNM	Fund for the Prevention of Major Natural Hazards (*Fonds de Prévention des Risques Naturels Majeurs)* or Barnier Fund (France)
GDP	Gross domestic product
GEMAPI	management of aquatic environments (*gestion des milieux aquatiques et prévention des inondations*) (France)
H(F)RAs	High Risk and High Flood Risk Areas (France)
HRA	High Risk Areas
IRV	Inter-cantonal Re-insurance Association (*Interkantonaler Rückversicherungsverband)* (Switzerland)
KatFonds	*Katastrophenfonds* (Austrian Catastrophe Fund)
LAINAT	Steering Committee Intervention in Natural Hazards (Switzerland)
MAPTAM	French law on modernising local public action and promoting metropolitan regions (*loi de modernisation de l'action publique territoriale et d'affirmation des métropoles)*
MEDDE	Ministry of Ecology, Sustainable Development and Energy (France)
MeteoSwiss	Federal Office for Meteorology and Climatology (Switzerland)

MLETR	*Ministère de l'Aménagement du territoire, de la Ruralité et des Collectivités territoriales* (Ministry of Territorial Equality, Housing and of Rurality (France)
NGOs	non-governmental organisations
NHP	United Kingdom's Natural Hazard Partnership
NPV	net present value (France)
NRA	National Risk Assessment
ÖBB	Austrian railway services
ÖeNB	Austrian National Bank
ONRN	*Observatoire National des Risques Naturels* (French National Risk Observatory)
ÖROK	Austrian Spatial Planning Conference
PAPI	Flood Prevention Action Program (*Programme d'Action de Prévention des Inondations)*
PER	new land use policy and urban development regulation (*Plans d'exposition aux Risques Naturels Prévisibles)* (France)
PGRI	Flood Risk Management Plan (Plan Gestion des Risques d'Inondation (France)
PIBs	Cantonal Public Insurance Companies for Buildings (*Kantonale Gebäudeversicherungen*) (Switzerland)
PLANALP	Natural Hazards Platform of the Alpine Convention
PLANAT	Swiss National Platform for Natural Hazards
PLU	*Plan Local d'Urbanisme* (France)
PPI	Particular Intervention Plan (*Plan Particulier d'Intervention)* (France)
PPR	Risk Prevention Plan (*Plan de Prévention des Risques)* (France)
PPRI	national and basin-level Flood Risk Management Plan (France)
PPRNs	Prevention Plans against Natural Risks (France)
ProClim	Forum for climate and global change (Switzerland)
PSR	Coastal/Flash Flood Plans *(Plan Submersion Rapide)* (France)
PSRs	Flood Prevention Action Programs
SAGYRC	*Syndicat Intercommunal du Bassin de l'Yzeron* (France)
SED	Swiss Seismological Service (*Erdbebendienst)*
SGDNS	General Secretariat for defence and national security (France)
SGG	Swiss society for public utility (*Schweizerische Gemeinnützige Gesellschaft*)
SHR	*Syndicat du Haut Rhône* (France)
SKKM	National Crisis and Disaster Protection Management (Austria)
SLF	Swiss Institute for Snow and Avalanche Research
SNGRI	National Flood Risk Management Strategy (*Stratégie Nationale de Gestion des Risques* d'Inondation) (France)
SVV	Swiss Insurance Association (*Schweizerischer Versicherungsverband)*
SYMADREM	*Syndicat Mixte Interrégional d'aménagement des Digues du Delta du Rhône à la Mer* (France)
UNISDR	United Nations Office for Disaster Risk Reduction

VKF	Association of Cantonal Fire Insurance Companies (Switzerland)
VVO	Austrian Insurance Association
WaG	Federal Law of Forestry (Switzerland)
WBG	Federal Law for Water Engineering (Switzerland)
WLV	Austrian Service for Torrent and Avalanche Control (Austria)
WSL	Federal Institute for Forest, Snow and Landscape Research (Switzerland)

Table of contents

Tables

Figures

Boxes

Executive summary

Countries have made significant progress in strengthening resilience to disasters and crises through prevention and mitigation, including an increased understanding of how critical risks can be managed. However, vulnerabilities persist in an ever-changing environment that creates gaps in countries' disaster risk prevention efforts. Existing protective infrastructure may no longer offer the level of protection for which the investments were initially made, due to inadequate maintenance. Regulatory frameworks may not keep pace with the changing risk environments, and enforcement tends to be inconsistent. Despite widespread recognition of the importance of whole-of-society efforts for improving resilience, implementing such broad initiatives requires significant energy and the capacity to mobilise a range of actors.

This report presents the findings of a cross-country comparative analysis designed to test policy recommendations from previous work in concrete country policy contexts. The three case studies (Austria, France and Switzerland) document, evaluate and compare progress in strengthening disaster risk prevention and mitigation efforts.

How can countries get the right policy mix to achieve successful disaster risk prevention?

While structural disaster risk prevention measures generally receive lower attention from central governments than in previous periods of growth and higher public investment, the results of the study show strong demand for such measures at the local level. In a resource-tight environment this tension is difficult to resolve.

Governments are confronted with growing liabilities arising from previous structural investment in disaster risk prevention. Austria, France and Switzerland have a large stock of protective infrastructure, but are now facing the challenge of ensuring those structures maintain their original level of protection. This will require investments in the maintenance and strengthening of works, but none of the cases included sufficient resources in initial financing plans.

National governments are gradually embracing a whole-of-society approach to strengthening disaster risk prevention. Austria, France and Switzerland increasingly recognise the value of non-governmental stakeholder participation in disaster risk prevention. Bottom-up initiatives, such as Austria's water boards, which include local beneficiaries, have unlocked additional prevention investments, while local ownership resulted in better maintenance of protective infrastructure.

Effective disaster risk management requires advanced hazard and risk assessment. All three countries provide central technical capacity and resources to subnational governments to ensure high-quality and widely available hazard information. Nevertheless, challenges persist in harmonising and updating hazard information. Furthermore, hazard assessments do not assess exposures and vulnerabilities of populations and assets – information necessary for informed policy decisions. Where available, risk assessments often fall short of assessing potential cascading impacts, which is the largest challenge in dealing with major critical risks across OECD countries.

The integration of hazard and risk information into land-use decisions remains problematic. In Austria, questions were raised about the effectiveness of putting local decision makers in charge of land-use decisions. In France, municipalities that ignored high-risk areas when issuing construction permits faced unprecedented legal action. Hazard-informed land-use planning has been most successful in high-risk areas, where construction bans were issued and enforced, while damages in lower-hazard zones in Switzerland have actually increased because of less stringent enforcement.

Resettlements out of high-risk areas are a disaster risk prevention measure of last resort. This option is the least used among prevention measures, due to its cost. The political and legal implications have been recognised as very challenging. Good practice cases, such as the Machland Dam in Austria, can provide guidance when resettlement becomes necessary. In cases of successful resettlements, governments have dedicated time to the process, instead of enforcing swift resettlement. Relocations were organised in a way that ensured community coherence and minimised costs for affected communities.

Maintaining momentum and strengthening awareness remains difficult. Although risk communication is considered the most important prevention policy across OECD countries, risk managers in the three countries studied still struggle with persistently low levels of risk awareness among their citizens, especially in the absence of recent major disasters.

Business continuity management is crucial to maintaining basic functions and facilitating a swift return to business as usual. Austria, France and Switzerland have recognised the essential role of business continuity planning for rapidly regaining functionality after a disaster. Technical guidelines and good practice toolkits are widely available, but implementation has been slow.

How can countries make disaster risk prevention work? The need for crossing boundaries

Remarkable progress has been made in bridging sectoral and geographical divides. Switzerland's PLANAT is a good example of a how a multi-stakeholder platform can co-ordinate cross-sectoral priorities for disaster risk management. Austria's ÖROK has been effective in co-ordinating cross-sectoral and cross-governmental priorities for spatial development. Geographical dimensions are also given more importance in risk management. Austria and France have embraced catchment-wide approaches for water-related hazards. In all three countries, arrangements are designed to ensure functional implementation of disaster risk reduction measures at a local level.

How can countries mobilise resources to finance disaster risk prevention?

Solidarity has been a guiding principle for financing disaster risk prevention measures. In France, the *Fonds Barnier*, sourced from a mandatory insurance contribution by holders of household, business and motor vehicle insurance, is an important source for prevention investments. In Austria, the *KatFonds* finances disaster risk prevention investments and post-disaster assistance through a contribution of 1.1% of total federal income, wage and corporate taxes. In Switzerland, the central government aims to equalise subnational governments' contributions by compensating for differences in exposure to risk.

Incentives are needed to increase private contributions to disaster risk prevention. The design of government compensation and insurance mechanisms to compensate for private losses is linked to the level of private investment in self-protection. If it is unclear how much governments will compensate private loss, individuals may be less inclined to invest in self-protection. Insurance schemes can be used to reward individual disaster risk prevention investments by reducing the amount of insurance premiums or increasing pay-outs. Swiss insurance companies have been starting to adopt pay-outs that reward private disaster risk prevention.

Going forward

This work is a first in-depth documentation of emerging country practices and solutions in disaster risk prevention. The reviewed practices will, in future work, be expanded to a larger set of countries and can inform concrete capacity building plans and actions to support countries disaster risk prevention management. The results inform the implementation progress report of the OECD Council Recommendation on the Governance of Critical Risks and practices will be recorded in the OECD "Toolkit for Risk Governance".

Chapter 1

Lessons from a cross country study

Despite the achievements of OECD countries to boost resilience to disasters, gaps in disaster risk reduction efforts continue to accentuate their social and economic vulnerabilities to such extreme events. This chapter provides an overview of the findings of a cross-country study of Austria, France, and Switzerland carried out to assess and compare progress and achievements in closing resilience gaps. It looks at how countries have ensured an appropriate policy mix between structural and non-structural measures to effectively reduce disaster risks. It highlights the increasing attention given to non-structural measures, and discusses the challenges associated with the maintenance of protective infrastructure and the associated increases to exposure. The chapter discusses how countries have strengthened organisational efforts to manage disaster risks, even if such measures have not always achieved the desired outcomes. To conclude, the chapter looks at how governance and financing arrangements could help boost the effectiveness of the proposed organisational measures.

Introduction

OECD countries are highly exposed to natural as well as man-made hazards, with storms, floods and earthquakes the sources of major natural hazards. Although OECD countries have been successful in minimising the fatality rates of major natural disasters, certain types of hazards can still cause significant social losses. Extreme weather events, such as the heatwave that swept over Europe in 2003, caused a significant number of deaths. The economic consequences of natural disasters have continued to rise over the past three decades, with single events causing as much as 20 percent of GDP in damages, such as the earthquakes in New Zealand in 2011 and the Chile earthquake in 2010. Man-made hazards, too, have become a growing concern to governments. Potential terrorist attacks are threatening many OECD countries and sophisticated cyber-attacks on critical infrastructure could cause widespread social and economic disruptions.

In 2014 the OECD carried out research on countries' resilience to major natural and man-made disasters. The ensuing report catalogued the social and economic consequences of major recorded disasters in recent decades, and discussed the measures countries have put in place to increase resilience, especially through disaster risk prevention and mitigation measures (OECD, 2014a).

The report found noteworthy some of the achievements in bolstering resilience through disaster risk prevention and mitigation measures in certain OECD countries. Past major disaster events have increased countries' understanding of hazards and vulnerabilities, and in turn improved the knowledge on how associated risk can be managed. Public information campaigns and the integration of risk management tenets in the standard curricula of education institutions has increased the level of disaster risk awareness overall. In many OECD countries governments have dedicated a central leadership function that ensures the integration and coordination of risk management responsibilities across sectors and levels of government.

Nevertheless, vulnerabilities to disaster risks persist across OECD countries, and gaps in disaster risk prevention management are made repeatedly apparent when disasters occur. OECD countries have invested in a significant stock of protective infrastructure, but the maintenance of these assets is often inadequate, which means these assets do not provide the level of protection for which they were initially designed. Regulatory reforms lag behind rapid changes to the built environment in which disaster risks arise. The challenges that countries encounter in enforcing land use and building code requirements has come to the fore. The contributions of the private sector and households to strengthen resilience could be higher despite widespread calls to mobilise all societal actors in this effort.

The OECD report pointed to several factors that explain this lack of engagement in disaster risk prevention and mitigation measures. Certain stakeholders may lack knowledge of measures they can take to increase disaster risk prevention and mitigation. Constrained resources may impede higher levels of investments in disaster risk prevention and mitigation, too. Ineffective institutions may have played a role also, undermining the incentives needed for a whole of-society approach to disaster risk prevention and mitigation to be effective. For example, individual households may have put few resources into protecting their assets against the impacts of disasters because they have had reasons to assume the government would step in to compensate for any eventual losses. Local governments may have invested more in disaster risk prevention and mitigation measures if there were mechanisms to share costs with beneficiaries in neighbouring jurisdictions. Policy makers at the central government level may be reluctant to increase investments in disaster risk prevention and mitigation, because their benefits are not as visible, especially in comparison to *ex post* support.

The OECD Recommendation on the Governance of Critical Risks (OECD, 2014b) promotes three main areas of disaster risk prevention and mitigation policy for OECD countries: (i) a whole-of-society approach to risk communication; (ii) an effective policy mix of structural and non-structural disaster risk prevention and mitigation measures; and (iii) business continuity planning.

Based on the policy recommendations put forward by the OECD and based on the findings of the OECD report, a cross-country comparative study was designed to document progress that countries have made in strengthening their disaster risk prevention and mitigation efforts. Three country case studies were carried out in Austria, France and Switzerland. As described in the methodology section below, these case studies were selected in part on the basis of similar hazard profiles and designed to ensure maximum comparability of the findings.

This report presents the findings of the cross-country comparative analysis, as well as the detailed results of the three case studies. Chapter 1 provides an overview of the methodology underlying the cross-country study. It then summarises the results of the synthesis analysis. Chapters 2-4 present the case study reports for each country.

Methodology

The cross-country comparative study was carried out in three OECD Member countries: Austria, France, and Switzerland. The research focused on public policies meant to manage the risks arising from natural hazards. The study sought to document, evaluate and compare countries' disaster risk prevention and mitigation efforts. The main national counterparts consulted in all three countries were the ministries of environment, with contributions from the national civil protection authorities and other key national and sub-national institutions that share responsibilities for disaster risk prevention and mitigation of natural hazards. Annex 1 provides a list of stakeholders who responded to questionnaires, participated in fact-finding interviews, and checked facts in the draft case study reports.

The design of each country case study followed practice observed in the OECD peer review methodology whereby peers from different OECD Member countries are invited to examine a defined scope of public policies and practices followed in the country under review. The peer examination facilitates exchanges between the country under review and the participating peers about what has worked in terms of policy making in other countries, which can save time, and costly experimenting, in crafting or reforming national policies.

For the purpose of this report's country case studies, officials from the 3 participating countries were invited to attend the various interviews in foreign countries in order to maximise knowledge exchange. The officials were subsequently asked to share their observations and recommendations with the OECD Secretariat. These observations in turn informed the Secretariat's case study reports, which included an assessment and a set of policy recommendations. A key objective of the exchanges organised during the study was to build a forum for policy discussions among country peers on how to boost resilience across countries. To this end, all study participants/peer reviewers were invited to discuss the results of the case studies during a dedicated session at the OECD High Level Risk Forum that took place in December 2016 in Paris.

To ensure comparability of the results of country case studies, the background country research, the country questionnaires that informed the background reports and the fact-finding missions were designed using the same structure and questions. The country questionnaire is included in Annex 2 of this report. The answers to these questions provide a comprehensive overview of the progress in disaster risk prevention and mitigation efforts across the OECD and will serve as an introduction to the synthesis analysis below.

The process to conduct each country entailed the development of a country questionnaire (Annex 2), the results to which informed the development of a background report. The background report, in turn, informed the questions for the fact-finding missions and gave the peers the necessary information to prepare their mission exchanges. On the basis of the findings of the missions, including summaries of observations made by the peers, case study reports were prepared and fact checked by countries. The final reports, including an overview of the assessment and recommendations, are included in chapters 2-4 of this report.

The cross-country study was designed to identify successful national policies and practices in strengthening disaster risk prevention and mitigation efforts. A selected set of policies and practices highlighted in this report will be included in the OECD's Toolkit for Risk Governance, which features an online portal of risk management practices from risk assessment and preparedness policies to effective disaster risk reduction measures (https://www.oecd.org/governance/toolkit-on-risk-governance/home/), targeted to risk management policy makers and stakeholders at large. The results of this study also inform the reporting on the implementation process of the OECD Recommendation on the Governance of Critical Risks (OECD, 2014b).

In the remainder of this chapter an overview of the risk profiles of the selected country case studies will be provided. It will show how the countries compare in terms of their hazard profiles and the similar disaster risk prevention needs they have. The chapter will then turn to discuss the countries' specific disaster risk prevention efforts, starting with investments in structural disaster risk prevention measures, followed by a comparison of the countries' non-structural measures to reduce exposure and vulnerability. The chapter continues with a discussion about the ability of countries to bring together all stakeholders concerned with disaster risk prevention and mitigation, i.e. their ability to promote a whole-of-society approach, which requires countries to go beyond traditional sectoral or jurisdictional-based approaches. The chapter will conclude with an overview of countries' strategies to finance disaster risk prevention and mitigation measures.

Overview country risk profiles

As mentioned in the methodology section the case study countries were identified and selected based on a comparable geography and set of natural hazards. In Austria and Switzerland around 60 % of the territory is mountainous, ranging from the Alps to the Jura Mountains on the Franco-Swiss border. In France, the Rhône River basin, too, is shaped by its varied topography, with much of the river passing through the mountainous terrain of the Alps and the Central Massif. As a consequence, in Austria, the study focused on Alpine hazards and floods. In France a specific geographic focus was on the Rhône River basin, where predominant natural hazards are floods, related Alpine hazards and earthquakes. In Switzerland, policies concerning all natural hazards were examined, with the predominant hazards very similar to those present in Austria and France.

Floods constitute the most prevalent natural hazard in all three countries. In Switzerland almost a quarter of the population lives in areas at risk of flooding, while in Austria, almost 8% of the population lives in flood risk areas. In the Rhône River basin (population of around 15 million), a third of the population faces flood risk directly or indirectly. Along with the exposed population, agriculture and industrial activity is often concentrated in areas at risk of flooding, particularly in the Rhône River basin and in Switzerland.

Table 1.1 Natural hazard profiles: Austria, France and Switzerland

Hazard types	Austria	France	Switzerland
Hydrological	Floods, flash floods, debris flow, torrential flood	Floods, flash floods, debris flow, torrential flood	Floods, flash floods, debris flow, torrential floods
Climate and meteorological	Extreme temperatures, wild fires, heavy rainfall, storms, hail, lightning, avalanches	Extreme temperatures, heavy rainfall, storms, hail, lightning	Extreme temperatures, wild fires, heavy rainfall, storms, hail, lightning, avalanches,
Geological	Soil erosion, sediment movement, earthquake, rockfalls	Sediment movement, earthquake	Soil erosion, sediment movement, earthquake

Source: OECD (2015); OECD (2016a); OECD (2016b)

Past disasters show the important negative impacts floods have had in the studied countries. The major floods that occurred in Switzerland in 2005 caused an estimated EUR 2.8 billion in damages. The 2002 floods in Austria caused around EUR 3.2 billion and the large-scale Rhône floods of 2003 an estimated EUR 1 billion in damages.

Extreme temperature events, especially in the form of heatwaves, have had significant impact across the three countries. In the 2003 European heatwave, for example, 1 000 people lost their lives in Switzerland, 180 to 345 in Austria, and in France, which was especially affected, around 20 000 deaths were recorded, although numbers vary widely across different sources. Most recently, during the summer of 2015, an estimated 800 people lost their lives to extreme heat in Switzerland.

Earthquake risk threatens the three case study countries in similar ways. Although earthquakes are extremely rare in their occurrence in the studied areas, their damage potential is significant. The 1356 earthquake in Switzerland's Basel region would cause an estimated EUR 46 – 94 billion (CHF 50 to CHF 100 billion) in economic losses if it were to occur nowadays (SED, 2016). An earthquake in the Provence-Alpes-Côtes-d'Azur region is considered to be among the top three major risks threatening France's society and economy.

In all three countries, hazards are assessed and mapped in regular intervals and the results are revisited after major disaster events. The hazard mapping results inform the work of risk managers, for disaster risk prevention as well as emergency preparedness and response purposes (more details on hazard assessments are provided below).

Successful disaster risk prevention: getting the policy mix right

As noted in the OECD Recommendation, an optimal disaster risk prevention and mitigation policy mix consists of both so called structural and non-structural measures (OECD, 2014). The Sendai Framework for Disaster Risk Reduction, too, highlights the need for both public and private investments in structural and non-structural measures to increase economic and social resilience to disasters (UNISDR, 2014). Structural measures, which often require significant public expenditure, seek to physically protect populations and assets through engineering works measures such as dykes and dams for floods or storm surges, retention walls, and so on. The direct costs of non-structural measures to governments tend to be lower, and encompass such efforts as s hazard zoning, spatial planning, building codes and their enforcement, risk communication measures and business continuity planning, but also measures like natural water retention, green infrastructure or expanding room for rivers to flow.

Table 1.2 Natural hazards, impacts and disaster risk prevention and mitigation measures

Type of Natural Hazards	Impact examples	Disaster Risk Prevention & Mitigation Measures	Description
Geophysical: Earthquakes, Volcanic Activity, Mass Movement (dry), Geomagnetic Storms)	Losses of human lives, impact on human health	Risk Identification and Assessment	Multi-hazard risk assessment; multi-stakeholder risk assessment; assessing future risks through scenario planning and other methods
Meteorological/ Climatological: Storms, Extreme Temperatures, Droughts, Wildfires	Destruction of physical (private and public) capital and critical infrastructure	Risk Awareness Measures	Public information campaigns, integration of risk in education curricula
Hydrological: Flood (storm surge, coastal), Mass Movement (wet)	Destruction of natural capital (natural resources, natural capital stock, loss of natural habitats, loss of animal stocks)	Technical and Engineering Measures	Dikes, flood gates, rock falls or landslide barriers, retrofitting of buildings, facilities to contain spread of epidemics, elevated roads; back-up and redundant infrastructure

Source: OECD (2014a)

Additional physical protection measures are used on an emergency needs basis, such as mobile protection measures used in the event of floods, or automatic weather stations to provide early warning information. Generally speaking both structural and non-structural measures aim at limiting the exposure of persons and core services to known hazards to reduce their vulnerability. Table 1.2 provides a set of examples of natural hazards, their potential negative impacts and exemplary disaster risk prevention and mitigation actions.

Risk patterns evolve over time, as they are in constant interplay with socio-economic, environmental and technological dynamics and changes. Therefore structural or non-structural disaster risk prevention and mitigation measures need to keep pace and have to be adapted to ever changing consequences that might not always be easy to appraise. The volcanic ash cloud that formed over Iceland in 2010, for example, demonstrated that experts had little understanding about just how much ash is dangerous to planes' engines. To overcome a reliance of policy makers and other stakeholders on past events to inform standards and recommendations, "anticipatory governance" allows for more real-time monitoring, and adapting disaster risk prevention and mitigation measures as swiftly as possible as new risk-related information is collected (OECD, 2014a). In this respect they contribute to the resilience of society.

Investments in physical disaster risk prevention and mitigation measures

In a flood risk financing survey carried out by the OECD as part of the work on the Financial Management of Flood Risk (OECD, 2016e), 17 out of 20 responding countries stated that physical disaster risk prevention investments led to a reduction in flood risks, with some respondents suggesting it is likely the largest contributor to reducing flood risk in their country. A recent survey on the Governance of Critical Risks, carried out in the process of reporting progress in the implementation of the OECD Council Recommendation on the Governance of Critical Risks (OECD, 2014b), assessed the relative importance of structural and non-structural measures as part of countries' policy mixes. The results show that for only 14 out of 35 responding countries "increasing investments in physical protective infrastructure" is a priority in their disaster risk prevention policy mix (Figure 1.1). These priorities may on the one hand reflect the view of central governments, which made up the majority of survey respondents. The view of local governments, that are often in charge of deciding on and co-financing disaster risk prevention investments (Box 1.1), may lead to different answers. On the other hand, these priority considerations may be subject to change. The country case studies provide some insights into this. In Austria, where the central government co-finances about half of structural disaster risk prevention investments, on average, demand from municipalities for protective measures has exceeded the supply that can be co-financed by the central government by about 40%. While in France the current demand and supply for investments in structural measures are more or less in equilibrium, French authorities expect future demands for protective infrastructure investments from the local levels to increase, partly because of increasing exposure to risks and partly because there has been a back log in terms of time it took sub-national authorities to put their requests and planning documents together to have access to central co-financing. In Switzerland, too, increases in demand are expected, as protective infrastructure ages and new and updated hazard maps indicate where additional structural works are needed.

The relatively lower importance that OECD countries seem to attach to structural investments compared to organisational disaster risk prevention measures (Figure 1.1) may also reflect historical legacies. In the studied case study countries, important investments in structural measures were made in the past decades, where an increasing challenge seems to be on how to maintain this large stock of infrastructure so as to ensure that the existing structures maintain the level of protection for which they had been conceived initially. In comparable terms, additional investments in new structural measures may hold lower gains in protection against natural hazards compared to the reinforcement of certain organisational measures.

Figure 1.1. Countries' priorities in strengthening disaster risk prevention and mitigation

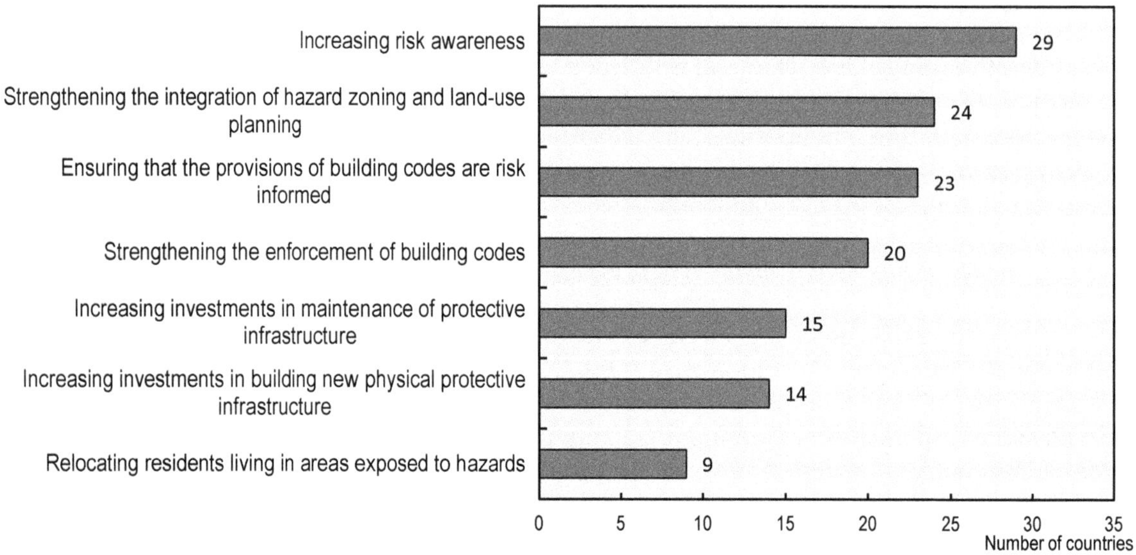

Note: Total number of responses 30/35
Source: OECD Survey on the Governance of Critical Risks

Maximising the benefits of structural infrastructure investments

Investments in structural protective infrastructure are costly, and their utility is often maximised through complementing them with non-structural disaster risk prevention measures. Figure 1.2 illustrates this in terms of the potential complementarity between the protection provided by hard infrastructure measures and insurance. The cost of hard infrastructure measures to physically protect against the most extreme events (i.e. low frequency, high impact events which would require a high standard of physical protection) is relatively high compared to the cost of purchasing insurance to provide financial protection against low frequency events. However, the relative cost of insurance is high for higher frequency events which normally can be prevented by more limited investments in hard infrastructure measures. As a result, a combination of the two types of measures may provide an efficient disaster risk prevention policy mix.

Box 1.1 Decision making for structural disaster risk prevention measures

Disasters are felt most strongly in the directly affected communities that suffer fatalities, and the physical destruction of homes, infrastructure and businesses. As a consequence, local stakeholders, such as municipalities and local interest groups, are in many countries considered well placed to signal the need for investments in structural disaster risk reduction measures. Austria and France delegate the initial responsibility to request a disaster risk reduction investment to the local level (e.g. local authorities, communities, or small beneficiary groups).

In Austria funding decisions are shared by the Federal Ministry of Agriculture, Forestry, Environment and Water Management, as well as the Federal Ministry of Transport, Innovation and Technology. Local level requests are made to one or the other depending on the river type, topography and the characteristics of the structural measure. For torrent and avalanche barriers, the need for structural measures are submitted to the regional service branch of the Austrian Service for Torrent and Avalanche Control (WLV), which assesses the protection needs and whether there is public interest in the investment in cooperation with the service's central office. If the assessment is positive, local parties are requested to develop and submit a co-funding proposal and to take the necessary steps to free up the land needed for the construction of a new structural measure. At this stage, the provincial level is also approached for co-financing. If all steps are passed, the WLV will conclude a formal agreement with the requesting party. For structural measures that address other water-related risks, the initial process is similar, although requests are made to the Federal Water Engineering Administration or the Federal Water Way Administration and then negotiated between the federal ministry and the provinces.

In France, local authorities signal the need for a structural measure to the deconcentrated regional service branches of the Ministry of Ecology, the Regional Directorates for Environment, Planning and Housing (DREALs). While requests for measures below EUR 3 million can be directly approved by the respective DREAL, bigger requests are evaluated by the central-level Joint Flood Commission (CMI). The final decision is then taken by the Ministry of Ecology, which typically follows the assessment done by CMI.

Sources: OECD (2015); OECD (2016a); OECD (2016b)

Figure 1.2. Illustration of trade-off between hard and soft disaster risk prevention and mitigation measures

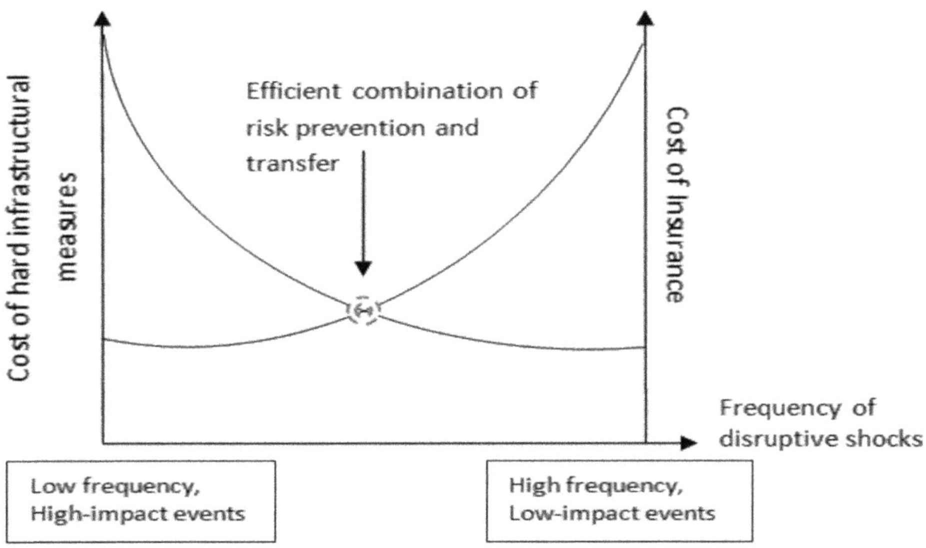

Source: OECD (2014a)

Decision-aiding tools, such as cost-benefit analysis can support policy-makers in deciding on whether and where to invest in structural measures, and hence to maximise the benefits from such investments. Such tools enable the comparison of costs and benefits of different investment alternatives, measured on a set of criteria, and in different decision contexts. They can aggregate the flows of advantages and disadvantages of decisions, and highlight distributional impacts (OECD, 2014a).

Given the importance of structural disaster risk prevention investments across the three case study countries, decision aiding instruments have been used widely. In Austria, for all disaster risk reduction investments exceeding EUR 1 million, exhaustive evaluations of direct as well as indirect costs and benefits are required. In Switzerland an in-depth evaluation of costs and benefits of disaster risk prevention investments is required for all investments above EUR 4,6 million. Standard cost and benefit measures include items such as construction and maintenance costs or on the benefits side items like avoided damages to buildings or critical infrastructures. Where countries are confronting more difficulties is how to address criteria that are important, such as the protection of lives, but that are difficult to evaluate monetarily. Austria has addressed this issue by including intangible benefits on a point scale as an add-on to the results of the standard monetised cost and benefits (Box 1.2). This makes comparison difficult, but at least ensures that this can be taken into consideration by decision makers. In France alternative methods are proposed, such as multi-criteria analysis that allow for commuting different value categories, such as for example the value of a human life or the value of environmental protection, and attaching different decision weights (usually defined by a pre-set point scale) to them. In Switzerland, the online tool, "EconoMe 4.0" [1] guides the evaluation of costs and benefits of complex projects, including social standards and environmental requirements, and in many cases the project proposal also undergoes a public consultation process.

Box 1.2 Evaluating the costs and benefits of disaster risk prevention investments: an example from Austria

Cost-benefit analysis (CBA) was first introduced formally in 1978 in Austria and has since been revised. Pursuant to article 3 of the legislation on the promotion of hydraulic engineering structures (*Wasserbautenförderungsgesetz*) established in 1985, CBA must be implemented to assess the financial feasibility of disaster risk prevention projects exceeding 1 EUR million in costs and having a significant impact on the population at risk. For all other projects, a standard benefit utility assessment is conducted.

CBA compares the cost and benefit stream of different project options (including status quo) over the 80 years that follow the start of a project. Costs include: construction costs (although generally there are no costs for the authorities to buy land as the interested persons are in charge of providing lots); maintenance and repair costs; costs for technological upgrades.

The benefits are linked to protection goals and hence calculated as the estimated average in avoided damages, including: damage to buildings; restoration costs; damage to streambed and receiving stream; damage to transport infrastructures; damage to supply and sanitation facilities; damage to tourism; damage in business/trade/industry/provision of services; damage to official belongings; intervention costs (civil and military forces).

Intangible and indirect benefits are included on a point scale according to the importance of each criterion. They include: protection of people's lives, prevention against an increase in exposure, feeling of safety, ensuring transport connections, protection of nature, landscape and culture related goods. An evaluation of 120 CBAs showed that intangible factors accounted for an

Box 1.2 Evaluating the costs and benefits of disaster risk prevention investments: an example from Austria *(continued)*

estimated 30% of the tangible benefits, which is why their overall weight was determined at 1.3.

Although it is important to include intangible benefits (such as the value of human lives) through, if possible, a point scale, the key question is how final decisions compare different values. Analytical tools such as multi-criteria analysis could be useful in ensuring equal assessment and clear weighting throughout the different evaluation criteria.

Source: BMLFUW (2006), *Richtlinien für die Wirtschaftlichkeitsuntersuchung und Priorisierung von Maßnahmen der Wildbach- und Lawinenverbauung gemäß § 3 Abs. 2 Z 3 Wasserbautenförderungsgesetz* 1985 [Legal guidelines for cost efficiency analysis and the prioritisation of torrent and avalanche barriers as defined in § 3 Para. 2 Z 3 legislation on the promotion of hydraulic engineering structures 1985].

The maintenance challenge

Over recent decades, Austria, France and Switzerland have created a significant stock of disaster risk prevention infrastructure. The challenge in all three countries has been to ensure the structures continue to provide the level of protection for which they were initially built, through adequate maintenance, rehabilitation and strengthening works.

While financial allocations for structural measures may be a fixed part of sectoral budgets, they do not, or only to a limited extent or for a limited amount of time, include a budget for the maintenance expenses for existing, or newly built, protective infrastructure. In Austria, for example, maintenance costs are budgeted into the initial project allocation that is co-funded by the central government, but after some years these costs have to be assumed by sub-national governments or the immediate beneficiaries of a protective infrastructure (e.g. citizens, communities, businesses). In France, there is no maintenance funding included in the initial project allocation for building protective infrastructure.

As a result of the lack of financial planning for maintenance of disaster risk prevention infrastructure, the levels of maintenance vary within countries. The heterogeneity has been caused by differing levels of fiscal and technical capacities at the local level. In the worst case, infrastructure frailty as become apparent during past disasters, e.g. when dams cannot hold water levels they were designed to withstand.

In an attempt to understand the scale of the maintenance problem, Austria, France and Switzerland have started to collect information on the level and adequacy of maintenance through a central fact finding process. In Austria, a central database was established by the Ministry of Agriculture, Forestry, Environment and Water Management that contains information on 270,000 protective infrastructures, with information on their physical dimensions, an assessment of their condition, documentation of monitoring and inspections, attendance, corrective maintenance, on rebuilding and potential other changes (Rudolf-Miklau et al., 2014). In France, local level initiatives, such as the SIRS-dike database created by the *Syndicat Mixte Interrégional d'aménagement des Digues du Delta du Rhône à la Mer* (SYMADREM) catalogues existing protective infrastructure along the Rhône downstream of Beaucaire, including inspection observations. In Switzerland, a database (ProtectMe) is currently being developed to monitor the aging process and vulnerabilities of existing protective infrastructure, which should include comprehensive information on the status of maintenance and protection capacity. Such databases have shown to be a useful tool in different countries including in the United States where the Army Corps of Engineers created the National Levee Database[2]. The database contains up-to-date and publicly available information on the location, condition and maintenance of the majority of dikes and dams built across the United States. The information can be illustrated with a mapping tool (OECD, 2013).

To address the uneven maintenance of local risk prevention infrastructure, France has been discussing a reform called GEMAPI (Box 1.3) that seeks to devolve this responsibility to local authorities and to provide them with authority to finance maintenance through taxes.

Box 1.3 Inter-municipal collaboration for flood risk management (GEMAPI)

The French law on modernising local public action and promoting metropolitan regions (*loi de modernisation de l'action publique territoriale et d'affirmation des métropoles*, MAPTAM), passed in 2014, gives the responsibility for managing aquatic environments and flood risk (*gestion des milieux aquatiques et prévention des inondations*, GEMAPI) to municipalities and to intercommunal services (EPCIs – see Box 3). This is intended to facilitate interventions at the local scale and ensure specific institutions are in charge of specified tasks related to the maintenance of protective infrastructure. Tasks for which the local level will be responsible under GEMAPI include:

- Hydrographic basin planning
- Installation and maintenance of water streams, canals and lakes, as well as access to them
- Flood and sea defence measures
- The protection and restauration of water ecosystems (such as flood plains)

To finance these new responsibilities, municipalities or inter-municipal services can raise a maximum tax of EUR 40 per citizen per year, attached to the local property or rental taxes. The municipalities and EPCIs may give the competence of GEMAPI or a part of it to unions that bring together different local-level groups. The law will come into force in 2018 with a transition period until 2020.

Source: http://www.rhone-mediterranee.eaufrance.fr/docs/gemapi/20140127_LoiGemapi.pdf; http://www.eaurmc.fr/fileadmin/grands-dossiers/documents/GEMAPI/2014_AERMC_resume_loi_GEMAPI.pdf

Mobilising non-governmental stakeholders in disaster risk prevention and mitigation investments

While providing safety and protection against damages from natural disasters for public and, to some extent private assets, has long been viewed as a responsibility of the government, in some OECD countries this responsibility is slowly being shared with non-governmental stakeholders. Especially the direct beneficiaries of disaster risk prevention investments have been involved in the decision-making, and the financing. Bottom-up initiatives, like the water boards in Austria (Box 1.4), have proven to be effective in unlocking additional investments for disaster risk prevention management and have also improved ownership, and hence maintenance, of the created assets.

Box 1.4 Bottom-up disaster risk prevention initiatives - the case of the water boards in Austria

Water boards are statutory corporations under Austrian law (Water Act of 1959) and can be composed of any number and combination of individuals, municipalities or companies. Each member contributes financially to a common fund, which is intended for use in the development and maintenance of mitigation or prevention measures. The readiness to financially contribute to infrastructure investment can be considerable. For example, in the case of the Saalbach (province of Salzburg) water board, which is relatively large with 600 members, individual contributions can be as high as EUR 50 000 annually. The level of contribution is determined by a point system derived from the exposure of a member's property or dwelling. The initial determination of membership fees is automatically transferred to new property owners.

Water boards may decide to take responsibility for co-financing sometimes costly protective infrastructure, instead of leaving this to local authorities. There are several advantages for taking such an initiative. Water boards can, for example, expedite the request for a protective infrastructure, which serves the interests of those directly impacted by potential hazardous events. Water boards, just like municipalities, can initiate and request the construction of protective infrastructure, and thereby oblige its members to finance the suggested measures. In the case of Austria, investment proposals by water boards receive a faster treatment of their request and a higher central co-financing rate than requests submitted by local government. The difference can be as high as 15% and should thereby reward individual willingness to contribute to financing protective infrastructure.

As water boards become the formal owners of the protective infrastructure they build, they are responsible for maintaining it This has led to significantly better results in the status of protective infrastructure over time, compared to infrastructure for which maintenance is the responsibility of other groups, such as municipalities, that have faced resourcing challenges. Considering the longer-term maintenance requirements of protective infrastructure investment, municipalities may encourage investment by water boards.

Source: OECD (2015)

In Switzerland, the insurance industry plays a strong role in mobilising private investments in disaster risk prevention and mitigation. In many cases, insurers inform their customers about the hazard exposures as well as about responsibilities and 'how-to' measures for self-protection. Many public insurers tie the amount of individual loss compensation in the event of a disaster to the prior implementation of disaster risk reduction measures. Financial support is offered by cantonal public insurance companies for investments in such self-protection measures.

Maximising the benefit of organisational disaster risk prevention measures

Non-structural or organisational disaster risk prevention measures are those that are focused on reducing exposure and vulnerability to natural disasters through longer term planning and adaptation to hazard patterns (OECD, 2014b). These include measures like risk communication, hazard zone mapping, risk mapping, spatial planning, building code enforcement or the restoration of natural functions of ecosystems to strengthen protection against natural hazards. These measures form an important element of an optimal policy mix for disaster risk prevention management, as mentioned in this chapter's introduction.

Box 1.5 Responsibilities for hazard assessments across levels of government: a cross-country comparison

Responsibilities for hazard assessment tend to be distributed across levels of governments. While the local levels tend to be in the driver's seat of hazard mapping, the central level oversees the process and ensures a common approach by providing guidelines and standards.

Across countries, this approach takes different forms. In Switzerland the Federal Office for the Environment (FOEN) provides national guidelines to conduct hazard assessments for all hazards except earthquakes, while the respective cantonal authorities oversee the hazard mapping done at the local level. In Austria and France, on the other hand, hazard mapping is done by the respective regional offices of the central Ministry in charge of disaster risk prevention. While in Austria, the Ministry finalizes the maps for publication, ensuring comparable high quality maps, in France the respective regional service that does the hazard mapping also decides the approach. As the central level only indirectly oversees the hazard mapping in France, this has resulted in differences in hazard mapping in different regions.

	Hazard assessments		Review and Updating frequency
	Guidance and oversight	Hazard mapping	
Austria	• Ministry of Agriculture, Forestry, Environment and Water Management	• Service for Torrent and Avalanche Control (WLV): provincial offices • Federal Water Engineering Administration (BWV): central office makes first drafts; provincial offices complement and detail them with local data	• WLV: on a ten-year basis and after changes in the catchment areas • BWV: every six years and after changes in the catchment area
France	Ministry of Ecology: • *Directions départementales des territoires (de la mer)*, DDT (M) • Regional Directorates for Environment, Planning and Housing (DREALs)	• *Directions départementales des territoires (de la mer)*, DDT (M) • Regional Directorates for Environment, Planning and Housing (DREALs)	• For floods (since implementation of UE Floods Directive) : national assessment of flood risks, updated every 6 years • typically updates follow major hazard events or socioeconomic changes • for new disaster risk prevention plans (PPR)
Switzerland	• Federal Office for the Environment (FOEN) • Cantonal authorities • Swiss Seismological Service (SED)	• Local authorities: floods, landslides, rockfalls, and avalanches • Cantonal authorities: spectral seismic zoning studies	• every 10-15 years and after major disaster events

Sources: OECD, 2015; OECD, 2016a; OECD, 2016b

Comparing policy priorities in disaster risk prevention management, the OECD Survey on the Governance of Critical Risks reveals that organisational disaster risk prevention measures, such as the integration of hazard zones in land-use planning (24 out of 35 respondents) or the enforcement of building code provisions (20 out of 35 responding countries) are ranked with a higher policy priority across OECD Members than structural prevention investments (14 out of 35 respondents) (Figure 1.1). These policy priorities reflect a historical legacy, i.e. that structural investments have taken priority in the past as compared to today, and hence very much the recognition that there is a limit to what structural disaster risk reduction investments can and should achieve in terms of protection against natural hazards. It could also reflect a cost consideration. Structural investments have, to a large extent, been shouldered by the government. Organisational measures have much lower upfront costs for the government. However, the indirect costs of organisational measures, for example the decrease in property values that might be caused by hazard zoning, can be substantial and have been borne by citizens, communities, or business owners. Policy considerations ideally should take account of the distributional impacts of the different measures being implemented.

Hazard (and risk) identification and assessment

In terms of identifying and assessing natural hazards OECD countries have made significant and rapid progress in covering their territories with up to date hazard information. In many countries a central government authority has ensured hazard assessments are carried out locally (Box 1.5).

In recognition of the importance of the availability of detailed hazard information, in Austria and Switzerland, for example, the central government authority co-financed, when necessary 100% of the hazard assessment process. In an effort to communicate the results of hazard assessments widely, Austria, France and Switzerland have made hazard information publicly accessible via online platforms that provide hazard information for exact address locations. In other countries, such as the United Kingdom, technical and scientific agencies and government partners cooperate to provide citizens and policy makers alike with regularly updated hazard information (Box 1.6). In an effort to communicate the results of hazard assessments to stakeholders France has proactively communicated this information to property buyers as part of the legally required documents in the purchasing process. The persisting challenges have been to keep hazard information regularly and sufficiently updated.

Box 1.6 Informing about Hazards – The United Kingdom's Natural Hazard Partnership (NHP)

The Natural Hazard Partnership (NHP) is a collaborative partnership between twelve technical and scientific agencies and five government partners. It provides a forum that allows the exchange of data, information and outcomes of all conducted risks analysis. The partnership also contributes to the National Risk Assessment (NRA), which identifies new hazards and advices on worst-case scenarios.

Through a comprehensive and accessible website, the public can access easily understandable information on all relevant hazards, ranging from flooding and extreme weather to earthquakes and wild fires. In addition to the general hazard information available on the website, the NHP provides Daily Hazard Assessment (DHA), which describes all potential natural hazards and health implications that could affect the United Kingdom over the following five days. The DHA is complemented by a general outlook that covers the following thirty days.

Since its creation in 2011, the NHP has significantly increased the coordination among different stakeholders, avoiding duplication and overlaps, which used to be a key challenge. During the 2007 floods, the overlapping mandates of the multiple involved agencies hindered efficient data and information sharing, causing a paradigm change in the aftermath of the floods.

Sources: OECD (2016), Toolkit for Risk Governance - UK Natural Hazard Partnership, https://www.oecd.org/governance/toolkit-on-risk-governance/goodpractices/page/uknaturalhazardpartnership.htm#tab_description;
NHP (2016), The Natural Hazards Partnership, http://www.naturalhazardspartnership.org.uk/

Hazard maps can be improved in the future to reflect the continuous changes and arising complexities in disasters by:

- Harmonising and integrating maps across different hazards: Hazard maps across OCED Member countries have often been developed by different authorities in charge of managing different types of hazards. This is true for different natural hazards, but also between natural and man-made hazards. In the United Kingdom, the Natural Hazard Partnership (NHP) (Box 1.6) has addressed the challenge of hazard mapping that is spread out across different agencies. The NHP acts as a forum of exchange and integrates hazard information provided by the participating public bodies and research institutes.

- Increasing the assessment of cascading impacts across different types of hazards: Since larger-scale disasters have shown their significant potential to trigger knock-on impacts, such as the Great East Japan Earthquake and the Fukushima power plant accident, there is also significant scope to integrate potential cascading effects in the traditional mapping process. Switzerland shows high awareness of such extreme disaster scenarios and has made concerted efforts to better identify and assess potential cascading disasters. The EXAR project described in Box 1.7 illustrates an example.

- Reflecting the evolution of hazards and risks due to climate change: Climate change is expected to affect both the intensity and the frequency of existing hazards and risks and might create new ones. Levels of precipitation and temperatures are expected to change, affecting among other things the probability of floods and droughts, the stability of slopes and bedrocks, and the intensity of storms. Comprehensive hazard maps should display climate impact to ensure a forward-looking understanding of risks and hazards.

Box 1.7 EXAR: Assessment of extreme flood risks along the Aare and Rhine rivers (Switzerland)

In 2013 the Swiss Federal Offices for the Environment, Energy, Nuclear Safety Inspectorate as well as Civil Protection launched the EXAR project that aims at establishing a common baseline to evaluate the risk of extreme flood events for infrastructures built close to the rivers Aare and Rhine. In the beginning phase of the project, data were collected and methodologies developed that enable a standard evaluation of extreme flood events along those two rivers, including gauge height, flow velocity, morphological changes of the river and recurrence probabilities. Projections are based on estimated return periods of 10 000 years.

Based on the initial ground work that established the evidence base for modelling extreme flood events of the Aare, in 2016 the Federal Office for the Environment commissioned a study to understand and evaluate interaction scenarios or cascading impacts of extreme flood risk events. These include erosion, landslides, blockages through floating refuse and dyke breaches. The objective of this study is to understand vulnerabilities of infrastructures to extreme flood events.

The results of this exercise are used to inform the implementation of protective strategies for infrastructures and other assets in the high risk area. Specifically, they are used to estimate the risk of an extreme event and cascading impacts for 15 damn structures and re-evaluate the risks for nuclear power plants in that area (Kühleberg, Gösgen, Beznau I and II).

Source: FOEN (2016), *Beurteilung der Gefährdung durch Extremhochwasser der Aare: Hauptstudie lanciert* [Evaluation of extreme flood hazards along the Aare: Main study launched], Federal Office for the Environment (FOEN), Switzerland
http://www.bafu.admin.ch/dokumentation/medieninformation/00962/index.html?lang=de&msg-id=60609

Although natural hazard assessments are indispensable for effective hazard management, they are insufficient in determining priorities for investments in disaster risk reduction efforts. Hazard assessments do not include information about the vulnerability and exposure of populations and assets to the identified hazards. Risk assessment describes the process that helps to "determine the nature and extent of risk by analysing potential hazards and evaluating existing conditions of vulnerability that together could potentially harm exposed people, property, services, livelihoods and their environment" (OECD, 2014b).

Risk assessments are increasingly in all three countries, although the available information is not always comprehensive, and the assessments are not carried out for all hazards. In Austria, individual studies have been carried out that looked for example at the exposure of buildings and residents to flood, torrent and avalanche risks (Fuchs and Zischg, 2014; Habsburg-Lothringen et al., 2009; BMLFUW, 2015). Switzerland has also relied on individual studies, such as the ongoing Mobilar project that seeks to map buildings exposed to natural hazards (http://www.mobiliarlab.unibe.ch/). Neither Switzerland, nor Austria has conducted a systematic risk assessment that includes an assessment of critical infrastructure and critical services for all existing sources of natural hazards. In France, and the Rhône River basin, more detailed risk assessments have been carried out as part of the obligatory development of national and basin-level flood risk management plans (PPRI). Table 1.3 illustrates the result of this elaborate flood risk assessment exercise, which included a comprehensive assessment of citizens at risk, private assets and public infrastructure, as well as environmental and cultural heritage sites.

Table 1.3 Assets at risk in the Rhône basin

	At risk from flooding	At risk from coastal flooding	Relative to total number of each indicator in France (%)	
Population	5,5 million	229,000	33	16
Number of health facilities	819	21	35	13
Potable water facilities	9,044	23	-	-
Total buildings	438 million m^2	21,2 million	34	15
Total business buildings	153,96 million m^2	5,4 million	36	13
Jobs	2,9 million	133,200	32	16
Infrastructure lines (roads and railways)	98,000 km	5,000 km	32	16
Nuclear power stations	57	0	-	-
Nature protection zones (Natura 2000)	6,500 k m^2	2,800 km^2	30	34
Cultural heritage buildings	1,6 million m^2	35,000	25	9
Museums	133	8	-	-

Source: DREAL Rhône-Alpes (2014), "*Plan de Gestion des Risques d'Inondation 2016-2021, Bassin Rhône-Méditerranée*" [Plan for Flood Risk Management 2016-2021, Rhône-Mediterranean Basin], Parties communes au Bassin Rhône-Méditerranée, Project submitted for public consultation Volume 1, http://www.rhone-mediterranee.eaufrance.fr/docs/dir-inondations/pgri/00_Projet_PGRI_volume1.pdf

In the absence of, or in complement to, prospective exposure and vulnerability analysis, data on the socio-economic impacts from past disasters can be highly instructive. Data on damages caused by past disasters are an essential building block of probabilistic vulnerability analysis. Evidence from a recent OECD survey on the costs of disasters (OECD, 2016d) shows that many OECD countries collect information on damages and losses from past disasters, but only few systematically register it in a central repository.

Switzerland stores data on economic disaster losses in a centralised data repository. In 1972 the Federal Institute for Forest, Snow and Landscape Research (WSL) was charged by the Federal Office for the Environment (FOEN) with the task of systematically recording both social and economic disaster losses in a central database. Starting out by collecting data on storms, the WSL now takes damage caused by floods, debris flows, landslides as well as rock falls into account. Damage resulting from other hazards, such as avalanches, snow pressure, earthquake, lightening, hail, windstorm and drought is not included in the database. The recording is based on newspaper articles for smaller events and official data from cantons and insurance companies for larger events. Damage records are relatively complete for the hazards listed above, particularly in regards to recorded insurance claims, facilitated by the mandatory natural hazard insurance for buildings and content.

While Austria and France do not currently have a centralised data collection system in place, information on the economic impact of major disasters tends to be collected in both countries in quite detail either prospectively or retroactively after a major disaster occurred. In the context of France and Austria the practice has focused on understanding major economic impacts with a view to preparing for a major event, whereas damages resulting from smaller scale events were perhaps viewed as less policy-relevant. In light of policy objectives agreed on in the context of the Sendai Framework for Disaster Risk Reduction, established practices for recording losses might change in the future.

Integrating the results of hazard assessments into land-use decisions

The integration of hazard maps into land-use planning is a core step in reducing the exposure of people and assets to hazards. Exposure is most effectively reduced or avoided through restrictions on land use development in hazard-prone areas or regulations on building design. However, scarcity of land for settlements, or a desire to increase densification to achieve higher economies of scale, have been factors in all three countries that contribute to tension between competing public policies for economic development and disaster risk reduction . It should be noted that in all three countries settlement in some exposed areas took place long before detailed hazard information became available. Such information can now guide the implementation of policies to reduce vulnerability through retrofitting measures, repairs and expansions.

As noted in the previous section, localised hazard information has been made available widely across OECD countries and in the case studies carried out for this report; countries have made concerted efforts to communicate this information widely through specific access friendly web platforms. Difficulties remain in translating hazard information into actual land-use planning and decisions. Where the use of hazard information for land-use decisions is not legally binding, such as in Austria, its integration depends on the final decision makers (such as government officials at the local level). Local interests can be particularly divided between a desire to safeguard the community and to support economic development.

The case studies have shown the integration of hazard information in land-use planning decisions has been most successful in high-risk areas, where construction bans have been issued and successfully enforced in countries like France (Box 1.8). Past disasters have confirmed that such measures reduced damages in those areas. However, countries like Switzerland, where the integration of hazard information in land use decisions is considered good practice, have in the meantime experienced a relatively higher accumulation of damage claims were filed in low hazard zones, where information about the hazard had been provided but no specific land-use requirement had previously been issued. This shows protection or more adapted regulations might have been overlooked in lower hazard zones.

Box 1.8 Integrating land-use planning in hazard assessments in France

In France hazard mapping results in the development of so-called Prevention Plans against Natural Risks (PPRNs). The plans outline hazard zones for possible earthquakes, floods, avalanches, wildfires or landslides. To assess flood risk PPRNs do not take into account the existence of protective measures, such as dykes, so as to account for the eventuality that these structures may fail. The hazard maps are publicly accessible and the public as well as local authorities and other stakeholders are involved in the hazard mapping process.

The responsibility for risk and hazard mapping lies in the hands of deconcentrated arms of the Ministry of Ecology at departmental level (*directions départementale des Territoires* (DDT(M)), with support from the Regional Directorate for Environment, Planning and Housing (*Direction Régionale de l'Environnement, de l'Aménagement et du Logement*, DREAL) and (public) engineering bureaus.

The hazard maps are regularly included in land-use planning. The spatial development code obliges local authorities to take hazard maps into consideration for spatial planning documents, with the Risk Prevention Plan (PPR) as an annex. The Flood Risk Prevention Plans (PPRIs) go even farther and establish clearly designated areas where construction is not allowed, leaving no room for ambiguity. To ensure that hazard maps are included in land-use planning, inspections are carried out up to three years after constructions are completed. Penalties follow if hazards maps were ignored.

Mayors are in the driver's seat of enforcing hazard zones in land use decisions and they are in charge of granting building permits. The department prefect monitors the integration of hazard zones in urban planning decisions. In case of doubts about whether hazard zones were respected in granting a building permit the prefect can initiate a legal procedure against municipalities. Mayors can and have been found liable for ignoring hazard zones. Regions also have a monitoring role and can positively encourage the integration of hazard zones in local land-use decisions.

To show commitment in enforcing this responsibility, mayors can and have been made liable for ignoring hazard zones. For example the mayor of La Faute-sur-mer was condemned to four years in prison for involuntary homicide after more than 50 fatalities were caused by the Xynthia storm in 2010 and some of them directly linked to the granting of construction periods in known zones at risk[3]. The condemnation was a strong signal to local planning authorities and mayors to take the integration of hazard zones in their land use decisions seriously.

Source: OECD (2016b)

Enforcing hazard informed land-use decisions has been a challenge throughout OECD countries. In the OECD survey on the financial management of flood risk (OECD, 2016e) only two countries (Estonia and Switzerland) of the responding 20 countries indicated that changes in land-use had led to a significant reduction in flood risk, while fourteen indicated that such changes had actually led to a substantial increase in flood risk. In Germany, for example, the increase in construction near rivers has outpaced the rate of construction outside flood zones, despite a 2004 law that forbids building and commercial usage in such zones. In the United Kingdom, one third of the projected three million properties to be built by 2020 are expected to be located on coastal and river flood plains. In Italy, the effectiveness of strong legislative requirements for assessing flood hazard in new developments has been limited by gaps in compliance and a number of exemptions provided for properties that were constructed without regard to flood hazard levels (OECD, 2016e).

Resettlement out of hazard zones

In areas subject to recurrent and large disaster impacts, or areas that could usefully serve to mitigate disaster impacts (such as flood retention areas), resettlement has been used as a disaster risk prevention instrument. Many OECD members have established a legal framework and set-up policies to support resettling populations outside of designated hazard zones, although in some countries this measure has been applied rarely and only as a last resort. Figure 1.1 reflects this, with only 9 of 35 responding countries listing resettlement as a priority policy area in their disaster risk prevention strategies. Since relocations can entail social hardships, good practices in handling this process can be informative for countries exploring or considering this option in the future. Box 1.9 describes a good practice of how Austrian authorities collaborated across levels of government in the process of a voluntary resettlement program that was organised around the Machland Dam project that saw the creation of a flood canal that expanded into settlement areas.

Box 1.9 Resettlement as a disaster risk prevention measure: the case of the Machland Dam in Austria

The Machland Dam is the biggest flood protective infrastructure work in Austria. The dam, constructed from 2008 to 2012, spans over 36.4 km to protect 22 400 inhabitants spread over 7 municipalities in the Machland region.

The project included the construction of an 8.7 km bypass, or flood canal, spreading from Naarn to Wallsee/Mitterkirchen that is meant to regulate small floods and constitute an element of the integrative flood risk management design of the project. It aims at protecting lives while re-establishing room for the river and preserving the environment. The creation of the flood canal also provided material (soil) for the dam construction.

The settlement structure in the flood-prone area, which was sparse and spread over a large area, made the protection against floods prohibitively expensive. It was therefore decided to offer citizens that were not going to be protected by the dam support to relocate. By 2015, 254 voluntary resettlement agreements for houses located in areas at risk of flooding were concluded, costing EUR 92 million in compensation payments. While resettlement began slowly, successive floods convinced the citizens to agree to move. The 2002 floods sparked a resettlement wave of 221 remaining properties.

Box 1.9 Resettlement as a disaster risk prevention measure: the case of the Machland Dam in Austria *(continued)*

Resettlement was successfully achieved because the conditions for citizens were relatively attractive in comparison to the status quo. Compensation for house owners was based on the replacement value of their houses as well as their demolition costs. The authorities provided 80% of the overall costs in compensation: the federal province paid 30% of total costs and the central level of government 50%. Property owners did not lose land titles of their initial belongings; however, land had to be re-dedicated to pasture land, revoking the possibility to construct on it. New lots for rebuilding houses were made available and were reserved in adjacent communities to protect relocated citizens from price hikes in land prices and to ensure that communities could be rebuilt in proximity.

Sources: http://www.machlanddamm.at; Oberösterreich Landesrechnungshof (2014), *LRH-Bericht, Initiativprüfung, Hochwasserschutz Machland Nord, LRH-100000-12/9-2014-LI.*

Risk Communication

Risk communication is a fundamental element of a sound risk management framework that seeks to reduce future losses and damages from disasters. Governments have a basic responsibility to engage with all actors in society, encouraging a whole-of-society approach, to notify them about their exposure to major hazards. Communicating risks effectively increases the awareness of households, businesses and communities about their exposure to risk and their vulnerabilities, and also informs them of what specific prevention, mitigation and preparation measures they could take. Such knowledge can also spur an informed debate on the need for public investment in prevention, mitigation and preparedness, and is thus a key element of good governance in risk management policy.

Even though risk communication and raising risk awareness has been the most important policy priority in terms of disaster risk prevention across OECD countries, all three studied cases have struggled with persistently low levels of risk awareness among their citizens, especially in the absence of recent major disasters. For example, a regular survey carried out in the Rhône River basin shows risk awareness levels have decreased after the major flood events in 2003, when the DREAL Rhône-Alpes decided to launch regular risk awareness surveys. The surveys, conducted in 2006, 2009, 2013 and 2016, showed only 18% of the population in risk zones took measures to protect themselves in 2016, against 21% in 2009. The results have been low despite significant efforts of local authorities to communicate to the population about risk exposures and the measures people can take to protect themselves. In France, a DICRIM is a local risk communication tool that can be highlighted as an effort in this regard (Box 1.10). Switzerland has observed low risk awareness levels especially among those citizens that have never been exposed to a natural disaster. This is especially challenging with regard to earthquake risks, since the last major earthquake occurred a long time before the current generation of Swiss was born.

Box 1.10 DICRIM – Local community information document about major prevailing risks (France)

DICRIM, introduced in 1990 in France, obliges every community, under the responsibility of the mayor and his municipal council, to draw up an information document about the safety measures to take in the event of a potential threat. The document is tailored to the locally prevailing hazards and includes information on:

- Locally prevailing natural and technological risks
- Measures taken by the municipality to reduce risk exposure
- Safety measures to be taken in the event of an emergency or an alarm (for example behavioural measures, securing assets from areas at risk, mounting electricity and gas meters above a potential flooding level)
- A list of critical public infrastructures (including retirement homes, schools etc.)
- How land owners and those renting premises have to communicate about the safety measures stipulated in the DICRIM

The objective of the DICRIM is to raise awareness among citizens about local major risks to which they could be exposed to. The DICRIM should inform about the nature of the threats, their potential consequences and the measures citizens can take to protect themselves or reduce their exposure and potential damages. The DICRIM recognises that the local administrative boundaries may not reflect the right scale for analysing hazards and encourages inter-municipal hazard analysis, based on which local prescriptions can be developed.

Source: http://www.risquesmajeurs.fr/le-document-d%E2%80%99information-communal-sur-les-risques-majeurs-dicrim

Low risk awareness levels have translated to a relatively low take-up of disaster risk prevention measures among citizens and businesses. For example, 17% of survey respondents in the Rhône River basin thought that preventive measures would be ineffective in providing individual protection. For risk management authorities in the studied countries such results indicate the continued reliance of individuals and businesses on the government to provide protection, undermining their efforts of establishing a whole-of-society approach to disaster risk prevention management. In Switzerland, authorities fear for further repercussions that low risk awareness may have. Owing to Switzerland's direct democratic culture, the risk awareness of citizens also is a crucial factor influencing the amount of public resources allocated towards disaster risk prevention management.

In an attempt to boost the effectiveness of risk communication efforts, countries have partnered with the private sector. In Switzerland, for example, cantonal insurance providers have played an instrumental role in informing citizens about disaster risk prevention measures they can take. Some of them provide automated text messages about weather warnings or imminent disasters. In France, through its *Mission Risques Naturels*, partnerships and platforms have been established that facilitate exchanges between public authorities and private sector actors to discuss risk communication strategies and to jointly train actors responsible for risk communication (*Mission Risques Naturels*, 2015). Similarly, the Austrian Civil Protection Association is a private organisation with nine regional branches which informs the public about risks and self-protection measures (Box 1.11).

Box 1.11 The Austrian Civil Protection Association: private sector risk communication on behalf of the government

The Austrian Civil Protection Association is a collective term comprising ten associations – one federal organisation and nine regional offices –, whose mission is to inform the population about civil defence in Austria, particularly on protective measures in emergency situations. According to the association´s statutes of 1993, its mission is the following:

- To promote the idea of self-protection through events, presentations and the dissemination of information to the population
- To coordinate and collaborate with the regional offices
- To train and advise the population in matters of civil defence, collaboration with the responsible authorities and intervention organisations
- To prepare and assess proposals for the creation of regulations within the framework of civil protection
- To exchange experience with foreign civil protection organisations.
- The association is, unlike the fire brigade and rescue organisation, not active on an operational level, but one whose main task is to disseminate risk-related information to the population. The association acts, in this matter, on behalf of the Federal Ministry of the Interior and forwards all information on self-protection to the public through two different channels:
- General public information on civil protection
- Organisation of safety and security information centres (SIZ) at a local community level.

Sources: Ministry of Interior, Austria (2016), Information on Austria's Civil Protection Agency, www.bmi.gv.at/cms/BMI_Zivilschutz_en/national/civil/start.aspx; Austrian Civil Protection Association, www.zivilschutzverband.at/home.

Policies to encourage businesses to take steps to ensure business continuity planning

Business continuity planning constitutes a key element to reduce the potential disruption of the supply of goods and services, especially in vital systems such as hospitals, water and energy, public security, transport and communications. The importance of business continuity for a country's resilience to disaster has been recognised in international policy guidance, including the OECD Recommendation on the Governance of Critical Risks (OECD, 2014b) and the UN Sendai Framework (UNISDR, 2015).

After a disaster, the economic recovery of a country or region may depend heavily on the continued productive capacities of such essential services. For public and private sector organisations alike, the first step in business continuity planning is to model the potential impacts and consequences of a hazard on the organisation's entire range of activities and identify its essential parts and functions as distinct from what can be discarded temporarily.

OECD countries have recognised the importance of business continuity plans, with governments providing strategic services, establishing standards or developing toolkits to manage risks. They also prepared capabilities to ensure the functioning of critical services in the aftermath of a disaster (Figure 1.3). However, there is little evidence yet available on the uptake and success in implementing these in practice. In Switzerland for example, the implementation of national guidelines is increasingly gaining speed. Although the Swiss "Guideline for the Protection of Critical Infrastructure" is not binding, economic associations and critical infrastructure providers increasingly apply it (Box 1.12).

Figure 1.3. Measures through which countries have encouraged the private sector to take steps in business continuity planning

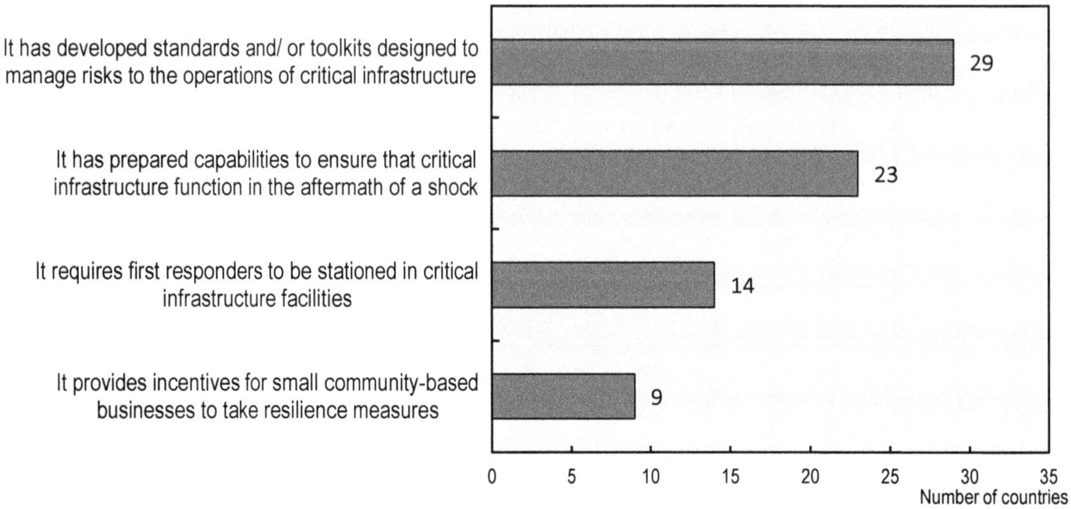

Note: Total number of responses 32 out of 35.
Source: OECD Survey on the Governance of Critical Risks

Despite the high cost disasters can inflict on businesses, many businesses have remained unaware of the prevention and mitigation measures available to them. Governments have therefore increasingly undertaken efforts to include businesses in their disaster risk reduction efforts. In some countries, such as France, programmes specifically tailored for businesses have shown success in increasing their resilience. The business vulnerability reduction programme to floods in the Loire river basin combined targeted risk communication with detailed on-site risk analysis and led to an increase in risk awareness and in preventive measures taken. In the Rhône river basin specific measures to make agricultural activity flood resilient were promoted and introduced (Box 1.13).

Box 1.12 Encouraging business continuity planning: a good practice from Switzerland

Switzerland has recognised that there is a joint responsibility by the operator of the critical infrastructure and the public authority to take potential consequences of a critical infrastructure failure that are of importance for the general public into account.

To support the critical infrastructure owners and operators in this endeavour, the Swiss Federal Office for Civil Protection (FOCP) has issued a "Guideline for the Protection of Critical Infrastructure". It applies a holistic approach for dealing with relevant hazards and considers all conceivable disaster risk prevention and mitigation measures. In the risk assessment process, natural hazards as well as man-made hazards and technical failures are considered. A broad variety of measures are evaluated, ranging from organizational adjustments to structural-technical provisions. As absolute protection is not possible, nor feasible, proportionality of cost and benefits as well as a continued process of disaster risk prevention and mitigation measures are important.

Box 1.12 Encouraging business continuity planning: a good practice from Switzerland *(continued)*

The more likely a risk occurs and the larger its potential damage to the community, the more extensive and comprehensive should protective and mitigation measures be. The Guideline includes a monitoring and evaluation step in order to evaluate the success of the measures implemented.

As the Guideline is non-binding and the FOCP is not a regulatory agency, critical infrastructure operators are not obliged to apply the Guideline. More and more economic associations and specific critical infrastructure owners are however interested in the application of the Guideline.

Source: FOCP (2012). *Nationale Strategie zum Schutz kritischer Infrastrukturen* [National Strategy for the Protection of Critical Infrastructure], Federal Office for Civil Protection, Bern, www.admin.ch/opc/de/federal-gazette/2012/7715.pdf; http://www.babs.admin.ch/en/aufgabenbabs/ski.html.

Box 1.13 Reducing business vulnerability along the Loire and Rhône basins

The business vulnerability reduction programme to flood in the Loire river basin is a basin-wide initiative that aims to accompany businesses situated in flood zones in taking disaster risk reduction measures in order to reduce a flood's impacts on business activity. The programme included a risk communication campaign and a risk awareness survey that was directly aimed at businesses in the Loire river basin. As a second step, businesses located in flood risk zones were offered an on-site flood vulnerability diagnosis with subsequent suggestions on concrete disaster risk reduction measures. To ensure the uptake of the suggested measures, local authorities provided financial support through co-funding.

The programme resulted in more than 20 000 businesses learning about their flood risk exposure, around half of which had not been previously aware of their exposure. An analysis of the on-site risk assessments showed that potential cumulative damages from flooding could reach up to EUR 3.3 billion, while implementing the proposed disaster risk reduction measures would reduce the cost by one third.

Given the importance of agriculture in the Rhône River basin for securing livelihoods and the importance of agricultural land in providing flood retention areas, the Plan Rhône introduced a diagnostic instrument to assess farmer's vulnerability to floods and suggests preventative measures for farms. In the first pilot phase the Regional Directorate for Environment, Planning and Housing (DREAL) Rhône-Alpes assessed around 230 farms. Following the assessment 85 farms decided to put prevention measures in place. Investments were co-financed at a maximum rate of 80%. Where necessary, new and more effective water pumps were installed, air conditioning was moved to higher ground and safe zones for important machinery were created. Finally, the DREAL Rhône-Alpes seeks to encourage farmers to put measures in place that avoid erosion (such as by planting grass).

Sources: OECD (2010), *Étude de l'OCDE sur la gestion des risques d'inondation: Bassin de la Loire, France 2010*, OECD Publishing, Paris.http://dx.doi.org/10.1787/9789264056817-en

Making disaster risk prevention work: the need for crossing jurisdictional and sectoral boundaries

Effective disaster risk prevention and mitigation management requires the involvement of local communities as much as that of central governments. As highlighted in the OECD Recommendation on the Governance of Critical Risks (OECD, 2014b), clear distribution of responsibilities and coordination across levels of government and with strong leadership at national level are key for effective risk governance. The Sendai

Framework for Disaster Risk Reduction (UNISDR, 2015), too, draws attention to the need and value of overcoming silo approaches and single-handed solutions.

Disaster risks are not confined to jurisdictional or sectoral borders. The limits of traditional governance structures have shown to be incapable of addressing the complexities that arise from events that affect multiple municipalities, regions and industrial sectors. In Austria, for example, the responsibility for managing flood risks from navigable rivers, which are the Danube, March and parts of the Thaya, lies with the Federal Ministry of Transport, Innovation and Technology Management, whereas small rivers are in the hands of the Federal Ministry of Agriculture, Forestry, Environment and Water. Particular vulnerabilities have appeared at the intersection of smaller rivers flowing into large rivers, where specific integrated hazard assessments and joint disaster risk prevention measures are needed. In terms of local jurisdictions the issue is a similar one. The risks stemming from natural hazards, such as floods, are most often shared by more than one local jurisdiction. This can become an issue especially in countries with a high number of small municipalities. Tackling flood risk just from one jurisdiction's perspective is hardly an efficient approach for all affected communities. Governance structures need to recognise and reflect these cross-jurisdictional and cross-sectoral issues to ensure that disaster risk prevention and mitigation operates at the adequate scales and to avoid fragmented approaches that undermine, instead of complement, each other. In the case of shared river areas, where up- and down-stream interests need to be coordinated, cross-jurisdictional governance arrangements are particularly important.

Bridging sectoral divides

Different types of natural hazards require different sets of expertise to be adequately identified, assessed, prevented and responded to. Many countries have therefore assigned responsibilities across different sectors or ministries. Table 1.4 gives an overview of the authorities in charge for different types of natural hazards in the countries studied. In Switzerland, for example, the Federal Office for the Environment is in charge of managing early warning for hydrological hazards. For climate-related and meteorological hazards this becomes a shared responsibility between Environment, the Federal Office for Meteorology and Climatology, and the Swiss Federal Institute for Forest, Snow and Landscape Research. The Swiss Seismological Service is in charge of managing seismic risks.

Cross-sectoral coordination and collaboration is important for several reasons. First of all, different sources of natural hazards interact with each other. One risk, such as for example earthquakes, can trigger risks of flooding or mudslides. A joint approach is needed to map knock-on effects and cascading risks, and design disaster risk prevention provisions accordingly. Second, heavy precipitation, for example, can lead to the flooding of both small and large rivers. A joint approach to managing such cascading risks is addressed in Austria with the help of the National Flood Risk Management Plan, which assesses risks at the basin level regardless of competences. Third, resources to manage risks are finite. Prioritisation in terms of the allocation of resources does not only have to be made within a specific sector, but also across different sectors in charge of managing different risks. This requires a coordinated approach and a central government lead to steer the cross-sectoral allocation decision process.

Table 1.4 Distribution of risk management responsibilities across sectors (and levels of government)

	Civil protection	Hydrological hazards	Climate-related & meteorological hazards	Geological hazards	Policy implementation
Austria	Ministry of the Interior (BMI)	Federal Ministry of Agriculture, Forestry, Environment and Water Management (BMLFUW); Federal Water Engineering Administration (BWV); Federal Ministry for Transport, Innovation and Technology (BMVIT)	Research Institute for Meteorology and Geodynamics (ZAMG)	Federal Service for Torrent and Avalanche Control (WLV); Research Institute for Meteorology and Geodynamics (ZAMG)	Sub-national branches of federal authorities (e.g. of WLV and BWV); Provincial governments; local governments/ municipalities
France	General Secretariat for defence and national security (SGDNS)	Ministry of Ecology, Sustainable Development and Energy (MEDDE) - Directorate General for Risk Prevention (DGPR); Joint Flood Commission (CMI);	Ministry of Ecology, Sustainable Development and Energy (MEDDE) - Directorate General for Risk Prevention (DGPR)	Ministry of Ecology, Sustainable Development and Energy (MEDDE) - Bureau for Geological Research and Mining (BRGM)	Prefectures & Departmental Commissions of Major Natural Hazards; Regional Directorates for Environment, Planning and Housing (DREALs); local governments/ municipalities
Switzerland	Federal Office for Civil Protection (FOCP)	Federal Office for the Environment (FOEN):	Federal Office for the Environment (FOEN); Federal Office for Meteorology and Climatology (MeteoSwiss); Swiss Federal Institute for Forest, Snow and Landscape Research (WSL)	Federal Office for the Environment (FOEN); Swiss Seismological Service (SED)	Cantonal governments; local governments/ municipalities

Source: OECD Survey on the Governance of Critical Risks 2016; OECD, 2015; OECD, 2016a; OECD, 2016b

In the three case study countries is an increasing recognition and concrete actions taken to manage policies across sectors in charge of different hazard types:

The Swiss National Platform for Natural Hazards (PLANAT)

The National Platform for Natural Hazards (PLANAT) in Switzerland is a good practice example in creating a multi-stakeholder platform to coordinate a cross-sectoral approach to managing disaster risks. PLANAT was founded as an extra-parliamentary commission to improve disaster risk prevention across Switzerland. It brings together representatives from the federal government, cantonal governments, the research community, professional associations, the private sector and insurance companies to work on strategic priorities in risk management, to introduce and foster a culture of risk that integrates ecological, social and economic aspects in disaster risk prevention management, and to coordinate disaster risk prevention efforts in Switzerland to avoid duplication and increase synergies between the different actors' activities. PLANAT's core objective is to ensure that the management of risks remains present in political and public discussions. The composition of PLANAT with members from the different national and sub-national agencies, but also research and insurers and other private sector actors has been important to achieve this.

The Austrian Spatial Planning Conference (ÖROK)

In Austria, the Austrian Spatial Planning Conference (ÖROK) has proved to be a useful platform for coordinating risk management across sectoral responsibilities, as well as levels of government. Founded in 1971, ÖROK was established by the federal government, the provinces and municipalities to co-ordinate spatial development at the national level. ÖROK is in charge of developing and publishing an Austrian spatial planning concept, last published in 2011, which represents a nationwide spatial planning strategy. The body is chaired by the Federal Chancellor and its members include all federal ministers and heads of the provinces, the presidents of the Austrian Association of Cities and Towns and the Austrian Association of Municipalities, and the heads of the social and economic partners that have a consulting vote. ÖROK plays an instrumental role in bringing all interest groups together to discuss how disaster risk prevention policies and actions can be better integrated into spatial planning decisions, building codes and other legal frameworks. As many of the past damages of floods have been attributed to weaknesses in enforcing disaster risk prevention measures in spatial planning practice, ÖROK plays a key role in increasing Austria's disaster risk management capacity by providing a platform for stakeholder dialogue and establishing key policy recommendations.

Bridging jurisdictional divides

The impacts of disasters are rarely confined to municipal borders and may not stop at regional or country borders. Therefore, governance structures should ensure that disaster risk management operates at the appropriate scale. Inter-communal collaboration is needed, especially for the development of joint spatial planning strategies for shared river areas and the development of compensation mechanisms between municipalities that pay for protection measures and others that may benefit or have additional costs. Collaboration methods include a range of partnerships, from establishing informal discussion fora and exchanging hazard information, to coordinating land-use planning activities or implementing joint protection measures.

A government's funding policies can influence the interest of local governments to cooperate across its jurisdictional borders. Austria's governance system for structural measures, as seen above, is organised around provincial service branches that are a deconcentrated arm of central service units (the case of the WLV and the BWV), which require local municipalities to request funding for projects. This governance structure may risk overlooking cross-jurisdictional risks and investment needs. In an attempt to address these issues Austria is increasingly using catchment-wide planning approaches, facilitated by the National Flood Risk Management Plan. Municipalities may have a stronger incentive to obtain the maximum amount of funding for their own projects, and investment by one municipality may create benefits (or costs) for others that could lead to an under-investment in protection. Aside from protection, potential environmental conflicts and potential synergies have to be considered flood risk management. Conflicts between up- and down-stream river communities can arise where retention zones developed by upstream municipalities created benefits for downstream municipalities who refuse to participate in the costs.

To address this geographical fragmentation problems, governments can change the way projects are financed, for example by rewarding joint project proposals with higher central level funding shares, and by regulating the way local risk assessments, prevention and preparedness measures are conducted and implemented. In Austria, the example of water boards (Box 4) is one that takes this direction and can be highlighted as a good country practice. Water boards are statutory can be composed of any number and combination of individuals, municipalities or companies, which together contribute financially to a common fund that finances the construction and maintenance of structural disaster risk reduction measures. Water boards have been rewarded with higher central-level co-funding and sometimes expedited processing of their co-funding request by the central government too. They have thereby been rewarded for working across jurisdictions and ensuring the appropriate scale for disaster risk prevention measures.

The subsidiarity arrangements in Switzerland are designed in a way that they ensure that disaster risk reduction measures are implemented on a functional level. To ensure coordination across administrative borders of cantons, cantonal authorities need to submit their proposals for protective infrastructure investments to the national level. Based on the degree of collaboration across cantons, different coordination models are used, where either both (or several) or just one canton takes the lead in the implementation process. Accordingly, co-financing arrangements are made. In case of differences between the cantons, the federal government acts as a mediator. When a protective measure is installed upstream, it needs to be proved that it does not worsen the situation further downstream.

Another emerging good country practice that illustrates the growing recognition of the importance of managing risks at the appropriate geographical or functional level can be found in France. The currently debated GEMAPI (the management of aquatic environments and flood risk prevention) law should equip France's existing inter-municipal collaborative bodies (EPCIs) with a strong role in flood risk management, which will include a responsibility for maintaining and building new structural measures in the EPCI's shared area, as well as a transfer of ownership of existing protective measures. To fund their activities, EPCIs will have the right to raise local taxes. EPCIs with local flood risk prevention plans (PAPI and PPR) also qualify for prevention funding through the *Fonds Barnier*[4]. Currently, shared Flood Prevention Action Programs (PAPIs and PSRs) are already in place to encourage joint flood risk management across municipalities that are grouped in the same risk area. As an additional layer of cross-jurisdictional cooperation between all relevant actors from along a shared river river plans have been adopted for all major river systems, including for the Rhône (*Plan Rhône*), supported by consolidated financing for joint projects.

The cooperation in the Natural Hazards Platform of the Alpine Convention (PLANALP), established in 2004 by the Alpine Convention[5], is a good example for ensuring trans-boundary risk management across multiple countries. In PLANALP eight countries[6], including Austria, France and Switzerland, as well as the European Union, work together to develop joint approaches to prevent natural hazards in the shared Alpine area. Through cross-border exchange of experiences PLANALP facilitates a coordinated and appropriate risk management across the Alps. To make sure that PLANALP is more than a 'toothless tiger', the participating parties mandated the platform to implement subsequent measures, including flood (risk) management plans. Other examples for good transboundary risk management include joint measures, such the European Flood Awareness System (EFAS). Since 2012, EFAS is fully operational and provides probabilistic, flood early warning information up to 10 days in advance to the participating National Hydrological Services.

Financing disaster risk prevention and mitigation

The OECD Recommendation stresses that governments should allocate sufficient resources throughout the risk management cycle and at all levels of government to build preparedness and reduce risks. Disruptions from disasters have an impact on individual households, businesses, and the public sector alike. Therefore, all actors should have an interest in investing in disaster risk prevention and mitigation. Governments across OECD countries face three main challenges when it comes to designing their approach to risk financing. The first entails determining the overall amount of resources to be allocated to managing risks, and what risks they choose to retain. The second constitutes the choice of how to finance risks, whereby a myriad of instruments are at the disposal of governments and each entails different distributional effects. The third is that in order to alleviate the financial burden on governments, countries need to leverage the private sector and individual households to participate in financing disaster risk prevention and mitigation measures or investing in individual risk transfer arrangements. They also need to collaborate with other countries to jointly finance risks (Figure 1.4). The recently adopted OECD Recommendation on Disaster Risk Financing Strategies (2017) provides guidance to governments on how to design a strategy for managing the financial impacts of disasters, including by leveraging the contribution of insurance and other risk transfer instruments.

Solidarity has been a key guiding principle when it comes to financing investments in disaster risk reduction in the three countries studied. Recognising that risk exposure is unevenly distributed, they share the financial burden of disaster risk reduction ensures that a more equal level of protection against natural hazards is achieved throughout their national territory. Among the insightful examples and lessons on how solidarity can be built into disaster risk prevention financing schemes are the following:

In France, risk financing builds on the natural catastrophes compensation scheme CATNAT (*Catastrophes Naturelles*) and the Fonds Barnier. It is sourced from an obligatory insurance contribution made by all holders of household, business and motor vehicle insurance policies and serves a double purpose. On the one hand it provides funds for compensating damages suffered from natural disasters to individual households and businesses, while on the other hand a share of its funds is reserved and used for disaster risk prevention investments under the Fund for the Prevention of Major Natural Hazards (*Fonds de Prévention des Risques Naturels Majeurs*), or "Fonds Barnier". 12% of the total premiums collected are invested in the Fonds Barnier. This corresponds to EUR 185 million per year.

What do governments spend on disaster risk prevention and how do they finance it?

Figure 1.4. Available risk financing tools

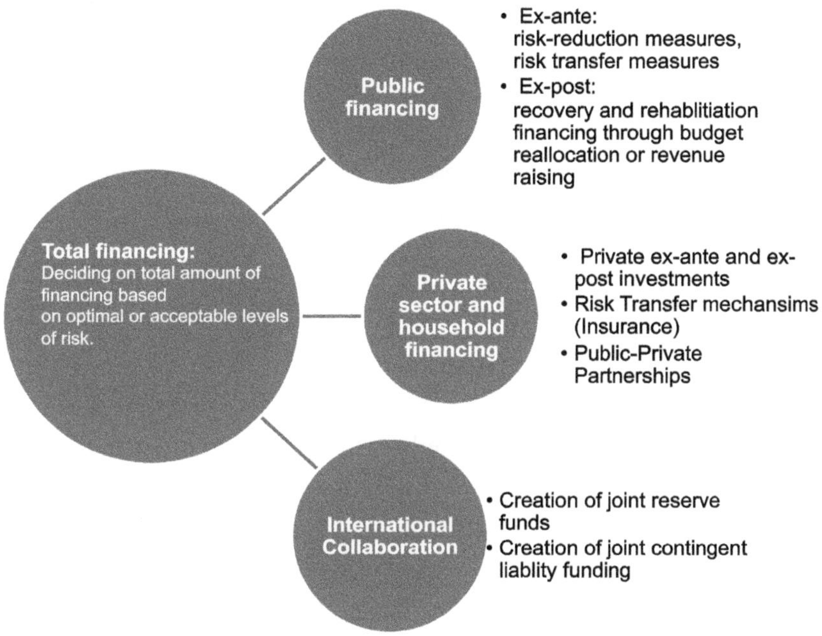

S

is also a reserve fund used to finance ex-ante disaster risk prevention investments and preparedness measures, as well as to provide post-disaster assistance. Contrary to the CATNAT in France, the KatFonds is financed by 1.1% of the total federal tax income, including income, wage and corporate taxes. Since 2010, an additional EUR 10 million is added annually from income tax receipts, which has been earmarked for state roads repairs. Three quarters of the available funding are allocated to the Federal Ministry of Agriculture, Forestry, Environment and Water and the Federal Ministry for Transport, Innovation and Technology for disaster risk prevention investments. The remaining funds are used to finance preparedness measures and for compensating losses incurred by households and businesses in the event of a disaster. At the federal level, on average EUR 250 million are spent annually on disaster risk prevention measures. So far, investments in prevention and mitigation measures have been sufficient to balance risk exposure, but if not increased soon the financing is expected to lag behind a growing municipal demand and need for protection against risks.

In Switzerland, the responsibility for financing disaster risk prevention has been shared across levels of government. The federal government bears at least 35% of the cost of disaster risk reduction measures. The cantons provide the same share, and the remainder is borne by the affected municipalities and beneficiaries. The budget for disaster risk prevention is positively correlated, given certain procedural delays in the budgeting process, to the occurrence of significant disaster events. The actual annual allocation for disaster risk prevention funding fluctuates in Switzerland, and responds strongly to the occurrence of significant disaster events. This is perhaps explained by the direct democratic elements built into the Swiss budgeting process and hence reflects the short term memory of citizens alike when major disasters occur. Studies have shown that in 2007, for example, the national government spent some EUR 450 million on prevention measures. It is expected that funding will become tighter in the coming years, given an increase in protective infrastructure investments and a potential central level funding requirement for maintenance costs.

Table 1.5 Annual federal spending on natural disaster risk prevention and mitigation

	Austria	France	Switzerland
Annual estimated average in million EUR	250	185	450

Source: OECD (2015); OECD (2016a); OECD (2016b)

The central governments are not the only source of financing disaster risk prevention measures. Sub-national governments that require such investments are co-financing them in all studied countries:

In France, an estimated 60% are paid by sub-national authorities for disaster risk prevention investments. Between 30 and 40% are shouldered by the central government. In Austria, the usual co-financing share from the central level is 50%, 20% are borne by the provinces and 30% by the local governments. In Switzerland, the national average co-funding share is at least 35%, but can be as high as 45% if investment projects show to embrace good risk management principles (such as considering participatory planning). Before 2008, central co-funding for disaster risk prevention took the relative income level of cantons into consideration, but this is no longer practiced given the new equalisation mechanisms that are built into national budget redistribution processes. Different to Austria and France, Switzerland's central government provides disaster risk prevention funding on a programmatic, 4-year basis, with the exception of large investment projects (above CHF 5 million), which require a separate funding approval process.

Table 1.6 Disaster risk prevention financing: average co-funding across levels of government

% of risk prevention funding provided by...	Austria	France	Switzerland
... the central government	50	40	35-45
... the sub-national government (i.e. provinces)	20	60	30-40
... the local government (i.e. municipalities)	30	60	15-30

Source: OECD (2015); OECD (2016a); OECD (2016b)

What can households and businesses expect in terms of damage compensation by the government in the event of a disaster?

The OECD Recommendation on Disaster Risk Financing Strategies (OECD, 2017) suggests developing public compensation and financial assistance arrangements that are coordinated across levels of government and that provide timely, targeted, transparent and equitable assistance for uninsurable losses to vulnerable segments of the population and/or economy and financial transfer mechanisms to provide support to sub-national levels of government facing fiscal constraints, with the aim of minimising economic disruptions and facilitating a stable supply of financing to the economy. In complement to this, the OECD Recommendation on the Governance of Critical Risks (OECD, 2014) emphasises the need for governments to promote a whole-of-society approach to risk management. Such an approach ensures the risk management efforts of the government are strengthened, instead of undermined, by contributions of non-governmental stakeholders such as households and business. The design of government compensation of losses and damages incurred by businesses or households during a natural disaster is a crucial determinant for the level of private contributions to self-protection. The case studies show practices that are not everywhere ideal in fostering the participation of non-governmental actors in disaster risk prevention and mitigation.

Ambiguity in the amount of compensation provided by the government is not effective in terms of encouraging self-protection investments by recipients of potential government compensation. In Austria there is no legal entitlement to receive government compensation in the event of a disaster, which is paid out of the *Katfonds*. Studies show that the average compensation rates vary between 20 and 100% of losses incurred by households or businesses during a natural disaster. Some individuals can be fully compensated at times, where others can be left with significant costs to repair damage they suffered. No clear compensation rules are applied. Compensation paid out by the *Katfonds* is complemented by payments made by provinces and local jurisdictions. Varying approaches to compensation by provinces and local jurisdictions, and variations between national compensation rates for different events, lead to significant uncertainty about expected compensation.

In France, despite the existence of an insurance scheme through the CATNAT, damage compensation is not always 100%. For example, the 2003 floods of the Rhône have shown that only half of the damages incurred by individual households were compensated by the state. The average compensation rates in France are estimated to be 60-80%. A significant amount of costs are incurred by temporary relocation of households, which are not covered by insurance. However, financial assistance for such expenses is often provided by local authorities.

In Switzerland, natural hazard insurance for buildings and content is linked to fire insurance and broadly acquired. In 19 cantons, building insurance is provided by cantonal monopoly insurers, which are public, non-profit companies. In the remaining seven cantons natural hazard insurance for buildings is provided by private insurance companies. Insurance must be provided for all buildings in a canton, regardless of their risk exposure. Coverage for building insurance is similar across the country and premium tariffs are affordable. In all but four cantons building insurance is mandatory. Deductibles can vary between 10% and 15% of damage, with a minimum of CHF 200 and a maximum of CHF 2000 per year. Finally, Switzerland created a fund for natural hazard damages that cannot be insured, which, in short, is called the elementary damage fund. It was founded by the Swiss Communal Society (*Schweizerische Gemeinnützige Gesellschaft*) and is funded by taxes and insurance premiums. The fund provides support for damages from natural hazards such as storms or floods that were not predictable or insurable.

Table 1.7 Average estimated damage compensation rates for individual households and businesses

	Switzerland	Austria	France
Federal damage compensation rates for individuals and businesses (including insurance)	85%-90% (cantonal insurance)	Variable (12% on average) (government compensation)[1]	60%-80% on average (insurance)
Sub-national complements	No	Yes (Amount undefined, average of 18%) (government compensation)	Yes (amount undefined)
Other insurance compensation	None	Less than 10% (based on sum insured)[2]	None

Sources: http://www.oecd.org/daf/fin/insurance/OECD-Conference-financial-management-flood-risk-presentation-session-5.pdf; http://www.vvo.at/vvo/vvo.nsf/sysPages/xFFDA3422FD062B89C1257FA200413B58/$file/VVO_JB_2015_220x280_WEB_Cover_Datenteil_Einzelseiten.pdf

There are several shortcomings in the funding schemes found in France and in Austria. The premium paid by insurance holders (12% of household and business insurance and 6% of motor vehicle insurance) in France is not adjusted to households' or businesses' actual risk exposure. It thereby discourages insured stakeholders to reduce their exposure or vulnerability to natural hazards by self-protection measures such as securing cellars or house walls against floods. In Austria, the *Katfonds*' funding through a fixed percentage of tax income earned by the government makes it disconnected from the levels of exposure of affected people as well. The ex-post compensation of losses, even if not clearly determined, provided through the *Katfonds* may act discouraging towards disaster risk prevention investments by households and businesses as well. Since the *Katfonds* compensation for businesses and individuals is channelled through local authorities, it is difficult to understand the actual level of compensation individuals receive and hence the efficacy of the instrument remains difficult to evaluate.

Swiss insurance authorities are conscious of the potential moral hazard risk that arises when insured clients rely on insurance pay-outs instead of investing in disaster risk prevention prior to a disaster. Therefore, insurance companies have been actively engaged in not only informing citizens about their individual responsibility in terms of adapting their behaviour in the event of a disaster, and in terms of investing in self-protection measures, but enforcing it when providing eventual pay-outs for damage compensation. For example, if expected disaster risk reduction measures were not installed, the provider would decrease the pay-out amounts.

Conclusion

This report's cross country investigation demonstrates that there is a wide recognition of the need to strengthen disaster risk prevention and mitigation efforts to boost countries' resilience against disasters. While the investment in structural disaster risk prevention and mitigation may have been the focus of countries' policies earlier on, a marked shift can be observed towards emphasising non-structural or organisational disaster risk prevention and mitigation. This has included:

- A country-wide coverage with high-quality, and publicly accessible hazard information to inform disaster risk prevention investments and disaster preparedness measures
- A recognition of the need to strengthen the integration of hazard assessments in land-use plans and decisions
- A continued focus on communicating risks to raise awareness, tapping into various channels including through the integration in standard education curricula
- An acknowledgement of the importance of business continuity planning to determine a society's ability to bounce back to normal and regain function after a disaster
- A policy discussion that spans beyond a country's sectoral responsibilities as well as beyond jurisdictional and country borders, to capture the functional area that a disaster may impact and the triggers of knock-on effects it may send across the globe
- An awareness that government financial assistance for post disaster needs has an influence on preventative action across society and levels of government

This report documents how countries have advanced in all of the above disaster risk prevention focus areas, and highlights areas where further progress could be made in the future.

Countries' focus on non-structural prevention measures is welcome and important. It demonstrates awareness by governments that disaster losses can be significantly reduced by measures that have relatively high risk reduction returns. Many of the non-structural measures discussed in this chapter require a re-focus in policies and how they are implemented and do not necessarily have a significant direct cost for governments. However, in assessing these measures, it needs to be acknowledged that substantial indirect costs may be shifted on to sub-national levels of government and non-governmental actors. Even though the sharing of costs is an effective step towards establishing a whole-of-government and a whole-of-society approach to disaster risk prevention, such policy shifts need to acknowledge the consequences this may have in terms of the level and quality of the implementation of disaster risk prevention measures.

In the process of shifting policy priorities, however, countries may have overlooked the continued, and perhaps in some areas growing need, for investing in structural protection. Even though a significant stock of protective infrastructure has been accumulated in all studied countries, this is an insufficient determinant for how much, in what form, and where this might be needed in the future. Risk patterns are changing. On the one hand socio-economic dynamics have shifted, often favouring concentration in some places at the expense of others. On the other hand environmental conditions are deteriorating and factors like climate change are expected to contribute to future changing risk patterns. These are important factors that require a shift in how structural protection is managed. In addition, the legacy of structural investments has become a liability at times, where failing maintenance and rehabilitation have exacerbated the losses suffered during a natural disaster, instead of reducing them. Countries will be confronted with managing both the stock of historical investments in protection, as well as carefully evaluating the need of allocating resources towards future new infrastructure investments.

Notes

[1] More information about the EconoMe 4.0 Platform: https://econome.ch/eco_work/index.php

[2] See website: http://nld.usace.army.mil/egis/f?p=471:1

[3] www.lemonde.fr/planete/article/2014/12/12/xynthia-l-ancien-maire-de-la-faute-sur-mer-condamne-a-quatre-ans-de-prison-ferme_4539436_3244.html

[4] Fund for the Prevention of Major Natural Risks (*Fonds de Prévention des Risques Naturels Majeurs*, FPRNM or short, *Fonds Barnier)*

[5] The Alpine Convention is an international treaty between Alpine countries (Austria, France, Germany, Italy, Liechtenstein, Monaco, Slovenia and Switzerland) as well as the EU that sets out to ensure the protection of the Alps and stresses the high value of sustainable development of the Alpine region. (http://www.alpconv.org/en/convention/default.html).

[6] Austria, Italy, France, Switzerland, Germany, Slovenia, Liechtenstein and Monaco

Bibliography

European Commission (2009), European Union Solidarity Fund: the Commission proposes to grant aid of € 109.4 million to France following Hurricane Klaus, http://europa.eu/rapid/press-release_IP-09-850_en.htm?locale=en

JRC (2014). Current status and Best Practices for Disaster Loss Data recording in EU Member States, European Commission - Joint Research Center, Ispra, Italy.

OECD (2003), OECD Peer Review: An OECD Tool for Co-operation and Change, OECD Publishing, Paris.

OECD (2010), Étude de l'OCDE sur la gestion des risques d'inondation: Bassin de la Loire, France 2010, OECD Publishing, Paris. http://dx.doi.org/10.1787/9789264056817-en

OECD (2013), Review of the Mexican National Civil Protection System, OECD Publishing, Paris. http://dx.doi.org/10.1787/9789264192294-en

OECD (2014a), Boosting Resilience through Innovative Risk Governance, OECD Publishing, Paris. http://dx.doi.org/10.1787/9789264209114-en

OECD (2014b), Recommendation of the Council on the Governance of Critical Risks, OECD Publishing, Paris.

OECD (2015), Boosting Resilience through Innovative Risk Governance: The Case of Alpine Areas in Austria, OECD Publishing, Paris.

OECD (2016a), Boosting Resilience through Innovative Risk Governance: The Case of Natural Disasters in Switzerland, OECD Publishing, Paris.

OECD (2016b), Boosting Resilience through Innovative Risk Governance: The Case of the Rhône River in France, OECD Publishing, Paris.

OECD (2016c), Progress and Challenges in Fostering Risk Prevention and Mitigation in a Cross-Country Comparative Perspective: Draft Case Study Report of the Rhône River in France, OECD Publishing, Paris.

OECD (2016d), Trends in Risk Communication Policies and Practices, OECD Reviews of Risk Management Policies, OECD Publishing, Paris.

OECD (2016e), Improving the Evidence Base on the Costs of Disasters: Key Findings from an OECD Survey, OECD Publishing, Paris.

OECD (2016f), Financial Management of Flood Risk, OECD Publishing, Paris. DOI: http://dx.doi.org/10.1787/9789264257689-en

OECD (2017). OECD Recommendation on Disaster Risk Financing Strategies. OECD Publishing, Paris. http://www.oecd.org/pensions/oecd-recommendation-disaster-risk-financing-strategies.htm

PLANAT (2004a), "*Sicherheit vor Naturgefahren. Vision und Strategie*" [Protection against Natural Hazards: Vision and Strategy], National Platform for Natural Hazards, Biel, www.planat.ch/fileadmin/PLANAT/planat_pdf/alle_2012/2001-2005/PLANAT_2004_-_Sicherheit_vor_Naturgefahren.pdf.

PLANAT (2004b), "*Strategie Naturgefahren Schweiz. Synthesebericht*" [Protection against Natural Hazards: Synthesis Report], National Platform for Natural Hazards, Biel, www.planat.ch/fileadmin/PLANAT/planat_pdf/alle_2012/2001-2005/Ammann__Schneider_2004_-_Strategie_Naturgefahren_Schweiz.pdf.

Rudolf-Miklau, F., Pichler, A., J. Suda, Rimboeck, Al, Hoehne, R., Mazzorana, B. and J. Papez (2014), "Persistence of Alpine natural hazard protection: Meeting multiple demands by applying systems engineering and life cycle management principles in natural hazard protection systems in the perimeter of the Alpine Convention", Platform on Natural Hazards of the Alpine Convention (PLANALP), Vienna.

SED (2016). *Earthquake risk in Switzerland,* Swiss Seismological Service, Bern, http://www.seismo.ethz.ch/en/knowledge/seismic-hazard-switzerland/

UNISDR (2015), Sendai Framework for Disaster Risk Reduction 2015-2030, United Nations, Geneva, http://www.unisdr.org/files/43291_sendaiframeworkfordrren.pdf.

Chapter 2

Boosting resilience through innovative risk governance: the case of Alpine areas in Austria

This chapter summarises the country case study findings of boosting resilience through innovative risk governance in Austria. After an overview over the prevalence of natural hazards, focusing on Austria's Alpine regions, and the past social and economic costs of disasters, the chapter documents Austria's progress in establishing resilience against major disasters through disaster risk prevention and mitigation measures. The chapter illustrates Austria's long-standing tradition in dealing with natural hazards and shows how responsibilities are shared across government sectors and levels. It also highlights the effective integration of citizens and communities in risk disaster risk management, from assessing hazards to financing disaster risk prevention. The chapter puts forward recommendations to confront future prevention challenges, such as meeting continuously increasing demand for new protection measures and the growing need to invest in the maintenance of existing infrastructure to sustain the intended protection levels.

Summary

Austria is very exposed to natural hazards, especially in the Alpine region. About 60% of Austria's territory is made up of mountains and large areas are covered by forests. Only about 34% of Austria's total land is suitable for human settlement. These areas are exposed to a variety of natural hazards, such as avalanches, torrents and floods. Climate change may contribute to the frequency and severity of natural disasters in the future.

The socio-economic costs of disasters in Austria are high. Floods in 2002 affected about 60 000 people and caused an estimated EUR 3 billion in direct damages. Around 14% of Austria's buildings, and the dwellings of 13% of its population, are exposed to natural hazards. Extreme temperature events, such as heatwaves, have caused a high number of deaths in the past. In the future these could potentially increase in frequency and intensity.

Key findings

Austria has developed a strong capacity to prevent and ease the impacts of natural disasters. After long-term exposure to various hazards and disasters, Austria has established solid risk management policies that are grounded in its constitution. Citizens exposed to natural hazards have actively engaged in helping to address risks, either through sharing knowledge about local hazards or initiating and contributing to protective infrastructure investments. Responsibilities for disaster risk prevention and mitigation are shared amongst the different government levels, and there has been a significant increase in capacity to enable co-operation for co-ordinating strategies and policies across ministries and sectors.

Investment in the protection of citizens is a priority for Austria. An estimated EUR 400 million is invested annually across ministries, levels of government and the private sector to prevent and alleviate the impacts of floods and Alpine hazards. This money has been used to finance disaster risk prevention and as relief funds to compensate for damages after disasters.

Maintaining this level of investment will be a challenge given the continued demand for new protective infrastructures and the increasing challenge of modernising the large stock of ageing infrastructures. Factors such as climate change may require investments to be scaled up to withstand greater degrees of disaster impacts.

Key recommendations

Adopt a broader risk-based governance system

- Use hazard zones rather than administrative borders as the principal guiding force in disaster risk prevention planning and financing. In this way, efforts across sectors and levels of governments will mutually reinforce each other. This approach will require increased co-ordination across administrative boundaries.
- Reward joint, cross-jurisdictional disaster risk prevention actions with more central-level funding.

- Regulate the way local risk assessments, prevention and preparedness measures are assessed and implemented across the hazard zones.
- Consider the use of compensation mechanisms between different municipalities affected by protective infrastructure investments and land-use decisions undertaken by adjacent jurisdictions.
- Apply clear and consistent prioritisation criteria to disaster risk prevention investment decisions.

Maintain an integrated approach to structural and non-structural measures

- Better translate information from hazard and risk assessments into land-use planning and actual land-use decisions.
- Systematically monitor the integration of hazard zones in actual land-use decisions. Significantly reduce the "grey" areas of new construction permits for existing buildings located in hazard areas. Include concrete disaster risk reduction targets in regional planning and land-use strategies.
- Continue the significant effort of re-dedicating land in the creation of flood expansion zones.

Embrace a whole-of-society approach to disaster risk prevention and mitigation

- Consider financial rewards for preventative actions by households and businesses. Ex-post loss compensation payments could equally reward individual preventative behaviour.
- Continue to increase risk awareness among property owners, explain their individual exposure to hazards and the solutions available to improve their resilience.
- Systematically collect evidence about the degree of vulnerability of private assets. Engage critical infrastructure operators by regularly assessing their vulnerabilities.

Design smart disaster risk financing mechanisms

- Increase clarity and transparency about ex-post loss compensations made by the central fund and the co-payments made by provincial and local governments.
- Address the financing gaps for the maintenance and rehabilitation of existing protective infrastructures.
- Consider the establishment of "joint maintenance bodies" that will work across jurisdictions and that are co-financed by different municipalities and potentially higher levels of government.

Introduction

Limited settlement space and significant, widespread exposure to natural hazards has formed a strong awareness in Austria for the need to prevent and mitigate natural disasters. Its key institutional foundations for disaster risk prevention and mitigation were established as early as 1884. To date, a significant amount of public funding has been made available to reduce disaster risks, with solidarity as a key guiding principle.

Among citizens there is a long established and strong volunteer force that can be mobilised during disasters, and a significant willingness to donate to help victims in the aftermath of a disaster. Strong, internationally renowned technical expertise, coupled with widespread local historical knowledge about prevailing hazards, has informed the development of advanced and detailed hazard information systems. These have guided investment in a large stock of physical protective infrastructure and the implementation of non-structural measures through land-use planning and building codes. Austria has adopted a forward-looking risk governance approach that integrates, for example, the potential impacts of climate change in the standard modelling of probability and impacts of disasters and in the adaptation needs of protective infrastructure technology.

However, recent large-scale disasters have brought to light some of the challenges Austria's disaster risk prevention and mitigation system faces that may impede its greater effectiveness and efficiency. In the aftermath of recent disastrous events, a large share of damage to buildings was found in previously known hazard-prone areas. Protective infrastructures (such as dykes) could not contain the impacts of floods because their initially conceived level of protection was too low or because they were potentially insufficiently maintained. In a multi-level governance context, underlined by Austria's federal administrative set-up, responsibilities for disaster risk prevention may not always be sufficiently delineated, and interests may differ between actors at different levels. In a context of tightening public coffers, increasing the impact of existing resources will become ever more important.

This report assesses the progress, achievements and potential challenges of Austria's disaster risk prevention system, with a particular emphasis on its governance or institutional design. Governance arrangements can significantly facilitate or hamper the effective engagement and investment of governmental and non-governmental stakeholders in disaster risk prevention and mitigation. For example, the decision of an individual household not to invest in protecting their own home may be the result of an expectation that the government will invest for them. Alternatively, a local government decision not to invest in a protective measure may be the result of neighbouring jurisdictions potentially benefitting without paying.

This study builds on previous work of the OECD (2014a) that sought to identify effective ways for OECD countries to boost their resilience against extreme disaster events, which informed the OECD Recommendation on the Governance of Critical Risks (OECD, 2014b). In a cross-country comparative study, of which this case study is one selected country, the OECD assessed and compared disaster risk prevention and mitigation systems across a set of OECD countries, based on the framework and recommendations previously developed. The objective of the study was to identify good practice and challenges across case study countries as they attempt to achieve greater resilience through a whole-of-society approach to disaster risk prevention and mitigation that involves a joint effort between government and non-governmental actors. The case study of Austria informs the comparative analysis and allows lessons to be shared widely in order to inform OECD countries' disaster risk prevention policies and practices.

This case study analyses whether the institutional roles, responsibilities, financial set-up and incentives of Austria's core disaster risk prevention institutions and actors are aligned so that each actor's expected contribution to a whole-of-society approach to disaster risk prevention is carried out adequately. Section II provides an overview of Austria's hazard landscape and its socio-economic relevance. It includes an assessment of recent significant disasters and the overall trend in socio-economic losses from disasters in Austria. Section III provides an overview of the principal legal frameworks and responsibilities governing Austria's disaster risk prevention and mitigation efforts. Section IV and V assess the effectiveness of current institutional and financial frameworks in fostering a whole-of-society approach to disaster risk prevention and mitigation. Section VI provides a final assessment and recommendations.

Austria's hazard sources and risk exposure

Section highlights

- On average, only 34% of Austria's territory is suitable for habitation; as little as 11% of territory is considered habitable in the province of Tyrol.
- 13 000 torrent catchments, 6 000 snow avalanche paths, 9 000 lakes and 100 000 km of rivers constitute the sources of flood, torrent, avalanche or rockfalls risks.
- The last major floods occurred in 2013, 2005 and 2002, the latter caused EUR 3 billion in damages and affected 60 000 people.
- Around 14% of Austria's building stock and 13% of its population are exposed to the potential of natural hazards.

Hazard sources

Austria's topography is characterised by mountainous terrain covering around 60% of its total territory. Moreover 50% of its land is covered by forests. As a consequence only about 34%, on average, of Austria's territory is considered as settlement area. In some provinces, such as Tyrol, this share is as low as 11%. A large part of Austria's settlement areas remains exposed to natural hazards such as avalanches, torrents or floods (see full list of prevailing hazards in Table 1). Some 13 000 torrent catchments and nearly 6 000 snow avalanche paths, in addition to numerous rivers, potentially threaten Austria's settlement areas. Some parts of the country are also exposed to significant earthquake risk, although the last major earthquakes date back a number of centuries.

Austria's most costly natural hazard is flooding because of its 100 000 km of rivers, creeks and about 9 000 lakes (Pichler, 2013). Together with torrents, flooding is the most recurring disaster (Figure 2.1) with the greatest potential for socio-economic impacts, followed by hail, storms, avalanches and rock falls or landslides. Heatwaves have had the most human impact: the 2003 heatwave caused roughly 180 deaths in Vienna alone (Hutter et al., 2007).

Table 2.1 Types of natural hazards prevalent in Austria

Natural hazard category	Types of natural hazards
Geological hazards	Soil erosion, landslide, rock falls, rock slides, debris slide, earthquake
Meteorological hazards	Heavy rainfall, hail, lightning, fog, drought, frost, storm, cold and heatwaves
Hydrological hazards	Flood, flash flood, debris flow, torrential flood, glacial lake outburst
Snow hazards	Avalanche, ice fall, glacier push, snow load (pressure)
Fire hazards	Forest fire
Biological hazards	Plant and animal disease, forest calamities by insects (e.g. bark beetle etc.)

Source: http://www.naturgefahren.at/karten.html

Climate change is increasingly recognised as a driver of a potential increase in the frequency or severity of some natural disasters, including: an increase in the frequency and intensity of floods, extreme low water periods and droughts coupled with heatwaves, an increased risk of rock falls and rock slides, intensified soil erosion, and heightened risks of forest fire (OECD, 2013). Perceived and observed increases in damaging events may also be linked to better documentation and increased exposure, including the increased occupation of land where potential disasters can occur. Independent of the actual cause or linkages between the causes, climate change has been recognised to lead to potentially damaging economic and social impacts, as well as ecological impacts (Pichler, 2010). Therefore, Austria has engaged in developing a forward-looking approach to its disaster risk prevention and mitigation management by ensuring a regular and dynamic updating of hazard zone maps and adapting protective infrastructure to the potential impacts of climate change.

Austria has recognised additional factors that could potentially drive its future and longer-term vulnerability to disasters. For example, significant demographic changes may have an immediate impact on its disaster risk management capacity, such as its aging population structure or diminishing population in some mountainous areas. These factors could reduce the availability of volunteers that have become an essential part of Austria's emergency response capacity.

Figure 2.1 Types and frequency of occurrence of natural disasters in Austria 1900-2014

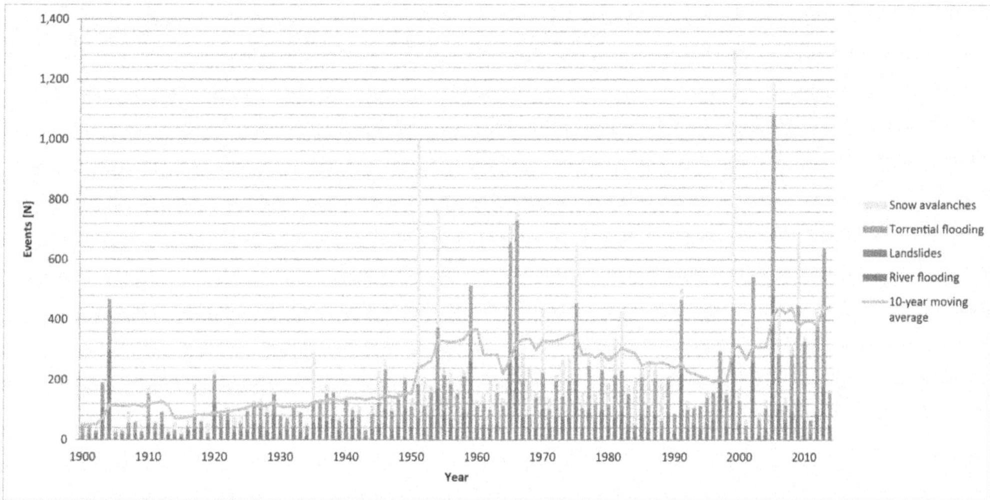

Source: BMLFUW cited in Fuchs, Keiler and Zischg (2015), "A spatiotemporal multi-hazard exposure assessment based on property data", Natural Hazards and Earth System Sciences, Vol. 15/9.

Disaster risk exposure

Due to the very limited territory that can be used for settlement, Austria's exposure to natural hazards is significant. Table 2.2 shows that 8% of buildings in municipalities that require a hazard zone plan for torrents and avalanches are exposed to torrent and/or avalanche risk. Table 3 shows that nearly 9% of all buildings in Austria are located in areas exposed to risk of flooding with a return period of up to 200 years.

Table 2.2 Exposure of Austrian buildings to torrent and avalanche hazards, 2013

	No. of buildings (2013)	In % of total	In % of buildings in municipalities that require a hazard zone plan
Total building stock in Austria	2 399 545*	100	
... Of which buildings in municipalities that need to have a hazard zone map	1 477 419	61.57%	100
... Of which exposed to torrents and/or avalanches	118 272	4.93%	8.01%

Note: * the grand total of buildings in Austria would be 3.7 million. However only those that have a digital ground plot and an unambiguous address location that can be linked with information of the building registry, as well as a digitalised hazard zone map, could be used for this calculation.

Source: Fuchs and Zischg (2014), "*Vulnerabilitätslandkarte Österreich, Kurzfassung*" " [Vulnerability Map Austria, Short Version], IAN Report 152, Institut für Alpine Naturgefahren, Universität für Bodenkultur, Vienna, (unpublished).

Table 2.3 Exposure of Austrian buildings to flood hazards, 2001

	No. of buildings (2001)	In % of total	Market value in million EUR	Reconstruction value in million EUR
Total building stock in Austria	1 995 027*	100		
.... Of which exposed to floods with a return period of 30 years**	162 716	6.78	117 025	119 967
.... Of which exposed to floods with a return period of 100 years**	193 337	8.06	139 382	146 815
.... Of which exposed to floods with a return period of 200 years**	215 545	8.98	156 703	163 530
.... Of which exposed to floods with a return period of over 200 years**	1 779 482	74.16	1 051 983	1 218 766

Notes: * the total of buildings in Austria in 2001 would be higher, but only those with a digital ground plot and an unambiguous address location were included.
** the return period of floods is based on Austria's HORA (*Hochwasserrisikozonierung* Austria – HORA [Flood Risk Zoning Austria]), which excludes torrents and avalanches covered by the Austrian Service for Torrent and Avalanche Control (WLV).

Source: Habsburg-Lothringen et al. (2009), "*Zonierung und Gebäudebewertung zur Bestimmung des Schadenpotentials für Hochwasser in Österreich*" [Zoning and building rating to determine potential damage levels of floods in Austria], in Prettenthaler, F. and H. Albrecher (eds.), *Hochwasser und dessen Versicherung in Österreich* [Floods and insurance in Austria], Austria Academy of Sciences and Joanneum Research, Vienna.

The following maps (Figure 2.2) show the location and spatial concentration of exposed buildings to avalanche, torrent and flood risks.

It has been estimated that the 8% of buildings exposed to torrent and avalanche risks amount to EUR 66 billion in economic value (Fuchs and Zischg, 2014). The maximum probable loss (Table 2.3) for flood risk in Austria, which corresponds to a flood return period of over 200 years, was estimated at EUR 1 218 billion (Habsburg-Lothringen et al., 2009).

Around 430 000 people are registered as residents in areas at risk of torrents and avalanches. In Austria's draft flood risk management plan (BLMFUW, 2015) 651 963 people live in areas flooded by a return probability of 300 years. This means that some 1.08 million people (or around 13% of the total population) are potentially affected by torrents, avalanches and floods in Austria. Tourist accommodation are among exposed buildings, which means the number of people at risk can be higher at given moments of the year (Fuchs and Zischg, 2014). During the winter season around 17 000 additional persons are exposed in buildings, and during summer time the number exposed increases to around 44 500 (Fuchs, 2015). As a result, one additional person is at risk per 1.7 exposed citizens during the winter and per eight to nine exposed citizens in the summer.

Figure 2.2 Buildings and residents exposed to avalanches and river flooding in Austria

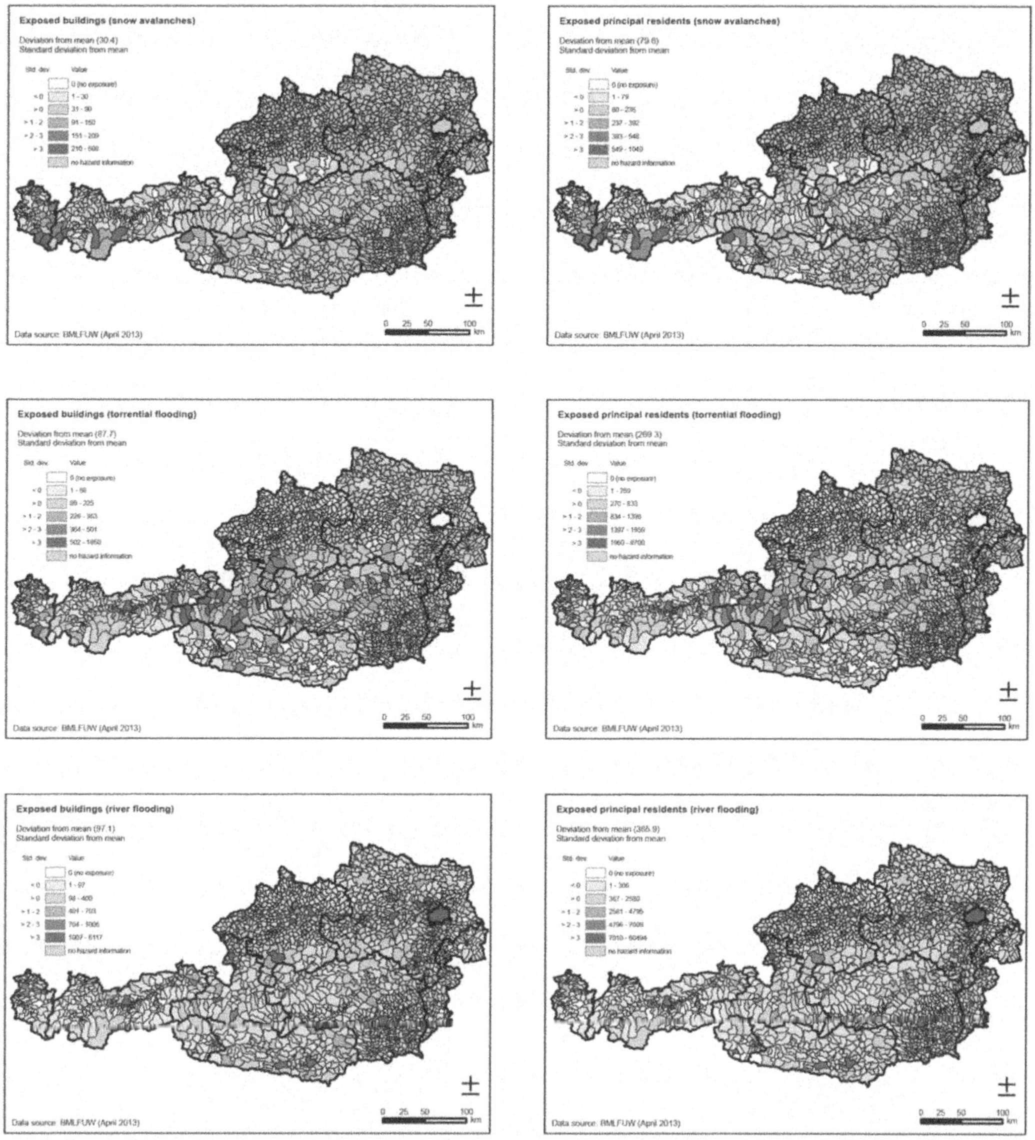

Source: Fuchs, Keiler and Zischg (2015), "A spatiotemporal multi-hazard exposure assessment based on property data", Natural Hazards and Earth System Sciences, Vol. 15/9.

Currently, there is no comprehensive information on the exposure of public assets and critical infrastructure to natural hazards. Given the direct importance and indirect consequences associated with service interruptions, it is vital that Austria expands this analysis to cover the exposure of these assets.

Socio-economic impacts of past disasters

Calculating and recording the socio-economic impacts of disasters is useful in many ways. It tracks trends in social and economic losses over time, thereby informing risk managers whether risk management policies have been effective in reducing risks and decreasing losses over time. It also informs the prioritisation of risk reduction investments by indicating areas that are most vulnerable to disaster events. Modelling and estimation methods that help determine the scale of losses have improved significantly, due in part to loss information that was collected in the past. Nevertheless, a continued effort to systematically collect this information can increase the effectiveness and efficiency of risk management policies and inform the refinement and improvement of loss modelling in the future.

Economic losses can be distinguished by direct and indirect economic losses. Direct economic losses reflect the monetary value of total or partial destruction of physical assets in the affected area. Indirect economic losses reflect the decline in value-added as a consequence of direct economic loss and/or human and environmental impacts (UNISDR, 2015).

Social losses, i.e. losses to life and affected people, have been well recorded. Figure 2.3 shows recorded deaths from avalanches since 1993, with an annual average of 25 fatalities. On average, some 150 persons are affected by avalanches every year. A detailed historical analysis reveals that until the 1970s, avalanches affected people in settlement areas or during work, following which an increase in mountain leisure activities led to affected people mostly being found in non-secured mountain areas. This trend has been reversed in winters of heavy snowfall, such as in 1989 and 1999 (Habersack et al., 2009).

Figure 2.3 Number of avalanche deaths in Austria, 1993-2012

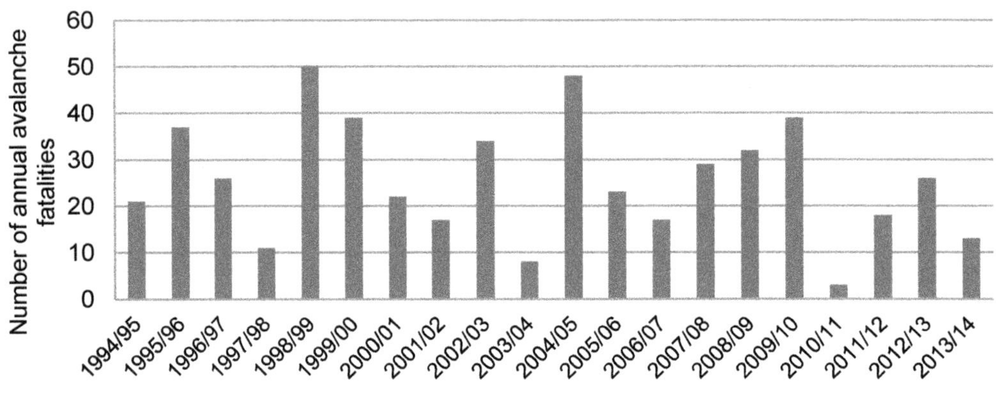

Source: Österreichisches Kuratorium für Alpine Sicherheit (2015), "*Analyse: Berg*" [Analysis: Mountain], Winter 2014/2015, Austria Alpine Safety Board, Innsbruck.

In terms of economic losses, no systematic records can be found for Austria. Some continued economic loss reporting can be found for torrents and avalanches, but recorded losses are not necessarily monetised and distinguished by direct and indirect losses and accrued to private or public stakeholders. For a set of major catastrophic events, in-depth studies of economic losses have been conducted and results recorded.

Austria has experienced a number of major disaster events in the past 15 years that caused significant negative socio-economic impacts. For these events, socio-economic losses have been well documented. Table 4 shows the most recent larger scale disasters.

The 2002 flood events affected some 60 000 people and caused approximately EUR 3.2 billion in damages. The floods of 2013 were comparably intensive, but caused significantly smaller damage sum: EUR 870 million. The major lessons learned of the 2002 floods likely contributed to decreasing the losses experienced in 2013.

Table 2.4.Socio-economic impacts of the largest disastrous events in Austria since 1999

Year	Disaster type	Deaths	Affected people*	Direct damages EUR	Affected regions
2013	Flood	4*	200	EUR 0.87 billion	Salzburg, Vorarlberg, Tyrol, lower and upper Austria
2005	Flood	1	900	EUR 0.5 billion	Vorarlberg, Tyrol, Styria, Carinthia
2003	Heatwave	345*	*N/a*	*N/a*	Country-wide
2002	Flood	9*	60 000	EUR 3.2 billion	Lower and upper Austria, Salzburg
1999	Avalanche	38	12 000**	EUR 10 million	Galtür (Tyrol)

Note: *data based on EM-DAT estimates; **number of people evacuated, based on BMLFUW.

Source: BMLFUW (2015), "*Entwurf Nationaler Hochwasserrisikomanagementplan* 2015" [National Flood Risk Management Plan 2015 (Draft)], Ministry of Agriculture, Forestry, Environment and Water Management (BMLFUW), Vienna.

Austria's records of relief payments by the Austrian *KatFonds* is a good source of information to approximate average past losses as they partly cover losses of uninsured households and public infrastructure (details on the functioning of the *KatFonds* can be found in Section V). Based on these recorded payments, Austria faces an annual average loss by torrents, avalanches and floods of around EUR 210 million. Figure 2.4 shows that average annual direct losses from torrents and avalanches amount to an estimated EUR 25-30 million. For floods, the annual average loss was calculated to be EUR 180 million (Habersack et al., 2009). Direct losses vary over the years and sometimes cause significantly more damages than the average annual government prevention spending.

Figure 2.4 Damages to buildings and infrastructure versus investments in prevention measures for torrents and avalanches, 1972-2004 (real prices 2004)

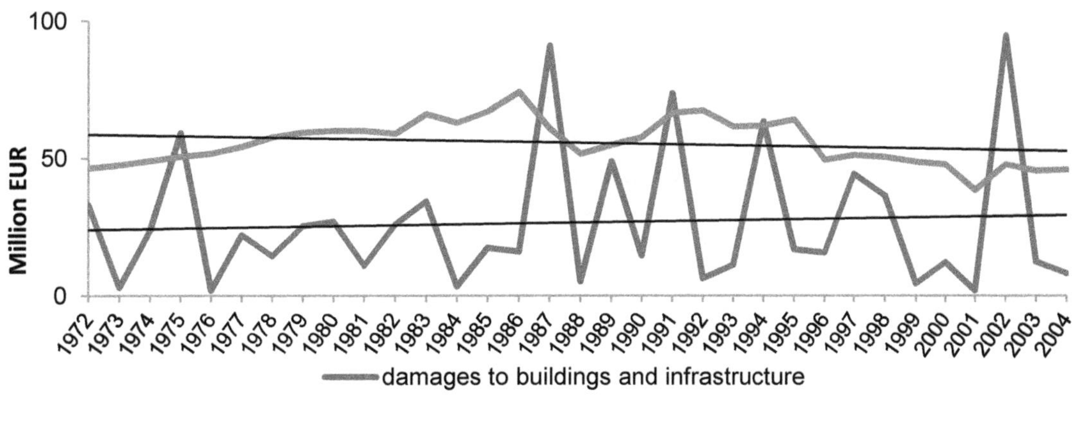

Source: Sinabell (2009) "*Eine volkswirtschaftliche Analyse der Wildbach- und Lawinenverbauung*" [An economic analysis of torrent and avalanche barriers], WIFO Austria, Vienna.

Investment in reducing risks from torrents and landslides has shown that it pays off over time. The number of exposed buildings in municipalities subject to torrent risks has increased by 66% since 1970. However, during this time the damages suffered from torrents were reduced by 22% (Habersack et al., 2009).

Conclusion

Although detailed estimations of socio-economic losses have been recorded for some hazards and major past disaster events, Austria could benefit from improving the systematic recording of social and economic losses of multiple types of disasters. Despite very good and comprehensive hydrographic documentation, little attention has been paid to systematically evaluating the socio-economic consequences of significant disaster events. Some pieces of information are gathered by different agencies, such as private sector data on exposure; however no systematic exchange or compilation of information is performed to record the socio-economic losses of disasters. Most of the available records are limited to direct economic losses; however, indirect losses, caused by the interruption of services, could be much more important as they cause damage to the regional, and sometimes national, economy.

The provincial governments in charge of assisting victims and handling the compensation process for households and businesses would be in a good position to carry out overall socio-economic impact assessments. In addition, the evaluations conducted by the Federal Chancellery, the commerce chambers and the insurance associations could complement the bottom-up data collection process (Sinabell and Url, 2006).

Risk governance in Austria

Section highlights

- Austria has a long established tradition in public disaster risk prevention and mitigation, with core policies anchored in Austria's constitution and the main institutions established in the 19th century.
- Like many policy areas in Austria's federal set-up, disaster risk prevention and mitigation is shared by different government levels, with the centre determining strategy and core funding and the local levels responsible for implementation.
- To ensure co-ordination across levels and between different sectors, platforms such as the Austrian Spatial Planning Conference (ÖROK) have been established that are also used to evaluate the system in place and discuss potential reforms.
- Austria's recently concluded national flood risk management plan is an example of a well-coordinated approach to developing an integrated and widely shared flood risk management strategy across national and sub-national levels of government.

Introduction

Disaster risk prevention and mitigation management is, like many other policy areas in Austria's federal system, a shared task across different levels of government. Disaster risk prevention and mitigation is principally led by the central level and carried out in close co-operation with the provinces. To complement this, provincial and local governments and other local interest groups carry out responsibilities, tasks and obligations related to disaster risk prevention and mitigation. For example, local interest groups are in charge of initiating the demand for a protective infrastructure against hazards, which is then co-financed and decided upon by all other levels of governments.

The legal frameworks guiding each actor's role and responsibilities are numerous and include the Forestry Law, the Water Law, the Hydraulic Engineering Assistance Act, the Building and Spatial Planning Codes and the *KatFonds* law.

Figure 2.5 Overview of Austria's main actors for risk management

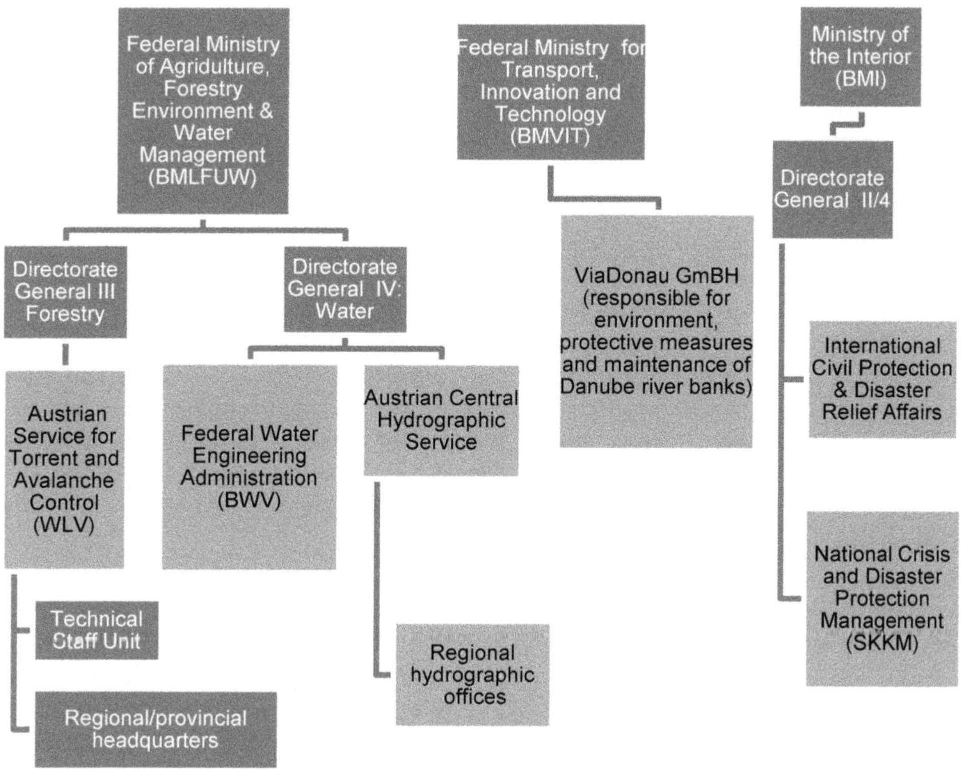

Source: BMLFUW (2015), https://www.bmlfuw.gv.at/english/ministry/organigramme.html ; BMVIT (2015), https://www.bmvit.gv.at/en/ministerium/downloads/chart.pdf; BMI (2015), http://www.bmi.gv.at/cms/bmi_zivilschutz/

Disaster risk prevention and mitigation management is anchored in Article 10 of Austria's constitution under public safety and services for the public, making it the responsibility of the central level, albeit stipulated as a shared task. Even though a clear legal framework is provided for disaster risk prevention and mitigation where the overarching aim is to secure and improve people's lives, it is important to highlight that there exists no legal claim for anyone to be protected from natural hazards by the state and hence there is no obligation for the state to provide protective infrastructure (Hecht, 2009).

Austria's risk governance structure is marked by shared responsibilities horizontally through different line ministries in charge and vertically between different levels of government. Disaster risk prevention and mitigation is separately managed from crisis management. Figure 2.5 provides an overview of Austria's core risk governance structure.

Disaster risk prevention management of floods (with the exception of three larger rivers) and hazards such as avalanches, torrents and smaller-sized rivers are under the responsibility of the Federal Ministry of Agriculture, Forestry, Environment and Water (BMLFUW). The three larger rivers, the Danube, the March and parts of the Thaya, are managed by the Federal Ministry of Transport, Innovation and Technology (BMVIT). Austria has a long-standing tradition in disaster risk prevention, for example the Austrian Service for Torrent and Avalanche Control (WLV) was founded in 1884 and the Hydrographic Service in 1893.

Governing disaster risk prevention and mitigation: Main institutions and actors

Within the BMLFUW, both structural and non-structural disaster risk prevention measures are managed. Two different departments share this work between them:

1. The Federal Service for Torrent and Avalanche Control (WLV) principally covers risks from torrents and avalanches (by law) and rockfalls and landslides (in practice).[1] The WLV is responsible for hazard identification and zoning, implementation and monitoring of protective measures, providing advice and analysis, and the monitoring of catchment areas of torrents and avalanches (carried out by regional service branches). WLV's headquarters are within the ministry and it carries out its work through regional service branches that correspond approximately to the federal provinces. These are further divided into local service branches that reflect administrative districts. The proximity of experts to municipalities at risk has been considered a key advantage in raising risk awareness and acceptance levels of disaster risk prevention measures.

2. The Federal Water Engineering Administration (BWV) covers risks stemming from rivers. There are some instances where its responsibilities overlap with The WLV and co-ordination between the two departments is crucial. Austria's national flood risk management plan includes a detailed list of rivers and outlines the responsible agency for managing flood protection (BMLFUW, 2015). The BWV is mandated with developing the national flood risk management plan in close co-operation with all relevant actors at the federal state, province and municipality levels. The plan is based on a comprehensive set of flood risk and flood hazard plans for all areas where a preliminary flood risk has been identified. It covers the entire flood risk management cycle and has a comprehensive set of measures as the basis of work carried out over the next six years (2015-2021). The BWV co-ordinates hazard identification and zoning (including designation of discharge areas) and the construction and operation of flood management structures. The BWV also handles the reimbursement of losses incurred by people in flood discharge areas. The BWV shares its responsibility with federal provinces.

The BMVIT is responsible for managing disaster risk prevention of flooding along the Danube and the March rivers.[2] The BMVIT also operates water gauges and maintains the river bed and fairway of the Danube and is responsible for the inland waterway fairway of these rivers as operator and authority.

Although the BMLFUW is the main co-ordinating body of risk and mitigation, the Ministry of Interior (BMI) represents Austria in the EU civil protection mechanism, which has included prevention aspects since 2014 (including a national risk assessment). The BMI is also responsible for disaster preparedness and response at governmental and international levels.

Austria's Ministry of Finance (BMF) is in charge of handling Austria's biggest source of prevention funding, the *Katastrophenfonds* (*KatFonds*), which collects its revenue from a number of tax streams (see Section V). Funding from the *KatFonds* is used to finance prevention measures and compensation for damages suffered by citizens, businesses and public authorities (see Section V).

Another important actor in Austria's risk management landscape is the Austrian Conference on Spatial Planning (ÖROK)[3]. Founded in 1971, ÖROK was established by the federal government, the provinces and municipalities to co-ordinate spatial development at the national level. ÖROK is in charge of developing and publishing an Austrian spatial planning concept, last published in 2011, which represents a nationwide spatial planning strategy. The body is chaired by the Federal Chancellor and its members include all federal ministers and heads of the provinces, the presidents of the Austrian Association of Cities and Towns and the Austrian Association of Municipalities, and the heads of the social and economic partners that have a consulting vote. ÖROK plays an instrumental role in bringing all interest groups together to discuss how disaster risk prevention management can be better integrated into spatial planning decisions, building codes and other legal frameworks that guide disaster risk prevention management. As many of the past damages of floods have been attributed to weaknesses in enforcing disaster risk prevention measures in spatial planning practice, ÖROK will continue to play a key role in increasing Austria's disaster risk management capacity by providing a platform for stakeholder dialogue and establishing key policy recommendations.

Austria's national flood risk management plan (BMLFUW, 2015), which came into force at the end of 2015, is a recent good practice example of bringing together flood risk management stakeholders across ministries and levels of government to develop a set of shared goals and implementation actions. The plan was also closely co-ordinated with the bilateral and international river commissions in which Austria participates. Based on the EU flood risk directive, Austria identified Areas of Potentially Significant Flood Risk (APSFR) based on its flood hazard and risk maps that were informed by past flood events, likely future events and existing protection levels (BMLFUW, 2015).

Sub-national governments, as well as critical infrastructure providers and the private sector, play a crucial role in managing disaster preparedness, responses to disasters and in disaster risk prevention management, as will be discussed below.

Research and development supports and informs Austria's rapidly evolving risk prevention management over time. Given the importance of disaster risk prevention, special natural hazard management branches have been created (such as at the University of Natural Resources and Life Sciences in Vienna) and degree courses developed to train future natural hazard engineers and managers for the public and private sectors. Action in this area also supports the development of new technologies for protective infrastructure to adapt to rapidly changing natural and social environments. Academia has been closely involved in studying the aftermath of disasters to improve their work and to critically reflect on the implementation of good practice by public and private agencies.[4]

Governing disaster risk preparedness and response: Main institutions and actors

The Federal Ministry of Interior (BMI) is the main actor in charge of civil protection and crisis management and has a key co-ordination function among all relevant actors locally and across borders in response to crises. There are two relevant departments within the Ministry: the International Civil Protection and Disaster Relief Affairs Department and the National Crisis and Disaster Protection Management (SKKM).

Depending on the scale of the disaster, the smallest administrative unit possible is charged with managing the situation. This can be the municipality, the district administration, the provincial administration or the federal government. The federal government is responsible for managing major crises through its SKKM. The federal level is also responsible for managing pandemics, rail or air accidents, and major forestry incidents. The SKKM brings together all ministries, federal provinces and emergency organisations (including rescue services, fire brigades, and other units, if required, such as the Austrian Broadcasting Corporation and the Austrian Press Agency). Closer co-ordination between all relevant groups has only been established since 2004.

The federal provinces are responsible for organising relief services and providing resources for emergency assistance. All provinces have enacted legislation to define responsibilities at local, district and provincial levels. Emergency relief is largely supported by volunteers: over 400 000 people are part of Austria's volunteer corps. Their efforts are supported by federal and provincial governments that provide resources for training and equipment, as well as for liability and accident insurance. The two biggest organisations in charge of emergency response are the Austrian Fire Brigade and the Austrian Red Cross.

The Ministry of Defence and Sports (BMLVS) is the governing body of the national army (*Bundesheer*) and also plays a central role in civil protection services, notably in mobilising the army corps to help set up emergency preparedness measures and handle emergency responses.

Sub-national responsibilities

In terms of disaster risk prevention and mitigation, federal authorities have sub-national branches (in the case of the WLV) or provincial government units that service provinces and municipalities to provide hazard information or install and advise on, as well as co-finance, protective infrastructure. Most importantly, local governments (or local interest groups) are in the driver's seat for requesting and negotiating the co-financing of protective infrastructure.

Land-use planning is another important disaster risk prevention and mitigation function of the sub-national levels. Although federal provinces establish a province-wide spatial plan and have a monitoring role over local land-use decisions, it is the municipal level that takes the final decision on land-use and that grants building permits, which has important implications for disaster risk prevention.

Box 2.1 The role of Austria's forestry services in disaster risk prevention

The forest services, particularly in the province of Tyrol, serve important biological disaster risk prevention functions by protecting the forest against hazards from torrents, rockfalls, landslides and avalanches. The Tyrolean Forest Service encourages forest owners to manage their forests by providing them with resources to prevent these natural hazards. In addition, forest supervisors have been upgraded and trained to fulfil a risk monitoring function where they document current conditions and set measures to prevent log jams.

The forest services work closely with the Austrian Service for Torrent and Avalanche Control and the Departments of Geology, Agriculture and Hydraulic Engineering of the provincial government and municipalities of Tyrol. Co-ordination meetings also take place between the different forest services of the provinces of Austria. Shared projects on the EU Interregional level were setup with Italy, Bavaria and Salzburg.

Sources: Amt der Tiroler Landesregierung (2011), *Waldstrategie 2020, Amt der Tiroler Landesregierung, Gruppe Forst, Innsbruck* [Forest Strategy 2020, Office of the Provincial Government of Tirol, Forest Group], www.tirol.gv.at/fileadmin/themen/umwelt/wald/waldzustand/downloads/waldstrategie2020_web.pdf.

The provision of disaster relief is primarily the responsibility of the federal provinces, which have adopted laws defining the management of interventions at community, district and provincial levels. This includes the organisation of disaster relief services and the provision of resources for emergency assistance and disaster relief measures. Operationally, the provinces rely on voluntary relief organisations: around 340 000 volunteers are engaged in local fire brigades and nearly 60 000 are engaged with the Austrian Red Cross. If disasters exceed the local or provincial service capacities, the national army intervenes.

The role of international collaboration

Austria works very closely and organises regular exchanges on disaster risk management issues (including disaster risk insurance models) with the European Commission (where Austria has been the co-chair of the Flood Working Group) and with the International River Commissions of the Danube,[5] the Rhine[6] and the Elbe[7]. Basin wide flood risk management plans are elaborated in collaboration with all neighbouring countries and stakeholders. For example, emphasis on the importance of transboundary collaboration is established in priority area five of the EU Danube Strategy, which is devoted to the management of environmental risks and flood risk management among neighbouring countries. This priority area highlights flood protection as an important element of transboundary collaboration.

A number of cross-border commissions have been created to co-ordinate economic, scientific and technical co-operation along shared rivers (Figure 2.6). For example, commissions were established between Austria and the Czech Republic, Austria and Hungary, and Austria and Slovenia for the Mur and the Drau Rivers, and with Germany for the Danube River. The BMVIT collaborates with Slovakia for the water road of the March River.

Austria also participates in the Alpine Convention[8] – an international treaty between Alpine countries (Austria, France, Germany, Italy, Liechtenstein, Monaco, Slovenia and Switzerland) and the EU – that aims to promote sustainable development in the Alpine area and protect the interests of residents. It embraces an integrated approach, including environmental, social, economic and cultural dimensions in developing the Alpine area's future. The Natural Hazards Platform of the Alpine Convention (PLANALP), established in 2004, aims to develop common strategies for the prevention of Alpine hazards as well as providing a platform for exchanging good practices on natural hazard management across borders. The initiative, currently presided by Austria, is mandated to formulate strategic concepts on integrated risk management against natural hazards and to coordinate the implementation of subsequent measures.

Conclusion

This section provided an overview of the main actors in charge of Austria's disaster risk prevention and mitigation management. It was demonstrated that there are several actors with often similar roles in disaster risk prevention and mitigation. In the following section, the objective will be to evaluate how each specific disaster risk prevention task (categorised in structural and non-structural measures) is approached by different actors and whether, in practice, the right incentives are in place for each actor to fully assume their roles and work together and co-ordinate tasks. It assumes that hazards often occur simultaneously and do not stop at local administrative or provincial borders.

Management of structural and non-structural disaster risk prevention and mitigation measures

Section highlights

- The demand for structural protective infrastructure seems to exceed supply that can be co-financed by the centre, especially under a tightening budget landscape. This makes prioritisation crucial if investments are to remain efficient and equitable.
- There is a large stock of protective infrastructure that needs to be maintained and for which additional investments currently exceed the available budget. Financial and technical capacities of municipalities may be limited, thereby increasing vulnerability.
- Water boards have inspired a "beneficiaries-pay-principle" on an equitable and solidary basis, complementing the traditional co-financing model.
- Cross-jurisdictional collaboration is indispensable to ensure the effectiveness and efficiency of disaster risk prevention investments; regulatory frameworks, financial incentives and facilitating platforms could be created to foster such collaboration.
- To maximise the benefits from disaster risk prevention investments, and to avoid the creation of new risks, accurate and up to date hazard information needs to be fully integrated into land-use decisions.

Introduction

To reduce disaster risks, a distinction between structural and non-structural or organisational measures is useful. Structural measures, which often require significant public expenditure, seek to reduce disaster impacts through physical constructions such as dykes and dams, retention walls, avalanche barriers, rock falls nets or slope stabilisation measures. Given the large percentage of Austria that is covered by forests, forestry measures (such as maintaining forests at high altitudes or forest management measures to strengthen the protection capacity of forests and afforestation) constitute equally important structural measures. Non-structural measures, whose direct costs are comparatively lower, encompass hazard zoning, spatial planning, building codes and their enforcement, risk communication measures or business continuity planning. Other physical measures are used on an emergency basis, such as mobile protection measures used in the event of floods, or automatic weather stations to provide early warning information.

Structural measures have long constituted a core of Austria's disaster risk prevention management to protect existing settlement areas. They have been conceived and implemented on the basis of solidarity, whereby the direct beneficiaries (which can be municipalities or other forms of interest groups, such as water boards or private owners) in local municipalities contribute to co-financing from higher levels of government.

There has been an increasing recognition of the importance of an integrated approach. Although structural measures make up most of Austria's disaster risk reduction investment, non-structural measures have become an increased focus, especially following several consecutive large-scale floods that highlighted the limits of structural measures and the potential benefits of non-structural measures. For example, a significant share of damages during the 2002 summer floods was caused by assets located in known areas at risk. Section II showed that a large share of Austria's building stock is presently located in areas at risk. Improving the integration of hazard zoning in land-use decisions may therefore yield a high return in terms of reducing exposure to risks. The progressive influence of the EU Flood Directive on national disaster risk prevention and mitigation policies has also increased Austria's engagement in fostering an integrated (flood) risk management approach, which suggests a key focus on overall capacity building and other non-structural measures as a complement to structural protective measures.

In Austria, structural and non-structural measures that protect against floods, torrents, avalanches, rock falls and landslides are largely the responsibility of the BMLFUW. Measures that protect against flooding from the Danube and the March rivers fall under the responsibility of the BMVIT. This section first focuses on structural measures, then discusses the different non-structural measures. The review of structural measures entails an analysis of general policies and practice and looks specifically at to what extent a functional approach to disaster risk prevention management is taken. A functional approach aims to take into account the entire area affected by and benefiting from disaster risk prevention measures, rather than taking decisions confined to the municipal level. This section will also look at how well Austria has developed a whole-of-society approach to disaster risk prevention management, which includes the responsibility and roles given to private sector actors and individuals and households.

Management and implementation of structural measures

Decision-making process

Structural measures implemented by the WLV within the BMLFUW are decided upon at the central level and co-financed by provinces and local beneficiaries (i.e. municipalities or water boards). However, the initial demand for investment needs to be placed by the local beneficiary or local interest groups (Figure 2.6).

Local interest groups make a request to the regional service branch of the WLV that, together with the central WLV unit, assesses the protection needs and whether there is public interest in the investment. This is subsequently prioritised among other requests received (Figure 2.6). In return, local authorities develop a proposal for a financial contribution to the measure. In addition to municipal financing, co-financing at the local level can come from other co-beneficiaries, including the road administration or railway operators. Upon receiving a request for a protective infrastructure, local authorities are charged with freeing up and dedicating land for the investment measure. The provincial government is then approached for co-financing and the WLV's central unit will conclude a formal agreement, including the amount of resources it will dedicate to the project. The usual distribution amounts to: 50% from the central level, 20% provincial level and 30% local level funding. Interest groups or direct beneficiaries have increasingly financed the local share. Figure 2.6 shows that since 1980, this share has increased from around 20% to 27%.

Figure 2.6 Average co-financing share for structural measures from local interest groups 1980-2014 (in % of total)

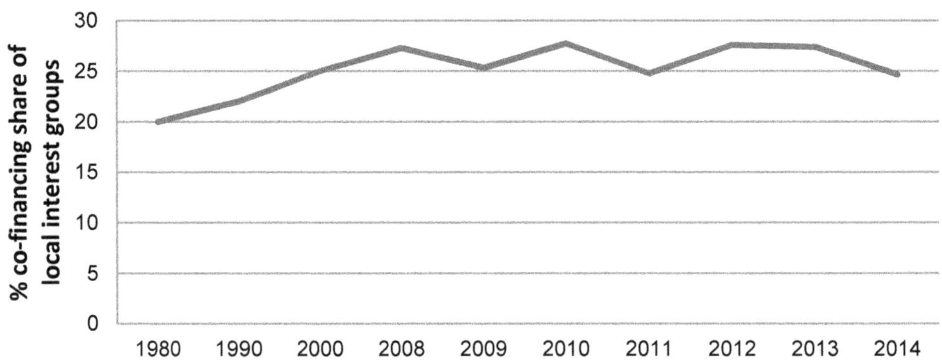

Source: OECD 2015 in-country mission meetings

BWV structural measures are also initiated by the interested party on the local level, which are generally municipalities, and then negotiated between the federal ministry and the provinces. BWV funding for projects, along with financial contributions from provinces and communities, depends on where damage is most likely to occur. Priority in the past has been given to projects that propose the creation of flood retention zones. On average, the central ministry pays 50%, the province 30% and the commune 20%. Maintenance costs are shared, with each level contributing a third of the agreed upon amount. Similarly, for measures implemented by the BMVIT along the Danube or the March, the central government contributes 50% of the costs, on average, while the province and local governments contribute 30% and 20%, respectively, on average (Table 2.5).

Generally speaking, demand from municipalities or other local interest groups for protective measures has exceeded the supply that can be provided and co-financed by the state. For example, for projects granted by the WLV between 2010 and 2015, 599 project requests were received and 366 (61%) were granted. An objective evaluation and prioritisation process is therefore indispensable. The central level prioritisation decision for measures provided by the WLV and the BWV is based on a Cost-Benefit Analysis for projects exceeding an investment amount of EUR 1 million (Box 2.2), although the methods of the two institutions differ slightly. For all others projects, a standardised benefit-utility valuation is conducted. It is unclear to what extent this analysis informs actual funding decisions to prioritise between projects. Clear prioritisation based on protection needs should help avoid the risk of allocating funding to projects where financial support from the local level may be stronger or where political interests (e.g. due to local elections) exert high pressure for projects to be realised.

Table 2.5 Average co-financing shares for disaster risk prevention investments across levels of government and by service unit

Average co-financing shares for disaster risk prevention investments			
	Central government	**Provincial government**	**Local government**
WLV	50%	20%	30%
BWV	50%	30%	20%
BMVIT	50%	30%	20%

Source: OECD 2015 in-country mission meetings

For the BWV, the law stipulates that protection investments have to be ranked according to priorities. Criteria that are to be considered for prioritisation are: legal obligations, damage potential, flood frequency, water management needs, official permits and maturity of project proposals. Any protective measure should minimise the impacts on natural water ecosystems, for example: passive flood protection should be preferable to active flood protection, and flood retention measures should be preferred in tributaries rather than the main river (BMLFUW, 2006).

BWV criteria can serve as an example of how clarity about criteria and prioritisation for funding can contribute to the efficiency and effectiveness of disaster risk reduction spending. An additional measure to boost investment efficiency could be to make allocation decisions for projects public. Although simple criteria catalogues may prove difficult to implement in practice, objective criteria need to be applied and published in order to guide municipal requests for funding and ensure equity that is independent of the financial capacity of the interested party or political urgency of the local government.

In the aftermath of a major disaster, criteria could be clarified as to how the re-construction of protective infrastructure is financed. To "build back better" it may often be required to strengthen or add additional measures while reconstructing buildings. It may be useful to jointly finance the costs of reconstruction and strengthening measures. The current arrangements of funding rehabilitation and reconstruction through the *KatFonds* could be adapted to allow for this kind of flexibility. This could avoid municipalities overstating individual compensation claims they received in order to obtain funding for additional needs in reconstruction of public infrastructure, which is what happened in the aftermath of the 2002 floods (*Salzburger Nachrichten*, 2015; BMF, 2015).

Box 2.2 Economic evaluation and prioritisation of Austria's prevention investments

Cost-benefit analysis (CBA) was first introduced formally in 1978 in Austria and has since been revised. Pursuant to article 3 of the legislation on the promotion of hydraulic engineering structures (*Wasserbautenförderungsgesetz*) established in 1985, CBA must be implemented to assess the financial feasibility of disaster risk prevention projects exceeding 1 EUR million in costs and having a significant impact on the population at risk. For all other projects, a standard benefit utility assessment is conducted.

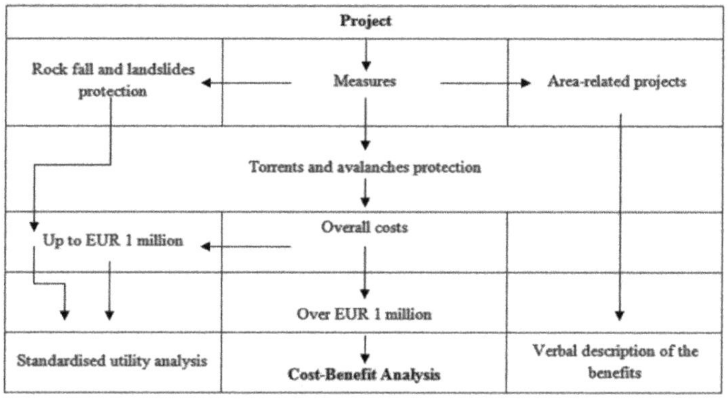

CBA compares the cost and benefit stream of different project options (including status quo) over the 80 years that follow the start of a project. Costs include:

- construction costs (whereby generally there are no costs for the authorities to buy land as the interested persons are in charge of providing lots)
- maintenance and repair costs
- costs for technological upgrades
- The benefits are linked to protection goals and hence calculated as the estimated average in avoided damages, including:
- damage to buildings
- restoration costs
- damage to streambed and receiving stream
- damage to transport infrastructures
- damage to supply and sanitation facilities
- damage to tourism
- damage in business/trade/industry/provision of services
- damage to official belongings
- intervention costs (civil and military forces)

Intangible and indirect benefits are included on a point scale according to the importance of each criterion. They include: protection of people's lives, prevention against an increase in exposure, feeling of safety, ensuring transport connections, protection of nature, landscape and culture related goods. An evaluation of 120 CBAs showed that intangible factors accounted for an estimated 30% of the tangible benefits, which is why their overall weight was determined at 1.3. Although it is important to include intangible benefits through, if possible, a point scale, the key question is how final decisions compare different values. Analytical tools such as multi-criteria analysis could be useful in ensuring equal assessment and clear weighting throughout the different evaluation criteria.

Source: BMLFUW (2006), *Richtlinien für die Wirtschaftlichkeitsuntersuchung und Priorisierung von Maßnahmen der Wildbach- und Lawinenverbauung gemäß § 3 Abs. 2 Z 3 Wasserbautenförderungsgesetz 1985* [Legal guidelines for cost efficieny analysis and the prioritisation of torrent and avalanche barriers as defined in § 3 Para. 2 Z 3 legislation on the promotion of hydraulic engineering structures].

Operating and maintaining structural measures

If the large stock of protective infrastructure that Austria has accumulated over past decades is to assure the level of protection for which it was initially conceived, implementing adequate maintenance, rehabilitation and strengthening projects is essential.

In Austria, significant investment was made in physical protective measures until the 1960s, after which expenditure went down and, as a consequence, the capital stock stopped increasing (Figure 2.7). Recent figures show that annual investment corresponds roughly to the annual depreciation rate of the capital stock of WLV protection measures. If the trend in decreasing expenditure continues, the capital stock will start to be depleted in the future (Sinnabell et al., 2009).

Figure 2.7 WLV investments in protective measures over time compared to capital stock and depreciation rate, real prices 2005

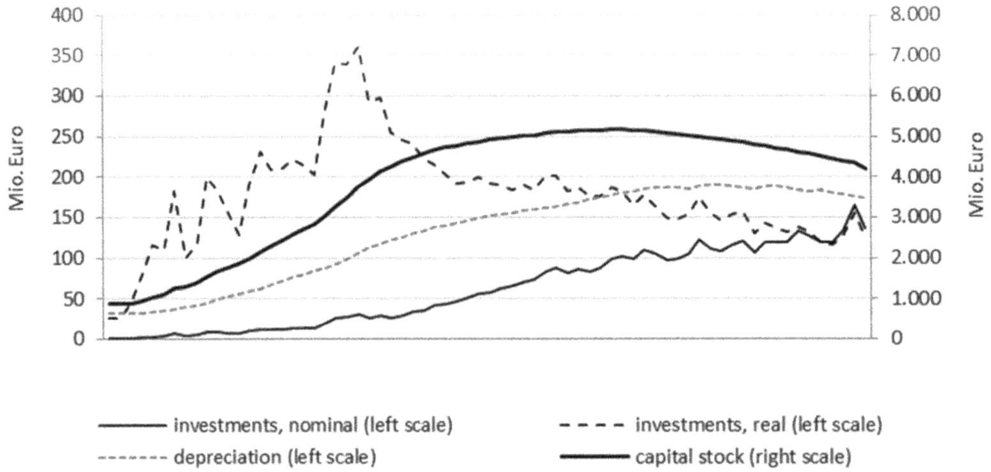

Note: Life cycle estimates of infrastructure: increase from 30 to 60 years between 1883 and 2006.
Sources: Suda, J. (2008), Abschätzung der durchschnittlichen Lebensdauer von Wildbachsperren [Estimate of the average life span of torrent dams], Universität für Bodenkultur, Wien, Mai 2008; Länger, E. (2003), Der forsttechnische Dienst für Wildbach- und Lawinenverbauung in Österreich und seine Tätigkeit seit der Gründung im Jahre 1884 [Forestry service and the construction and maintenance of mountain torrent and avalanche barriers since its establishment in 1884]. Dissertation an der Universität für Bodenkultur Wien.

In Austria, current operations and maintenance costs for existing torrent and flood protective infrastructure amount to 15% of annual investment costs, or around EUR 20 million. For avalanches and rockfallss, operations and maintenance costs are up to 5% of annual investment costs, or approximately EUR 2 million and EUR 1 million, respectively. WLV-financed projects for torrents, landslides, avalanche and rockfalls protection measures integrate 15 years of maintenance costs into their initial project budget to ensure seed funding for maintenance works. After this period, maintenance costs have to be covered by the owners of the protective infrastructure. For avalanches and rockfallss, the provincial forest services or land owners (with public subsidies) are responsible for maintenance work. Extraordinary maintenance work for protective infrastructure against torrents and floods can be supported by the central unit of the WLV or the BWV beyond the initial 15 years after construction (Rudolf-Miklau et al., 2014).

Ensuring maintenance of protective measures at the local level has proven challenging. Even with the initial seed funding for 15 years and the central government support for financing extraordinary maintenance or repair work of protective infrastructure, municipalities that own the majority of infrastructure are often financially overwhelmed by maintenance costs. In addition, a significant capacity level needs to be assured to be able to monitor protective infrastructure and assess it for potential repair works. It has been suggested that during recent disasters, the lack of adequate maintenance of protective infrastructure led to some infrastructure breaking down, resulting in high damages for settlements that could have otherwise been protected. In some cases, liability questions have arisen, where the owners of the protective infrastructure needed to prove that maintenance was carried out properly or else face charges.

There is an increased recognition that ensuring adequate maintenance of the large stock of protective infrastructure in Austria is a challenge. There is a central WLV-led database containing some 270 000 protective structures, including their physical dimensions, an assessment of their condition, documentation of monitoring and inspections, documentation of attendance and corrective maintenance, and documentation of rebuilding and potential other changes (Rudolf-Miklau et al., 2014). This serves as an effective planning and prioritisation tool to address maintenance needs. To resolve the current maintenance shortcomings, municipalities have called for this role to be carried out by the WLV. Since the WLV's budget is limited, this responsibility could only be financed by diverting resources away from additional infrastructure investment.

Similar to other European countries, notably France, the province of Salzburg has addressed the problem of maintaining protective infrastructure against torrents and avalanches through its long-standing tradition of water boards. Water boards (described in more detail below) are co-operatives of a number of interest groups or entire municipalities. They allow certain capacity costs for maintenance to be shared among several infrastructure owners, which has proven an effective way of ensuring the maintenance of protective infrastructure. Scaling-up the system of water boards for maintenance works of torrent and avalanche protection may not be a feasible policy option, especially in the short term, as they are bodies that have grown as bottom-up movements over a significant amount of time and in a specific regional context. However, it may be worth exploring policy options that facilitate the establishment of "joint maintenance bodies" that work across jurisdictions and are co-financed by different municipalities and potentially higher levels of government.

The role of water boards

Aside from local government authorities, local interest groups, in the form of water boards, play an important role in some parts of Austria by providing disaster risk prevention measures against water-related risks and assuring the adequate maintenance of infrastructure.

Water boards are statutory corporations under Austrian law (Water Act of 1959) and can be composed of any number and combination of individuals, municipalities or companies. Each member contributes financially to a common fund, which is intended for use in the development and maintenance of mitigation or prevention measures. The readiness to financially contribute to infrastructure investment can be considerable. For example, in the case of the Saalbach (province of Salzburg) water board, which is relatively big with 600 members, individual contributions can be as high as EUR 50 000 annually. The level of contribution is determined by a point system derived from the exposure of a member's property or dwelling. The initial determination of membership fees is automatically transferred to new property owners.

Water boards can take three organisational forms: a voluntary board with voluntary membership; a board with obligatory membership (determined by the majority of interested members and considering the number of opposing members in a given hazard area); or an obligatory board enforced by the provincial governor. Obligatory boards are the minority, with only seven currently existing. Water boards can be as small as 10 members or encompass an entire valley with all its inhabitants. In Austria, 270 water boards are relevant for torrents and avalanche-related hazards. A large share of these water boards are located in the province of Salzburg, with some dating back to 1830 (Box 2.3), where they have traditionally been in charge of providing access to (potable) water.

Water boards may decide to take responsibility for co-financing sometimes costly protective infrastructure, instead of leaving this to local authorities. There are several advantages for taking such an initiative, for example, water boards can expedite the request for a protective infrastructure, which serves the interests of those directly impacted by potential hazardous events. Water boards, just like municipalities, can initiate and request the construction of protective infrastructure, and thereby oblige its members to finance the suggested measures. In the case of the WLV, investment proposals by water boards receive a faster treatment of their request and a higher central co-financing rate than requests submitted by local government. The difference can be as high as 15% and should thereby reward individual willingness to contribute to financing protective infrastructure.

As water boards become the formal owners of the protective infrastructure they build, they are responsible for maintaining protective infrastructure. This has led to significantly better results in the status of protective infrastructure over time, compared to infrastructure for which maintenance is the responsibility of other interest groups, such as municipalities, who have faced resourcing challenges. Considering the longer-term maintenance requirements of protective infrastructure investment, municipalities may encourage investment by water boards. In Kaprun (province of Salzburg), the local government agreed to co-finance protective infrastructure, under the condition that the water board takes charge of the maintenance.

A further evaluation of the effectiveness and transferability of water board arrangements for boosting the maintenance level of protective infrastructure across Austria is important for assessing the wider policy relevance of water boards. The national flood risk management plan assesses the existence of water boards across Austria and encourages their creation to address flood risk specific disaster risk reduction investments. Due to regional specificities and differences in tradition, co-operatives to resolve some of the challenges in disaster risk prevention management, such as maintenance, may not be suitable for scale-up across Austria. However, some elements could be used and perhaps encouraged, especially in terms of establishing the capacity for joint maintenance bodies across municipalities.

Cross-jurisdictional collaboration

Risks are rarely confined to municipal borders and may not halt at provincial or country borders. Therefore, governance structures should ensure that disaster risk management operates at an adequate scale. Inter-communal collaboration is needed, especially for the development of joint spatial planning strategies for shared river areas and the development of compensation mechanisms between municipalities that pay for protection measures and others that may benefit or have additional costs. Collaboration methods include a range of partnerships, from establishing informal discussion fora and exchanging hazard relevant data, to co-ordinating land-use planning activities or implementing joint protection measures (Habersack et al., 2009).

Box 2.3 Bottom-up disaster risk prevention initiatives – the case of the water board of Schmittenbach

The water board Schmittenbach was created in 1883 to protect the catchment area of the Schmittenbach against natural hazards. Hazard events, particularly floods and torrents, have long been documented in the catchment area, as far back as 1737. The first protective infrastructure was built some 100 years ago, for which extensive repair and maintenance work has been required. The water board was re-established in 1973 to adapt to the changes in the Austrian water law. Its membership has fluctuated between 350 and 700 members, numbering nearly 400 in 2015. Membership fees have been calculated on the basis of property size and hazard exposure. The collective membership fees have contributed some 6.5% of the total repair work costs, which have been complemented by other local interest groups (the municipality, the federal road administration, two forestry communities) and the province with 18% and the central level with 69%.

The latest project submitted by the water board was to secure a local torrent catchment area with an investment cost of EUR 2.4 million, to be completed in December 2016. The water board's website provides a list of the most recent maintenance and repair works that have been carried out. The water board congratulates and continues to encourage its members to participate by underlining the success they have had in avoiding disasters compared to neighbouring communities that may have not had the same membership engagement. Members are reminded that they contribute to the water board's preventative measures so as to not regret non-action in the aftermath of a disaster.

Source: WG – Schmittenbach (2016), www.wg-schmittenbach.at/ (accessed 21 February 2016).

Austria's governance system for structural measures, as seen above, is organised around provincial service branches that are a deconcentrated arm of central service units (the case of the WLV and the BWV), which require municipalities to request projects. This governance structure may risk overlooking cross-jurisdictional risks and investment needs. Municipalities may have a stronger incentive to obtain the maximum amount of funding for their own projects, and investment by one municipality may create benefits (or costs) for others that could lead to an under-investment in protection. Austria has experienced such conflicts between up- and down-stream river communities, where retention zones developed by upstream municipalities created benefits for downstream municipalities who refused to participate in the costs. The large-scale lessons learned evaluation, in which a wide range of Austrian stakeholders participated, suggested that this problem should be addressed.

To address this collective action problem, governments can change the way projects are financed, for example by rewarding joint project proposals with higher central level funding shares, and by regulating the way local risk assessments, prevention and preparedness measures are conducted and implemented (OECD, 2014a). The Austrian Spatial Planning Conference (ÖROK) proposed a policy reform to address this issue that stemmed from the lessons learnt as part of the 2002 and 2005 large-scale floods evaluation. The reform suggests establishing co-ordination and compensation mechanisms between the different municipalities impacted by protective infrastructure investments and land-use decisions undertaken by adjacent jurisdictions (ÖROK, 2005). This would require developing guidelines for cross-jurisdictional and jurisdictional spatial planning (ÖROK, 2015) that would provide the basis for co-ordination and potential collaborative projects. Some good practice examples that lead the way towards a greater harmonisation of disaster risk prevention activities across jurisdictions include:

- The national flood risk management plan is a new instrument based on a nationwide assessment of flood risks that follows the criteria in the EU Flood Directive. Its core policy objective is to encourage flood risk planning efforts to be undertaken at the level of the river basin (BMLFUW, 2015).
- The water boards discussed above have, in a number of cases, brought several municipalities together to form one common water board that addresses the installation and maintenance of common protective infrastructure. The national flood risk management plan identifies this model as a way of further encouraging cross-jurisdictional collaboration on disaster risk prevention measures (BMLFUW, 2015).
- Working across provincial borders, the "*Machland Nord*" dyke construction, which is part of a treaty between three federal provinces (Upper Austria, Lower Austria and Vienna) and the Republic of Austria, was initiated in 2006 (under "Article 15a B-VG Treaty"). EUR 182.6 million was invested and co-financed by the three provinces to construct a dam protecting some 22 000 citizens in 7 municipalities from potential flooding, while at the same time maintaining the river's retention capacities (Hackel, 2012).

The role of the private sector in providing protective infrastructure

To manage disaster risk prevention and mitigation effectively, inclusive policy-making, based on a whole-of-society approach, is needed. Part of this approach requires the effective involvement of the private sector and critical infrastructure providers in disaster risk prevention and mitigation management.

At present, there is little systematic evidence of the specific vulnerabilities of the private sector and/or critical infrastructures in Austria and how they are addressed. For effective management, a systematic and regular assessment of vulnerabilities is needed to co-ordinate and strengthen the implementation of disaster risk reduction and business continuity measures. Some practices highlight that considerable effort is undertaken by individual actors. For example, the Austrian railway services (ÖBB) assessed that 20% of their railway network is exposed to natural hazards. In response, 4-5% of its reinvestment budget is allocated to natural hazard management on an annual basis.

In terms of business continuity planning, the Federal Chancellery and the BMI are collaborating on critical infrastructure protection. After ministers decided to create the Austrian programme in 2008 to protect critical infrastructure, the authorities developed an electronic guidance document to help critical infrastructure (CI) providers self-evaluate their provisions for safety and business continuity. The main objective is to support CI providers in their risk, crisis, and safety management.

The role of individual households

Individual households' investment and behavioural decisions have a significant impact on the effectiveness of public disaster risk prevention action. Public efforts in preventing risks may be undermined by individuals or households if there is a widespread reliance on the state for damage compensation. For example, a slope stabilisation measure implemented to protect a settlement area can only provide adequate protection if individual house walls are also reinforced. If individuals rely on the state for compensation it could be that the state not only pays for the structural measure, but also for the individual compensation of households if a large scale disaster occurs.

Austria's disaster risk prevention and mitigation system is strongly rooted in solidarity. For example, a large volunteer force and generous donation efforts are mobilised following a disaster. Although such solidarity is welcome, there may be scope for increasing individual preventative action to ensure that the benefits from public disaster risk reduction investment efforts are reaped.

Previous risk management evaluations in Austria (Habersack et al., 2009) have shown that there are many technical options for strengthening and reinforcing existing building stock and improving the integration of these measures into new constructions. Incentives such as tax breaks, subsidies or interest-free loans can be created to encourage property owners to reinforce their assets against the potential impact of a natural disaster. For this to work effectively, information and awareness levels need to be raised and building codes and building permit processes need to be strengthened to integrate individual investments into protection. To increase the effectiveness and efficiency of the Austrian *KatFonds* mechanism (described in Section V), individual compensation payments could integrate criteria based on previous protective investments. There are current examples in Austria that show how the uptake of reinforcement measures is fostered. They do not, however, target ex-ante installations. For example, there are tax incentives for rebuilding and renovating businesses after disastrous events, but not for strengthening or reinforcing business buildings ex-ante.

A building certification scheme has been discussed in Austria in order to increase awareness and share an understanding of what can be done to make buildings more resistant to potential impacts from natural hazards. Since building certificates indicate whether a building is "safe" from natural hazards they could help building owners understand what they can do to make their assets more resistant to the impacts of hazards, while at the same time minimising transaction costs among building permit providers and necessary building inspections. To be effective, such an initiative is ideally tied to the mode of compensation payments by the *KatFonds* to ensure that individual investments are rewarded.

Management and implementation of non-structural measures

There is a limit to what structural measures can and should do in preventing risks. As the Austrian case demonstrates, an ever-increasing stock of structural measures can become a significant liability for maintenance and repair works in the medium- to long-term after their construction. It is important to limit an accumulation of assets that then have to be protected by physical measures. Important complements to structural measures are organisational non-structural measures, such as hazard zone mapping, risk mapping, spatial planning or building code enforcement. They form an important element of the optimal policy mix for disaster risk prevention management. The importance of non-structural measures has been recognised and highlighted in Austria's national flood risk management plan, where two of the four main goals have been exclusively dedicated to the reduction of new risks through non-structural measures and the reinforcement of risk and hazard awareness among citizens to counter the rapid decline in awareness as time passes after a disaster event (BMLFUW, 2015).

The regulatory framework of non-structural measures is the key basis for ensuring that actors carry out their roles and responsibilities with the full information and the right incentives. In the following sub-section, the achievements and potential challenges in designing and implementing policies for non-structural disaster risk prevention measures will be discussed in the Austrian context.

Hazard assessment and mapping

Updated hazard information is crucial for informing often fast-paced land-use developments. For torrents and avalanches, Austria has achieved a full coverage of areas at risk with hazard maps. For water-related risks under the responsibility of the BWV, hazard information is fully available by means of hazard maps. Risk maps are available for all Areas of Potentially Significant Flood Risk (APSFR). The remaining challenge for Austria is to keep hazard maps sufficiently updated and fully integrated in land-use decisions.

The responsibility for hazard identification, assessment and mapping lies, as for structural measures, in the respective branches of the BMLFUW. The WLV is responsible for mapping hazards in torrent and avalanche catchment areas,[9] and the BWV for the remaining water-related risks. The WLV revises hazard assessments upon request, such as when a significant change in exposure arises or after a hazard event, or else on average every 10 years. Outside of the planned revision period of hazard maps, the installation of protective measures or disaster events can lead to a revision of the hazard map before the planned revision period.[10] The WLV assessments are technically hazard and not risk assessments as they do not evaluate the assets that are at risk. The BWV continuously improves, revises and updates its hazard assessments, especially when there have been changes in the catchment area. The EU Flood Directive stipulates that all hazard maps have to be updated at least every six years. This directive was incorporated into national law in 2011 and led the BWV to harmonise and conduct a nationwide flood risk assessment. Based on this programme, hazard maps[11] were developed for all areas where an initial assessment had revealed a preliminary flood risk.

The process for conducting hazard assessments and drawing up hazard zone maps is the following:

- The WLV regional branches submit draft hazard assessments that are reviewed by the ministry. This is followed by a public consultation period where comments are collected and assessed by a commission. Gamper (2008) argues that, particularly in areas where settlement space is scarce, this instrument has led to active public participation. The experience in the municipality of Galtür, which was hit by a large avalanche that caused 38 deaths in 1999, shows that citizens do not necessarily participate in the hazard zoning process to ensure the maximum restriction of hazard zones and protect the value of their assets, but rather have an interest in knowing whether they are at risk and to what extent. They may even take a prudent approach by enlarging estimated hazard zones (ÖROK, 2015).
- The WLV hazard mapping process is tied in with the mapping of forest functions in order to integrate the protective forest functions with their hazard assessment processes. The forest mapping process is supported by airborne laser scanning data that helps map priority activity areas.
- In the risk mapping process of the BWV, a number of risk indicators are distinguished and integrated, such as: population at risk, economic activity at risk, installations that can cause environmental damage in case of flooding, areas where mudslides are likely, and points of interest (cultural heritage sites, critical infrastructures, etc.). Contrary to the WLV, the BWV central service makes a first draft map, followed by provincial branches re-working the draft using regional data. The draft is returned by provinces for the federal unit to finalise and publish (BMLFUW, 2014c). This was also the standard procedure for drafting the national flood risk management plan (BMLFUW, 2015), which was enshrined in the National Water Act to ensure nationwide comparability and consistency.
- Accessibility of hazard information: The web portal of www.hora.gv.at shows flood hazard by exact address location. The hazards include earthquake risks, storm and lightening risks, and weather warnings. The portal www.naturgefahren.at includes all other risks covered by the WLV, based on exact address locations.

To ensure the impartiality of experts, the BWV administers an oath and the WLV employs close scrutiny through rigorous training and ensuring sufficient practical experience.

In Austria, hazard maps cover 100% of avalanche and torrent-threatened municipalities. However, some of the available maps may be older than 15 years. For example, in the provinces of Upper Austria and Salzburg in 2004, more than half of the hazard maps were older than 15 years, despite full coverage of all municipalities (ÖROK, 2005). The first BWV-developed hazard zone maps for the province of Salzburg were only developed in 2008, after floods in 2002 and 2005 increased awareness and political stakes. In terms of hazard and risk maps for water ways, maps are available for more than 30 000 km of water ways, which encompasses nearly all rivers larger than 10 km^2 in catchment size.

Integrating hazard assessments in land-use planning

Hazard-based land-use planning is a core instrument for reducing the exposure of people and assets to natural hazards. However, in Austria, as in many other countries, scarcity of land for settlements, the increased consumption of space, and the significant reduction of retention zones have all been factors that have contributed to the rising tension between land-use and hazard zone planning.

Exposure is most efficiently reduced or avoided if the built environment is restricted in hazard-prone areas or if areas are left undeveloped, for example to create flood retention zones. However, in many cases, especially in Austria where potential settlement areas have been scarce, the built environment existed long before detailed hazard information became available. Nevertheless, such information can also guide retrofitting measures and any repair or expansion works that may otherwise continue to increase risk exposure in the future. To work effectively, hazard information needs to be available at the local level by parcel of land and frequently updated to reflect potential changes in prevalent risks and risk levels. Since land-use is quickly evolving, and many land areas may be rapidly developing, up to date hazard information may be challenging to maintain.

As seen earlier, Austria has made significant strides in making hazard information available for all hazard-prone areas and updating this information based on new land-use developments or after a disaster. The challenge, however, seems to lie in translating information into actual land-use planning and decisions.

In the aftermath of the 2002 large-scale floods in Austria, it emerged that existing hazard maps may have not been sufficiently considered in local land-use decisions, which resulted in a high number of properties being exposed to and destroyed during the floods (Habersack et al., 2004). For example, in the municipality of Fürstenfeld, houses and shops have been built in flood-prone areas, meaning that 30% of the flood retention area has been lost over past decades. Examples like these highlight questions surrounding the responsibility taken by planners and final decision makers at the local level, and have led to an increased understanding that a forward-looking approach to planning decisions must be taken (Kanonier, 2004). The extent of problems caused by misled land-use decisions after a disaster event has taken place suggests that there is no systematic monitoring and oversight of the integration of hazard zones in land-use decisions (ÖROK, 2005).

The spatial planning laws of Tyrol and Styria explicitly request hazard maps as a criterion for land-use decisions. In Upper Austria there is an absolute ban on construction in areas lying in a zone of the 30 years flood return period, allowing some potential construction in areas at risk of a 100 years flood return period (Habersack at al., 2009). In Lower Austria there is a ban on any new construction within the 100 year flood return perimeter.

In 2005, the Austrian spatial planning conference (ÖROK) recommended that hazard zones be fully and legally integrated into land-use codes, essentially prohibiting construction in high hazard zones. It was also recommended that regional planning and land-use strategies include disaster risk reduction targets. Furthermore, final decision makers should document their efforts to implement risk reduction objectives in their planning decisions. They should be provided with support and monitoring from experts in this process.

To inhibit further land-use expansion into existing retention zones, and to stop the rapid decline in expansion zones, it has also been widely recommended to consider re-dedicating land to recreate flood retention zones.

What have been the barriers for better integrating hazard zones into land-use planning?

Provinces and municipalities take final decisions on land-use planning and it is at their discretion to take the recommendations from hazard maps into account. However, decision makers in charge of providing land-use and construction permits can be made liable for the consequences of a disaster if construction permits were granted in a hazard zone.

Mayors are the final local land-use authority, and despite potential liability charges they have good reasons not to restrict land-use in their municipalities. For example, large industrial zones (often developed in flood retention zones) provide a significant stream of revenue for municipalities that otherwise have very restricted revenue-raising authority in Austria. To overcome such local level conflicts of interest, it has been proposed to shift responsibility for final land-use decisions to the province. It could be argued that mayors know local level environments best and hence this responsibility should stay with them. Alternatively, the province may be better placed to ensure land-use decisions integrate hazard considerations and take into account cross-jurisdictional hazard mitigation considerations.

There are no established systematic monitoring mechanisms of land-use decisions in hazard zones across municipalities, although policies suggest that this monitoring function should be carried out by provinces. Since the responsibility of implementing hazard zones in spatial planning lies in the hand of provinces, both mayors and provincial governors could face liability charges. Therefore, provinces should have an incentive to carry out their monitoring role of ensuring that hazards are integrated into land-use decisions.

Most provincial land-use codes include absolute restrictions to expanding existing building stock in high hazard areas. This includes the construction of new buildings and the expansion of existing building stock. However, even this absolute restriction seems to have been subject to exceptions. Although planning laws stipulate that the land area of buildings in hazard zone areas may not be further extended, they do not specify, for example, the number of residents allowed to live in such buildings. As a consequence, changes to housing stock may entail the conversion of a family house into a hotel, thereby multiplying the damage potential.

Resettlement

To recreate and increase flood retention zones, relocating settled areas has often been considered. Relocating settled areas is not explicitly regulated in Austria and no resident can be forced to resettle. Nevertheless, a number of resettlement programmes have been successfully implemented.

For example the *Donau Machland*[12] project saw around 260 houses removed to create retention areas for the Danube River (Box 2.4), amounting to a total of EUR 92 million in compensation payments (Table 2.6). As a result, a large area along the Danube was protected through the construction of a large dam, while other areas were purposefully left empty to create retention zones as complementary protection. The initial process started in 1993 and saw a slow uptake of compensation offers, with residents reluctant to agree to move. Consecutive flooding events increased the number of residents that agreed to move. The next large resettlement project currently planned in Austria is ongoing in the province of Upper Austria, where around 400 buildings shall be resettled in the *Eferdinger Becken*.

Table 2.6 Recent Austrian resettlement examples

Project	and (upper Austria)	Schildried (Vorarlberg)
Share of costs	Centre: 50% Province: 30% Municipality: - Owner: 20%	Centre: 60% Province: 30% Municipality: 10% Owner: -
Total compensation payments (in million EUR)	91.99	3.63
Assets to be compensated	Building	Building and land
Acquisition of ownership of land	No	Yes
Alternative land area provided	Yes	Support in search

Source: Habersack et al. (2009), "FloodRisk II: Vertiefung und Vernetzung zukunftsweisender Umsetzungsstrategien zum integrierten Hochwassermanagement. Synthesebericht". Ministry of Agriculture, Forestry, Environment and Water Management, Vienna.

Building codes

As with spatial planning, building codes are the responsibility of provinces. Building authorities execute the building code provisions. Several policy documents highlight the potential improvements that could be made to strengthen the contribution of building codes in boosting the resilience of disaster-affected areas in Austria. For example, the ÖROK Recommendation of 2005 underlines the importance of prohibiting new construction in the most hazard exposed zones, and of applying stringent building codes for construction in medium exposed zones. In addition, it recommends that new building codes are more imposed on existing constructions to enable them to adapt them to potentially new hazards, adopt newly available technology that improves protection, or simply to bring them up to standard (ÖROK, 2005).

Building code objectives could be spelled out more explicitly in provincial spatial planning law, as some provinces only specify general civil protection goals and not those specific to natural hazards protection. This gives planners a larger margin for discretion and flexibility (ÖROK, 2005), especially during new construction where the benefit of integrating hazard-resistant measures would be the greatest.

As previously highlighted, Austria's widespread solidarity in disaster response may have discouraged preventative action individually, and possibly also for building stock enforcement. Therefore, it is necessary to raise awareness among property owners about their individual exposure to hazards and the solutions that are available to improve resilience against potential disasters. Campaigns to provide information and individual technical advice, such as that provided by the WLV, should be continuously scaled up. Financial support to property owners for retrofitting their houses could further encourage protective investments.

Box 2.4 Integrative flood risk management: The Machland Dam in Austria

The Machland Dam is the biggest flood protective infrastructure work that has been undertaken in Austria, and also in comparison to other projects in neighbouring Europe. The dam, constructed from 2008 to 2012, spans over 36.4 km to protect 22 400 inhabitants spread over 7 municipalities in the Machland region.

The dam was complemented by an 8.7 km bypass, or flood canal, spreading from Naarn to Wallsee/Mitterkirchen that should prevent smaller scale floods and constitute an element of the integrative flood risk management design of the project, aimed at protecting lives while re-establishing room for the river and preserving the environment. The creation of the flood canal also provided material (soil) for the dam construction.

The creation of the flood canal expanded into settlement areas, which required citizens to relocate. Currently, 254 voluntary resettlement agreements for houses located in areas at risk of flooding were concluded, costing EUR 92 million in compensation payments . The process began in 1993, where initially only 5 resettlement agreements were made in the first 5 years. Successive floods convinced the remaining citizens to agree to move. Finally, the 2002 floods led to a rapid resettlement of 221 remaining properties.

Compensation for house owners was based on the replacement value of their houses as well as their demolition costs. The authorities provided 80% of the overall costs in compensation: the federal province paid 30% of total costs and the central level 50%. Property owners did not lose land titles of their initial belongings; however, land had to be re-dedicated to pasture land, revoking the possibility to construct on it. New lots for rebuilding houses were made available and were reserved in adjacent communities to protect relocating citizens from price hikes in land prices and to ensure that communities could be rebuilt elsewhere.

Source: Oberösterreich Landesrechnungshof (2014), "*LRH-Bericht, Initiativprüfung, Hochwasserschutz Machland Nord*" [LRH Report, Audit, Flood Protection Machland North], LRH-100000-12/9-2014-LI, www.machlanddamm.at.

Risk communication

Communicating about prevailing risks is the first, and probably one of the most important, steps when initiating whole-of-society engagement in disaster risk prevention and mitigation action. In Austria, the BMLFUW is one of several agencies responsible for communicating about risks and is tasked with publishing all hazard-relevant information. Publicly accessible Internet portals, such as www.naturgefahren.at and www.hora.gv.at, provide easily accessible information tailored to a wide audience. Individual exposure to multiple hazards (such as floods, avalanches and torrents) can be explored based on individual addresses.

In addition to communicating about existing hazards, the BMLFUW seeks to enhance knowledge about: what citizens can do to protect themselves against risks, promote the acceptance of risk management measures, inform about behavioural measures during catastrophic events, build trust, involve actors, and establish a mutual dialogue. The below images (Figure 2.8) are two examples of how information is communicated about the impacts of hazards and what house owners can do to protect their properties.

Figure 2.8 Excerpt of a brochure on raising awareness about risks in Austria

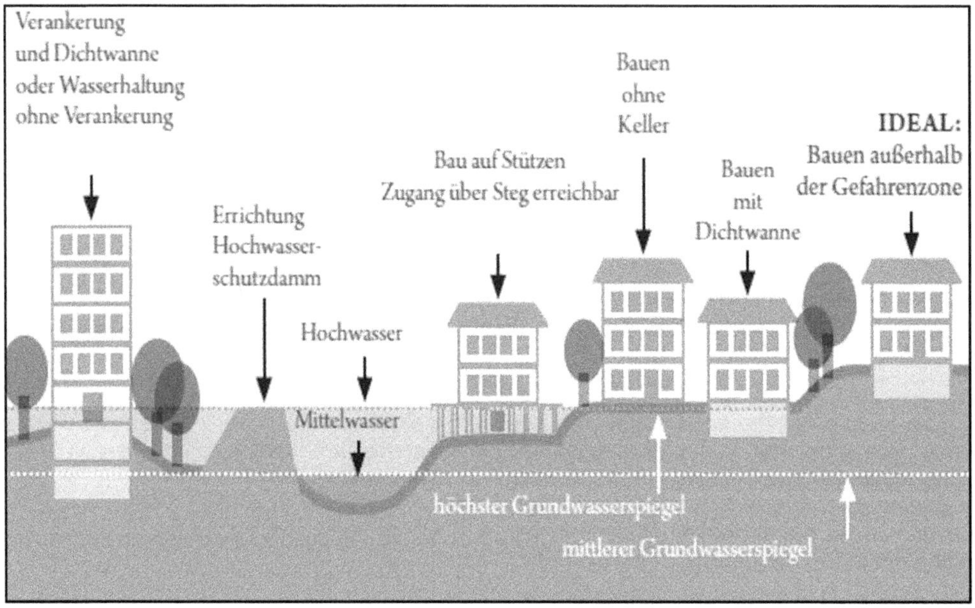

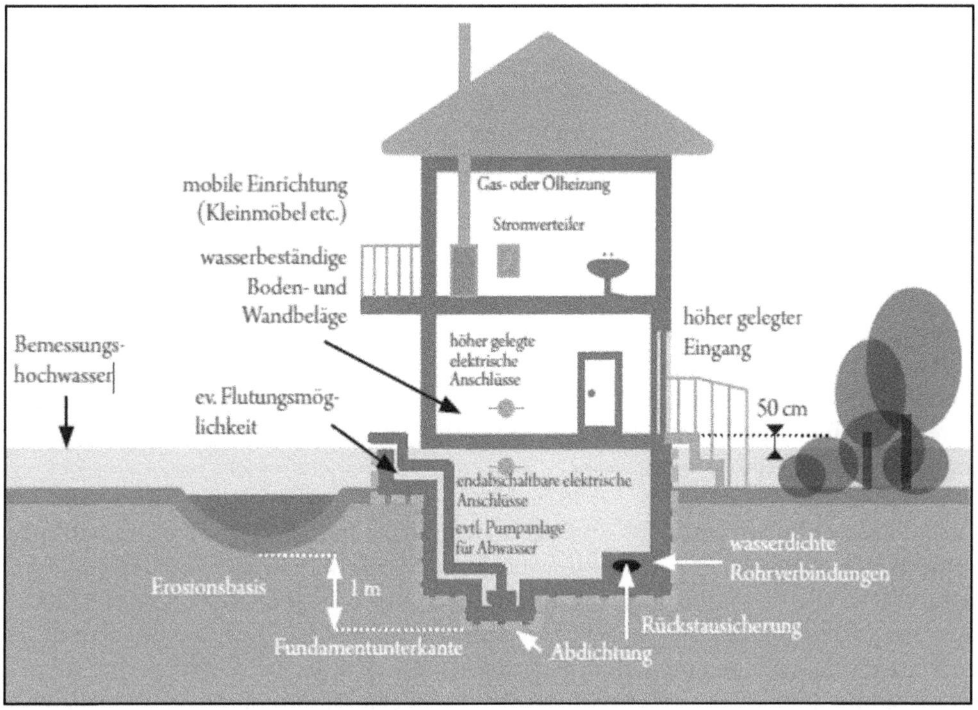

Source: BMLFUW (2015), "*Leben mit Naturgefahren: Ratgeber für die Eigenvorsorge bei Hochwasser, Muren, Lawinen, Steinschlag und Rutschungen*" [Living with natural hazards: guidance for self-protection in case of floods, debris flows, avalanches, rockfalls and landslides], Ministry of Agriculture, Forestry, Environment and Water Management (BMLFUW), Vienna.

Information is transmitted through brochures, booklets and leaflets. In addition, there are initiatives targeting risk awareness in children aged 9-10, such as the "*Biber Berti*" programme.[13] There is scope and potential to make more use of new media, such as information communication technology (including applications on risk information) or social networks. The public consultation process in the development of hazard maps and the consultation for the draft national water management plan are both instruments that aim to increase risk awareness of the wider public.

For earthquake risks, the Federal Ministry of Interior (BMI) has published information documents that outline hazard exposure areas across the country and protective measures that can be invested in ex-ante, during and after an earthquake (BMI, 2011). For non-natural hazards, the BMI has several risk communication initiatives, including online information services[14] and collaborations with non-governmental organisations (NGOs), such as the Austrian Civil Protection Association,[15] to provide information to the general public about self-protection and individual preparedness.

Direct engagement in dialogue with citizens is deemed most effective by authorities in charge of risk communication, especially during negotiations for construction permits. An evaluation of the effectiveness of risk communication measures is ongoing and will be presented in the third national evaluation program called FloodRiskE.

Despite efforts to communicate about risks and raise awareness of existing hazards, a very low uptake of protective measures by individual households and businesses can be observed. The absence of complementary incentives (e.g. tax credits and subsidies for investments) may hamper an increased level of private investment in disaster risk prevention and mitigation. The national flood risk management plan points out that the attention span and awareness levels sharply reduce as time passes after a disaster event. As a consequence, one of the four major goals of the national plan seeks to address risk awareness gaps in Austria (BMLFUW, 2015).

Conclusion

This section examined whether and how institutions or governance arrangements in Austria's disaster risk prevention and mitigation management facilitate actions by public and private actors in implementing disaster risk reduction measures. Austria has continuously and significantly invested in boosting its resilience against natural hazards. As a result, it has developed advanced capacities and accumulated a sizable amount of protective infrastructure.

The increasing demand for available resources requires a clear prioritisation of allocations for disaster risk reduction projects. Such a process should identify key vulnerabilities and the most urgent investment needs. Transparency in the allocation process is crucial to ensure equity and trust in public authorities. Moreover, better solutions for adequate maintenance and rehabilitation must be found or the significant stock of public protective infrastructure that has been accumulated in Austria will risk losing its protective capacity.

Austria's disaster risk prevention and mitigation system is still very much organised around jurisdictional responsibilities, instead of taking a more functional, hazard-zone approach. This could impede more effective distribution of resources or lead to underinvestment in disaster risk prevention and mitigation measures by local jurisdictions.

There has been a remarkable and widespread solidarity during and after a disaster in Austria that has been focused on helping citizens most impacted by adverse events. Although this solidarity is remarkable and should not be discouraged, preventative measures by individual households and businesses could be more effectively encouraged. This would ensure that the full benefits of public disaster risk reduction investments are enjoyed by the affected population.

Austria has a well-established capacity in hazard mapping and sharing this information with the public. Hazard assessments have been subject to regular revisions, whereby authorities ensure they take into account changing land-use patterns and future uncertainties in disaster occurrence, such as disasters influenced by climate change. To fully realise the gains of these advanced hazard assessment systems, better integration into land-use decisions and building code applications would be desirable.

Risk management financing

Section highlights

- An estimated EUR 400 million is invested annually across ministries, levels of government and private actors to prevent and mitigate floods and Alpine hazards in Austria.
- At current expenditure levels, there may be a risk of depleting the existing capital stock of prevention infrastructure. There is a need to boost and find innovative ways to maintain the protective function of existing infrastructure and manage the needs for the future, potentially increasing the requirement for new infrastructure investment.
- Austria's disaster risk prevention financing framework could encourage more contribution from individuals and households in increasing their own resilience. This would ensure the full benefits of public disaster risk prevention and mitigation investments are enjoyed in the long term.

Disruptions from disasters have an impact on individual households, businesses, and the public sector alike. Therefore, all actors have an interest in investing in disaster risk prevention and mitigation. Governments across OECD countries face three main challenges when it comes to designing their risk financing strategies. The first entails determining the overall amount of resources to be allocated to managing risks, and what risks they choose to retain. The second constitutes the choice of how to finance risks, whereby a myriad of instruments are at the disposal of governments and each entails different distributional effects. The third is that in order to alleviate the financial burden on governments, countries need to leverage the private sector and individual households to participate in financing disaster risk prevention and mitigation measures or investing in individual risk transfer arrangements. They also need to collaborate with other countries to jointly finance risks (Figure 2.9).

In this section, the main financing sources and the overall government expenditure of Austria on disaster risk prevention and mitigation will be summarised and assessed.

Austrian Catastrophe Fund (KatFonds)

Austria's key source for financing disaster risk prevention and mitigation measures is the *Katastrophenfonds*, or *KatFonds*. It serves a double function as it is used to finance disaster risk prevention and mitigation measures provided by the responsible authorities, and is also used as a relief fund to compensate for damages after a disaster (Figure 2.10). The distribution share across its uses is set out in the *KatFonds* law of 1996 (BMF, 2015).

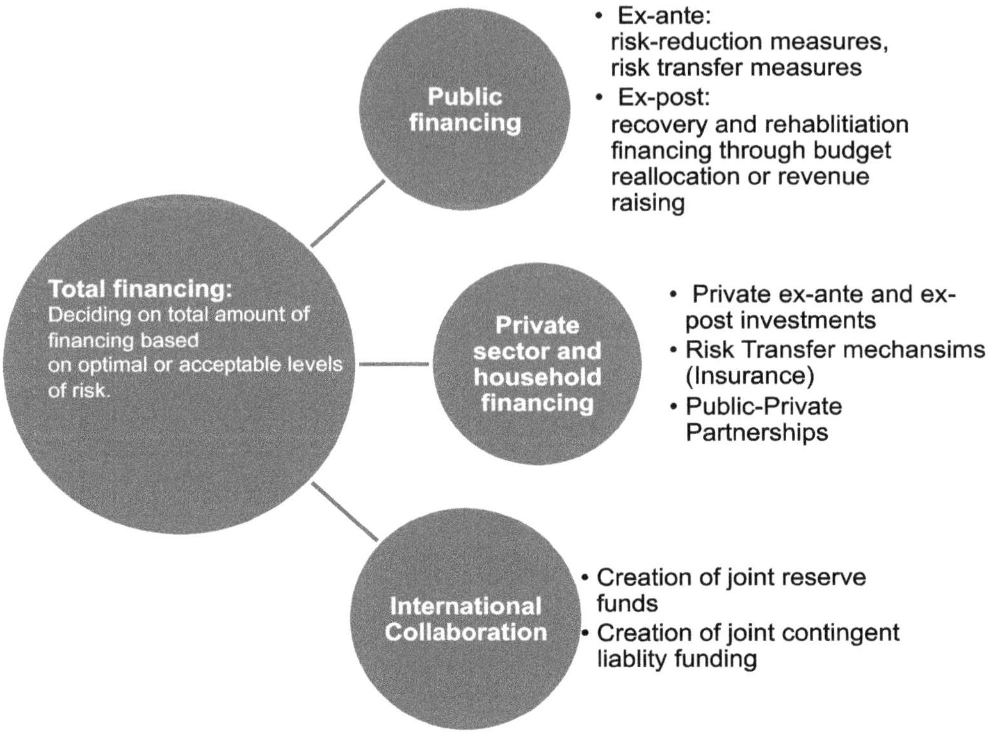

KatFonds was enacted after severe flood events in Austria in 1965 and 1966. It is funded by an annual contribution by the federal government of 1.1% of total federal tax income (including income and wage taxes and corporate tax). Since 2010, an additional EUR 10 million per year is added from the taxes on income earnings. This contribution is earmarked to repair damages to rural roads. A revision of its provisions in 1996 led to its reserves being limited to a maximum of EUR 29 million (Figure 2.11).

Three quarters of the annual prevention and mitigation investment funding (Figure 2.10) is allocated to the authorities in charge of prevention and mitigation of natural hazard risk: the WLV, the BWV, and the BMVIT. The remaining funding is used to support preparedness functions (e.g. equipment for fire departments and early-warning systems) and for compensating losses incurred by households and businesses in the event of a disaster.

Figure 2.10 Share of KatFonds allocation used for disaster risk prevention, loss compensation and fire brigades

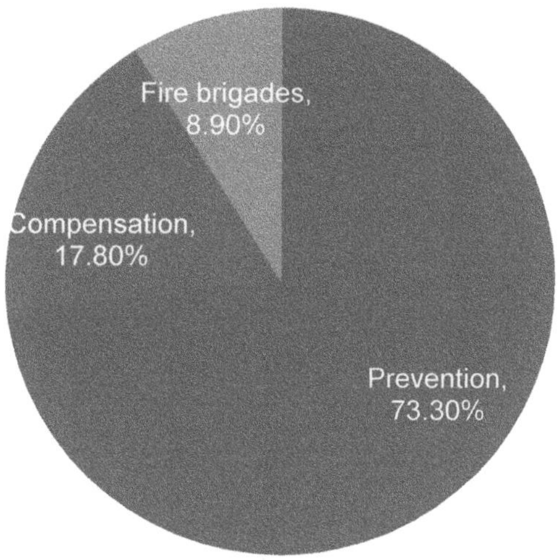

Source: BMF (2015), "Katastrophenfondsgesetz 1996: Daten zum Jahr 2014" [Catastrophe Fund Law 1996: Data for the year 2014], Ministry of Finance (BMF), Vienna.

Figure 2.11. The Austrian KatFonds: The effect of annual absorption of funds, 1990-2010

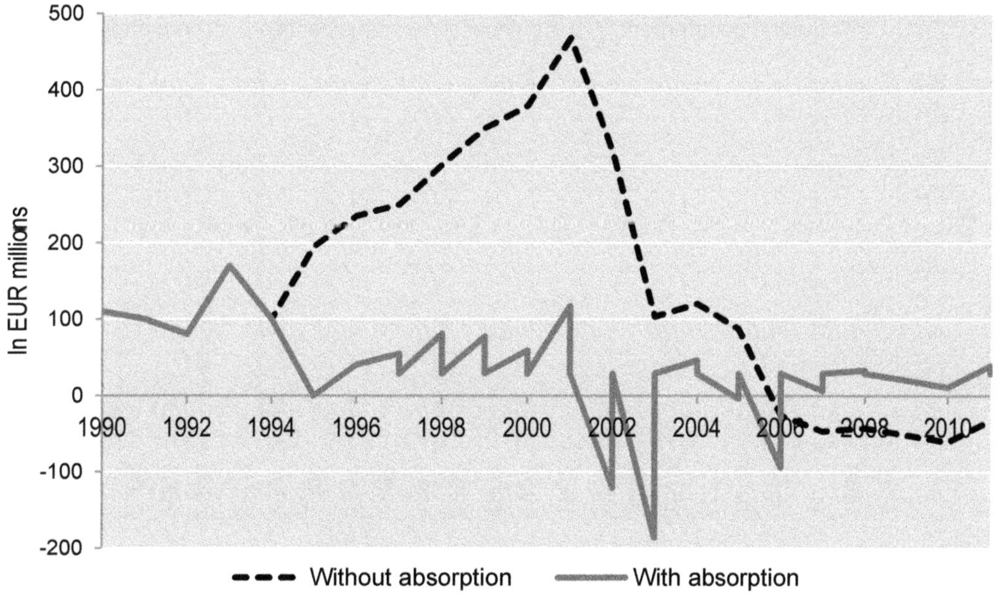

Source: Prettenthaler, F., et al. (2015), "Catastrophe Management: Riverine Flooding", in Steininger, K.W. et al. Economic Evaluation of Climate Change Impacts: Development of a Cross-Sectoral Framework and Results for Austria, Springer International Publishing, Switzerland.

Figure 2.12. Damage compensation paid to private individuals and households from the Austrian KatFonds, 1967-2015

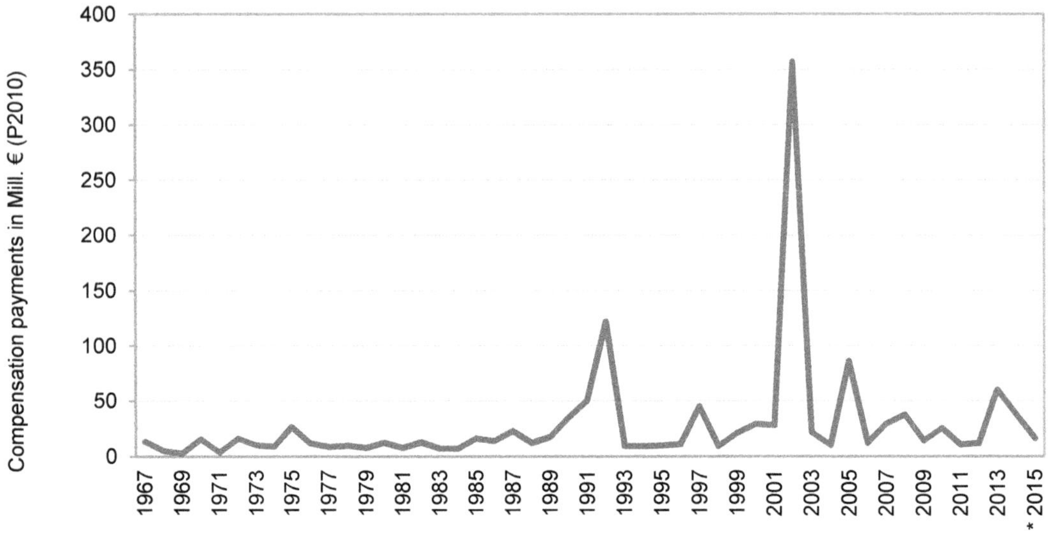

Note: *Estimated budget. Expenditures include payments based on the compensation fund and rehabilitation law (HWG) Values in real prices of 2010.

Source: Austrian Institute of Economic Research (WIFO) calculations on the basis of the Ministry of Finance (BMF), Austria.

Figure 2.13 Compensation payments to private agents, municipalities, provinces and the state by the KatFonds (real prices 2010)

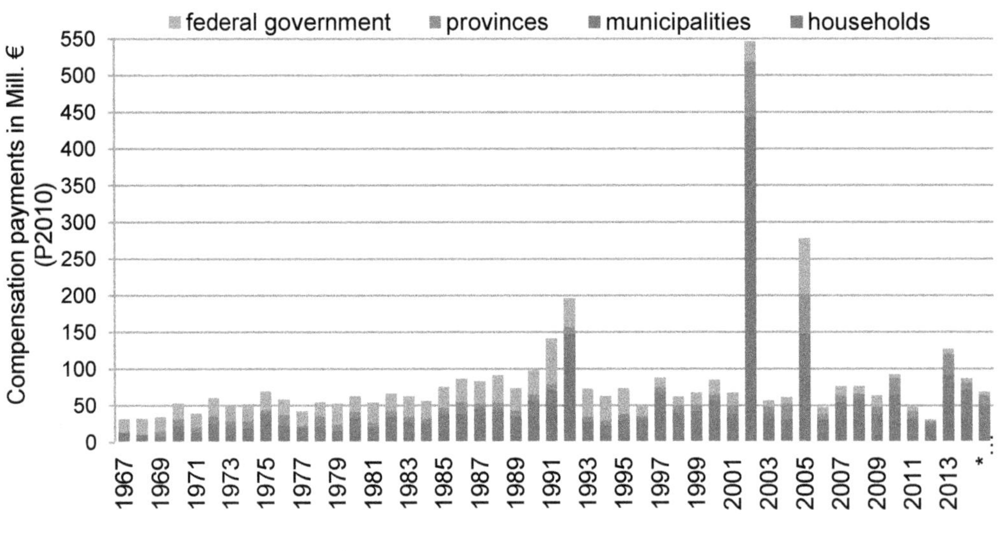

Note: *Estimated budget Expenditures include payments based on the compensation fund and rehabilitation law (HWG); Values in real prices of 2010.

Source: WIFO-calculations on the basis of Ministry of Finance (BMF) Austria.

Figure 2.12 shows the amount of money paid to individuals and households from the *KatFonds* over time.

Between 20% and 100% of losses suffered by a natural disaster can be reimbursed by the government. Of this total compensation, 60% is covered by *KatFonds* and 40% by sub-national governments. Average total compensation rates lie between 20% and 30%, but can reach up to 80% in exceptional cases (Raschky et al., 2013). During the floods in 2002 and 2005, an average of 20% of damages had to be paid by private households and businesses; the rest was compensated by public assistance, including donations. This average hides significant differences: some households and businesses in some provinces had their damages fully compensated, while others had to pay for most of the damages themselves (Sinabell and Url, 2006). Up to 50% of damage to public infrastructure in sub-national jurisdictions is financed by *KatFonds*. The fund also reimburses expenses related to recovery and protective measures. Special laws have been enacted during previous disasters to provide additional compensation, such as grants for the replacement of goods and tax relief measures (OECD, 2015).

Figure 2.14 shows the estimated total damages caused by the flood events of 2002 (EUR 2.9 billion) and 2005 (EUR 592 million), as well as the estimated amounts and different sources that compensated for private losses. For the 2002 floods, compensation payments for private damages by *KatFonds* totalled EUR 301 million, compared to EUR 225 million paid by private actors, EUR 83 million paid in donations, EUR 170 million paid by the provinces, and EUR 420 paid by insurance companies. In total loss payments to compensate private damages amounted to EUR 1.2 billion.

Figure 2.14 Estimated total damages of flood events in 2002 and 2005 (in million EURO)

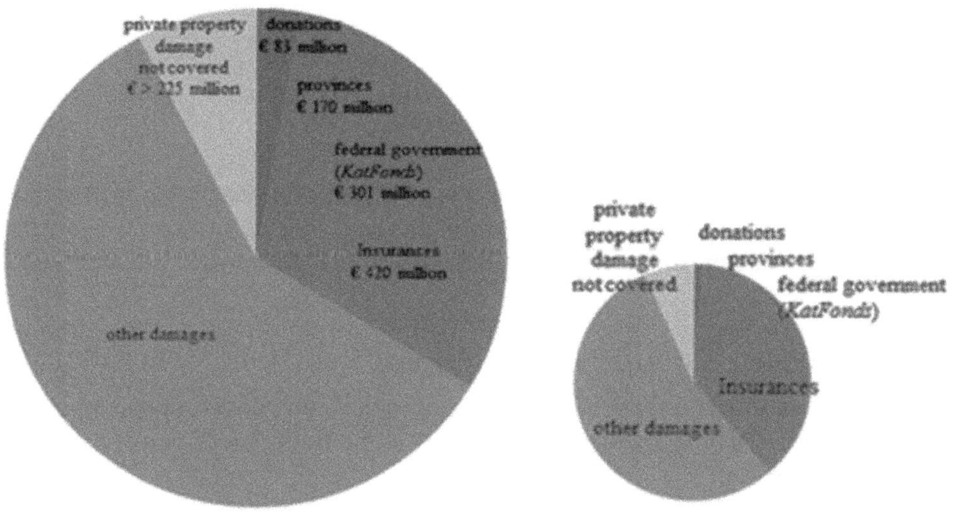

2002 Floods: EUR 2.9 billion estimated total damage (November 2003)

2005 Floods: EUR 592 million estimated total damage (June 2006)

Source: WIFO calculations based on Ministry of Finance (BMF).

There are some shortcomings of *KatFonds* that may raise questions about its economic efficiency:

- Since there is no legal entitlement, *KatFonds* entails ambiguity and uncertainty about how much the state will provide in individual assistance. *KatFonds* may leave some affected citizens with low or no compensation at all.
- The funding by tax money leaves *KatFonds* with no connection between raising and distributing financial assistance according to risk exposure of persons affected, which may be a disincentive to ex-ante individual disaster risk prevention investments.
- Providing financial relief ex-post may hinder ex-ante investments in disaster risk prevention by individuals and companies.
- Compensation by *KatFonds* is channelled through local authorities, which adds to the piecemeal process and the difficulty in understanding eligibility versus pay-outs.
- As a consequence of the severe summer floods in 2002, the Austrian government cancelled a planned tax reform and added EUR 500 million to *KatFonds* to handle the exceptional amount of damages (Prettenthaler et al., 2005). Such top-ups of *KatFonds* can be made at any moment and when circumstances require. This ad-hoc option can bring uncertainty and exposure to Austria's public finances, depending on the extent of the needed amounts.
- Over the past two decades, Austria's *KatFonds* paid out an average of EUR 50-75 million in compensation of damages to households, enterprises and public authorities (Figure 2.14). This figure does not include the complementary payments by the provinces and municipalities, nor other sources of compensation. It also shows that payments of more than EUR 200 million per year are rare, and payments to private actors often make up a small share of the overall amount.

Private insurance

In Austria, insurance against natural catastrophes can be purchased as an extra package within household insurance. This insurance includes floods, rockfalls, earthquakes, avalanches and backwater.

Sinabell and Url (2006) find that the majority of private households in Austria are insufficiently financially protected against natural hazards. Private insurance is available, although there are a number of shortcomings impeding a greater uptake (Sinabell and Url, 2006). These include:

- There is no insurance coverage for high-risk areas.
- Insurance policies usually only offer standard products that cover a percentage of the sum insured or a flat sum (between EUR 4 000 and 7 000), hence insured people are largely under-insured.
- Insurance companies set an upper limit to their total damage compensation, which means that benefits for insured households could vary depending on the number of total affected insured people and the total amount of damages.
- In some provinces, indemnities paid by private insurance reduce the compensation amounts provided by the state, which could decrease the incentive to take up insurance.

KatFonds can be a potential obstacle to insurance purchased by consumers given the significant, albeit unsure, pay-outs it offers in the event of a disaster.

In an attempt to address these private insurance gaps, the BMLFUW and the Ministry of Finance have proposed a quasi-obligatory insurance system that would be attached to existing fire insurance policies. The model suggests risk-based premiums and allows for some government compensation, based on a fixed threshold and clearly determined conditions. The Austrian Insurance Association (VVO) was involved in the development of the draft model and made an effort to consult a wide stakeholder base. To date, the model has not been considered for implementation in Austria.

Current incentive structures may not be conducive to changing the role of disaster risk insurance in Austria. All levels of government enjoy a strong solidarity movement in the event of a disaster, with a large volunteer body helping in response to a disaster and a widespread willingness to donate money to support disaster victims. A possible insurance solution may reduce people's desire to demonstrate such solidarity. In addition, the hand-out of assistance in the aftermath of a disaster by different levels of government has significant political symbolism. From a citizen's perspective, the current situation allows them to receive some damage compensation, without having to pay an insurance premium. These prevailing conditions may continue to make it difficult to obtain more effective disaster risk insurance provision.

European Solidarity Fund

The European Union Solidarity Fund (EUSF) was created as a re-financing facility (rather than an emergency response instrument) to assist countries that experience major disruptive shocks. The fund was created as a reaction to the severe floods in Central Europe in the summer of 2002. Since then, it has assisted 24 countries during 63 catastrophic events including floods, forest fires, earthquakes, storms and drought. It has providing an estimated EUR 3.7 billion in financial support. Austria has received around EUR 170 million (from a total estimated damage of EUR 3.2 billion) to compensate for damages incurred from past floods (Table 2.7), especially during the 2002 summer floods. In comparison, for the earthquake of L'Aquila in 2009 and Emilia-Romagna in 2012, Italy received nearly EUR 500 and 670 million respectively in compensation from the fund.

Table 2.7 European Solidarity Fund interventions, 2002-2015

Disaster	Estimated direct damage, EUR	Compensation amount granted, EUR
Summer floods 2002	3.2 billion	134 million
Summer floods 2005	592 million (Tyrol, Vorarlberg)	14.8 million
Lavamünd floods 2012	10 million	240 000
Floods 2013	866 million	21.7 million

Source: European Commission (2015), EU Solidarity Fund Interventions since 2002, European Commission, Brussels, http://ec.europa.eu/regional_policy/sources/thefunds/doc/interventions_since_2002.pdf.

European Recovery Fund

In an effort to help the recovery and re-establishment of businesses after the 2002 summer floods, the Austrian National Bank (ÖeNB) and the European Recovery Fund (ERP) provided interest-free loans of around EUR 400 million to industrial, commercial and tourism enterprises that were affected by the floods. Repayments of provided loans were not requested until after three years.[16]

Public expenditure in disaster risk prevention and mitigation

At the federal level, on average EUR 250 million is spent annually for prevention and mitigation measures against flood and Alpine hazards by the three main authorities: WLV, BWV, and BMVIT (Figure 2.15). The WLV allocations have been relatively stable at around EUR 76 million, except in 2013 and 2014 when they raised to EUR 88 million. A continuous reduction can be observed in WLV allocations over time and in real terms (Figure 2.16). BMVIT allocations were around EUR 50 million until 2006, when they increased to nearly EUR 100 million and afterwards reached an average level similar to WLV. For the BWV, there was an increase in 2013 and 2014 to EUR 108 million and EUR 99 million, respectively. Counting cross-governmental and private investments together, the total amount of annual prevention spending is estimated to be around EUR 400 million.

Figure 2.15 Annual federal disaster risk prevention and mitigation expenditure from 2002-2014 (in 2010 prices)

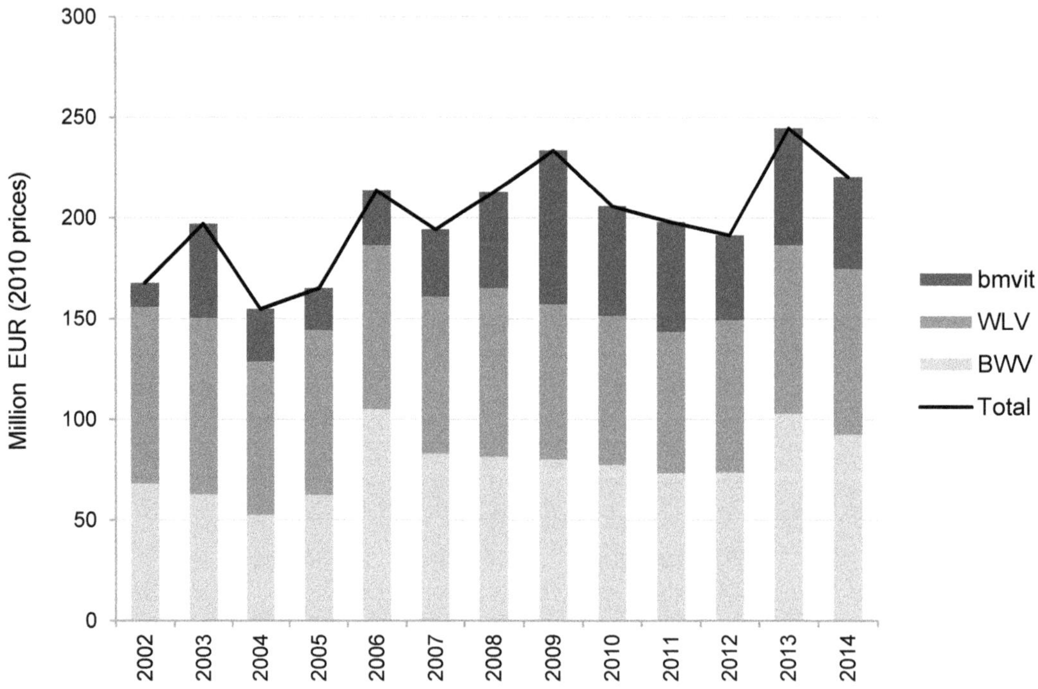

Source: OECD 2015 in-country mission meetings

Figure 2.16 WLV expenditure (across levels of government) in real terms, 1945-2007, real prices 2010

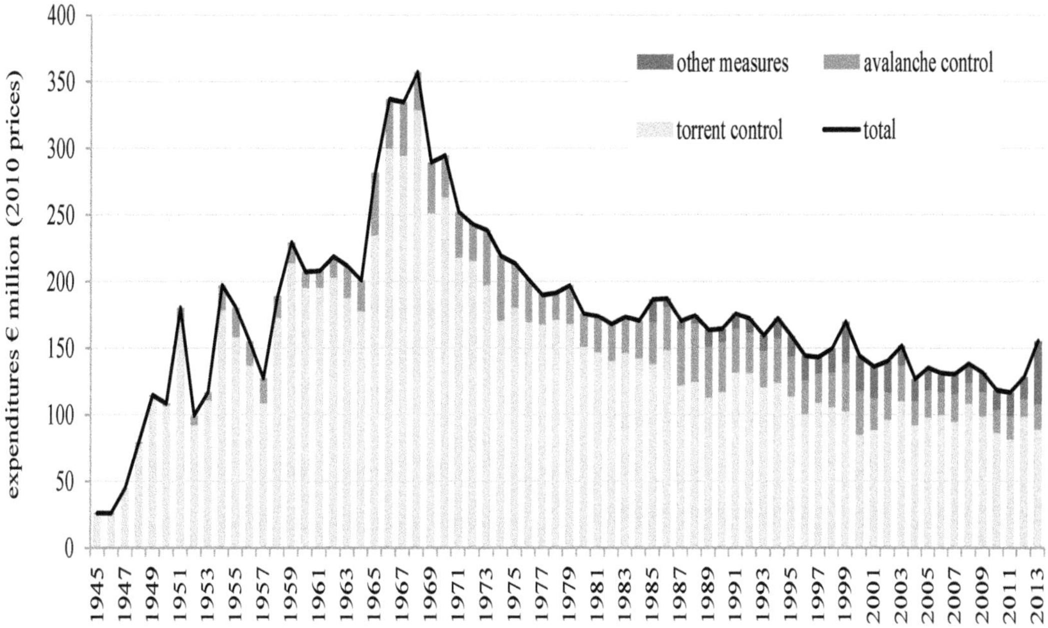

Source: graph provided by Franz Sinabell based on data of WLV

Within the WLV, 76% of investment is allocated to torrent prevention, 10% to avalanche prevention, and 10 % to rock falls and landslides. The remaining 5% is invested in forest protection.

The allocation for the BMVIT is mostly used for structural protective measures along the Danube and March rivers, such as dams and walls. One of the biggest protective dams was constructed and finalised in 2012: the Machland Nord.

As mentioned earlier, over the past four decades, Austria's investment in disaster risk prevention and mitigation, including protective infrastructure, has managed to offset the impacts of increased exposure through a greater number of buildings in hazard prone areas. Nevertheless, the amount of financing available for disaster risk prevention and mitigation is increasingly only sufficient to cover the depreciation rate of existing infrastructure. With current resources, creating protection for new areas, or increasing protection in existing areas, is only possible at the expense of diminishing protection levels elsewhere (Habersack et al., 2009).

Looking at the allocation of prevention spending across Austria, Figure 2.17 shows the expenditure by the two different disaster risk prevention services within provinces. The majority of expenditure by the WLV is concentrated in mountainous provinces, such as Tyrol, Salzburg and Styria. Whereas the largest part of BWV spending is undertaken in low-lying provinces with large rivers, such as Lower Austria.

Figure 2.17 Federal disaster risk prevention and mitigation expenditure by province in 2014

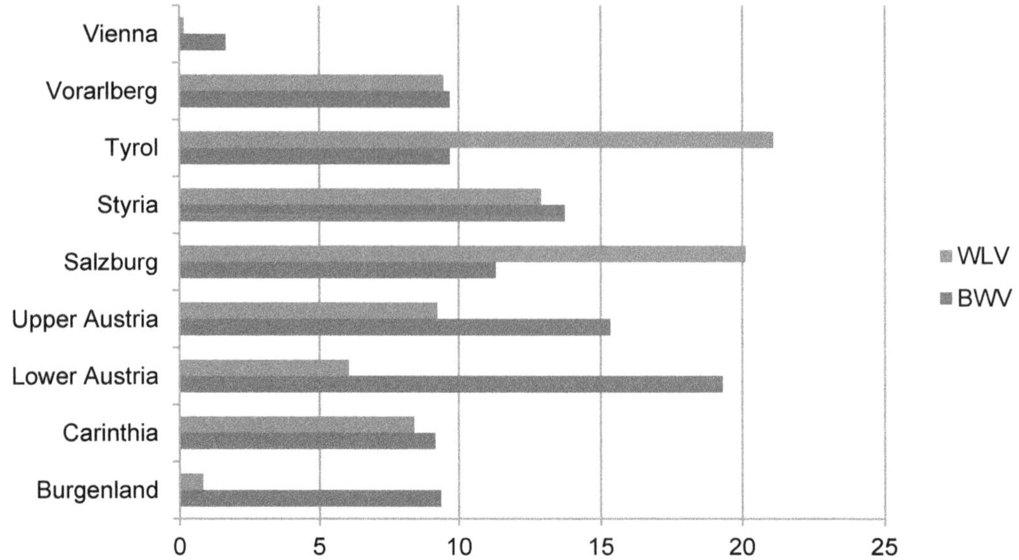

Source: OECD 2015 in-country mission meetings

Tables 2.8 and 2.9 illustrate that the largest disaster risk prevention expenditures per household are made in the region with the lowest number of properties in flood risk zones (Burgenland), whereas investments in preventive measures are relatively low in the province with the most properties in risk zones (Lower Austria) (Sinabell and Url, 2006).

Table 2.8 Total disaster risk prevention investments per household per province in Austria (2001-2005 average)

		Investment in flood prevention measures in EUR per household
1	Burgenland	191
2	Salzburg	128
3	Vorarlberg	128
4	Tyrol	118
5	Carinthia	104
6	Styria	62
7	Upper Austria	52
8	Lower Austria	47
9	Vienna	25

Source: Sinabell and Url (2006), "Versicherungen als effizientes Mittel zur Risikotragung von Naturgefahren, Studie des Österreichischen Instituts für Wirtschaftsforschung im Auftrag des Verbandes der Versicherungsunternehmen Österreichs" [Insurance as an efficient tool for risk transfer, Study by the Austrian Institute of Economic Research (WIFO) on behalf of the Austrian Association of Insurance Companies (VVO)], WIFO Austria, Vienna.

Table 2.9 Number of properties in high risk zones in 2005

	Province	Number of properties in high risk zones
1	Lower Austria	73 531
2	Upper Austria	35 755
3	Styria	26 785
4	Vienna	24 829
5	Tyrol	22 044
6	Salzburg	19 732
7	Carinthia	15 594
8	Vorarlberg	15 527
9	Burgenland	8 254

Source: Sinabell and Url (2006), "Versicherungen als effizientes Mittel zur Risikotragung von Naturgefahren, Studie des Österreichischen Instituts für Wirtschaftsforschung im Auftrag des Verbandes der Versicherungsunternehmen Österreichs" [Insurance as an efficient tool for risk transfer, Study by the Austrian Institute of Economic Research (WIFO) on behalf of the Austrian Association of Insurance Companies (VVO)], WIFO Austria, Vienna.

Conclusion

This section showed the significant amount of resources that have been dedicated to reducing disaster risks in Austria over time. These investments have contributed to avoiding higher damages in disasters. For those damages that did occur, *KatFonds* has provided damage compensation for private losses and for public infrastructure damages.

The significant public financial assistance in Austria has provided ex-ante support in reducing risks and also ex-post disaster assistance. However, through doing this it may have deterred a higher contribution of individual households and businesses to increasing overall resilience levels.

A whole-of-society approach to disaster risk prevention requires everyone to share the burden of financing disaster risk management to ensure that all risk reduction investments yield their expected benefits. A number of instruments could be introduced to encourage more preventative investments by individual households and businesses, such as tax credits, public financial support for preventative investments, or rewards in the way compensations are paid out.

Assessment and recommendations

Austria is significantly exposed to Alpine natural hazards. Mountains cover around 60% of its territory and large areas are covered by forests, leaving only about 34% of land suitable for settlements. A large part of this space is exposed to a variety of natural, especially Alpine, hazards, such as avalanches, torrents or floods. Extreme temperatures, such as heatwaves, have caused significant death tolls in the past and could increase in frequency in the future through potentially changing climatic conditions.

Around 14% of Austria's building stock and 13% of its population is potentially exposed to natural hazards. Recent major flood events have shown that natural disasters may have considerable socio-economic impacts. The floods that occurred in 2002 caused some EUR 3 billion in damages and affected 60 000 people.

Given its history with natural disasters, Austria has a long tradition in public disaster risk prevention and mitigation management, with core policies anchored in its constitution and its main authorities established in the 19th century. From early on, citizens exposed to natural hazards have actively engaged in helping to address risks, either through sharing knowledge about local hazards or initiating public protective infrastructure projects. This sharing of knowledge complemented and fostered advanced technical capacity and contributed to an exemplary whole-of-society approach to risk management.

Identification and monitoring of current and future risks

Austria has a long-standing tradition in identifying and assessing natural hazards. Its technical capacity has developed state-of-the-art hazard monitoring systems, which have ensured nationwide, systematic and regular assessments of hazards. Austria is highly aware that current hazard patterns are continuously evolving and has embraced the importance of factoring in uncertainty and the potential impacts of climate change when estimating the future severity and frequency of natural disasters. Austria also recognises the importance of changes in exposure driven by the increased occupation and changes in the use of land in hazard zones, and the ecological, economic and social implications of disasters. It has therefore engaged in developing a prospective approach to its disaster risk prevention and mitigation management, ensuring a regular and dynamic updating of hazard zone maps and adapting protective infrastructure to potential impacts of climate change.

To improve hazard models, and to inform effective disaster risk prevention and mitigation policies, it is crucial to know the socio-economic impacts from past disasters. This information also serves as a key variable in assessing the effectiveness of disaster risk reduction investments over time.

Although some detailed estimations of socio-economic losses have been recorded for some hazards and major past disaster events, and despite very good and comprehensive hydrographic documentation, Austria could benefit from improving the systematic recording of social and economic losses of disasters. Some information is gathered by different agencies in order to carry out their work, for example the private sector gathers data on exposure. However, most of the available records are confined to direct economic losses, whereby indirect losses causes by the interruption of services could be much more important and damaging to regional and potentially the national economy.

The provincial governments in charge of assisting victims and handling the compensation process for households and businesses would be in a good position to carry out such overall socio-economic impact assessments. In addition, the evaluations conducted by the Federal Chancellery, the commerce chambers and the insurance association could complement bottom-up data collection.

Legal and institutional frameworks for disaster risk prevention management

Austria's significant exposure to natural hazards and past experiences with disasters has contributed to its well-established knowledge of and capacity in preventing and mitigating disaster risks. This is well reflected in its legal and institutional framework for disaster risk prevention management. A number of ministries and departments share the task of addressing different disaster risks, with a lead function situated in the BMLFUW, the BMVIT and the BMI. As with many policy areas in Austria's federal arrangement, disaster risk prevention and mitigation is a task that is shared by different government levels, with the centre most often determining strategy and core funding and the local levels driving implementation and co-financing investments. To ensure good co-ordination across levels of government and between different ministries, platforms such as the Austrian Spatial Planning Conference (ÖROK) should be encouraged and further strengthened. They can develop and strengthen co-ordinated strategies and, through regular evaluations, issue recommendations for continuously improving existing policies and practices.

The division of tasks among different ministries and levels of governments relies on an approach that is narrowly based on specific hazards or specific locations delineated by administrative borders, rather than actual hazard zones. Austria should ensure that disaster risk reduction measures across sectors mutually reinforce each other, and that hazards are viewed in their potential cascading nature, instead of as isolated events. This is important during the identification of risks and should be taken into account in relation to the organisational structure (e.g. to facilitate cross-jurisdictional collaboration) and the planning and financing of disaster risk prevention and mitigation measures.

Managing structural and non-structural measures to foster disaster risk prevention

Structural measures have long constituted a core of Austria's disaster risk prevention management to protect existing settlement areas. They have been conceived and implemented on the basis of partnerships with local communities, whereby the direct beneficiaries have contributed to co-financing from higher levels of government. In Austria, there has been an increasing recognition of the importance of an integrated approach to disaster risk prevention and mitigation. Although structural measures have made up the majority of disaster risk reduction investments, there has been an increased focus on non-structural measures, especially following several consecutive large-scale floods that highlighted the limits of structural measures and the potential benefits of non-structural measures.

Austria's large stock of protective infrastructure has greatly protected its population and economic assets, but there are challenges for the future

Despite the significant and continued investment in physical infrastructure protection, its demand consistently exceeds the supply that can be co-financed by central government units. This will become particularly challenging under tightening public budgets and the potential reallocation of resources towards operation and maintenance tasks. Under these conditions it will be crucial for Austria to apply clear and consistent prioritisation criteria to its investment decisions, making sure to address the most important protection needs first. Although simple criteria catalogues may prove more difficult to implement in practice, objective criteria need to be applied and published in order to guide municipal requests for funding and ensure equity that is independent of the financial capacity of the interested party or political urgency of the local government. Transparency will be the key to ensuring equity, efficiency and continued trust in the government carrying out this function.

Maintaining and rehabilitating the significant stock that has been accumulated over past decades will also be a challenge for Austria, especially if measures aim to ensure the stock maintains it original levels of protection. The financing of these tasks has become an increasing issue, as the financial and technical capacities of municipalities that currently own the majority of infrastructure have proven limited. The challenge of ensuring adequate maintenance is increasingly recognised in Austria. Promising practices have been introduced to address this issue, such as the centrally led WLV database that contains information on some 270 000 protective structures, including an assessment of their condition, documentation of monitoring and inspections, and corrective maintenance works that have been carried out. However, the challenge to be addressed is the responsibility and the long-term financing of these works.

Similar to other European countries, notably France, this problem has been addressed in the province of Salzburg through its long-standing tradition of water boards, which are co-operatives between a number of interest groups or entire municipalities that provide the capacity for shared maintenance among several infrastructure owners. Scaling-up the system of water boards across Austria may not be a feasible policy option as they are bodies that have grown as bottom-up movements over a significant amount of time and in a specific regional context. However, it may be worth exploring policy options that facilitate the establishment of "joint maintenance bodies" that work across jurisdictions and are co-financed by different municipalities and potentially higher levels of government.

Collaboration across jurisdictional borders will be key to continue ensuring protection against future disasters

Austria's governance system for structural measures, as seen above, is organised around provincial service branches, which are a deconcentrated arm of central service units that receive project proposals from local municipalities. This governance structure may risk overlooking cross-jurisdictional risks and investment needs. As previously highlighted, risk prevention management should take into account zones where either one or several hazards could occur and cause damage. This requires taking a cross-jurisdictional approach to map potential risks and the impacts of disaster risk reduction measures across the hazard territory. Given the importance of local level actors in disaster risk prevention management, cross-jurisdictional collaboration is indispensable for ensuring the effectiveness and efficiency of disaster risk reduction investments.

To address this collective action problem, governments can both change the way projects are financed, for example by rewarding joint project proposals with higher central level funding shares, and regulate the way local risk assessments, prevention and preparedness measures are assessed and implemented. An alternative, and perhaps complementary, policy reform was proposed by the Austrian Spatial Planning Conference

(ÖROK) as a result of lessons learnt from the evaluations of the 2002 and 2005 large-scale floods. The reform suggested establishing co-ordination and compensation mechanisms between the different municipalities impacted, including for protective infrastructure investments and land-use decisions undertaken by adjacent jurisdictions. This would require developing guidelines for cross-jurisdictional and jurisdictional spatial planning. Good practice cases already exist, such as the water boards in the province of Salzburg, where cross-jurisdictional hazard assessments and disaster risk reduction investments have been carried out through the cross-jurisdictional collaboration of different interest groups.

The growing importance of non-structural disaster risk prevention measures

Non-structural or "soft" disaster risk prevention measures are important complements to physical disaster risk reduction investments. They can be often low cost measures, in comparison to the costs of physical infrastructure, which yield potentially high returns. Non-structural measures include hazard identification and mapping, land-use planning or risk communication.

Austria has highly advanced technical capacities and technologies to identify and map the multiple hazard types that potentially threaten its population and economic assets. Systematic hazard mapping has been conducted since the 1970s, but only in recent years has Austria started to ensure that hazard maps are regularly updated and, if necessary, adjusted by specific local developments. Austria has made significant progress in making hazard information available to the public for all hazard-prone areas. There could be improvements made in overlaying different hazard maps so that end users have a clear understanding of the potential multiple hazards to which they could be exposed. However, the real challenge lies in translating this information into actual land-use planning and decisions.

Hazard-based land-use planning is a core instrument to reduce the exposure of people and assets to natural hazards. However, in Austria, as in many other countries, scarcity of land for settlements, the increased consumption of space, and the significant reduction of retention zones have all been factors that have contributed to the rising tension between land-use and hazard zone planning. In the aftermath of the 2002 large-scale floods in Austria, it emerged that existing hazard maps may have not been sufficiently considered in local land-use decisions. This resulted in a high number of properties being exposed to and destroyed during the floods. The actual extent of problems caused by misled land-use decisions has only been visible in Austria after a disaster event has taken place. This suggests that there is no systematic monitoring and oversight of the integration of hazard zones in actual land-use decisions.

To improve the integration of hazard zoning in land-use decisions it is essential to ensure that new constructions are not permitted, but also that the "grey" areas of new works to existing building stock in hazard areas is better monitored to avoid a further increase in damage potential. Furthermore, regional planning and land-use strategies should include disaster risk reduction targets. To aid this process, decision makers should document their efforts to implement disaster risk reduction objectives in their planning decisions. They should be provided with support and monitoring from experts in this process. It is recommended that provinces work more closely with local governments on this task to ensure that disaster risk reduction targets are implemented and damage potential is not increased in the future.

Austria should be applauded for its recognition and concrete actions to re-dedicate land to create flood expansion zones. Austria has shown exemplary work in engaging in highly complex legal procedures, together with land owners, to accomplish this difficult task.

There is scope to increase the private sector's and individual households' responsibility to boost Austria's resilience against future disasters

Austrians have enjoyed exemplary and widespread solidarity in response to disasters. For example, a large volunteer force and generous donation efforts have been mobilised following a disaster. While this practice demonstrates strong human capital that benefits other parts of Austrians' lives, it may contribute to impeding much needed increases to individual preventative action measures. Public compensation mechanisms may also have a similar effect.

While citizens' solidarity and compensation mechanisms should not be abolished, more attention could be paid to policies that would encourage complementary individual preventative action. This may reinforce public action ex-ante and ex-post of disasters to make sure that public investment in disaster risk reduction is fully enjoyed by the affected population. Measures could include raising awareness among property owners about their individual exposure to hazards and the solutions available to improve resilience against potential disasters. Campaigns to provide information and individual technical advice, as provided by the WLV, should be continuously scaled up. Financial support in the form of tax credits or subsidies to property owners for retrofitting their houses could further encourage protective investments. Compensation payments could reward individual preventative behaviour.

It is presumed that businesses have invested more in protecting their assets against the impacts of potential disasters, but there is little supporting systematic evidence. It is recommended that risk managers systematically engage with the private sector, including critical infrastructure operators, to assess their vulnerabilities, their disaster risk reductions needs and potential regulatory mechanisms that contribute to reinforcing resilience.

Risk financing – the challenge of achieving whole-of-society engagement in disaster risk prevention

The disruptions disasters can cause have an impact on individual households, businesses, and the public sector. Hence all actors have to decide to which degree and how they will invest in disaster risk prevention and mitigation. A whole-of-society approach to disaster risk prevention requires everyone to share the burden of financing disaster risk management in order to ensure that public disaster risk management investments yield their expected benefits.

In Austria, an estimated EUR 400 million is invested annually across ministries, levels of government and private actors to prevent and mitigate floods and Alpine hazards. Although risk management expenditure is high in comparison to other OECD countries, there is a risk, at current expenditure levels, of depleting the existing capital stock of prevention measures. Current maintenance and rehabilitation work cannot be sufficiently carried out by owners of protective infrastructure, which means alternative arrangements have to be found to ensure that protective infrastructure investments are not forfeited because resources have to be shifted to other purposes. Joint maintenance bodies, organised as co-operatives by several municipalities or interest groups, could be a way to overcome the financial burden and ensure technical capacity at the local level.

Austria's key source of financing for disaster risk prevention and mitigation measures, the *Katastrophenfonds*, serves as a double function as it is used to finance disaster risk prevention and mitigation measures and also as a relief fund to compensate for damages after a disaster. To improve its efficiency, there should be more clarity and transparency about actual compensations by the central fund and the co-payments made by provincial and local governments. Complementary pay-outs by potential insurance or other sources should also be published and clearly integrated into compensation pay-out decisions. Compensation mechanisms could better reward individual investments in disaster risk reduction measures in order to increase private preventative action.

Notes

[1] Formal responsibilities are outlined in Austria's Forestry Law: *Forstgesetz* (1975).

[2] Formal responsibilities are outlined in the water construction law: *Bundeswasserbaugesetz* (1985).

[3] http://www.oerok.gv.at/

[4] See for example: Flood Risk I and II evaluation reports that were conducted in the aftermath of the 2002 and 2005 floods.

[5] https://www.icpdr.org/main/.

[6] http://www.iksr.org/en/index.html.

[7] http://www.ikse-mkol.org/index.php?id=1&L=2.

[8] http://www.alpconv.org/en/convention/default.html.

[9] Of the 2 354 Austrian municipalities (2013), 1 545 need to have a hazard zone plan (*ForstG* 1975).

[10] Revisions due to the installation of protective infrastructure may lead to a change of a high hazard zone to a medium one, but the medium zone will always remain a medium-hazard zone, rather than a zone that becomes hazard-free.

[11] Maps include low (300 year return period), medium (100 year return period) and high probability (30 year return period) for flood exposure.

[12] http://www.machlanddamm.at/de/3/26.html.

[13] www.biberberti.com/de/index.php.

[14] http://www.bmi.gv.at/cms/BMI_Zivilschutz/broschueren/start.aspx.

[15] www.zivilschutzverband.at.

[16] http://www.ots.at/presseaussendung/OTS_20130613_OTS0065/hochwasserhilfe-oenb-und-erp-fonds-stellen-400-mio-eur-der-wirtschaft-zur-verfuegung.

Bibliography

Amt der Tiroler Landesregierung (2011), *Waldstrategie 2020, Amt der Tiroler Landesregierung, Gruppe Forst*" [Forest Strategy 2020, Office of the Provincial Government of Tirol, Forest Group], Innsbruck, https://www.tirol.gv.at/fileadmin/themen/umwelt/wald/waldzustand/downloads/waldstrategie2020_web.pdf.

BMF (2013), "*Steuerliche Maßnahmen bei Katastrophenschäden*" [Tax measures in case of disaster damage], Ministry of Finance (BMF), Vienna.

BMF (2015), "*Katastrophenfondsgesetz 1996: Daten zum Jahr 2014*" [Catastrophe Fund Law 1996: Data for the year 2014], Ministry of Finance (BMF), Vienna.

BMI (2011), "*Erdbebenschutzratgeber: Erbebensituation in Österreich, Anleitung für vorbeugende Massnahmen*" [Earthquake Guide Book: Earthquake situation in Austria, guidance for preventive measures], Ministry of Interior, Vienna.

BMI (2013), Austrian Security Strategy: Security in a new decade – Shaping security, Federal Chancellery of the Republic of Austria, Vienna.

BMLFUW (2006), "*Richtlinien für die Wirtschaftlichkeitsuntersuchung und Priorisierung von Maßnahmen der Wildbach- und Lawinenverbauung gemäß § 3 Abs. 2 Z 3 Wasserbautenförderungsgesetz 1985*" [Legal guidelines for cost efficieny analysis and the prioritisation of torrent and avalanche barriers as defined in § 3 Para. 2 Z 3 legislation on the promotion of hydraulic engineering structures 1985].

BMLFUW (2015), "*Leben mit Naturgefahren: Ratgeber für die Eigenvorsorge bei Hochwasser, Muren, Lawinen, Steinschlag und Rutschungen*" [Living with natural hazards: guidance for self-protection in case of floods, debris flows, avalanches, rockfalls and landslides], Ministry of Agriculture, Forestry, Environment and Water Management (BMLFUW), Vienna.

BMLFUW (2014a), "*Schutz Wirkung Lebensraum: Die Wildbach und Lawinenverbauung – Wirkungs - und serviceorientierte Organisation zum Schutz vor Naturgefahren*" [Protection impact living area: torrent and avalanche barriers – effect and service-oriented organisation for the protection against natural hazards], Ministry of Agriculture, Forestry, Environment and Water Management (BMLFUW), Vienna.

BMLFUW (2014b), "*III/5, Projektcontrollingbericht 2014*" [Project Controlling Report], Ministry of Agriculture, Forestry, Environment and Water Management (BMLFUW), Vienna (unpublished).

BMLFUW (2014c), *Hochwasser Risikokarten. Fachlicher Leitfaden*, [Flood Risk Maps. Technical Guidance]. Ministry of Agriculture, Forestry, Environment and Water Management (BMLFUW), Vienna.

BMLFUW (2015), "*Entwurf Nationaler Hochwasserrisikomanagementplan 2015*" [National Flood Risk Management Plan 2015 (Draft)], Ministry of Agriculture, Forestry, Environment and Water Management (BMLFUW), Vienna.

BMVIT (2009), "*FloodRisk II Vertiefung und Vernetzung zukunftsweisender Umsetzungsstrategien zum integrierten Hochwassermanagement*" [FloodRisk II Deepening and Cross-linking of future-oriented Implementation Strategies for integrated Flood Management], Synthesebericht, Ministry of Agriculture, Forestry, Environment and Water Management, Vienna.

Ecker, M. and F. Hrebik (2012), "*Machlanddamm: Jahrhundertbauwerk in Rekordbauzeit*" [Machland Dam: A once-in-a-century structure constructed in record time], World of Porr 161/2012, Porr Allgemeine Baugesellschaft, Vienna. EM-DAT (n.d.), The OFDA/CRED International Disaster Database, Université catholique de Louvain, Brussels, www.emdat.be.

European Commission (2012), Report from the Commission to the European Parliament and Council on the Implementation of the Water Framework Directive (2000/60/C) River Basin Management Plans: Austria, Commission Staff Working Document, European Commission, Brussels, http://ec.europa.eu/environment/water/participation/map_mc/countries/austria_en.htm.

European Commission (2015), EU Solidarity Fund Interventions since 2002, European Commission, Brussels, http://ec.europa.eu/regional_policy/sources/thefunds/doc/interventions_since_2002.pdf.

Fuchs, S. (2015), "*Vulnerabilität und Restgefährdung Österreich*" [Vulnerability and Residual Risk Austria], IAN Report 172, Institut für Alpine Naturgefahren, Universität für Bodenkultur, Vienna, (unpublished).

Fuchs, S. and A. Zischg (2014), "*Vulnerabilitätslandkarte Österreich, Kurzfassung*" [Vulnerability Map Austria, Short Version], IAN Report 152, Institut für Alpine Naturgefahren, Universität für Bodenkultur, Vienna, (unpublished).

Fuchs, S., Keiler, M. and A. Zischg (2015), "A spatiotemporal multi-hazard exposure assessment based on property data", Natural Hazards and Earth System Sciences, Vol. 15/9, pp. 2127-2142.

Gamper, C.D. (2008), "The political economy of public participation in natural hazard management: A theoretical review and an exemplary case of the decision framework of the Austrian hazard zone mapping", Natural Hazards and Earth System Sciences, Vol. 8, pp. 233-241.

Gamper, C.D. and C. Turcanu (2009). "Can public participation help managing risks from natural hazards?", Safety Science, Vol. 47/4, pp. 522-528.

Habersack, H. et al (2004), "*Analyse der Hochwasserereignisse vom August 2002 – FloodRisk (Kurzfassung)*" [Analysis of Flood events in August 2002 – FloodRisk (Short Version)], Ministry of Agriculture, Forestry, Environment and Water Management, Vienna.

Habersack, H., J. Bürgel and A. Kanonier (2009), "*FloodRisk II: Vertiefung und Vernetzung zukunftsweisender Umsetzungsstrategien zum integrierten Hochwassermanagement. Synthesebericht*" [FloodRisk II: Deepening and linking of forward-looking strategies to implement an integrated flood risk management. Synthesis Report]. Ministry of Agriculture, Forestry, Environment and Water Management, Vienna.

Habsburg-Lothringen, C., A. Amrusch and F. Prettenthaler (2009), "*Zonierung und Gebäudebewertung zur Bestimmung des Schadenpotentials für Hochwasser in Österreich*" [Zoning and building rating to determine potential damage levels of floods in Austria], in Prettenthaler, F. and H. Albrecher (eds.), Hochwasser und dessen Versicherung in Österreich [Floods and insurance in Austria], Austria Academy of Sciences and Joanneum Research, Vienna.

Hackel (2012), "*Hochwasserschutz Machland Ein Jahrhundertbauwerk*" [Flood Protection Machland- A once-in-a-century structure], Presentation for Flussbautagung, Ministry of Transport, Innovation and Technology, Vienna.

Hecht, M. (2009), "*Workpackage Recht TP10.7: Errichtungsverpflichtungen, Entschädigungspflichten, Parteistellung und Genehmigungspflichten (nach WBFG, WRG und UVP-G) bei Errichtung und Sanierung von Hochwasserschutzmaßnahmen*" [Workpackage Law TP10.7: Obligations for Installation, Indemnities, Recognition of Parties and Authorisation Requirements (as determined by WBFG, WRG and UVP-G) in Case of the Construction and Maintenance of Flood Protection Measures], in "*FloodRisk II: Vertiefung und Vernetzung zukunftsweisender Umsetzungsstrategien zum integrierten Hochwasserschutz*" [FloodRisk II: Deepening and linking of forward-looking strategies to implement an integrated flood risk management], Final Report. Vienna.

Hutter, H.P., H. Moshammer, P. Wallner, B. Leitner and M. Kundi (2007), "Heatwaves in Vienna: effects on mortality", Wiener Klinische Wochenschrift, Vol. 119/7-8, pp. 223-227.

Kanonier, A. (2004), "Naturgefahren im österreichischen Raumordnungsrecht: Übersicht hinsichtlich der raumordungsgesetzlichen Bestimmungen bezüglich Naturgefahren im Raumordnungsrecht der Länder"[Natural Hazards in Austrial Planning Law: Overview over spatial planning regulations relating to natural hazards in provincial planning law], study commissioned by the Austrian Spatial Planning Conference, Vienna.

Länger, E., 2003, "*Der forsttechnische Dienst für Wildbach- und Lawinenverbauung in Österreich und seine Tätigkeit seit der Gründung im Jahre 1884*" [Forestry service and the construction and maintenance of mountain torrent and avalanche barriers since its establishment in 1884]. Dissertation an der Universität für Bodenkultur Wien.

Oberösterreich Landesrechnungshof (2014), "*LRH-Bericht, Initiativprüfung, Hochwasserschutz Machland Nord*" [LRH Report, Audit, Flood Protection Machland North], LRH-100000-12/9-2014-LI

OECD (2013), OECD Environmental Performance Reviews: Austria 2013, OECD Publishing, Paris, http://dx.doi.org/10.1787/9789264202924-en.

OECD (2014b), Recommendation of the Council on the Governance of Critical Risks, OECD Publishing, Paris.

OECD (2014a), Boosting Resilience through Innovative Risk Governance, OECD Publishing, Paris, http://dx.doi.org/10.1787/9789264209114-en.

OECD (2015), Disaster Risk Financing: A global survey of practices and challenges, OECD Publishing, Paris, http://dx.doi.org/10.1787/9789264234246-en.

ÖROK (2004), "*Naturgefahren im österreichischen Raumordnungsrecht*" [Natural Hazards in Austrian Planning Law], Endbericht, Austrian Conference on Spatial Planning, Vienna.

ÖROK (2015), "*Risikomanagement für gravitative Naturgefahren in der Raumplanung: Fachliche Empfehlungen & Materialienband*" [Risk Management for Gravitational Natural Hazards in Spatial Planning: Expert Recommendations and Materials Volume], Austrian Conference on Spatial Planning, Vienna.

ÖROK (2005), "*Präventiver Umgang mit Naturgefahren in der Raumordnung, Materialienband*" [Preventive Dealing with Natural Hazards in Spatial Planning: Materials Volume], ÖROK Schriftenreihe Nr. 168, Austrian Conference on Spatial Planning, Vienna. Österreichisches Institut für Raumplanung (2004), "*Präventive Raumordnung gegen Folgeschäden aus Naturkatastrophen*" [Preventive Regional Planning against Consequential Damage from Natural Hazards], Endbericht, Austrian Institute for Regional Studies and Spatial Planning, Vienna.

Österreichisches Kuratorium für Alpine Sicherheit (2015), "*Analyse: Berg*" [Analysis: Mountain], Winter 2014/2015, Austria Alpine Safety Board, Innsbruck.

Pichler, A. (2010), *Handlungsempfehlungen zur Anpassung an den Klimawandel in Österreich: Aktivitätsfeld "Bauen und Wohnen" und "Schutz vor Naturgefahren"* [Recommendations for climate change adaptation in Austria: Activity Field "Construction and Living" and "Protection against Natural Hazards"], AustroClim, October 2010, Vienna.

Pichler, A. (2013), "Governing Disasters: Challenges, Limitations, Lessons learnt. An Austrian Perspective", presentation submitted to the OECD Expert Meeting on Risk Prevention and Mitigation, Paris, www.oecd.org/gov/risk/governingeffectivepreventionandmitigationof disruptiveshocks.htm.

Prettenthaler, F. and N. Vetters (2005), "*Finanzielle Bewältigung von Naturgefahren: Vorschläge zur Reform des Österreichischen Modells*" [Financial Management of Natural Hazards: Suggestions for Reforming the Austrian Model], InTeReg Working Paper Nr. 21-2005, Joanneum Research, Graz, Vienna.

Prettenthaler, F., D. Kortschak, S. Hochrainer-Stigler, R. Mechler, H. Urban and K.W. Steininger (2015), "Catastrophe Management: Riverine Flooding", in Steininger, K.W. et al. Economic Evaluation of Climate Change Impacts: Development of a Cross-Sectoral Framework and Results for Austria, Springer International Publishing, Switzerland.

Prettenthaler, F., W. Hyll and N. Vetters, N. (2010), "*Nationale Risikotransfermechanismen für Naturgefahren, Analyse der Problemlagen für Individuen, Versicherer und Staat*" [National Risk Transfer Mechanisms for Natural Hazards, Analysis of Problematic Situations faced by Individuals, Insurers and the State], InTeReg Working Paper Nr. 19-2004, Joanneum Research, Graz, Vienna. Raschky, P.A., Schwarze, R., Schwindt, M. and F. Zahn (2013), "Uncertainty of Governmental Relief and the Crowding out of Flood Insurance", Environmental Resource Economics, 54:179-200.

Rudolf-Miklau, F., Pichler, A., and J. Suda (2014), "Persistence of Alpine natural hazard protection: Metting multiple demands by applying systems engineering and life cycle management principles in natural hazard protection systems in the perimeter of the Alpine Convention", Platform on Natural Hazards of the Alpine Convention (PLANAT), Vienna.

Salzburger Nachrichten (2015), "*Trotz des Finanzskandals mehr Hochwasserschutz*" [Despite finance scandal increasing investments in flood protection], article published on January 16, 2015, Salzburg.

Sinabell, F. and T. Url (2006), "*Versicherungen als effizientes Mittel zur Risikotragung von Naturgefahren, Studie des Österreichischen Instituts für Wirtschaftsforschung im Auftrag des Verbandes der Versicherungsunternehmen Österreichs*" [Insurance as an efficient tool for risk transfer, Study by the Austrian Institute of Economic Research (WIFO) on behalf of the Austrian Association of Insurance Companies (VVO)], WIFO Austria, Vienna.

Sinabell, F., O. Fritz, W. Puwein and G. Streicher (2009), "*Eine volkswirtschaftliche Analyse der Wildbach- und Lawinenverbauung*" [An economic analysis of torrent and avalanche barriers], WIFO Austria, Vienna.

Suda, J., 2008, "*Abschätzung der durchschnittlichen Lebensdauer von Wildbachsperren*" [Estimate of the average life span of torrent dams], Universität für Bodenkultur, Wien, Mai 2008.

UNISDR (2015), "Concept note on Methodology to Estimate Direct Economic Losses from Hazardous Events to Measure the Achievement of Target C of the Sendai Framework for Disaster Risk Reducation: A Technical Review", the United Nations Office for Disaster Risk Reduction (UNISDR), Geneva. www.preventionweb.net/documents/framework/Concept%20Paper%20-20Direct%20Economic%20Loss%20Indicator%20methodology%2011%20November%202015.pdf.

WG – Schmittenbach (2016), Website, www.wg-schmittenbach.at/ (accessed 21 February 2016)

Chapter 3

Boosting resilience through innovative risk governance: the case of the Rhône river in France

This chapter summarises France's progress in bolstering resilience against natural disasters through innovative risk governance across the Rhône River Basin. Due to the basin's large size, natural hazards include river and coastal floods, but also torrents, storms and earthquakes. The chapter shows that a major Rhône flood is considered a critical risk for France, given the basin's size and economic importance. The chapter explains that recent floods have sparked a number of disaster risk prevention reforms, emphasising the need for a basin-wide approach, as well as giving local communities an important role in engaging in local risk management. It is shown that during reform processes it is key to dedicate adequate financial and technical competences to those with new disaster risk prevention responsibilities. Finally, the chapter emphasises the large untapped potential of a whole-of-society approach to risk management, where clear roles are assigned and risks are effectively communicated to all stakeholders.

Summary

The Rhône River basin is one of France's largest river systems. Due to its size it covers a wide range of different topographies and diverse climatic conditions. These subject the areas around the river to a variety of natural hazards, including river and coastal floods, torrents and sediment movements, storms and storm surges, but also earthquakes are a potential threat.

The socio-economic vulnerability of the Rhône River basin against major disaster events is high. The basin area accounts for a major share of France's energy production. Around 5.5 million basin inhabitants are potentially exposed to the risk of flooding. Critical infrastructure and industrial sectors located in close proximity to the river render a potential flood a critical risk for France. The last large-scale floods of 2003 caused an estimated EUR 1 billion in damages.

Key findings

The Rhône's flood risk prevention management has a long history, with some of its major structures established as early as 1856, in response to devastating floods. Although flooding and related events have been relatively frequent along the Rhône, a large-scale flood comparable to the one of 1856 has not occurred in the recent past. This makes it important to assess whether current disaster risk prevention levels are sufficient to confront similar events that are expected to take place in the future.

A number of governance reforms have been implemented to improve disaster risk prevention management. In response to the devastating 2003 floods in the Rhône River basin, a basin prefect has taken the role of coordination of all basin level activities. Strategic frameworks like the Plan Rhône or the Plan Gestion des Risques d'Inondation have provided an important basis for achieving a better basin-wide flood risk prevention management. At the national level reforms have been underway to strengthen local level responsibilities in risk management. It is therefore a good moment to assess the progress and challenges in disaster risk prevention management in the Rhône River basin.

Key recommendations

Improve the evidence base on the potential occurrence and on the costs of disasters

- Harmonise hazard evaluation criteria and maps across the basin area, across different local jurisdictions so as to ensure effectiveness and efficiency when deciding on disaster risk reduction investments. To further improve the understanding of the type and scale of potential disaster events, it could be useful to more systematically assess the concomitance of different disaster types as well as the impact of potential disasters on the basin's critical infrastructures.
- To inform policy making for disaster risk prevention in the Rhône River basin, a more systematic accounting of social and economic losses of past disasters is needed. This evidence does not only help in identifying potential disaster hot spots, but they also inform the refinement of hazard models over time and give policy

makers an understanding of whether their disaster risk reduction measures are effective in reducing losses from disasters over time.

Strengthen risk governance mechanisms

- Ensure clear lines of responsibilities between national and sub-national actors and enhance ownership and accountability for disaster risk prevention.
- To implement ongoing territorial reforms effectively, it is important to build technical capacity and ensure financial resources to carry out new responsibilities.
- Consider the establishment of a basin-level authority for stronger coordination and integration of disaster risk prevention efforts.

Continue to foster an integrated approach between structural and non-structural measures.

- Clarify and consistently apply central-level prioritisation for co-financing local disaster risk prevention investments. This will become more important as funding requests are expected to increase, without central funding necessarily being adjusted.
- Strengthen the quality of maintenance of protective infrastructure across the basin area. Ensure that current reforms do not stop at clarifying ownership and maintenance responsibilities of protective infrastructure, but that they provide the necessary technical capacity building measures and financial solutions.

Embrace a whole-of-society approach to disaster risk prevention and mitigation

- Increase the investments in self-protection by private stakeholders, such as households and businesses. Consider setting financial incentives, such as tax credits or subsidies, to encourage such investment efforts.
- Boost risk awareness measures in a way that informs stakeholders about the value and effectiveness of investing in individual self-protection measures.
- Systematically collect evidence on the degree of vulnerability of private assets. Engage critical infrastructure operators in regularly assessing their vulnerabilities.

Design smart disaster risk financing mechanisms

- Increase clarity and transparency about ex-post loss compensations, not only by the central fund, but also for the co-payments made by provincial and local governments.
- Address the financing gap for maintenance and rehabilitation works of existing protective infrastructures.
- Consider the establishment of "joint maintenance bodies" that work across jurisdictions and that are co-financed by different municipalities and potentially higher levels of government.

Introduction

The Rhône River basin[1] is the largest river system in France. It covers a wide range of topographies making it subject to important flood risks, but also risks from coastal flooding, torrents, sediment movements, storms and storm surges. Earthquakes are an additional risk in the region of Provence-Alpes-Côte d'Azur.

The Rhône River basin accounts for a significant share of France's economy, which has been facilitated by the river's multiple uses: as a key navigation route, as a key source of irrigation for its large agricultural industry, but also by supporting an important share of France's hydro and nuclear power production. The socio-economic importance of the Rhône River basin makes a potential large-scale flood a critical risk for France, similar to a major flood of the Seine River in Paris or a significant earthquake in the Provence-Alpes-Côte d'Azur region.

Although flooding and related events have been relatively frequent along the Rhône a large-scale flood comparable to the one of 1856 has not happened in the recent past. The equally large-scale floods of 2003 were geographically more limited, but nonetheless highlighted the challenges accompanying Rhône River floods once more. This makes it important to assess whether current disaster risk prevention engagements are sufficient to confront similar events in the future.

The Rhône River's flood risk prevention management has a long history with some of its major structures established as early as 1856, in response to the devastating floods. Given the large territory of the Rhône, its many actors with often very different legacies, flood risk prevention levels are heterogeneous throughout the basin area. The floods in 2003 made some of this apparent as important protective infrastructure gave in to the floods and contributed to devastating damages mounting to over EUR 1 billion. These floods were a wake-up call and led affected regions to establish a more formal collaboration to jointly work on reducing existing vulnerabilities. A basin prefect should from then on take the role of coordination of all basin level activities. Strategic frameworks like the *Plan Rhône* or the *Plan Gestion des Risques d'Inondation* have provided an important basis for achieving a better basin-wide flood risk prevention management.

The present case study report assesses the progress, achievements and potential challenges of the Rhône River's disaster risk prevention system, with a particular emphasis on its institutional design. The latter plays a significant role in facilitating or hampering the effective engagement and investments of governmental and non-governmental stakeholders in disaster risk prevention and mitigation. For example, the decision of an individual household not to invest in protecting their own home may be the result of an expectation about the government doing so for them. A local government decision not to invest in a protective measure may be the result of neighbouring jurisdictions potentially freeriding on them. On the central government level, for example, actors may be reluctant to invest more in disaster risk prevention and mitigation, because ex-ante investments are not visible for their electorate and hence individual rewards too low.

This report is part of an OECD cross-country comparative study that assesses and compares disaster risk prevention and mitigation systems across a set of OECD countries. The objective of the analysis is to monitor the progress in countries' disaster risk prevention policies, to identify good practices as well as challenges that may persist and that may impede a whole-of-society approach to disaster risk prevention and mitigation, bringing both governmental and non-governmental actors together. The case study of France's Rhône River informs this comparative analysis.

The following case study report will first provide an overview of the Rhône River's hazard landscape as well as its socio-economic relevance (Section II). This will inform the remainder of the document, where France's and the Rhône River's core disaster risk prevention institutions, actors and their financial set-up will be reviewed to analyse whether roles and responsibilities as well as incentives are aligned to ensure each actor's expected contribution to a whole-of-society approach to disaster risk prevention. Section III will provide an overview of the principal legal frameworks and responsibilities and Section IV and V will look at how this plays out in the actual disaster risk prevention implementation processes.

Hazard sources and risk exposure of the Rhône river basin area

Section Highlights

- The Rhône River basin, the largest river system in France, has a varied topography and diverse climate making it subject to hazards such as (coastal) flooding, torrents and sediment movements, storms and storm surges and earthquakes.
- On average, the region experiences three floods a year; the largest recent floods were those of 2014, 2010 and 2002, with floods rarely affecting the entire basin area; the floods of 2003 that occurred in Valence, downstream of Lyon caused damages worth more than EUR 1 billion.
- The Rhône River basin accounts for a major share of France's economy, with two thirds of hydropower supply and one fourth of nuclear power produced there.
- A major flood of the Rhône River basin and a major earthquake in the region of Provence-Alpes-Côte d'Azur constitute two critical risks that France could be confronted with, similar to a large-scale flood of the Seine River in the Paris region.
- 5.5 million basin inhabitants are potentially threatened by floods, with a significant exposure of critical infrastructure and the industrial sectors in close proximity to the river; 6 of the 16 identified areas of high flood risk that are of national importance are located in the basin of the Rhône.

Hazard sources

France's topography is one of the most varied in Europe. It ranges from sea landscapes of the Atlantic and the Mediterranean over hilly landscapes in Brittany and Normandy to Europe's highest elevations, such as the Mont Blanc. A number of mountain ranges cover the country, including the Ardennes Plateau in the northeast, the Vosges, the Alps and the Jura Mountains towards the east of the country and the Pyrenees in the south. The Massif Central, topped by extinct volcanoes, occupies the south-central area. At the centre of France is the Paris basin. It occupies one of France's main river systems, the Seine. Besides the Seine, the Rhône, the Loire, the Rhine and the Garonne are major river systems in France.

The Rhône is one of France's major river systems. It extends over 813 kilometres and its major tributary, the Saône, over 480 kilometres. The Rhône basin covers an area of 96 500 km2. It provides a pass way (Figure 3.1) from the Paris basin and eastern France to the Mediterranean (Bravard and Clémens, 2008).

Figure 3.1 The Rhône river basin

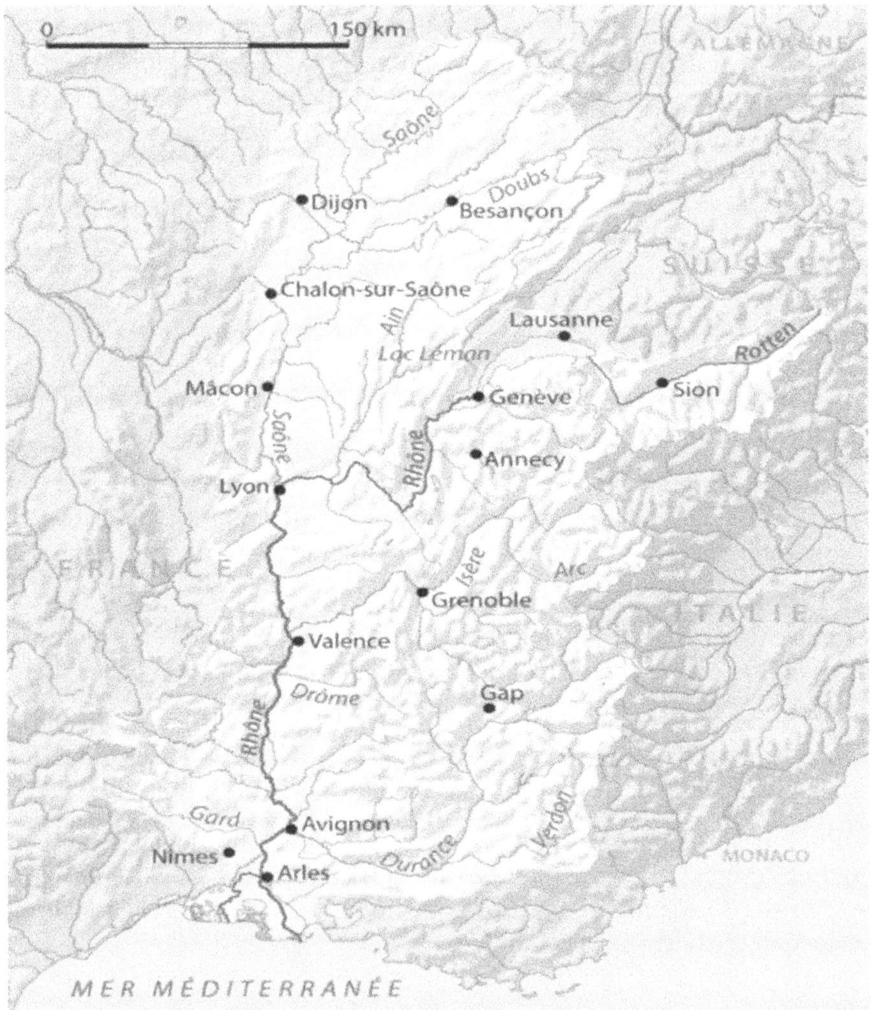

Source: GTOPO-30 Elevation Data by USGS via Wikimedia Commons: https://commons.wikimedia.org/wiki/File:Rhone_bassin_versant.png#/media/File:Rhone_bassin_versant.png

The Rhône river basin (also referred to as the *Rhône-Méditerranée* basin) is located in the southeast of France, encompassing 5 of France's 22 Metropolitan[2] regions and 25 departments (Figure 3.2). Prior to the territorial reform (see Box 3.4) implemented in

January 2016, the regions were Burgundy, Franche-Comté, Rhône-Alpes, Languedoc-Roussillon and Provence-Alpes-Côte d'Azur (PACA). Since January 2016 the regions surrounding the Rhône river basin are Burgundy-Franche-Comté, Auvergne-Rhône-Alpes, the Occitania Region and Provence-Alpes-Côte d'Azur (PACA). Approximately 15 million people inhabit the area of the Rhône basin.

Figure 3.2 Regions and departments in the Rhône river basin (in 2015)

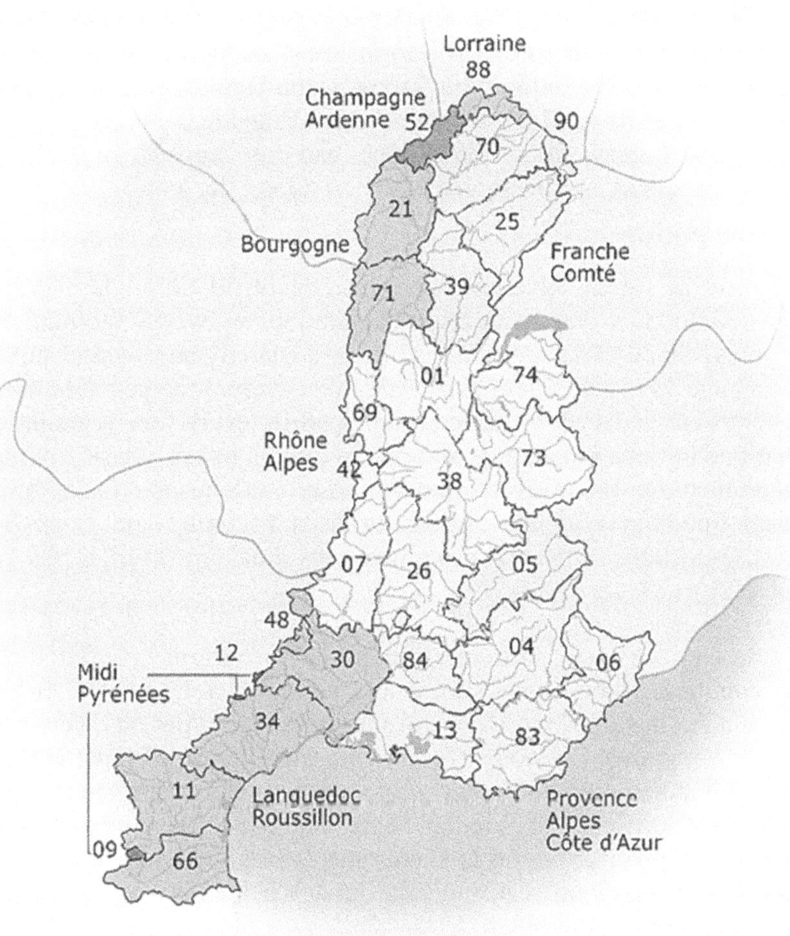

Source: Water Agency Rhône Méditerranée Corse (2016), http://www.eaurmc.fr/le-bassin-rhone-mediterranee/les-caracteristiques-du-bassin-rhone-mediterranee/perimetre-administratif-du-bassin-rhone-mediterranee.html

The Rhône is not only among the largest rivers, but especially one of the most complex river systems in France. Rising in the Swiss Alps and passing through Lake Geneva, it gathers its major tributary, the Saône, at Lyon, the biggest agglomeration along the river. It continues southward through France into the Mediterranean Sea. In Arles, the river divides into the Great Rhône and the Little Rhône, creating a delta of the Camargue region. The Rhône passes through mountain ranges of the Massif Central and the Alps. Its water stems from several lakes as well as from Alpine glaciers and underwater sources (Bravard and Clémens, 2008).

The Rhône is a river that has been subject to significant regulatory action to ensure its multiple uses as a resource for hydro power, as a key navigation route, a source for agricultural irrigation, but also potable water and various environmental and leisure services.

As a consequence of its varied topography and its diverse climate, the Rhône basin is confronted with various hazards in its different regions. River flooding is a great concern in the upstream Rhône, whereas the downstream part is also confronted with coastal flooding. Various hydro-meteorological hazards exist along the area. Slow on-set floods can develop over a large area along the Saône or the Rhône rivers, whereas rapid flash floods can occur along its smaller catchment areas, together with torrents and sediment movements. Finally, areas along the Rhône can be exposed to strong periods of precipitation, storms and storm surges such as along its coast line causing coastal flooding.

The basin of the Rhône River is prone to frequent flooding. On average the region experiences three floods a year, with crisis declarations in over 6700 municipalities over the last 30 years. Since 1982 19 municipalities declared[3] on average one flood event every two years and 147 municipalities declared one every three years. In terms of coastal floods, disasters were declared by eleven municipalities every four years on average. It is estimated that one in three inhabitants and one in three jobs are at risk from flooding. Put in a national context the Rhône river is most exposed to floods and ranks third in terms of risk of coastal flooding (after the regions of Escaut-Somme and Loire-Bretagne). 95 municipalities, especially in the more mountainous areas are at high risk from torrents (PGRI, 2014, p.26).

The Camargue region is particularly exposed to hazards. Its flat topography and potential concomitance with storm surges and coastal flooding make floods persistent risks. Floods and storm surges tend to occur during the same periods, between September and November. Areas remain flooded for an extensive period of time, as pumping flood water into the sea is complex and other disaster risk reduction options are limited. Dike breaches, that are difficult to predict, can aggravate the impacts of floods, as demonstrated during the 2003 flood in Camargue, where the wetlands around the Rhône were saturated from the flood, causing dike breaches that increased the impact of the flood (Bravard and Clémens, 2008, p. 131).

Disaster risk exposure

Given its varied topography and different land uses near its banks, vulnerability and exposure characteristics differ quite significantly along the Rhône River. There is a difference in exposure between the heavily urban areas (such as Greater Lyon) and the rural ones as well as in the areas of the Rhône's tributaries compared to the main river. Vulnerability also differs on the Rhône's right and the left bank, as well as between the areas channelled by dams and those where floods can expand into agricultural land. Again other vulnerability aspects arise in industrial sites where technological hazards are a major threat such as the chemical industry around Lyon or the nuclear power plants in Donzère.

Generally speaking the Rhône River basin has been an important area for development in human habitat and economic activity in France. Counting just the regions of Rhône-Alpes and Provence-Alpes-Côte d'Azur they account for a fifth of France's GDP, which makes them economically speaking the most important regions after the Paris Metropolitan Area. A major flood in the Rhône River basin therefore constitutes a critical national risk in France, similar to a major flood of the Seine River in Paris or a major earthquake in the region of Provence-Alpes-Côte d'Azur.

The basin's core economic activities are closely intertwined with the Rhône River. Agriculture, for example, accounting for 16.7% of the basin's regional GDP, is largely located in flood plain areas. Industrial activity, contributing some 20% to the regional GDP, is concentrated along the river. Tourism, which makes for 30% of the region's GDP, peaks particularly during seasons where floods are most likely to occur (PGRI, 2014).

Table 3.1 Assets at risk in the Rhône basin

	At risk from flooding	At risk from coastal flooding	Relative to total number of each indicator in France (%)	
Population	5,5 million	229,000	33	16
Number of health facilities	819	21	35	13
Potable water facilities	9,044	23	-	-
Total buildings	438 million m^2	21,2 million	34	15
Total business buildings	153,96 million m^2	5,4 million	36	13
Jobs	2,9 million	133,200	32	16
Infrastructure lines (roads and railways)	98,000 km	5,000 km	32	16
Nuclear power stations	57	0	-	-
Nature protection zones (Natura 2000)	6,500 k m^2	2,800 km^2	30	34
Cultural heritage buildings	1,6 million m^2	35,000	25	9
Museums	133	8	-	-

Source: DREAL Rhône-Alpes (2014), "Plan de Gestion des Risques d'Inondation 2016-2021, Bassin Rhône-Méditerranée" [Plan for Flood Risk Management 2016-2021, Rhône-Mediterranean Basin], Parties communes au Bassin Rhône-Méditerranée, Project submitted for public consultation Volume 1, http://www.rhone-mediterranee.eaufrance.fr/docs/dir-inondations/pgri/00_Projet_PGRI_volume1.pdf

A significant amount of power is produced along the Rhône River, which is exposed to several sources of risk. Along the Rhône River two thirds of hydropower supply of France is produced, as well as one fourth of France's nuclear power. Vulnerabilities arise from two particular sources. First, energy production along the Rhône is influenced by Switzerland, which is using the river upstream for its own energy production, having an impact on the speed and volume of the flow of the river as well its temperature further downstream. These elements are crucial especially for the cooling capacity of nuclear power stations along the Rhône. Second, a number of nuclear power production facilities are located in flood risk areas. (Bravard and Clémens, 2008)

With regard to human habitat Figure 3.3 demonstrates that population density is particularly high in close proximity to the river. Since the 1960s flood retention zones have had to increasingly give way to settlements, through urban expansion, which was sparked by an increase in population of 11% since 1999, and facilitated by infrastructure development (e.g. roads). Furthermore, urban vulnerability has significantly increased by allowing the residential use of basements. Although urban areas along the Rhône are relatively well protected, exceptional flood events could cause major damages (DIREN Rhône-Alpes, 2009).

Figure 3.3 Population density in the Rhône River basin

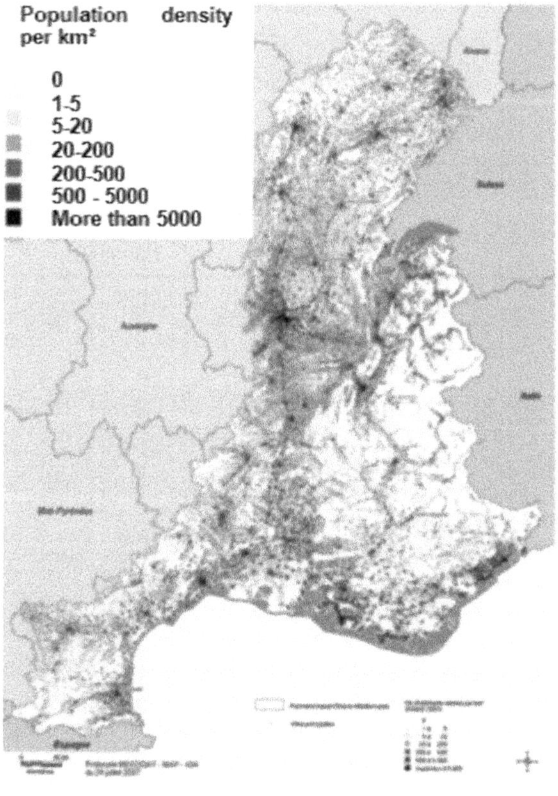

Source: DREAL Rhône-Alpes (2014), "Plan de Gestion des Risques d'Inondation 2016-2021, Bassin Rhône-Méditerranée" [Plan for Flood Risk Management 2016-2021, Rhône-Mediterranean Basin], Volume 1: Parties communes au Bassin Rhône-Méditerranée, project submitted for public consultation

A significant flood in the Lyon agglomeration could cause an estimated EUR 1.25 billion in direct damages and EUR 6.2 billion in indirect damages (Bravard and Clémens, 2008) (Table 3.1), not accounting for existing protective barriers. A preliminary evaluation concluded that this flood scenario would translate into the following estimates in the Rhône-Méditerranée hydrographic district (PGRI, 2014):

- 5.5 million inhabitants, a third of the basin's population are directly or indirectly at risk from floods, including coastal flooding;

- A sizable number of health facilities, over 800, are exposed to floods and coastal floods;
- Above 9 000 potable water facilities are at risk;
- Around 3 000 businesses, with 100 000 jobs and more than 1 000 000 hectares of agricultural land are threatened by potential floods.

Figure 3.4 depicts areas identified as having a high risk of flooding (HRAs), based on the national risk catalogue4. The zones at risk were identified based on hazard levels, demographics, taking into account seasonal flux of population based on tourism. Among the high risk zones are the urban areas of Aix-en-Provence, Avignon, Chambéry, Lyon, Marseille, Montpellier, Nice, Nimes and Perpignan. The national risk catalogue identified a total of 122 high flood risk areas (HRAs) in France, out of which 16 are of national importance given the potential impacts. The Rhône basin amounts for 31 of the 122 flood risk areas, out of which 6 are of national importance.

Figure 3.4 Areas at significant risk of flooding

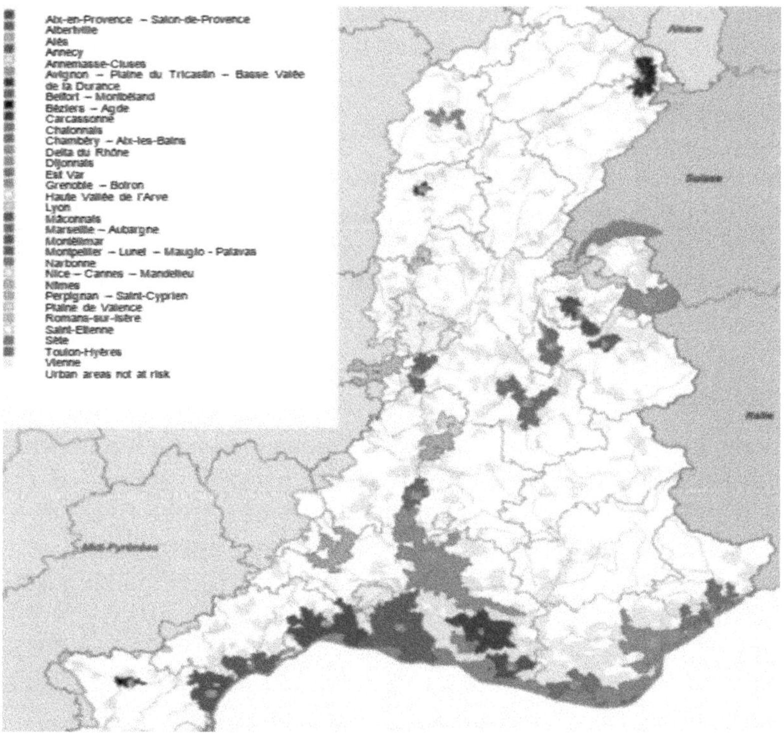

Source: DREAL Rhône-Alpes (2014), DREAL Rhône-Alpes (2014), "Plan de Gestion des Risques d'Inondation 2016-2021 [Plan for Flood Risk Management 2016-2021, Rhône-Mediterranean Basin], Bassin Rhône-Méditerranée", Volume 1: Parties communes au Bassin Rhône-Méditerranée, Project submitted for public consultation

As mentioned above, the Rhône's river flow has become heavily regulated. This implies a long history of construction of dams and dikes to protect socio-economic activities along the river. As a consequence and generally speaking protective infrastructure along the Rhône River has provided a relatively high protection level. There are however certain particular vulnerabilities:

First of all, the large number of dikes has led to a varying degree in their maintenance. Some were built in the last decades by the National Company of the Rhone (*Compagnie Nationale du Rhône*, CNR), and are primarily used to produce hydropower and facilitate navigation. Others are older, mostly constructed throughout the 19th century in reaction to the floods of 1840 and 1856to protect against flooding.

Some of them, especially the ones operated and maintained by the National Company of the Rhone have provided a very strong protection level against one-in1000-year floods. Other infrastructures provide protection levels that are much lower, such as against the flood levels of a 100-year flood, or of 30-year-floods and of floods with lower probabilities of occurring in a given year. The dikes built by the CNR were built to keep the water levels that have been increased to create the flow for the generation of hydropower. As an unintended consequence the land upstream of the hydropower plant enjoy better protection against floods, often to the level of a 1000-year flood. The remaining dikes (those not managed by the CNR) are often either the property of municipalities or owned by public enterprises. Some are also owned by private entities, grouped in dike unions (*associations syndicales autorisées,* ASA*)*. Besides these, some dikes are abandoned and not officially owned by municipalities or dike unions. No clear responsibility for maintenance exists for these abandoned structures and it is not clear, if they still offer protection.

Moreover, although floods occur frequently along the Rhône River, the absence of a major river flood may have blurred the collective risk memory. This has contributed to the emergence of a sense of safety that lowers continued commitment and investment in flood risk management. This may be particularly threatening for large metropolitan areas such as Lyon.

Socio-economic impacts of past disasters

Larger scale hazard events occur relatively frequently in the Rhône River basin. The most important flood events since records exist are listed in Figures 3.5 and 3.6. Some past floods of the Rhône had an impact on the entire area of the river, such as the 1856 flood, a 250-year-flood, with the highest peak discharge rate recorded at 12 000 m^3/s. Other significant floods have only affected a part of the river's area, such as the 1957 flood that impacted the area downstream of Lyon or those of 1910, 1928, 1944 and 1990 that affected the area upstream of Lyon. The floods of 1994, 2002 and 2003 affected the regions downstream of the river, including the Camargue (Bravard and Clémens, 2008).

Although multiple hazard events have occurred and were recorded in the past, little systematic knowledge about the extent of their negative socio-economic impact exists. Particularly in the Rhône basin this is the case. On average France experiences an estimated EUR 650 to 800 million in damages from floods each year. Floods along the Rhône are frequent and have caused damages above EUR 1 billion, such as the floods in 2002, 2003 and 2010, the latter of which also accounted for 23 casualties. The floods of Nîmes in 1988 caused an estimated EUR 610 million in damages, while the flood of the Aude in 1999 cost around EUR 500 million (Bravard and Clémens, 2008).

Table 3.2 Significant floods measured in discharge rates of m3/s of the Upstream Rhône

	Pougny 1925-2006		Bognes 1853-2006		Lagnieu 1891-2006		Perrache 1900-2006	
1	24/11/1944	1 520	20/01/1910	2 000	16/02/1990	2 445	25/11/1944	4 250
2	15/11/2002	1 440	23/12/1918	1 920	27/11/1944	2 400	16/02/1928	4 150
3	13/01/2004	1 300	03/10/1888	1 900	25/12/1918	2 100	25/12/1918	3 900
4	14/05/1999	1 300	30/05/1856	1 800	22/01/1910	2 090	26/02/1957	3 700
5	22/09/1968	1 280	25/09/1863	1 800	16/02/1928	2 025	21/01/1910	3 550

Source: Bravard Jean-Paul and Anne Clémens (2008), "Le Rhône en 100 questions" [The Rhône in 100 Questions], http://mediterranee.revues.org/6386.

Table 3.3 Significant floods measured in discharge rates of m3/s of the Downstream Rhône

	Ternay 1895-2006		Valence 1855-2006		Viviers 1910-2006		Beaucaire 1840-2006	
1	26/02/1957	5 320	31/05/1856	8 300	03/12/2003	8 000	31/05/1856	12 000 12 500
2	16/02/1928	5 120	01/11/1896	7 400	09/10/1993	7 715	03/12/2003	11 500
3	20/01/1955	5 075	08/10/1993	6 700	07/01/1994	7 590	08/01/1994	11 000
4	26/11/1944	4 850	16/11/2002	6 620	17/11/2002	7 580	11/11/1886	10 200
5	02/11/1986	4 830	11/11/1886	6 620	21/11/1951	6 660	10/10/1993	9 800

Source: Bravard and Clémens (2008), "Le Rhône en 100 questions" [The Rhône in 100 Questions], http://mediterranee.revues.org/6386.

Even though systematic evidence regarding floods in the basin is not available, the economic losses caused by the major events have mostly been studied in quite some detail. For example during the 2003 floods that occurred downstream of the Rhône the assets destroyed by the flood were recorded in great detail (SIEE, 2005). The floods seriously impacted downstream cities, such as Arles, Comps, Codolet or Bellegarde, which were submerged in water for an extensive period of time. In Arles and in Laudun-l'Ardoise, two important industrial zones were flooded, with significant local economic consequences. A number of infrastructures were also affected by the floods, including some major transport routes between Arles and Bellegarde that were closed off for 11 days. In total, an estimated 30,000 houses were flooded and 32,000 persons had to be temporarily relocated. The floods also caused 4 dikes to breach. Of the overall estimated damages of over EUR 1 billion Figure 3.7 shows that a great share of damages was suffered by households (53%), followed by businesses (32%) and the agricultural industry (7%).

Figure 3.5 Damages among stakeholder groups of the floods 2003, Rhône

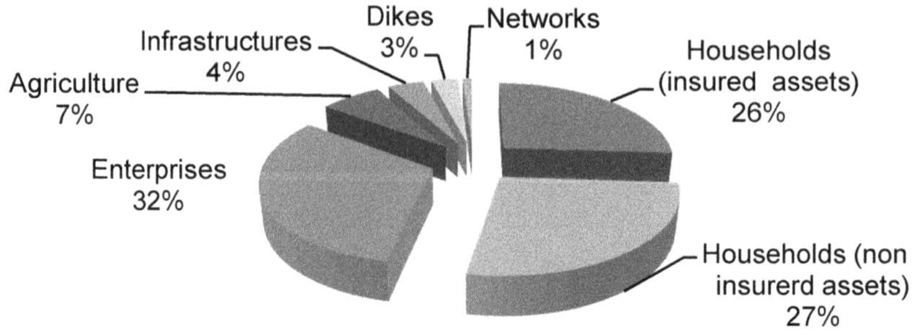

Sources: Bravard and Clémens (2008), "Le Rhône en 100 questions" [The Rhône in 100 Questions]; Société d'Ingénierie pour l'Eau et l'Environnement (SIEE) (2005), "Inondations du Rhône et de ses principaux affluents de décembre 2003 en aval de viviers dans les départements de la Drôme, de l'Ardèche, du Gard, du Vaucluse et des Bouches-du- Rhône"

In a more forward-looking manner a detailed ex-ante evaluation of potential damage was undertaken briefly before the 2003 floods. A 10-year-flood was estimated to cause direct damages worth nearly EUR 500 million. A 100-year flood could cause nearly EUR 2 billion in direct damages, and a major flood nearly EUR 5 billion (see Box 3.1).

Box 3.1 Potential direct damages of major floods along the Rhône

A study of the entire Rhône River (*Etude Global pour le Rhône*), conducted between 1993 and 2003, aimed at developing a flood plain management plan to improve flood predictions and associated early warnings. It also aimed at informing and improving flood-based land use management, including the designation of flood expansion zones. Also part of this study was an evaluation of potential damages under different flood scenarios occurring along the Rhône.

Table 1 shows the results of this analysis. The potential direct damages could range from EUR 500 million, for a 10-year-flood, up to nearly EUR 5 billion for a flood with a reoccurrence period of above 100 years. Agricultural damages are expected to be particularly high, accounting for more than half of the total expected damages. It is expected that this would already be the case under the least-impact scenario.

The calculations in Table 1 only include direct damages linked to an increase of water levels. They do not include the potential increase in damages caused by dike breaks (with the exception of the Camargue). These figures are therefore expected to underestimate potential direct damages, especially in light of the floods that followed in 2003, where a number of damages were caused by the breach of protective infrastructures.

Direct damages of different flood scenarios along the Rhône River

Direct damages (not taking into account dike breaches)	Intermediary flood (10-year return period)	Strong flood (100-year return period)	Major flood (above 100-year return period)
Agriculture	150-300	260-530	400-800
Businesses	140	770	2150
Individuals/Households	110	630	1860
Total Direct Damages	400-550	1660-1930	4410-4810

Note: Figures in million Euros

Source: Compagnie Nationale du Rhône (CNR)/ Etablissement Public Territoire Rhône (2003): *Étude Globale pour le Rhône* [Rhône Study] (not published officially)

Conclusion

A number of efforts have been undertaken to identify and map natural hazards in the basin area of the Rhône. An overview of hot spots of potential hazards and important risks that emerge out of it, for example, due to the density of economic activities, has been well established. In the future, it could be useful to have a more understanding of the existing risks in relation to the existing protective infrastructure. This section highlighted a number of cases, where different types of protective measures could significantly reduce the negative socio-economic impacts of a disaster. It is important to link vulnerability with public and private assets at risk to prioritise disaster risk reduction measures. Taking the potential occurrence of two simultaneous hazard events, for example a flood triggers an industrial accident, into account, would also help to enhance the understanding and management of the potential future a complex disaster.

Finally, the basin area could benefit from a better understanding of the potential socio-economic impacts of major disasters. Although detailed ex-post assessments of socio-economic losses have been conducted after some floods, for example following the 2003 floods, this could be done in a more systematic manner. Ex-post assessments could make greater use of existing information and more strongly involve national and regional actors already engaged in this effort. A basin-wide understanding of such vulnerabilities is key to prioritise joint actions at along the entire river.

Risk governance in the Rhône river basin

Section Highlights

- France's disaster risk prevention policy framework is guided by the principles of solidarity on the national level and of subsidiarity across levels of government, whereby a complex web of national and sub-national actors has emerged that all play a role in the planning and implementation of flood risk policies of the Rhône basin.
- Ongoing territorial reforms could help regrouping many of the more fragmented sub-national actors and to maximise the pay-offs of disaster risk prevention efforts, to increase ownership by the direct beneficiaries and to improve accountability of the responsible actors to their citizens.
- The process of decentralising flood risk management responsibilities may face several challenges: in a country with a mostly unitary tradition, sub-national actors may not all have the technical and financial capacities to fulfil their new responsibilities; the regrouping of local jurisdictions will not solve cross-jurisdictional conflicts arising from negative and positive spill over effects of disaster risk prevention investment up- and downstream of the Rhône River, but also between the main river and its tributaries.
- The strategic framework provided by the Plan Rhône has been an effective and successful instrument to integrate economic development and flood risk management, bringing all relevant actors together to work on commonly agreed priorities, supported by consolidated financing across levels of government. However the absence of a governance body for disaster risk management questions for the entire river basin reinforces the challenges of balancing interests across different parts of the river.

Main legal and strategic frameworks governing disaster risk prevention

From the Barnier Law to the "Great River Plans"

After devastating floods in 1982, 1995 and 2003 a number of new laws to improve disaster risk prevention management in France were passed. These new regulations were guided by a disaster risk prevention policy framework based on the principles of subsidiarity between the various tiers of government and of national solidarity to help France's exposed population cope with prevailing risks.

The 1982 law on Compensation for Victims of Natural Disasters introduced an insurance system, the CATNAT (*Catastrophes Naturelles)* compensation scheme (see more in the financing section) that was coupled with a new land use policy and urban development regulation (*Plans d'exposition aux Risques Naturels Prévisibles,* PER) to decrease exposure to hazards.

A requirement for local strategic action plans for flood risk management was subsequently introduced. In 1995 the Barnier law was passed to better manage urban development in floodplains. It introduced the requirement of Flood Risk Prevention Plans (*Plan de Prévention du Risque Inondation,* PPRIs) that should be created at the local level, overseen by the prefect of the department. The plans will include maps delineating hazard zones as well as, in a second step, assets at risk. Mining disaster risk prevention plans were introduced in 1999, followed by technological disaster risk prevention plans that were introduced in 2003 in response to an industrial accident at a fertiliser plant in the city of Toulouse that caused nearly 30 casualties.

To finance local strategic disaster risk prevention actions a central disaster risk prevention fund was established. Under the Barnier law the Fund for the Prevention of Major Natural Hazards (*Fonds de Prévention des Risques Naturels Majeurs,* FPRNM) or "Barnier Fund" was created to finance disaster risk prevention measures, including the resources involved in drawing up PPRIs. PPRIs constitute the basis of flood risk management between the local and central level. Based on the PPRIs Flood Prevention Action Programs (*Programmes d'Action de Prévention des Inondations,* PAPIs) are developed at the local level. They identify the prevention measures to be financed through the central Barnier Fund, administered by the Ministry of Ecology and, for projects above EUR 3 million, also approved by the Joint Flood Commission (*Commission Mixte Inondations,* CMI). The PAPIs rally central government stakeholders and local authorities to co-operate on integrated, comprehensive prevention projects for flood-prone river systems. Local contracting authorities develop the programmes and submit them to central government for financial support in a competitive selection process. Preventative measures under PAPIs can include improved risk knowledge and awareness of risks, forecast and early warning systems, vulnerability reduction through land-use and urban planning and protective infrastructure. The OECD Seine study (2014) found that the selection of projects (90% of which are structural measures) may not always have been based on previously identified High Flood Risk Areas (HRAs), a key requirement for allocating funds.

In recognition of the need to address flood risk management at the appropriate geographical and functional scale basin-level, strategic action frameworks were established. The great river plans aim at coordinating flood prevention initiatives at the territorial or basin level. Launched in 1994 with the Loire River, the great river plans have been adopted for all major river systems, including for the Rhône (*Plan Rhône*). They are intimately linked with France's State-Region Contracts (*Contrats de Plan État-Région,* CPER). These contracts constitute the basis of an agreement between the central government and the regional council on the tasks to be accomplished over a certain period, for which the central government provides co-financing (Box 3.2). In the case of the Plan Rhône, the Plan aims at consolidating disaster risk prevention action at the basin level and negotiates one central co-financing agreement, rather than for several local-level PAPIs scattered throughout the basin.

Box 3.2 France's State-Region Contracts

France's State-Region Contracts (*Contrats de Plan Etat-Région,* CPER) are planning instruments particularly key in accompanying the recent territorial reform of France launched in 2014. They are a tool for local investment whereby the State and the regions jointly set up a multi-annual (for 5 to 7 years) funding and programming document ("contract") to identify development projects at the territorial level. The contracts aim at generating and multiplying local investments. The process is steered by a general commission under the prime minister's office that aims at fostering territorial equality and managing spatial planning.

Several regions can group together in the same contract with the State, which in turn serves as leverage for obtaining additional funding from the European Union's regional development funds (particularly on issues relating to rivers and mountains, as well as for regional cross-border cooperation projects).

The previous contracting period during which the Plan Rhône received over EUR 600 million (see more in financing section) ended in 2013. The current planning phase spans from 2015 to 2020 with an expected funding envelope of EUR 850 million. This new generation of contracts, with a total funding of EUR 12,5 billion, fosters 6 goals that seek to foster employment as an overarching goal:

- Multimodal mobility (EUR 6.7 billion)
- University education, research and innovation (EUR 1.2 billion)
- Ecological and energetic transition (EUR 2.9 billion)
- Digital (EUR 32 million)
- Innovation (EUR 50 million)
- Territories (EUR 994 million)

Source: OCDE (2014), " Seine Basin, Île-de-France, 2014: Resilience to Major Floods "OECD Publishing, Paris. DOI: http://dx.doi.org/10.1787/9789264208728-en.

The Plan Rhône

In terms of funding the Plan Rhône[5] is the best equipped amongst the basin plans in France (Table 3.4). Following several damaging floods along the Rhône in the 1990's and the large floods in 2003 a strong consensus on the need for strategic action across the river basin to improve disaster risk prevention management emerged. The elaboration of a global strategy for flood risk prevention along the Rhône, which was informed by a large-scale study on how to reduce risks in the basin, laid the foundation for the plan. The Plan

Rhône builds on these previous studies and seeks to foster sustainable development in the region, of which flood prevention is one key pillar.

Three regions (Rhône-Alpes, Provence-Alpes-Côte d'Azur and Languedoc-Roussillon6) agreed to implement the Plan together. The regions of Bourgogne and Franche-Comté as well as the National Company of the Rhône (CNR) became additional partners of the Plan Rhône. The French energy producer Électricité de France (EDF) became a partner in 2015. All partners agreed that the activities implemented under the Plan Rhône should aim at preserving solidarity both up- and downstream of the river but also across its tributary arms.

Table 3.4 Flood risk prevention funding envelopes of France's major river plans

		Financial contribution by level of government (€ million)		
	Flood prevention funding (million €)	State	Regions	Others
Rhône Plan	310	108	83	38
Loire Plan	127	72	45	8
Seine Plan	70	42	24	3
Garonne Plan	42	33	9	-

Sources: adapted from OCDE (2014), "Seine Basin, Île-de-France, 2014: Resilience to Major Floods" OECD Publishing, Paris. DOI: http://dx.doi.org/10.1787/9789264208728-en.

Like the other basin level plans in France, the Plan Rhône aims at developing a strategy for the sustainable economic, environmental and social development of the basin level regions. Under the leadership of coordinating Prefect of the Rhône basin the regions and partners have been collaborating to establish an integrated development approach between river and flood risk management and the economic activities in the region to achieve a sustainable future. The region Rhône-Alpes also plays a special role as authority in charge of the management of the interregional programme of the European Regional Development Fund (*Programme Opérationnel Pluri-Régional Fonds européen de développement regional*, POP FEDER) implemented in the 2014/2020 period. The Plan is currently being renewed for the next five years until 2020, with a total allocation of EUR 849 million (see section V for details). Of the five regions that originally contributed to the flood risk management pillar only two have committed to continue their contribution (Provence-Alpes-Côte d'Azur and Languedoc-Roussillon). The current plan identifies 6 fields of action:

1. Culture along the River
2. Floods
3. Water quality, resources and biodiversity
4. Energy
5. River transports
6. Tourism and cultural heritage

The flood risk management pillar (2) is coordinated and managed by the Regional Directorate for Environment, Planning and Housing (*Direction Régionale de l'Environnement, de l'Aménagement et du Logement,* DREAL) Rhône-Alpes. Its specified objectives for the flood part are:

- Reducing the exposure to risks;
- Reducing vulnerability for better managed urban planning;
- Increase risk awareness and preparation for better living with flood risk.

The Plan Rhône's key governing bodies are the executive committee and the steering committee. The executive committee is composed of the basin coordinator prefect, the president of the basin committee and the three presidents of the regional councils of Rhône-Alpes, Provence-Alpes-Côte d'Azur and of Languedoc-Roussillon. The executive committee ensures that the implementation of the Plan follows its general orientations. The steering committee has a broader membership and includes representatives from the urban agglomerations of the Rhône, as well as from regional chambers of commerce and inter-municipal unions. The central government and the local communities work together to implement the Plan Rhône and to coordinate with partners across national borders, such as in Switzerland. A close collaboration is also ensured with a key partner on the Rhône, the National Company of the Rhône (CNR).

The Plan Rhône is grounded in open and democratic consultation processes that include stakeholders from citizens to journalists, unions and the founding partners of the Plan. Stakeholders are organised in committees, whereas each part of the river (upstream, middle and downstream) has its own stakeholder committee, presided by the prefect and an elected official of the basin committee. The geographical distinction takes account of the specific features of each zone along the river.

The Plan Rhône's major success lies in its ability to bring all key actors together that share a common interest in preserving the Rhône River's core functions for sustainable economic development of the Rhône River basin. Through the Plan Rhône regional and local actors created a key coordinating platform that jointly leverages disaster risk prevention investments.

Nonetheless challenges in the Plan Rhône's governance system at the basin level remain. The below governance overview will demonstrate that there are numerous different actors in flood risk management in the Rhône basin that operate on different scales and with different political affiliations and historical legacies. This has led to heterogeneous outcomes in the flood risk protection levels across the basin. It has also fostered the development of silos that undermine the better coordination of up- and downstream, as well as tributary versus main river interests along the Rhône. In the following this point will be more closely elaborated.

The Rhône Flood Risk Management Plan (PGRI)

In addition to the Plan Rhône a Flood Risk Management Plan (*Plan Gestion des Risques d'Inondation*7, PGRI) was established, covering the Rhône-Méditerranée basin from 2012-2016 (Table 3.5). The plan comes as a result of the implementation of the EU Floods Directive that prescribes the development of a flood risk management strategy at basin level. Based on the basin level plan, local flood risk management strategies have to be developed for the identified High Risk Areas (HRAs) (Figure 3.8).

Figure 3.6 Overview of the French national flood risk policy formulation process

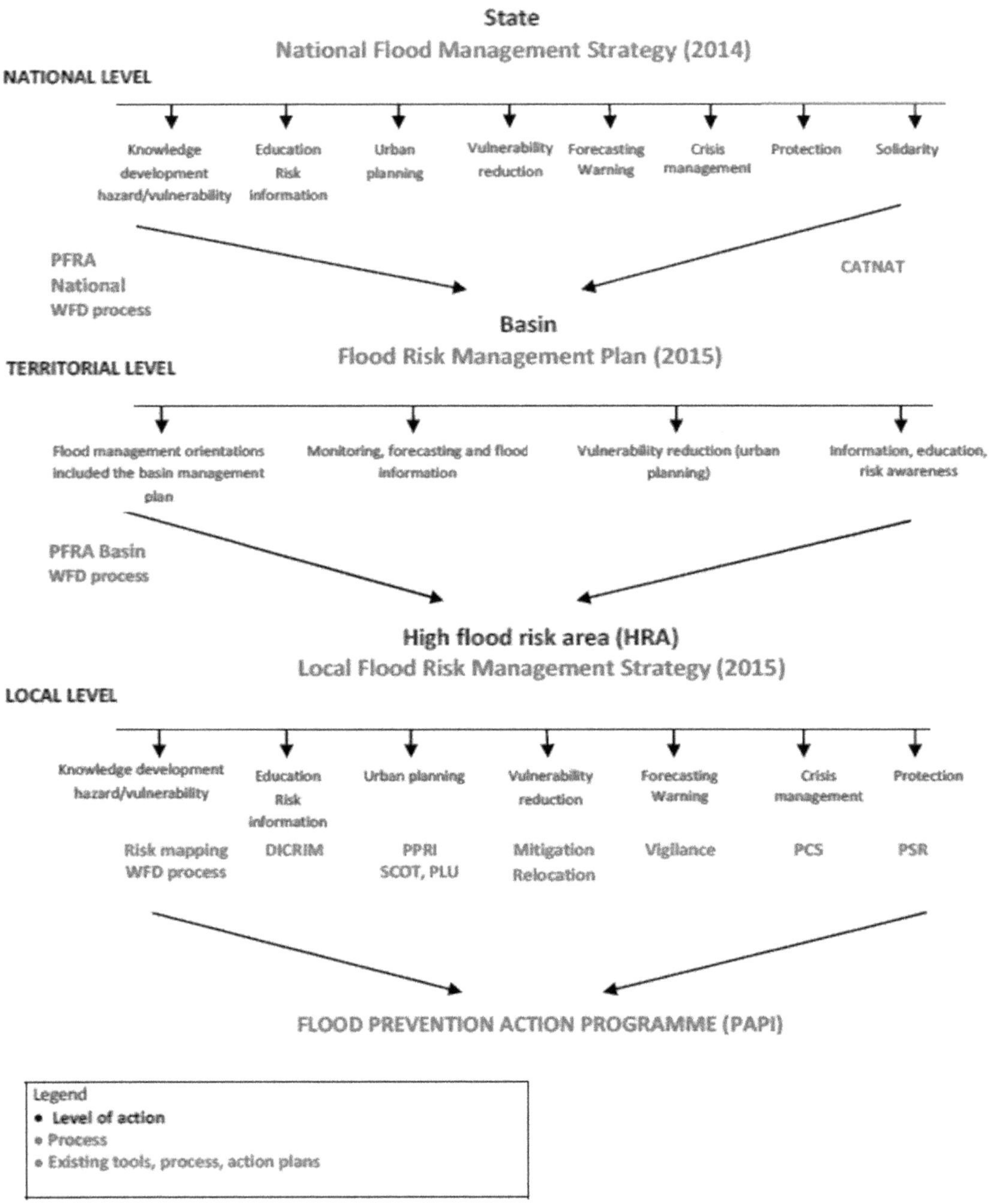

Source: OECD (2014), "Seine Basin, Île-de-France, 2014: Resilience to Major Floods", OECD Publishing, Paris. DOI: http://dx.doi.org/10.1787/9789264208728-en; based on Direction générale de la Prévention des risques (2011), "La politique nationale de gestion des risques inondation: Ce qui change aujourd'hui" [National flood management policy : What changes today], Ministry of Ecology, Sustainable Development, Transport and Housing, Paris.

Table 3.5 Strategic documents for flood risk management of the Rhône

Document	Period	Area	Key stakeholders	Objectives
Rhône Flood Risk Management Plan for the basin (PGRI)	2016-2021	Rhône-Mediterranean basin; Rhône and Saône rivers and tributaries	• Regional Development Agency (DREAL) Rhône-Alpes • Departments • Ministry of Environment	• Better integration of risks in urban planning; • Increase safety of flood exposed population; • Improve resilience of exposed territories; • Organise actors and skills • Foster knowledge of flood and their risks
Plan Rhône	2005-2025; renewed in 2010, 2015, 2020;	Rhône basin	• Rhône-Alpes region • EU • Other regions (Burgundy, Franche-Comté, Languedoc-Roussillon, Provence-Alpes-Côte d'Azur) • Regional Development Agency (DREAL) Rhône-Alpes, Economy and Employment Agency Rhône-Alpes, Navigation Routes of France, Water Agency of Rhône-Méditerranée-Corse, Environment Agency and the Energy Management Agency; • The basin committee • The electricity provider EDF • The National Company of the Rhône (CNR)	• Reinforce capacities to confront flood risk • Support river transport • Preserve and restore wetlands, the flow of the water and promote heritage

Source: Plan Rhône, www.planrhone.fr; Plan Gestion des Risques d'Inondation, http://www.developpement-durable.gouv.fr/Les-plans-de-gestion-des-risques-d,40052.html

In line with the priorities spelled out in the France's National Flood Risk Management Strategy (*Stratégie Nationale de Gestion des Risques* d'Inondation, SNGRI), the PGRI for the Rhône River basin includes five priority pillars:

- Better taking risk into account when deciding for urban planning and keeping costs under control: decrease the territory's vulnerability and improve the knowledge about it; respect the principles of spatial planning integrating flood risks;

- Increase the safety of the population exposed to floods while taking into account the natural functioning of the aquatic environments, the torrential risks, coastal erosion, and ensuring the performance of protective infrastructure;
- Improve the resilience of the exposed territories: act on surveillance and forecasting, prepare for crises and learn to better live with floods, foster risk awareness among the population through awareness campaigns, fostering of a memory of risk and information sharing;
- Organise the actors and skills: enable the synergy between the different public policies: risk management, environmental management, spatial planning and coastal management;
- Foster knowledge about flood risks; foster knowledge sharing.

The Rhône Flood Risk Management Plan is well positioned to become an effective complementary planning instrument to the Plan Rhône. It puts an important emphasis on improving organisational measures in risk management such as urban planning and vulnerability, safety, preparedness and risk culture.

Risk awareness: A key weakness that has been observed is the low risk awareness of the Rhône River basin's inhabitants. Although the state and sub-national authorities may be the main investors in core disaster risk prevention infrastructure, citizens have a key role to play in decreasing vulnerability. Citizens are in the driver's seat of limiting or reducing damage potential in existing built-up areas in risk zones. This includes organisational measures to take when a flood event is imminent, but also *ex ante* measures that improve the resistance of properties against flood damages, for example. For all these contributions to happen risk awareness is a key foundation.

Risk Governance: The governance gaps have appeared as a consequence of the multitude of disaster risk prevention actors. This has created key discrepancies in the level of protection achieved along the Rhône River. Bringing actors together to create synergies and to work across sectoral frontiers can be key to fill some of the prevailing governance gaps to harmonise flood risk management approaches across the basin and to ensure negative and positive spill overs are accounted for. The Rhône Flood Risk Management Plan aims at overcoming existing governance obstacles.

In the following we will zoom into the multi-level governance context that characterises the disaster risk prevention efforts in France in general, and that of the Rhône basin in specific. With a traditional unitary administrative culture France has recognised the need to transfer more disaster risk prevention responsibilities to local levels, as they are the core beneficiaries of disaster risk prevention measures and hence the owners of such investments. The challenge however will be to gradually address the gap that has been arising between new local level responsibilities and the availability of the necessary technical and financial capacities.

Governing Disaster Risk Prevention and Mitigation: Main National Institutions and Actors across Levels of Government

Given its traditional unitary culture, the central government in France also plays a key role in disaster risk prevention management. Central government services are in charge of drawing up national flood prevention policies, but do not play a direct role in implementing policies on the ground. However, the tools, apparatus and funding mechanisms they develop to implement laws and regulations directly affect policies implemented at the local level (OECD, 2014).

In France, the main central level responsibility for disaster risk prevention and mitigation sits with the *Ministry of Ecology, Sustainable Development and Energy (Ministère de l'Ecologie, du Développement durable et de l'Energie* (MEDDE*)* and within it the Directorate General for Risk Prevention (*Direction Générale de la Prévention des Risques* (DGPR)) is in charge. Within the MEDDE an interministerial delegation is in charge of coordinating the management of major risks across France's ministries. The DGPR manages three types of hazards, which constitutes its three main services:

- The hydraulic and natural hazards service
- The technological hazards service
- The environmental pressure and environmental quality service

The hydraulic and natural hazards service is composed of:

- A central hydrometeorologic and flood forecasting service in charge of national flood prediction. It coordinates and centralises the sub-national prevention services;
- A technical service in charge of electric energy of big dams;
- The Office of Territorial Action in charge of the deconcentrated services (including the regional development agency of Rhône-Alpes);
- The Office of Meteorological Risks in charge of the national flood risk policy;
- The Office of Natural Earth Risks in charge of the national policy of seismic, volcanic, mountain, forest fire and landslide risks;
- The Office of preventative information, coordination and prospection in charge of risk awareness.

The DGPR coordinates policies for developing disaster risk prevention plans and has drawn up calls for funding local level prevention plans (*Programmes d'Action de Prévention des Inondations* (PAPIs) and *Plan Submersion Rapide*, PSR) established as a new contractual instrument (see section IV) to obtain funding from the Barnier Fund (see financing section for more details). The DGPR is in charge of implementing the EU Flood Directive. It conducted a nation-wide flood risk assessment, developing the criteria for determining High Risk and High Flood Risk Areas (H(F)RAs).

The Ministry of Territorial Equality, Housing and of Rurality (MLETR) coordinates regional development and planning matters. In terms of disaster risk prevention the ministry ensures that risk is taken into account in urban and spatial planning and that building codes are adapted to prevent or reduce risks to the built environment.

Through the Insurance Markets and Products Bureau, the *Ministry of the Economy and Finance* is involved in regulating the principal preventive funding tool in France, the CATNAT compensation scheme and the associated Fund for the Prevention of Major Natural Hazards, or Barnier Fund (see financing section for more details) (OECD, 2014).

Other ministries that contribute to disaster risk prevention are the Ministries of Research and Education, Cultural Affairs, Foreign Affairs and International Development.

The Joint Flood Commission (*Commission Mixte Inondation*, CMI) was established in 2011 to draw up national strategy options for implementing the EU Flood Directive. The CMI is in charge of steering the national policy for flood risk management, notably the monitoring of the implementation of the National Flood Risk Management Strategy and the Flood Prevention Action Programs (PAPI) as well as the Coastal/Flash Flood Plans (*Plan Submersions Rapides* (PSRs)). The CMI also considers and approves financing for prevention projects submitted by local governments under the PAPI/PSR scheme, opening the way to state funding under the Barnier Fund (see financing section for more details). The Joint Flood Commission is composed of state bodies, local government and civil society bodies.

Governing preparedness and response: main institutions and actors

The *Ministry of the Interior* is in charge of crisis management matters. Its General Directorate for Civil Protection and Crisis Management (*Direction Générale de la Sécurité Civile et de la Gestion des Crises,* DGSCGC) is responsible for developing public policy instruments for crisis management and crisis preparedness. These instruments have important links with managing business continuity plans. This directorate also has an operational role in managing major crises that require coordination of resources at national or international level (for all others the local levels are in charge).

The Operational Centre for Interministerial Crisis Management (*Centre Opérationnel de Gestion Interministérielle des Crises*, COGIC) is activated as soon as local emergency responses so require. The unit has powerful information systems and databases on hazards and the vulnerability of populations and regions. The Disaster and Emergency Response Organisation (*Organisation de la Réponse de Sécurité Civile*, ORSEC) was created as a single structure that mobilises and coordinates the whole network of emergency response stakeholders under the sole authority of the Prefect at the administrative level appropriate to the crises. The same law that created this single structure also obliges all municipalities that have a PPR to draw up a local level emergency response plan (OECD, 2014).

Sub-national disaster risk prevention and preparedness responsibilities in the Rhône River basin

Given France's rather unitary state set-up, sub-national responsibilities are shared between deconcentrated service arms at sub-national level and decentralised, i.e. locally elected, public authorities. Until now, the central government has been essentially prescribing flood risk prevention policy, implementing it through its deconcentrated service arms. Due to the ongoing territorial reform process, local decentralised authorities have recently also started to assume more responsibility in flood risk prevention management.

Deconcentrated services

The *prefecture* is the sub-national representative of the central government overseeing a department or region, or basin or (defence) zone, and ensuring the adequate implementation of central level policies. The prefectures are an arm of the Ministry of Interior in charge of managing crises if they surpass the borders of a municipality. In terms of disaster risk prevention the prefect presides over the Departmental Commission of Major Natural Hazards (*Commission Départementale des Risques Naturels Majeurs* (CDRNM)). As part of his role the Prefect can inform municipalities about the Particular Intervention Plan (*Plan Particulier d'Intervention* (PPI)) for industries and the Natural hazards and Technological Risks Prevention Plan (*Plan de Prévention des Risques*, PPR). The regional prefecture coordinates flood risk prevention policies at the sub-national level.

The Regional Directorate for Environment, Planning and Housing *(Direction Régionale de l'Environnement, de l'Aménagement et du Logement* (DREAL); DEAL in overseas territories), as well as their *departmental arms* are the deconcentrated arm of the central Ministry's (MEDDE) disaster risk prevention services. The DREAL Rhône-Alpes and the DREAL of the Rhône-Méditerranée basin are the deconcentrated service arms at the regional level responsible for implementing the *Plan Rhône*. Its complement exists at the departmental level. They play a key role in implementing the EU Flood Directive, through risk assessment and mapping, and flood forecasting. On the regional scale, they also coordinate with all DREALs and with the sub-national service arms at the department level (*directions départementales des territoires (de la mer)*, DDT (M)).

The Interregional Zonal Operations Centre assembles the Prefect for Defence and Security, the Prefects of the Departments, the regional director of public finances, whose scope includes the administrative centres of the defence and security zones, the general officer of the defence and security zones, when appropriate also the general in command for the territorial zone, the commanding admiral for the maritime district, the general in command for air defence and air operations, the general in command for the gendarmerie of the defence and security zone, the head(s) of military staff of the defence and security zone, the delegates of the defence and security zone representing the deconcentrated services of ministers, as well as the director general of the regional health agency.

The Rhône-Méditerranée Corse Water Agency is the public body regulated by the MEDDE. Its role is to help elected representatives and local communities, economic stakeholders and inhabitants use water resources rationally and fight against the pollution and deterioration of aquatic environments. To achieve its goals, it collects charges based on the "polluter-pays" principle. It also funds initiatives for the conservation and exploitation of aquatic environments, in the form of subsidies paid to public or private developers.

The Flood Commission of the Basin *(Comité Inondation de Bassin*, CIB) is the sub-national version of the Joint Flood Commission, bringing together all district hydrographical services. This commission participates in drawing up the Flood Risk Management Plan for the basin level (PGRI).

Decentralised authorities

Up until now, the powers of the three tiers of local government, as stipulated in French law, are so that local levels can become involved in any public policy issue in which their interests are at stake. Municipalities, departments and regions can thus play important roles in flood risk prevention along the Rhône River:

- Regions have no formal disaster risk prevention role. They nonetheless often make important contributions to improving local level resilience. First of all regions are in charge of transport and have thus a key interest and an important role in improving the resilience of their transport infrastructure. Second, in financial terms the regions play a significant role in establishing the state-region contracts (Box 2), which – through the Plan Rhône - enable sub-national actors to have access to key disaster risk prevention financing from central resources (such as the Fonds Barnier), but also through European structural funds. Third, regions also have an observer and monitoring function over spatial planning, which enables them to encourage mayors to integrate hazard zones in their land-use decisions. Fourth, regions have the liberty to finance disaster risk prevention projects at their own discretion, which some of them have used to invest for example in risk awareness campaigns. Finally, regions can be an important intermediary between the local and the central level, which can be useful to channel feedback for better policy making.

- The departments and their elected representatives of the general council (*Conseil Général*) do not have any specifically defined responsibilities on disaster risk prevention. However, they have been contracting authorities for structural measures or have managed sewerage systems against the risks of flooding. Some departments have made significant investments into the prevention of flood risks by co-financing related projects in their territory.

- The municipalities (*communes*) have a number of key functions regarding disaster risk prevention management. They are responsible for protecting their citizens from risks and for planning and development matters in their jurisdiction. They need to draw up local emergency response plans for crisis management and continuity of public services and to annex the risk prevention plan (PPR) to their local urban development plan. Where required, they are responsible to integrate the risk prevention plan developed by the state into their communal or intercommunal urban planning documents. They are also required to inform citizens of the risks to the municipality in local community information documents about major prevailing risks (*Documents d'Information Communal sur les Risques Majeurs*, DICRIM). Besides this, municipalities are also responsible for the provision of potable water and sanitation services, with several municipalities often choosing to share responsibilities in so called inter-municipal collaborations (*Établissement Public de Coopération Intercommunale*, EPCI - Box 3). It is expected that this inter-municipal collaboration through the EPCI will become mandatory on 1 January 2020.

- Finally, the mayors are responsible for spatial planning and the security of their territory. The mayor thereby has to monitor risk information, take risk information into account of spatial planning and has to organise evacuation in times of crisis.

Inter-municipal cooperation has become an important form of governance in disaster risk prevention management. In addition to the inter-municipal collaboration body established through the EPCIs (Box 3.3), unions have become a frequent form for municipalities to work together to address certain aspects of risk management.

Along the Rhône a number of large unions have emerged that have become key players and experts in local disaster risk prevention management. This includes for example the *Syndicat du Haut Rhône* (SHR), the *Syndicat Intercommunal du Bassin de l'Yzeron* (SAGYRC) or the *Syndicat Mixte Interrégional d'aménagement des Digues du Delta du Rhône à la Mer* (SYMADREM) :

Box 3.3 Inter-municipal collaboration in France (Établissement Public de Coopération Intercommunale, EPCI)

Between France's different tiers of sub-national government (regions, departments and municipalities) EPCIs are an intermediate form that groups municipalities into "public establishments for inter-communal co-operation". Due to their specific purpose EPCIs are distinct from the other sub-national collectives whose mandates are more general. To encourage inter-municipal cooperation the state in 1999 decided to increase the basic grant given to local authorities forming an EPCI. While voluntary in the beginning, it has since become obligatory for municipalities to be part of an EPCI. In 2014 36.614 French municipalities (of 36.680 in total in 2014) were part of an EPCI.

EPCIs are created either to operate large-scale infrastructure facilities or to make major investments (such as shopping malls, office spaces), with a view to benefit from economies of scale and to avoid negative externalities arising to some while accruing benefits to other municipalities. It has yet to be shown that cost reductions were realized, as EPCIs have often led to parallel administrative structures, that of the municipalities and that of the inter-municipality body, the EPCI. Instead of reducing positions new ones were created.

EPCIs can either be financed by budget contributions from the municipalities or from their own taxation powers. The later can either be "additional" in form of a levy on local taxes or exclusive, whereby the business tax is attributed to the EPCI instead of the municipalities. The exclusive business taxation became the most common form of EPCI financing. Since the EPCI business tax harmonisation led to some municipalities having to share significant business tax revenue with others whose revenue may have been a lot smaller equalization rules for redistributing resources have been introduced. Corresponding to their increased responsibility and revenue raising authority, the members of the EPCIs with own taxation powers are directly elected since 2014. The executive body is steered by a president assisted by vice presidents.

Sources: OECD (2006), OECD Territorial Reviews, France, OECD, Paris. http://www.collectivites-locales.gouv.fr/files/files/BIS_98.pdf

SYMADREM is a union (and an EPCI) in charge of the construction, reinforcement and the maintenance of protective infrastructure along the Rhône, including dikes and protection against coastal flooding the Rhône delta. The SYMADREM also intervenes for the implementation of environmental measures (e.g. in the creation of wetlands) in compensation of structural projects, such as the construction of dikes. The SYMADREM owns over 250 km dikes in the downstream Rhône, which makes it one of the biggest such unions in France. The second mission of SYMADREM is to implement the Plan Rhône in their area, which includes building new dikes as well. The SYMADREM came together as a result of participating municipalities wanting to work together, sparked by the Camargue floods in 1983. To operate and maintain their dikes a budget of EUR 4 million is available annually.

Empowering the local level in flood risk management – the impact of France's territorial reform on flood risk governance

The ongoing reform for the territorial reorganisation of France has important consequences on how flood risks are managed locally. The reform (Box 4) reduced the number of regions from 22 to 13, which affects 6 former regions along the Rhône that will be merged into 3, namely Auvergne-Rhône-Alpes, Midi-Pyrénées-Languedoc-Roussillon and Bourgogne-France-Comté. Regions will take up a key role in driving the regional economy and overseeing important sectoral work across the region. The former responsibilities of departments will be split between the region and local authorities. In terms of risk management local authorities will become the key players.

Another ongoing reform called GEMAPI (Box 3.5), which stands for the responsibility for managing aquatic environments and flood risk, entails transferring more responsibilities for flood risk management to municipalities and to inter-municipal collaboration bodies (EPCIs). Through this reform more municipalities and EPCIs will be given the ownership of existing structural measures in their localities (such as for dikes that currently belong to the department council or to the state) and will be in charge of building and maintaining new structural measures. To finance their new responsibilities the local authorities will have the option to introduce a local tax of a maximum of EUR 40 per citizen and year.

The role of unions will likely remain the same under the current territorial reform. Municipalities and inter-municipal bodies will have the option to delegate their responsibilities to existing or newly created unions. This will ensure that currently well-functioning inter-municipal collaboration based on unions can continue the work.

Although the reform has the potential to increase the efficiency of flood risk management through clarifying roles and determining local ownership, there are several potential gaps that still need to be addressed:

- The first concern is reform speed. With a strong unitary tradition it is important that the transition to more local responsibilities is carefully managed. A number of local authorities may still have some way to go to acquire the necessary technical capacities to fulfil their new functions, which is why the GEMAPI reform will only come into force in 2018.
- The second concern is resourcing. The reform recognises that there has been a gap in ownership and maintenance of existing protective infrastructure that has contributed to an increased vulnerability in recent flood events. Although local ownership is a desirable outcome, this new competence needs to be backed by adequate resources.

While the local level receives a revenue raising opportunity through a potential tax, it has been highlighted that this may neither be a feasible nor a sufficient instrument for all local authorities to cover their financial resource needs.

- The third concern is persisting fragmentation. Resolving local governance questions is crucial and the reform makes a good attempt in solving this. However, the problem of governance fragmentation along the Rhône River will remain unsolved and will continue to make coordination between interests up- and downstream of the river areas as well as between the main river and its tributary arms on both sides very difficult. It is important that any new reform is designed in tandem with a basin-level orientation of interests.

Box 3.4 France's Territorial Reform of 2004

A territorial reform was started by the French government in 2014 aiming at simplifying and rationalizing sub-national competences at the regional, departmental, municipal and inter-municipal level. The envisaged reform entails three core objectives:

- Reduce the number of regions from 22 to 13.

  Reinforce the role of the regions and gradually decrease the role of departments: the regions will be responsible for their economic development, including the promotion of small and medium enterprises, innovation and professional training. Regions will also be in charge of fostering sustainable development, especially spatial development, mobility, environmental pollution, energy, housing and waste management. Regions will take over the competences that belonged to departments: such as ownership of colleges, road and school transportation.
- Reinforce the role of inter-municipal collaborations (EPCIs) by increasing their number of inhabitants by reducing their total number and organizing them around functional areas. They will gain more competences (such as tourism, waste treatment, as well as from 2020 on also wastewater treatment) too. Departments can delegate competences to the EPCIs.
- Transform urban agglomerations into metropolitan areas, which means that inter-municipal cooperations (EPCI – Box 3) can become metropolitan areas, if they have more than 400.000 inhabitants. They will have a special status, responsible for economic, social and cultural development as well as spatial planning, the environment and the management of local public services (such as water). The new urban agglomerations will be distinct from the inter-municipal cooperations (EPCIs) and will include the functional areas of Paris, Aix-Marseille and Lyon. The Greater Lyon metropolitan area that was created in January 2015 takes over the competences of the Great Lyon EPCI and those of specified areas in the Rhone department.

Sources: http://www.gouvernement.fr/action/la-reforme-territoriale; http://www.vie-publique.fr/actualite/dossier/reforme-collectivites-territoriales/collectivites-territoriales-nouvelle-reforme-2014.html

Additional state operators and state-controlled businesses

The Central Reinsurance Fund (*Caisse Centrale de Réassurance,* CCR) is a business governed by private law, fully owned by the French state. It provides insurers with reinsurance solutions guaranteed by the French central government. The CCR participates in the CATNAT compensation scheme by offering reinsurance for the scheme while collecting a levy on the premium surcharge for disaster risk prevention that the insurance companies transfer to the CCR to place in the Barnier Fund. The CCR conducts significant work in risk assessment and disaster-related damage estimations (OECD, 2014).

The National Company of the Rhône (*Compagnie Nationale du Rhône* - CNR), created in 1933, is a company funded mostly by public capital. Its three historical tasks are electricity, navigation and irrigation. The CNR is the second most important electricity producer in France and the most important producer of renewable energy. Half of its investments are public (*Caisse des Dépôts*, local governments). The CNR is also constructor and owner of (and thereby responsible for) the structure protective measures along the Rhône, including hydropower stations, dams and dikes. The CNR would be well placed to play a key role in managing and especially reducing flood risk through its infrastructure. There is potential for reinforcing this role that could perhaps be more exploited in the future.

Box 3.5 Inter-municipal collaboration for flood risk management (GEMAPI)

The French "MAPTAM" law on modernizing local public action and promoting metropolitan regions, passed in 2014, gives the responsibility for managing aquatic environments and flood risk (GEMAPI) to municipalities and to intercommunal services (EPCIs – see Box 3). This should facilitate interventions at the right scale and ensure specific institutions are in charge of specified tasks, where responsibility has not been clear (as has e.g. been the case for the maintenance of protective infrastructure). Tasks for which the local level will be responsible under GEMAPI include:

- Hydrographic basin planning
- Installation and maintenance of water streams, canals and lakes, as well as access to them
- Flood and sea defence measures
- The protection and restauration of water ecosystems (such as flood plains)

To finance these new responsibilities, municipalities or inter-municipal services can raise a maximum tax of EUR 40 per citizen per year, attached to the local property or rental taxes. The municipalities and EPCIs may give the competence of GEMAPI or a part of it to unions that bring together different local-level groups. The law will come into force in 2018 with a transition period until 2020.

Sources: http://www.rhone-mediterranee.eaufrance.fr/docs/gemapi/20140127_LoiGemapi.pdf; http://www.eaurmc.fr/fileadmin/grands-dossiers/documents/GEMAPI/2014_AERMC_resume_loi_GEMAPI.pdf

Various network providers (such as the French Railway Corporation SNCF), energy sector (RTE, EDF and ERDF) are key actors in securing business continuity and avoiding knock-on impacts of floods. Moreover, EDF has provided important funding for the renewed Plan Rhône.

Associations

The European Centre for Flood Risk Prevention (*Centre Européen de Prévention du risque d'inondation* (CEPRI)) assists local governments in their prevention initiatives.

The role of citizens

With the development of recent new legislation, the responsibility for citizens has been increasing, aiming at a culture of risk for better preparedness for risks. In France information is available to citizens on:

- Various documents on the major existing risks and their consequences for citizens, assets and the environment. They can be consulted at the city hall or on the internet. They also provide information on measures that citizens can take to protect themselves and to act when an emergency situation arises.[8]

- Since 2006 owners or renters of a home have to be informed about their asset's exposure to potential risks; this includes the location in an unsafe zone or the radius of a disaster risk prevention plan.

International actors and institutions

France cooperates in the Alpine Convention[9] and is engaged in a cross-border dialogue with Switzerland on the border management of the Rhône. France envisages putting in place a coordinating body with Switzerland that can work on an agreement framework on the management of the Rhône. An important aspect of this collaboration will be on the management of the quantity and continuity of water flowing downstream.

Conclusion

This section's aim was to provide an overview of the main governance arrangements and actors in charge of the Rhône's disaster risk prevention and mitigation management. This section has delineated each actor's formal role and responsibilities, with a focus on establishing the facts. A number of observations can be made:

First, in terms of strategic frameworks the Plan Rhône and the basin-level disaster risk prevention management plan (PGRI) are effective instruments in determining flood risk priorities based on hazard and risk assessments at the basin level. Given the increased shift in responsibilities to the local level it is crucial that strategic frameworks are consulted with, translated to and co-owned by the local authorities, if they are to achieve actual results and induce changes on the ground.

Second, although many strategic frameworks exist for flood risk management, little has been done to create integrated risk management strategies, based on an all hazards approach and considering important interactive and cascading impacts between risks. Such a strategy could also be useful to improve the prioritisation of disaster risk prevention funding in the Rhône River basin. Although local level disaster risk prevention plans aim at establishing a local multi-risk strategy, such an approach could be equally useful for the elaboration of basin-level plans.

Third, there has been a wide recognition in the Rhône River basin that flood risk is best managed when resources are pooled and flood risk is managed across municipalities. A number of differently sized unions have emerged that have established effective and successful cross-jurisdictional collaboration. Unions have been effective in increasing the public's engagement and solidarity and should therefore be strengthened and reinforced in future reform programs.

Fourth, the high number of actors across levels of government has blurred the clear lines of responsibilities and ownership for risk management on the ground. This dynamic has led to the weak or sometimes fully absent maintenance of a number of protective infrastructures and has contributed to the increased vulnerabilities during recent flood events. The current reform processes are set out to address some of these issues.

Fifth, the absence of a single governance body at the Rhône River basin level has amplified the effect of fragmented governance structures. The Rhône river basin does not have a governance body that oversees the entire basin area. This has impeded the coordination of interests in disaster risk prevention investments between up- and downstream users as well as between the main river and its tributaries. Positive and negative externalities arise from flood risk prevention investments and if they are not addressed they can undermine the efficiency and effectiveness of disaster risk prevention investments. Similarly, at the international level, there is no governance body that can coordinate interests along the Rhône across national boundaries, although bilateral agreements with Switzerland are currently discussed.

Lastly, the ongoing territorial reform discussions envisage the local level to take the driver's seat in future disaster risk prevention management. This reform is laudable as it brings clarity of ownership and responsibilities and also determines the right functional level at which core disaster risk prevention interventions should be managed, namely the local one. It also comes as a direct and logical sequence of the increased responsibilities at the local level for disaster risk prevention since the regulatory changes in 2003. Nevertheless important accompanying measures need to be put in place to ensure local authorities will have adequate technical and financial resources to live up to their responsibilities.

In the following the objective will be to evaluate how each specific disaster risk prevention task (categorised in structural and non-structural measures) is approached by different actors and whether in practice the right incentives are in place for each actor to fully assume their roles, as well as to work together and coordinate tasks, assuming that hazards occur neither isolated, but often rather simultaneously, nor that they stop at local administrative or provincial borders.

Management of Structural and Non-Structural Disaster Risk Prevention and Mitigation Measures

Section Highlights

- The programmatic, bottom-up approach to central disaster risk prevention co-funding under PAPIs and PSRs has been particularly successful in rallying subnational disaster risk prevention stakeholders to join forces in reducing flood risks and to jointly mobilise co-funding by the state.

- Although PAPI and PSR funding proposals for disaster risk prevention investments are evaluated against a set of criteria, priority so far seems to have been given on a first come first serve basis; instead of allocating funding to areas at highest risk this may have favoured those local authorities with stronger financial and technical capacities; allocation mechanisms could be further strengthened to better reflect equity concerns and different levels of exposure to risk.

- The territorial reform process puts inter-municipal bodies (EPCIs) in the driver's seat of disaster risk prevention, which gives clear ownership structures at the local level. Two challenges will remain: (i) in a traditional unitary state careful sequencing of reforms will be required to ensure that local level bodies will have time to acquire the necessary financial and technical capacities to fulfil their new responsibilities; (ii) the consolidation of responsibilities at the local level will not resolve conflicts arising from disaster risk prevention investments up- and downstream of the Rhône River and between the main river and its tributaries; complementary governance arrangements that ensure coordination may still be necessary at the basin level.

- Hazard maps build the core for effective flood risk management, the delineation of high risk areas through a national hazard mapping exercise is a very good practice; the same homogeneity and coherence in terms of hazard criteria should be applied to develop local level hazard maps across the same river system. Hazard maps in the Rhône River basin could also benefit from integrating multiple hazards and cascading impacts on e.g. critical infrastructure such as nuclear power stations.

- Although businesses and households have been mobilised through various disaster risk prevention activities in the Plan Rhône, awareness and as a consequence investments in self-protection remain rather low. A whole-of-society approach should seek to mobilise contributions from all disaster risk prevention actors to increase the effectiveness and the multiplying effect of public disaster risk reduction investments.

Flood prevention funding at the national level in France is mainly provided by the obligatory insurance-based CATNAT system and its Fund for the Prevention of Major Natural Risks (*Fonds Barnier;* see financing section for details). Eligible for using this fund are municipalities or inter-municipal bodies (EPCIs) that have a flood risk prevention plan (*Plan de Prévention des Risques,* PPR) and that have, based on this, developed a local level flood prevention action plan (*Programmes d'Action et de Prévention des Inondations,* PAPI) or the equivalent for coastal flooding or flash floods (*Plan Submersions Rapides* PSR[10]) that includes concrete project propositions for disaster risk prevention. The central level can co-finance up to 50% of the costs of prevention measures.

France has moved from a project- to programme-based funding for disaster risk prevention. The motivation for introducing PAPIs in 2002 - and later also PSRs - was to move away from a project-by-project funding mechanism to a more programmatic approach that bundles several disaster risk prevention measures in one action plan. This should incentivise the proposition and financing of complementary measures, such as infrastructure investments alongside flood plain extensions or organisational measures such as risk awareness campaigns.

Management and implementation of structural measures

In recent years a paradigm shift has emerged calling for more room for the Rhône River. Originally, a considerable stock of protective infrastructure has been accumulated along the Rhône, with the first big dams constructed in the aftermath of the 1856 floods. Large areas of the Rhône River are so heavily protected by built infrastructure that they leave little space for new protective measures. A further limitation to increasing safety by physical protective infrastructure has been the limited utility of dams to retain water in the event of floods given the sheer size of the river.

As a consequence, in recent years the focus has changed towards prioritizing more room for the Rhône River. Maintaining and enlarging existing flood retention areas has thus become a key priority for disaster risk prevention investments in the Rhône River basin. This paradigm change has been embraced by the Plan Rhône.

Securing land as retention areas has been a major challenge in implementing this new paradigm. Firstly, it focuses on preventing the urbanisation of the land identified as retention areas that for a great part is currently in agricultural use. In the framework of the Plan Rhône, agricultural land has been identified for water retention purposes and farmers get support for disaster risk prevention measures to protect their livestock and machinery. In certain areas of the Rhône-Méditerranée outside the coverage of the Plan Rhône, a process of over flooding certain areas usually flooded during floods with the goal of optimizing its water retention capacity. In that case, the compensations aim especially at indemnifying the losses in harvest, as well as the damages to fields, material and livestock.

Decision making process

The need for a structural measure as part of a prevention action plan (PAPI) is identified by the project owner (*porteur de projet)*, such as a municipality, based on technical surveys that are often conducted by private engineering bureaus. The project documents are then submitted to the deconcentrated regional service branches of the Ministry of Ecology, the Regional Directorate for Environment, Planning and Housing (DREAL). The DREAL can directly approve projects that cost less than EUR 3 million. For projects above EUR 3 million the DREAL has to send the proposals for evaluation by the central-level Joint Flood Commission (*Commission Mixte Inondation,* CMI), that consists of a number of central- and local-level stakeholders (see section III for a detailed description). Formally the final decision lies in the hand of the state, represented by the Ministry of Ecology, however the recommendations of the Joint Flood Commission are usually followed.

Financing is allocated based on an assessment of 12 criteria, including safety and economic efficiency. Economic efficiency is determined by a Cost Benefit Analysis that was introduced in 2011 and that includes all current project and longer term operational costs (Box 6). Given the analytical constraints of this method, especially the difficulty of monetising all important costs and benefits, has proven to undermine a project's complete and thorough assessment. To allow for a better integration of all the possible costs and benefits of disaster risk prevention measure projects a new Multi-Criteria Analysis[11] tool will be implemented to overcome shortcomings experienced with Cost Benefit Analysis (CBA).

Box 3.6 Cost-benefit and multi-criteria analysis

The cost-benefit method described in PAPI project specifications provides for project promoters to follow a minimum range of criteria. The study must focus on the structural measures of projects, if they exceed EUR 2 million or 25% of the project. In terms of cost, it must consider both the initial costs as a whole from the time of the study until commissioning, and maintenance and operating costs over time. In terms of damage assessment, the method adopted involves assessing the average annual damage with or without planning in order to obtain the average annual damage avoided.

To achieve this, the minimum direct tangible damage must be assessed for four types of asset (housing, economic activity, agriculture and public infrastructure) and three flood scenarios (frequent, average – ~100 years – and extreme). The cost-benefit ratio will then be obtained by dividing the total discounted benefit by the total updated cost in the timeframe of the analysis, which must not exceed 50 years, and by using the discount rates established by the French planning authorities. This is referred to as the net present value (NPV). This calculation must be completed by a sensitivity analysis. This figure thus allows the economic efficiency of a project to be determined. It also enables several development options in the same basin to be compared.

It is, however, more difficult to use to compare projects in different basins, since the methods involved are generally too dissimilar. In order to also factor in the more intangible impacts highlighted by the Floods Directive in particular, the Ministry of Environment developed a multi-criteria analysis method to complete the cost-benefit analysis. This method considers impacts on human health, the environment or cultural heritage without having to monetise them. Some 20 indicators were thus defined, and a guide for project managers is has been drawn up (published in July 2014).

Source: OECD (2014)

Central-level steering for large disaster risk prevention projects needs to ensure equitable allocation of available resources. There is a clear advantage of having a central decision making process for large disaster risk prevention projects to ensure that high risk areas across the country are identified and addressed accordingly and that funds are distributed in an equitable manner. Despite the catalogue of criteria that has been elaborated funding allocations have tended to be made on a "first come first served" basis. This has certainly been enabled by the fact that available funding at the beginning of the PAPI funding process more or less equalled the demand for projects that needed funding. However this process cannot be sustained in the future, for two main reasons:

- First central-level funding is projected to become more constraint, since demand for disaster risk prevention investments will rise as more areas will be in the position to present a PAPI. This will necessitate the application of stringent evaluation criteria and a clear and transparent prioritisation process.

- Second the current process gives rise to considerable inequities. Instead of favouring the allocation of funds for the areas most exposed to risks, it has favoured disaster risk prevention investments on a first come serve basis. For those areas where the determination of local priorities and negotiation among interest groups has taken more time funding will become much more difficult and competitive to obtain in the future.

The balancing of interests up- and downstream, but also between the main river and its tributaries is crucial to ensure equity in disaster risk prevention management. The programmatic approach to deciding on disaster risk prevention funding allocation has been effective in rallying local level stakeholders to draw up a disaster risk prevention action programme (PAPIs or PSR), often across municipalities. However, the approach has not addressed the challenge of balancing interests of those communities upstream that may for example invest collaboratively in protective infrastructure and others that may gain further downstream without contributing to its financing. That is a challenge that for example a union upstream of Lyon (*Syndicat du Haut Rhône,* SHR) has been confronted with. The Plan Rhône could envisage the development of a PAPI that covers the entire area between Lyon and the Rhône's Delta or at least a way to coordinate existing PAPI's with a view to balance interests, but without a governance body in charge of the entire basin area this type of larger scale collaboration among interests along the river will be difficult to achieve.

Operating and Maintaining Structural Measures

Operating, maintaining and rehabilitating protective infrastructure is as crucial as their construction. The Rhône River basin, as many other areas in Europe, has had to witness key weaknesses in the existing infrastructures during recent flood events. The 2003 floods of the Rhône saw several dike breaches that aggravated the negative socio-economic impact. Inadequate maintenance does not only lead to failed protection, but can also increase the negative consequences of hazardous events by producing unexpected cascading impacts.

In France, the responsibility for operations and maintenance of protective infrastructure has been a shared one. Responsible at the state level has been the Ministry of Environment. At the department level under the control of the prefect the water police has been in charge of inventorying hydraulic works and of classifying them according to the assets that they protect. At the regional level the regional deconcentrated services of the environment ministry (DREAL) have been in charge of monitoring this task, under the supervision of the regional prefect. Figures indicate that across France the state has managed 750 kilometres of dikes[12], local authorities 3700 kilometres and other organisations (such as unions, associations etc.) manage some 4700 kilometres. Even for dikes where the state has not been the official owner it still has a duty to oversee the maintenance work, which is usually assured by its deconcentrated services (DREAL).

At present a significant heterogeneity in the level of maintenance of existing protective infrastructure can be observed in the Rhône River basin. Of the river's 1000 kilometres of dike infrastructure 57% are managed and well maintained by the National

Company of the Rhône (*Compagnie Nationale du Rhône,* CNR) and 21% by the SYMADREM union (*Syndicat Mixte Interrégional d'Aménagement des Digues du Delta du Rhône à la Mer*). The remaining 22% are not clearly owned and maintained by anyone (Table 3.6). The dikes managed by the CNR are recent whereas the dikes that are not well maintained are old ones built in the middle of the 19th century. The level of protection they had been designed to provide also differs. While CNR dikes are prepared to deal with flood events of 1000 years return period, the others have a maximum protection level of 100 year return period floods. The dikes managed by the CNR were not actually built primarily to protect from flooding but rather to manage hydro power production.

Table 3.6 Management of dikes of the Rhône River basin

Dikes managed by...	... km of dikes managed	% of total
CNR	570	57
SYMADREM	210 (+ 25 along the sea)	21
"Orphaned and otherwise managed dikes"	220	22

Source: Bravard and Clémens (2008)

Several contributing factors can help explain the significant difference in the level of maintenance of protective infrastructure:

- The initial project funding by the central government does not include coverage of the future maintenance costs of the infrastructure. Instead this is expected to be covered by the local level, which is the designated owner of the infrastructure.
- Different levels of local capacities have led to heterogeneous maintenance outcomes. In areas where a strong union or other type of organisation (such as the National Company of the Rhône, CNR) has taken charge of maintenance works the protective infrastructure tends to be in better shape than in areas where no such equivalent exists. Unions thus have a significant leverage effect on bundling resources and technical capacities to ensure adequate maintenance.
- Local ownership of infrastructure has not always been clear-cut. Over time a considerable stock of protective infrastructure has accumulated that was built in different periods and under different regulations. As a result there is a significant stock of infrastructure that is not officially owned by any municipality, inter-municipal body or union. As a consequence these infrastructures have degraded and can no longer be expected to provide the level of protection for which they were originally designed.

The ongoing territorial reform process, especially the law on the management of aquatic environments (GEMAPI[13]) provides a clear guidance for solving the existing problem. GEMAPI prescribes a clear responsibility of operations and maintenance of protective infrastructure that is to be given to inter-municipal bodies (EPCIs) that can in turn contract for example unions to carry out the work. GEMAPI can thereby clarify ownership questions of existing, including "abandoned", dike structures. In doing so there could be a risk that currently engaged actors feel no longer in charge, which risks losing valuable existing capacity. It is important that the re-structuring of responsibilities is coupled with the necessary financial capacities. Although GEMAPI introduces a new tax raising power for local authorities (ca. EUR 40 per person per year) a large finance gap could arise as local authorities may face constraints in imposing an additional tax and unions may begin to compete for potential funding raised through the tax.

In the meantime, a number of local initiatives have started to address problems of inadequate maintenance in the Rhône River basin area:

The *Syndicat du Haut-Rhône* (SHR), in line with the national laws regulating hydraulic works' operations and maintenance, has recently conducted a survey, with support of the Plan Rhône, to establish the current ownership of each structural measure upstream in the Rhône and, in its absence determine the operator that will take charge of the infrastructure in the future. Similarly the DREAL Rhône-Alpes financed a study carried out in Donzère Mondragon by the local union (SIAGAR) to study the functioning of protective measures not belonging to the *Compagnie Nationale du Rhône* (CNR). This study gave an important impetus to major renewal works of structural measures.

As part of the Plan Rhône the DREAL Rhône-Alpes has been dedicated to the securitisation of the protective infrastructure of the delta sector of the Rhône. This has been carried out through the *Pré-schéma Sud* approved in 2006 and adopted also in the flood risk management scheme of the downstream Rhône in 2009. This scheme is implemented by the *Syndicat Mixte Interrégional d'Aménagement des Digues du Delta du Rhône à la Mer* (SYMADREM). An innovative practice that comes out of that work is a database created by the SYMADREM that catalogues all existing protective infrastructure (called SIRS-dike[14]), including inspection observations to optimise monitoring of structural measures.

To counter the arising local technical capacity gap the catalogue that was developed on the construction, operations and maintenance requirements by the MEDEE and in collaboration with multiple stakeholders can guide regional and local efforts (MEDEE, 2015).

Cross-jurisdictional collaboration

Given its large number of municipalities France has recognised the importance for cross-jurisdictional collaboration. The creation of inter-municipal collaborative bodies (EPCIs) has been an attempt to address local public policy issues at a functional scale, to maximise efficiency and economies of scale.

With the creation of the Flood Prevention Action Programs (PAPIs and PSRs) flood risk management has been addressed jointly by municipalities that are part of the same risk area and that jointly develop an action programme that has received priority funding through the central Barnier Fund.

The new territorial reform enhances cross-municipal collaboration, but it does not necessarily address flood risks at a functional scale. To enhance flood risk management across municipal borders the GEMAPI law places EPCIs in the driver's seat for local disaster risk prevention by giving them, among others, the ownership of protective infrastructure as well as the responsibility for maintaining them. This provision will be made mandatory starting from 2018. However, GEMAPI may continue to address disaster risk prevention problems at an administrative rather than a functional scale. Equally, without anticipating the structural governance reform, GEMPAI will not solve some important flood risk governance issues, such as balancing interests up- and downstream of the Rhône River and between the main river and its tributaries.

The role of the private sector, critical infrastructure providers and citizens in providing protective infrastructure

With regard to structural measures the electricity provider EDF and the *Compagnie Nationale du Rhône* (CNR) have and will support the financing of structural measures to be implemented under the Plan Rhône. For the next financing period of the Plan Rhône the EDF will contribute approximately EUR 11 and the CNR EUR 8.5 million respectively. These amounts correspond more or less to the financing of measures protecting industrial areas. Apart from the Plan Rhône industrial companies have invested in protective measures to protect their assets without benefiting from public financial support.

The role of the CNR as a potential key investor in flood risk prevention has not been fully embraced. As described earlier the CNR has been investing in flood risk prevention infrastructure without this being directly its mandate. The CNR's core mission is to produce hydro power, but its works especially in terms of securing its dams is at the heart of flood risk management of the Rhône. The CNR's important role has to be fully embraced and requires a close collaboration between basin level and other local actors to ensure the right measures are implemented, especially in the event of a flood (e.g. adjusting discharge rates). For the time being the CNR participates in measuring discharge rates and monitoring flood risk.

Generally speaking citizens have invested very little in their self-protection and financial support does not seem to be the only impediment. In the Rhône River basin a number of surveys demonstrated that few citizens invest in self-protection measures against natural hazards. The reasons given by survey respondents is most often that they think they are not concerned by suggested prevention measures of the Risk Prevention Plan (PPRI) and many believe the suggested measures may not be effective. Only some survey respondents mention money has been the barrier to their investments in self-protection.

How are non-structural measures managed?

Hazard assessment and mapping and land-use planning

France's hazard mapping results in the development of so-called Prevention Plans against Natural Risks (PPRNs). Those plans delineate hazard zones, regarding earthquakes, floods, avalanches, wildfires or landslides. To evaluate flood risk PPRNs take obstacles into account that could prevent the river to flow, including in rivers' retention zones. Sometimes maps are renewed on the basis of a new risk prevention plan (PPR), after a major hazard event justifies a re-zoning or if major socio-economic changes necessitate an expansion of the existing maps to take into considerations new developments. Hazard maps are not adjusted once protection measures are built; thereby new constructions behind protective infrastructures are discouraged.

Hazard maps can be accessed by the public[15]. The public, as well as local authorities and other stakeholders, are implicated in the hazard mapping process by being consulted in public meetings and by responding to surveys conducted after the consultation meetings.

The responsibility for risk hazard mapping lies in the hands of deconcentrated arms of the Ministry of Ecology. PPRNs have to be drawn under the auspices of the department prefect, either at the municipal or inter-municipal level. The deconcentrated services of the ministry at departmental level (DDT(M)), supported by their regional services (DREAL), carry out hazard mapping. The actual mapping is often outsourced to (public) engineering bureaus and afterwards controlled by various stakeholders. It has happened that counter-assessments have been requested. Finally the DREAL verifies the adequacy of maps developed. This ensures that maps are developed impartially and are technically accurate.

Since the responsibility for hazard mapping is not fully centrally guided, heterogeneity in the quality of hazard mapping exists, impeding comparability across existing hazard maps. Given that hazard mapping is a local responsibility it can happen that along one and the same river one finds different specifications in hazard mapping. For example, in accordance with the national doctrine, a part of the river's hazard maps may be based on flood events with a return period of 100 years, whereas other parts, where more extreme events have happened, are based on longer return periods of up to 200 years. This essentially leaves the maps along the same river hardly comparable. Taking this into account, methodological work was conducted in partnership with departmental stakeholders in order to develop a hazard map based on homogenized water levels and data. With the implementation of the EU Flood Directive France carried out a national flood risk assessment based on which 122 areas of important flood risks (HRAs) have been identified and for which maps have been established identifying all hazards. These maps have been developed at the national level, with the help of sub-national service arms (DREAL, DDT(M)). The hazard mapping exercise carried out for the Rhône River basin identified six High Risk Areas (HRAs) from a national perspective, which include Lyon, Vienne, Valence, Montélimar, Avignon and the plain of Tricastin as well as the Rhône delta. Based on this national identification process six detailed hazard maps were developed. Both national and regional mapping exercises can be accessed online[16].

There are several instruments that aim at integrating hazard maps in land use decisions. To integrate hazard mapping in spatial planning decisions, the spatial development code obliges local authorities to take into consideration hazard maps in their spatial planning documents, the so called *Schéma de Cohérence Territorial*, the *Plan*

Local d'Urbanisme (PLU) and the *Carte Communale*. The Risk Prevention Plan (PPR) has to be annexed to the local planning documents. This allows making zones either unfit for construction or developable under certain prescriptions. Penalties can be given if such prescriptions are ignored and discovered during control visits. These control visits can be carried out by the prefect, the mayor or his delegates as well as officials and commissioned agents of the ministry in charge of urban development. These control visits can be carried out up to three years after constructions were completed. A stronger integration yet of hazard zones in planning decisions has been achieved through the Flood Risk Prevention Plans (PPRIs) that create a hard constraint on constructions in hazard zones. Whereas previous annexations of hazard maps to planning documents was rather lose, the PPRIs clearly designate areas that are unfit for construction. The PPRI should thereby leave no more room for ambiguity, at least in those municipalities that have a PPRI.

The responsibility for respecting hazard zones in land use decisions lies with mayors, whereby department prefects have a monitoring function. The mayor has the responsibility of informing the population of existing hazards and risks. The mayor is in the driver's seat of enforcing hazard zones in land use decisions the mayor is in charge of granting construction permits. The department prefect is in charge of monitoring the integration of hazard zones in urban planning and can launch a legal procedure against a municipality at the administrative tribunal if (s)he has doubts about whether hazard zones were respected in granting a construction permit. The prefect can impose works to protect planned constructions from hazards or call a project off if it is suggested to be built in a high risk zone.

Mayors can and have been made liable for ignoring hazard zones. For example the mayor of *La Faute-sur-mer* was condemned to four years in prison for involuntary homicide after more than 50 fatalities were caused by the Xynthia storm and some of them directly linked to the granting of construction periods in known zones at risk[17]. The condemnation was a strong signal to local planning authorities and mayors to take the integration of hazard zones in their land use decisions seriously.

Regions have a monitoring role and can positively encourage the integration of hazard zones in local land-use decisions. Regions are in charge of developing regional spatial plans. They can exercise their oversight role by encouraging mayors to respect hazard zones when taking land-use decisions. The region of *Provence-Alpes-Côte d'Azur* for example sees it as its role to ensure that no new constructions are built in risk prone zones, including for example behind new protective infrastructure. The challenge though for the region seems to be avoiding additional constructions to existing building stock in areas at risk.

For the Rhône River basin it would be desirable to not just have high risk areas delineated through a general mapping exercise, but to also strengthen the efforts to ensure more homogeneity and coherence across the local hazard maps that are being developed. Hazard maps build the core of effective flood risk management and it is therefore of key importance to ensure the same hazard mapping criteria and models as well as the same hazard criteria or levels of intensity of projected hazard events.

Hazard mapping for the Rhône should eventually be expanded to include the potential impacts of climate change on the local level, but also to better understand the cascading impacts and resulting complex risks emerging from the concomitant occurrence of hazardous events. This includes studying not only the impacts of one natural hazard on another (such as landslides and floods) but also the impact of for example floods on critical infrastructure such as nuclear power stations or an ensuing tsunami as a result of an earthquake.

It would be desirable to have clear prescriptions in terms of building codes in hazardous areas for all hazards. Clear building code regulations exist for different levels of assessed seismic risks. Building code consequences for other risks are less clear.

Risk Communication

General responsibility for informing about natural hazards and increasing risk awareness lies within the department through the *Dossier Départmental sur les Risques Majeurs*. Mayors are obliged to publish risk information documents in the city hall, which includes the risk prevention plan (PPR) and the local community information documents about major prevailing risks (DICRIM – Box 3.7).

Risk awareness in the Rhône River basin seems rather low. Following the large downstream floods in 2003 the DREAL Rhône-Alpes decided to launch regular risk awareness surveys, which have been conducted in 2006, 2009 and 2013. The surveys show that in the absence of major floods risk awareness is relatively low: Only 18% of the population in risk zones took measures to self-protect them, against 21% in 2009. Reasons provided for this low engagement are varied. 36% of respondents do not see themselves as concerned by this, 17% thought that such preventive measures would be ineffective and only 5% give financial constraints as a reason for not having invested in individual disaster risk reduction measures. These developments show the difficulty of establishing a culture of risks and underline the prevailing notion that disaster risk prevention is the sole responsibility of the state and not of individual actors (DREAL, 2013).

The DREAL Rhône-Alpes through its *Mission Rhône* supports risk communication activities in various ways. First it supports and engages in more traditional ways of communication such as the organisation of risk exhibitions or newspaper information campaigns. More innovative actions include a project call for creating a culture of risk in 2008-09 as well as a photography campaign of the Rhône River. It has also been dedicated to publishing research studies, providing website information and engaging in consultations for the flood risk pillar of the *Plan Rhône*.

Risk awareness is not only key to make sure all actors have the information they need to act individually to invest in self-protection, but also to ensure people are aware about why for example a tax is raised locally to finance prevention measures. This is key to forming acceptance, for example for local revenue raising measures for disaster risk prevention investments, such as the introduction of local taxes through GEMAPI.

Box 3.7 DICRIM – Local community information document about major prevailing risks (France)

DICRIM, introduced in 1990 in France, obliges every community, under the responsibility of the mayor and his municipal council, to draw up an information document about the safety measures to take in the event of a potential threat. The document is tailored to the locally prevailing hazards and includes information on:

- Locally prevailing natural and technological risks
- Measures taken by the municipality to reduce risk exposure
- Safety measures to be taken in the event of an emergency or an alarm (for example behavioural measures, securing assets from areas at risk, mounting electricity and gas meters above a potential flooding level)
- A list of critical public infrastructures (including retirement homes, schools etc.)
- How land owners and those renting premises have to communicate about the safety measures stipulated in the DICRIM

The objective of the DICRIM is to raise awareness among citizens about local major risks to which they could be exposed to. The DICRIM should inform about the nature of the threats, their potential consequences and the measures citizens can take to protect themselves or to reduce their exposure and potential damages. The DICRIM recognizes that the local administrative boundaries may not reflect the right scale for analyzing hazards and encourages inter-municipal hazard analysis, based on which local prescriptions can be developed.

Source: http://www.risquesmajeurs.fr/le-document-d%E2%80%99information-communal-sur-les-risques-majeurs-dicrim

Business continuity planning

The DREAL has initiated actions to increase the resilience of public services and critical infrastructure providers. In some initial experiments two health facilities, a clinic and a medical centre near Valence have engaged in evaluating their business continuity in case of a flood event. Based on this measures have been identified to increase their resilience as part of a business continuity plan.

Similarly a number of water energy and transport providers have engaged in working groups on business continuity planning with a view to identify potential vulnerabilities and creating an action plan.

Business continuity planning has also been introduced in the agricultural sector, where losses due to natural disasters have been more important in the Rhône River basin than in other basin areas such as for example the Loire River basin. Disaster risk prevention and mitigation measures for agricultural land do not only aim to secure agricultural livelihoods, but are also an important part of conserving agricultural land as flood retention areas. Since farmers have no access to conventional prevention funding under PAPIs and PSRs special disaster risk prevention and mitigation activities have been supported by the Plan Rhône (Box 3.8).

It will be important to mainstream these initial actions across all critical infrastructure providers and business in the basin area. The pilot introduction of disaster risk prevention and mitigation measures for critical infrastructure providers and businesses at large are an ideal opportunity to evaluate the effectiveness of proposed measures and to improve actions as they are being mainstreamed.

Box 3.8 Measures to making agricultural activities flood resilient in the Rhône River basin

The 2003 floods of the Rhône caused so significant damages to farmers that some of them had to shutter their businesses. Given the importance of agriculture in the Rhône River basin for securing livelihoods but also its importance for providing important flood retention areas, the Plan Rhône introduced a diagnostic instrument to assess farmer's vulnerability to floods as well as preventative measures they could undertake. This exercise was inspired by the Plan Loire that recognised the importance of raising awareness of farmers that their agricultural land serves as an important flood retention area, thereby discouraging them from building dikes to protect their assets.

The DREAL Rhône-Alpes assessed some 230 farmers in the first pilot phase based on which 85 farmers decided to put prevention measures in place. Investments were co- financed at a maximum rate of 80%. Measures included:

- The installation of new and more effective water pumps (while inhibiting the purchase of bigger pumps that could increase productivity);
- Moving air conditioning for refrigeration from underground to higher ground;
- Building of a safe zone where important machinery (such as tractors) could be stored in the event of flooding;

Finally, the DREAL Rhône-Alpes seeks to encourage farmers to put measures in place that avoid erosion (such as by planting grass), but the DREAL is in no position of mandating farmers to do so.

Source: http://www.planrhone.fr/front/277-252-0-Reduire-la-vulnerabilite-des-exploitations-agricoles

Risk Management Financing Section Highlights:

- It is difficult to establish figures indicating the total amount of investment for disaster risk prevention on the national level, but also on the Rhône River basin level, across levels of government and across different sectors.

- The CATNAT obligatory disaster risk insurance scheme is an important solidary mechanism in France's risk financing system. The CATNAT insurance premiums are paid by each contributor independent of their risk exposure, which has disincentivising effects on individual disaster risk prevention efforts. Complementary policies should be considered that support individual households and businesses in investing more in self-protection measures. This could increase the efficiency and effectiveness of public investment in risk reducing measures.

- Although until present the available funding from the Barnier Fund was sufficient to cover the demands from local authorities for co-funding of protection measures, this is expected to change in the near future as more funding requests will be made based on the wider adoption and elaboration of disaster risk prevention plans. Considering that sub-national co-funding rates have been quite considerable already (around 60%), other options and sources of additional financing may have to be explored.

- The territorial reforms require sub-national authorities to be in charge of not only managing but also financing considerable disaster risk prevention tasks, such as maintenance of protective infrastructure. The ongoing reforms need to ensure sufficient funding for sub-national actors for co-financing disaster risk prevention investments through the Barnier Fund. A thorough disaster risk prevention financing mechanism has to be elaborated to ensure the reform can at least maintain, if not increase, the level of disaster risk prevention in France and of the Rhône basin in particular.

France's main natural catastrophes compensation & disaster risk prevention funding scheme - CATNAT

The natural catastrophes compensation scheme CATNAT (*Catastrophes Naturelles*) builds the core of France's risk financing system. It is sourced from an obligatory insurance contribution made by all holders of household, business and motor vehicle insurance policies and serves a double purpose. On the one hand it provides funds for compensating damages suffered from natural disasters to individual households and businesses, while on the other hand a share of its funds is reserved and used for disaster risk prevention investments under the Fund for the Prevention of Major Natural Hazards (Barnier Fund):

The CATNAT insurance scheme is a public-private partnership inscribed in France's constitutional principle of solidarity. The CATNAT scheme was established in 1982 to offset shortcomings of the insurance market by making insurance available to cover all individuals and businesses against disaster risks. It does not cover losses suffered by municipalities through destroyed infrastructure. The scheme is funded by an additional premium at a mandatory uniform state-fixed rate, which applies to any insurance contract for damage to or loss of property, irrespective of its exposure to natural disaster risks. Its proceeds go to the CATNAT reserve and a state guarantee is provided by the Central Reinsurance Fund (*Caisse Centrale de Réassurance,* CCR).

The CATNAT insurance scheme has proven its effectiveness since its foundation. The CATNAT has allowed broad coverage and compensation for disaster events where a state of emergency was declared. Disputes and appeals have not been common, and civil society stakeholders and insurers agree on the usefulness of the mechanism. Initially established at 2.5%, the premium has now risen to 12% for all-risk home and business insurance and 6% for motor vehicle insurances (Grislain-Letrémy and Calvet, 2012). The CATNAT covers insured assets only. This excludes damages to public assets, as well as damages accrued by people that are not insured. In Metropolitan France 99% of assets are insured, whereas only 52% of assets are insured in France's oversea territories. Insured losses are only a part of total economic losses. It is estimated that insured assets make up 50-60% of disaster-related economic losses (EPRI *nationale*).

The CATNAT insurance scheme by its design also has a number of shortcomings. The lack of insurance premium adjustment in line with risk levels creates moral hazard by discouraging insured parties to reduce their exposure or vulnerability to natural hazards by investing in self-protection measures such as securing cellars or house walls against floods. Similarly, prevention efforts by individuals are not rewarded by lower premiums.

In addition, the too-frequent triggering of the mechanism, even for events with a low recurrence interval of up to a mere ten years, hinders prevention measures (French Senate, 2012; OECD, 2006). This system, initially envisaged for extreme events, deludes the public and decision makers into assuming that they can take advantage of it irrespective of the circumstances. These consequences have brought about a number of minor modifications to the system and many recommendations over the years, plus an unsuccessful bill drafted to overcome its failings.

To back the CATNAT insurance scheme a wholly state-owned reinsurance, the CCR, was established as a state guarantee to fund compensation in extreme events. Despite its substantial reserves, the CATNAT resources could be heavily restricted by two other major risks in metropolitan France: a major flood of the Loire (OECD, 2010) or an earthquake on the Côte d'Azur. In that event, the call for the state guarantee could then come into play. The state guarantee was used following multiple natural disasters in 1999. This led to the additional insurance premium to be raised from 9% to 12%.

Apart from serving as an insurance fund the CATNAT has since 1995 funded France's core Fund for the Prevention of Major Natural Hazards (*Fonds de Prévention des Risques Naturels Majeurs* FPRNM), or short *Fonds Barnier* (Barnier Fund). A fixed percentage of sums collected has since been retained to provide funding for disaster risk prevention investments. The *Fonds Barnier* thereby has the advantage of being disconnected from direct state budget resources. Initially established at 2.5% of the total additional premiums collected via CATNAT, the 2003 Bachelot Law allowed this rate to be adjusted by decree, which led to its gradual increase to 4%, 8% and at present 12%. EUR 185 million have been retained (Figure 3.9) through this contribution.

The Barnier Fund became the principal instrument for co-funding disaster risk prevention measures proposed by sub-national government levels. The Barnier Fund has been used to fund the drawing-up of disaster risk prevention plans (PPRs) and structural as well as non-structural, organisational measures against (coastal) flood risks. It generally involves co-funding from local authorities, with a fixed rate by type of activity ranging from 100% for preparing PPR-type regulatory instruments or departmental documents on major risks, and 40-50% for all other measures.

The system's strength lies in the reliability of its funding, but fund disbursements have been more variable. Although the Barnier Fund has consistently retained EUR 185 million for disaster risk prevention investments, disbursement rates are variable as they dependent both on recent disasters and on public prevention policy guidelines. The variations in disbursement are shown in Figure 3.9. To continue fulfilling the CATNAT's double function of insurance compensation and prevention funding it has been projected by the Ministry of Economy that its reserves will eventually require higher contributions.

It seems that the level of damage compensation has remained constant over the past 20 years. This takes into account new constructions. This shows that prevention investments have been somewhat effective in reducing damages over time.

A financing gap for disaster risk prevention measures may arise in the next years. To date the central level Barnier Fund has been big enough to finance all project proposals that were received. It is projected though that in the current phase of financing that lasts until 2022 demand for central level financing will exceed the Fund's capacities to finance projects. This will necessitate either an increase of insurance contributions that feed the central Fund or a higher number of projects whose proposal for funding will have to be declined. The Joint Flood Commission (CMI) will have to ensure that only projects focusing on flood risk prevention will be financed through the Barnier Fund and refuse projects, like they did in the past already, whose flood risk prevention focus is only a minor aspect of the project proposal. Furthermore rigorous selection criteria will have to be applied to enable a clear prioritisation of project proposals.

Figure 3.7 Development of the Barnier Fund budget and forecast, 2008-2015

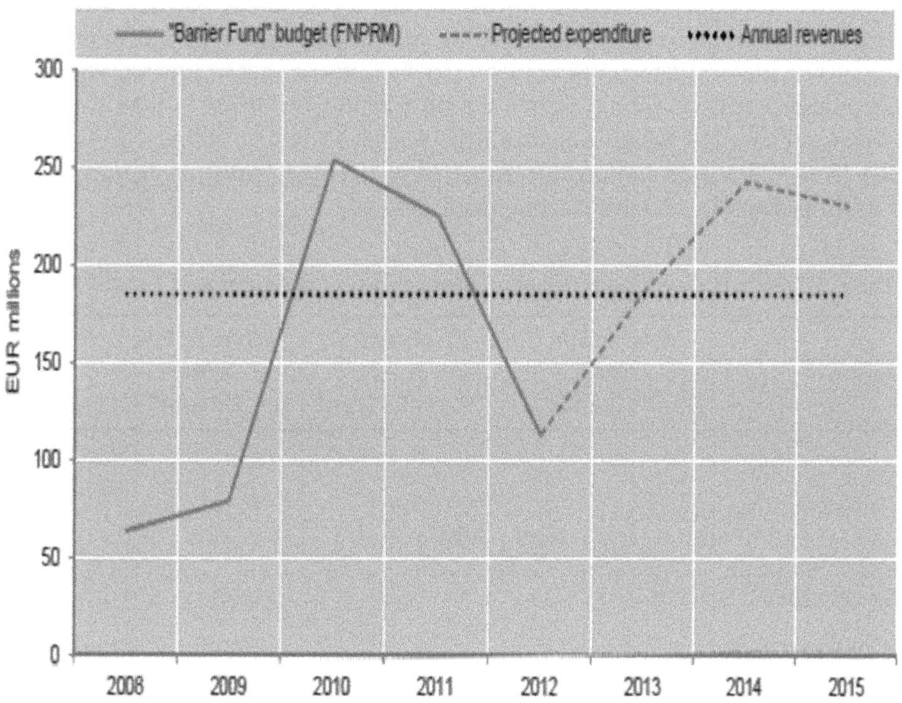

Source: OCDE (2014), " Seine Basin, Île-de-France, 2014: Resilience to Major Floods "OECD Publishing, Paris. DOI: http://dx.doi.org/10.1787/9789264208728-en.

Co-financing arrangements

The calls for proposals under PAPI and PSR have put local authorities in the driver's seat for initiating disaster risk prevention investments. As highlighted earlier, contracts between the state and local authorities (*Contrats de Plan État-Région*, CPER) enable local flood risk protection funding to be mobilised in tandem with central state funding. For natural hazard risk management such co-funding agreements can be established during the development of Disaster Risk Prevention Plans (PPRs) and Flood Risk Prevention Action Programmes (PAPIs or PSRs) at basin level and via the major river plans at catchment level, including the departments and regions and their different groupings.

Financing of the Plan Rhône

The major river plans, including the Plan Rhône, use the state-region contracts to mobilise local and state level financial contributions for the implementation of the plan. The Plan Rhône seeks complementary funding from the European Regional Development Fund (ERDF), which are funds dedicated to support collaboration on watercourse planning and flood risk prevention in particular.

The Plan Rhône was a key instrument to leverage funding for flood risk prevention among regional and local interest groups. In the period of 2007 to 2013 EUR 137,2 million of the Plan Rhône financing were dedicated to structural measures, of which the majority (EUR 128 million) went towards the implementation of the *Pré-schéma Sud*. The central government co-financed EUR 41 million and gave budget loans over EUR 12.7 million. For the next financing period (2014-2020) EUR 223 million will be invested in disaster risk prevention management, of which EUR 76 million will be financed by the central government, EUR 60 million from the region Provence-Alpes-Côte d'Azur, EUR 13 million from the region Languedoc-Roussillon, EUR 8.5 million from the CNR (and EUR 11 million from the electricity provider EDF.

Table 3.7 Plan Rhône financing from state-region contracts and EU 2007-2020

	Total (in EUR million) 2007-2013	...of which	Total (in EUR million) 2014-2020	...of which
State-Region Contracts	613.8	State: 228.41 Regions 200.44 CNR: 185	849	State: 170.31 Regions 153 CNR: 200 EDF: 65
EU funding 2007-2013	33.8	-	32.01	-
Total funding flood risk prevention	321.1		259	

Sources: Document de préfiguration du contrat de plan interrégional état régions plan Rhône 2014-2020 [Blueprint for the interregional state region plan Rhône 2014-2020], http://www.planrhone.fr/module/00003/19/data/Files/ACTUS2014/Actu_2/CPIER/Projet_cpier_Plan_rhone_2014 2020.pdf; *Projet de Contrat de Plan Interrégional État Régions Plan Rhône 2015-2020* [Contract Project of the interregional state region plan Rhône 2015-2020], http://www.planrhone.fr/module/00003/19/data/Files/ACTUS2014/Actu_2015/Projet_Cpier20152020_15042015.pdf; *Contrat de Projets Interrégional Plan Rhône 2007-2013* [Contract Project of the interregional state region plan Rhône 2007-2013], http://www.datar.gouv.fr/sites/default/files/datar/plan-rhone-2007-2013.pdf ; *Objectif compétitivité régionale et Emploi, Programme Opérationnel Interrégional FEDER Rhône Saône 2014-2020* [Regional competition objectives and employment, Interregional Programme Feder Rhône Saône 2014-2020], www.europe-en-france.gouv.fr; *Objectif compétitivité régionale et Emploi , Programme Opérationnel Plurirégional FEDER Plan Rhône, 2007-2013* [Regional competition objectives and employment, Interregional Programme Feder Rhône Saône 2007-2013], http://www.planrhone.fr/data/Files/Plan_rhone/POPMODIFVALID_mai2014.pdf; *Accompagnement du volet inondations 2007-2013* [Flood support component 2007-2013], http://www.rhone-alpes.developpement-durable.gouv.fr/IMG/pdf/AP_Valorisation_BDT-20-06-2010_cle749a5e.pdf

The Rhône River basin receives a large share of central level funding, albeit a high sub-national co-financing rate. Three calls for programmes have been launched since the introduction of PAPI's, with the first one in 2003. An audit report in 2009 showed that of the total of EUR 884 million spent during a first financing phase, 60% were co-financed by sub-national authorities. Figures for the Rhône suggest a co-financing rate that is slightly above this average. Of the EUR 739 million that were invested during the first phase of PAPI projects in the Rhône River basin EUR 268 were funded by the central fund. This corresponds to a co-financing rate of the sub-national level of 64%. In the second phase 18 PAPIs were financed for a total of EUR 329, of which EUR 128 million were funded by the state. This corresponds to a sub-national co-financing rate of 61% (DREAL Rhône-Méditerranée, 2013). These figures demonstrate that a large share of the central level funding for flood risk prevention was allocated to the Rhône River basin.

Who bears the cost in the aftermath of a disaster?

By looking at the 2003 floods of the Rhône (that occurred downstream of Lyon), Figure 3.7 (in section II) shows that half of the total estimated damages accrued to individual households. Of these damages, it seems only half of them got compensated by insurance. This figure seems relatively low and on average one would expect the damage compensation of households to be at least 60-80%. A significant amount of costs to households are temporary relocation costs, which are not covered by insurances. They could explain, at least to some extent, why the insured costs make up a lower share of the total costs accrued to households. Temporary relocation costs are often covered by local authorities, rather than households themselves.

When looking at France's overall level of disaster risk insurance penetration, it looks like more than 95% of private assets are insured in metropolitan France (FFSA, 2013), which contrasts with 52% in France's oversea territories. How much is compensated in terms of damages suffered by a household depends on the clauses of the insurance contract.

Assessment & Recommendations

The Rhône River basin is one of France's largest river systems. Due to its size it covers a wide range of different topographies and diverse climatic conditions. These make the areas around the river subject to a variety of natural hazards, including river and coastal floods, torrents and sediment movements, storms and storm surges, but also earthquakes are a potential threat.

The Rhône River basin accounts for a major share of France's economy, with two thirds of hydropower supply and one fourth of nuclear power produced in the area. It is estimated that around 5.5 million basin inhabitants are potentially exposed to the risk of flooding. Critical infrastructure and industrial sectors located in close proximity to the river make a potential flood a critical risk for France. six of the 16 identified areas of high flood risk of national importance are located in the basin area of the Rhône.

The Rhône's flood risk prevention management has a long history, with some of its major structures established as early as 1856, in response to devastating floods. Although flooding and related events have been relatively frequent along the Rhône, a large-scale flood comparable to the one of 1856 has not occurred in the recent past. This makes it important to assess whether current disaster risk prevention levels are sufficient to confront similar such events that are expected to take place in the future.

Identification and monitoring of current and future risks

Hazard maps build the core for effective disaster risk management. There is a relatively good understanding of the nature of different prevailing threats in the basin area of the Rhône. France's effort to identify areas of particularly high flood risk has also informed the identification and prioritization process in the basin area of the Rhône that includes 6 of the 16 identified national high flood risk areas. It would be desirable to apply the same homogeneity and coherence in terms of hazard evaluation criteria for the development of local level hazard maps across the Rhône river system. To improve hazard maps in the Rhône River basin further, it would be helpful to assess the potential concomitance of hazards in the same areas, including their potential cascading impacts on critical infrastructure such as nuclear power stations.

To refine hazard models and maps over time, and to inform future effective disaster risk prevention and mitigation policies, it is crucial to understand the socio-economic impacts of past disasters. This information also serves as a key variable in assessing the effectiveness of disaster risk reduction investments over time. Although some detailed estimations of socio-economic losses have been recorded such as for the 2003 flood events, the basin area of the Rhône could benefit from more systematically recording social and economic losses of disasters. France has a long-established insurance and re-insurance system to compensate for losses and damages from disasters accrued by individual households and businesses. Recorded insured losses can be an important starting point to eventually get a better understanding of total direct economic, and eventually also indirect economic losses in the basin area. To improve this evidence base for the Rhône, collaboration with national and regional public and private sector partners already active in this field could be useful.

Legal and institutional frameworks for disaster risk prevention management

France's risk governance system has been tested during a number of major natural disasters. Past lessons learned informed reforms aiming at improving the national disaster risk prevention management system. As many other countries' disaster risk prevention governance frameworks, France has set-up one that is guided by solidarity on the national level, which the national compensation scheme CATNAT represents, for example, and subsidiarity across levels of government, whereby local level actors are in charge of identifying locally prevailing risks and developing local prevention action plans. France has also recognised the importance of managing risks at the appropriate geographical or functional level, which led to the development of its great river plans, including the Plan Rhône.

Over time however, a complex web of national and sub-national actors has emerged that has blurred the lines of responsibilities. Fragmented governance arrangements at the sub-national level have contributed to the heterogeneous protection levels one can observe across the Rhône River basin, which have been made apparent during recent major flood events. The ongoing territorial reforms of France could help regrouping many of the more fragmented sub-national actors and efforts to maximise the pay-offs of sub-national and national disaster risk prevention efforts, while strengthening the ownership of disaster risk prevention actions by direct beneficiaries, thereby improving accountability of the responsible actors to their citizens.

The ongoing reform process, which aims at increasing the level of decentralised functions for flood risk management may face several challenges that need to be addressed, if the reform were to yield its expected outcomes. In a mostly unitary tradition, subnational actors that will receive more flood risk management responsibilities may not all have the technical and financial capacities in place today to fulfil their new duties. The reform should therefore allow for sufficient time in the transition process to acquire the necessary capacities to fulfil their new roles, as well as take into account the possible political economy obstacles that could arise with new, albeit limited, revenue raising authority by sub-national actors.

The strategic framework provided by the Plan Rhône has been an effective and successful instrument to integrate economic development and flood risk management, bringing all relevant actors together to work on commonly agreed priorities, supported by consolidated financing across levels of government. However, the absence of a governance body for disaster risk management questions for the entire river basin reinforces the challenges of balancing interests across different parts of the river. The ongoing territorial reform that seeks to regroup local jurisdictions will not solve cross-jurisdictional conflicts arising from negative and positive spill over effects of disaster risk prevention investments up- and downstream of the Rhône River, but also between the main river and its tributaries. Further governance or coordination mechanisms that aim at covering the entire river or basin area could be useful.

Managing structural and non-structural measures to foster disaster risk prevention

The programmatic, bottom-up approach to central disaster risk prevention co-funding under PAPIs and PSRs has been particularly successful in rallying subnational disaster risk prevention stakeholders to join forces in reducing flood risks and to jointly mobilise co-funding by the state. Although PAPI and PSR funding proposals for disaster risk prevention investments are evaluated against a set of criteria, priority so far seems to have been given on a first come serve basis. This has been facilitated by a more or less equal demand and supply of risk protection financing. However, the number of demands for financing is expected to increase in the future as more local authorities will start to develop their disaster risk prevention strategies. This will necessitate a stronger and equitable prioritisation of funding allocation decisions, as otherwise those local authorities will have an advantage that have stronger and more readily available financial and technical capacities to put their disaster risk prevention programmes together.

The significant stock of protective infrastructure is becoming increasingly difficult to maintain

Given the Rhône River basin's multiple and vital functions for the social and economic development of its inhabitants, investments in structural protection measures date back a long time and the stock that exists today is testimony to continued investment in protecting lives and economic development along the river. In order to keep the level of protection, for which structures were initially conceived, up, maintenance works are necessary. Weaknesses in maintenance levels have been made apparent during past flood events, such as the ones in 2003, which showed heterogeneity in the level of maintenance of protective infrastructures across the basin area. Some of this heterogeneity can be explained by the number of different actors, with sometimes different levels of technical and financial capacity, that are in charge of maintenance along the river. For some protective infrastructures there might not even be a specific actor in charge. Recent efforts to address this shortcoming, including the recording of all existing infrastructures, their owner and maintenance level, show the recognition of the underlying problems.

Although the ongoing territorial reform process seeks to clarify ownership of protective structures at the local level, it is important that this is accompanied with the necessary technical and financial capacity to carry out this responsibility in the future.

Emphasising the importance of non-structural disaster risk prevention measures

Non-structural or "soft" disaster risk prevention measures are important complements to physical disaster risk reduction investments. They can be often low cost measures, in comparison to the costs of physical infrastructure, which yield potentially high returns. Non-structural measures include hazard identification and mapping, land-use planning or risk communication.

The integration of hazard zones into land-use planning and land-use decisions is a key non-structural measure that serves to avoid a future increase in risk exposure, while also informing about the potential adjustments that can be made to existing land-uses to render them more resilient. France has developed a number of effective instruments that allow for a systematic and effective integration of hazard information into land-use planning, such as the flood risk prevention plans (PPRIs). Monitoring and subsequent penalisation of mayors that grant construction rights in known zones at risk have shown France's strong commitments to this measure.

There is scope to more strongly engage all societal actors in disaster risk prevention management along the Rhône

The disruptions disasters can cause have an impact on individual households, businesses, and the public sector. Hence all actors have to decide to which degree and how they will invest in disaster risk prevention and mitigation. A whole-of-society approach to disaster risk prevention requires everyone to share the burden of financing disaster risk reduction in order to ensure that public disaster risk reduction investments yield their expected benefits.

Although businesses and households have been mobilised through various disaster risk prevention activities in the Plan Rhône, investments in self-protection remain rather low. Surveys have shown that this low engagement may be due to a number of reasons, but most concerning of all a belief that individual risk protection investments are ineffective. Risk awareness raising campaigns must inform not only about the individual exposure of risks, but the also the potential options there are to invest in reducing this exposure.

The public compensation scheme of the CATNAT may not necessarily be conducive to achieving a whole-of-society engagement in disaster risk prevention. Its premium structure does not differentiate between different levels of risk exposure. This means that in the event of a disaster individual investments may not be rewarded - neither in the premium structure, nor in the eventual pay-outs. This necessitates complementary policies that support individual households and businesses in investing more in self-protective measures. This could increase the efficiency and effectiveness of public investment in risk reducing measures.

Current risk financing arrangements may be insufficient in meeting medium- to long-term disaster risk prevention investment needs

Although it is difficult to establish a global picture of total available disaster risk prevention investments at national and sub-national levels, there are indications that existing funding available through France's national prevention fund may not be sufficient to meet future demands for prevention investments. As sub-national levels increasingly gear up to establish their disaster risk prevention plans and financing needs, more demands for co-funding from the central prevention funds are expected. To ensure that France's risk protection levels can be maintained over time, a risk financing plan should be elaborated that identifies investment needs and potential additional or alternative sources of prevention funding.

The impacts of ongoing territorial reforms on sub-national financial capacity to perform their given tasks remain uncertain. It needs to be ensured that the reform does not reduce the financial resources for carrying out important prevention investments or maintenance tasks. At the very least the reform should ensure that financial resources maintain the same level, or increase them where possible and where needed.

Notes

[1] In this document Rhône River basin corresponds to the Rhône-Méditerranée River Basin.

[2] Excludes regions in overseas territories of France. In total there are 18 regions and 101 departments.

[3] Note: "declared" here means an event that triggers the French CATNAT compensation scheme.

[4] Note: the process of elaborating the Rhône flood risk management plan called PGRI (mandated by the central level and based on the EU flood directive) prescribes the identification of high risk areas (HRAs), based on a preliminary flood risk assessment (called EPRI)

[5] www.planrhone.fr

[6] Since the territorial reform implemented in January 2016, the regions are part of Auvergne-Rhône-Alpes, Provence-Alpes-Côte d'Azur and Occitanie.

[7] http://www.developpement-durable.gouv.fr/Les-plans-de-gestion-des-risques-d,40052.html

[8] www.prim.net is a portal that informs about the prevention of major risks; www.georisques.gouv.fr is a portal that provides dynamic risk maps.

[9] The Alpine Convention is an international treaty between Alpine countries (Austria, France, Germany, Italy, Liechtenstein, Monaco, Slovenia and Switzerland) as well as the EU, aimed at promoting sustainable development in the Alpine area and at protecting the interests of the people living within it. It embraces an integrated approach, including environmental, social, economic and cultural dimensions in developing the Alpine area's future (http://www.alpconv.org/en/convention/default.html).

[10] After the damages caused by the storm Xynthia an additional funding and project decision mechanism has been established particularly for coastal flooding, called the PSR. Structural measures providing protection against coastal flooding are thereby prioritised and put under particular technical scrutiny.

[11] Multi Criteria Analysis allows comparing different scenarios, including the status quo, integrating monetary and non-monetary values incorporating environmental, cultural heritage and social criteria along economic ones.

[12] It is envisaged that the state no longer owns any dikes by 2024.

[13] GEMAPI was supposed come into full force in January 2016 but it seems it will require two more years for the EPCIs to prepare themselves for such responsibilities.

[14] www.france-digues.fr/sirs-digues/

[15] www.georisques.gouv.fr; http://carmen.naturefrance.fr; http://carmen.developpement-durable.gouv.fr/index.php?map=risques_naturels.map&service_idx=8W; http://cartelie.application.developpement-durable.gouv.fr/cartelie/voir.do?carte=cartelie_ADS&service=DDT_72

[16] www.rhone-mediterranee.eaufrance.fr/gestion/inondations/artes.php#carto

[17] www.lemonde.fr/planete/article/2014/12/12/xynthia-l-ancien-maire-de-la-faute-sur-mer-condamne-a-quatre-ans-de-prison-ferme_4539436_3244.html

Bibliography

Bravard, J.-P. and Clémens, A. (2008), "Le Rhône en 100 questions" [The Rhône in 100 Questions], in Revue géographique des pays méditerranéens/Journal of Mediterranean geography, No. 118. ZABR, GRAIE, Villeurbanne, pp. 295. http://mediterranee.revues.org/6386.

Compagnie Nationale du Rhône (2013), "Rapport d'activités 2013" [Activity Review 2013], Lyon.

Cour des Comptes (2014), "Les finances publiques locales" [Local public finances], www.ccomptes.fr/Publications/Publications/Les-finances-publiques-locales2.

DIREN Rhône-Alpes (2009), "Monographie de la crue du Rhône de décembre 2003" [Monograph of the December 2003 Rhône Flood], Direction Régionale de l'Environnement Rhône-Alpes, French Ministry of Ecology, Energy, Sustainable Development and Spatial Planning, France.

Douvinet, J., Defossez, S., Anselle, A., & Denolle, A. S. (2011), "Les maires face aux plans de prévention du risque inundation" [Mayors and Flood Risk Prevention Plans], L'Espace géographique 1/2011 (Tome 40), pp. 31-46, www.cairn.info/revue-espace-geographique-2011-1-page-31.htm.

DREAL Rhône-Alpes (2014), "Plan de Gestion des Risques d'Inondation 2016-2021, Bassin Rhône-Méditerranée" [Flood Risk Management Plan 2016-2021, Rhône-Méditerranée Basin], Volume 1: Parties communes au Bassin Rhône-Méditerranée, Project submitted for public consultation, www.rhone-mediterranee.eaufrance.fr/docs/dir-inondations/pgri/plaquettePGRI.pdf.

DREAL Rhône-Alpes (2013a). Perception des Risques d'Inondation par les Riverains du Rhône de la Frontiére Suisse à la Mer [Flood risk perception by residents of the Rhône and the frontier from Switzerland to the sea], www.planrhone.fr/content/download/1431/10992/file/DREAL_Sondage2013_plaquette_BD.pdf.

DREAL Rhône-Méditerranée, (2013b). "Mise en oeuvre de la Directive Inondations sur le bassin Rhône-Méditerranée. Bilan d'avancement du dispositive PAPI-PSR sure le basin." [Implementation of the Flood Directive in the Rhône-Méditerranée basin], Comité Inondation de Bassin, 6 décembre 2013, www.rhone-mediterranee.eaufrance.fr/gestion/inondations/reunions/cib.php.

DREAL Rhônes-Alpes (2010), "Accompagnement du volet inondations 2007-2013" [Monitoring floods between 2007 and 2013], www.rhone-alpes.developpement-durable.gouv.fr/IMG/pdf/_AP_Valorisation_BDT-20-06-2010_cle749a5e.pdf.

DREAL Rhônes-Alpes (2011), "Évaluation préliminaire des risques d'inondation sur le bassin Rhône-Méditerranée" [Preliminary evaluations of flood risk in the Rhône-Méditerranée basin], www.rhone-mediterranee.eaufrance.fr/docs/dir-inondations/epri/14_Synthese_ConsutaltionPP.pdf.

European Union (2007), "Objectif compétitivité régionale et Emploi, Programme Opérationnel Plurirégional FEDER Plan Rhône, Accompagnement du volet inondations 2007-2013" [Regional competition objectives and European Regional Development Fund FEDER Plan Rhône, Monitoring floods between 2007 and 2013], http://feader.rhone-alpes.agriculture.gouv.fr/IMG/pdf/POI_Rhone_cle81b921.pdf.

European Union (2013?), "Objectif compétitivité régionale et Emploi, Programme Opérationnel Plurirégional FEDER Plan Rhône, 2007-2013" [Regional competition objectives and European Regional Development Fund FEDER] (modified version).

FFSA (2013). European Commission "Green Paper on the insurance of natural and man-made disasters": response by the French Federation of Insurance Companies (FFSA), Paris, France, http://ec.europa.eu/finance/insurance/consumer/natural-catastrophes/index_en.htm.

French Government (2010), "Programmes d'action de prévention des inondations (PAPI). De la strategie aux programmes d'action" [Flood Prevention Action Programs. From strategy to action programmes], Cahier des charges, French Ministry of Ecology, Energy and Sustainable Development, www.developpement-durable.gouv.fr/IMG/pdf/110215_PAPI_vdef.pdf.

French Government (2009), "Assurance des risques naturels en France: sous quelles conditions les assureurs peuvent-ils inciter à la prévention des catastrophes naturelles?" [Natural Disaster Risk Insurance in France: Under which conditions can insurers stimulate prevention measures against natural disasters?], French Ministry of Ecology, Energy, Sustainable Development and Spatial Planning, www.developpement-durable.gouv.fr/IMG/pdf/01-14.pdf.

French Government (2011), "Plan submersions rapides: submersions marines, crues soudaines et ruptures de digues" [Flash Flood Plans: Coastal flooding, flash floods and dike breaches], French Ministry of Ecology, Energy and Sustainable Development, www.developpement-durable.gouv.fr/IMG/pdf/Le_plan_submersion_rapide.pdf.

French Government (2013a), "La démarche française de la prévention des risques majeurs" [The French approach to the prevention of critical risks], French Ministry of Ecology, Energy and Sustainable Development, www.developpement-durable.gouv.fr/IMG/pdf/10010-1_Demarche-francaise-prevention-risques-majeurs_DEF_Web.pdf.

French Government (2013b), "Les dépenses publiques et les bénéfices de la prévention des risques naturels" [Public expenditure and the benefits of natural risk prevention], French Ministry of Ecology, Energy, Sustainable Development and

Spatial Planning, www.developpement-durable.gouv.fr/IMG/pdf/E_D94_depenses_publiques_et_benefices_PRN.pdf

French Government (2014a), "Note concernant l'État gestionnaire de digues dans le contexte nouveau de la GEMAPI (version 2)" [Note on the state of maintenance of dikes in the context of the new GEMAPI], French Ministry of Ecology, Energy and Sustainable Development, http://www.driee.ile-de-france.developpement-durable.gouv.fr/IMG/pdf/DGPR_Etat_gestionnaire_digues-2.pdf.

French Government (2014b), Présentations de Jean-Baptiste Butlen "Création de la compétence GEMAPI, implications et enjeux" [Presentation by Jean-Baptiste Butlen "Creation of GEMAPI: implications and challenges], French Ministry of Ecology, Energy and Sustainable Development, www.actus.rhone-mediterranee.eaufrance.fr/IMG/File/actus2014/1_JBButlen_DEB_MEDDE_seminaire_GEMAPI_11avril2014.pdf.

French Government (2015a), "Décret no 2015-526 du 12 mai 2015 relatif aux règles applicables aux ouvrages construits ou aménagés en vue de prévenir les inondations et aux règles de sûreté des ouvrages hydrauliques" [Decree no 2015-526 of May 12, 2015 relating to the applicable rules for infrastructure constructed or adapted for flood prevention and in line of the safety rules for hydraulic buildings], French Ministry of Ecology, Energy and Sustainable Development (2015), www.legifrance.gouv.fr/affichTexte.do?cidTexte=JORFTEXT000030591079&dateTexte=&categorieLien=id%20.

French Government (2015b), "Référentiel technique digues maritimes et fluviales" [Technical reference for maritime and river dikes], French Ministry of Ecology, Energy and Sustainable Development. www.barrages-cfbr.eu/IMG/pdf/referentiel_technique_digues_maritimes_et_fluviales.pdf

French Senate (2012), "Projet de loi de finances pour 2013 : Protection de l'environnement et prévention des risques" [2013 Finance law project : Environment Protection and Risk Prevention], www.senat.fr/rap/a12-153-2/a12-153-2.html.

Grislain-Letrémy, C., and Calvet, L. (2012). "L'assurance habitation dans les départements d'Outre-mer: une faible souscription" [Building insurance in overseas territories : A weak subscription], http://basepub.dauphine.fr/bitstream/handle/123456789/11676/ES447C.pdf?sequence=1.

OCDE (2014), "Seine Basin, Île-de-France, 2014: Resilience to Major Floods", OECD Publishing, Paris. DOI: http://dx.doi.org/10.1787/9789264208728-en.

OECD (2006), "Competitive Cities in the Global Economy", OECD Publishing, Paris. DOI: http://dx.doi.org/10.1787/9789264027091-en.

Société d'Ingénierie pour l'Eau et l'Environnement (SIEE) (2005), "Inondations du Rhône et de ses principaux affluents de décembre 2003 en aval de viviers dans les départements de la Drôme, de l'Ardèche, du Gard, du Vaucluse et des Bouches-du-Rhône" [Floods of the Rhône and her main tributary rivers in December 2003 in the downstream departments Drôme, Ardèche, Gard, Vaucluse and Bouches-du-Rhône], www.planrhone.fr/data/Files/Inondations/1_thematique/5_Savoir_mieux_vivre_avec_le_risque/2_Developper_la_connaissance_sur_le_fleuve/1_Crue_du_rhone_2003_inventaire_zones_et_dommages/rapport_de_presentation_dec2003.pdf.

Syndicat du Haut-Rhône (2015), "Étude historique et juridique sur les digues orphelines du Haut-Rhône", [Historic and legal study on orphaned dikes in upstream Rhône], www.planrhone.fr/data/Files/Inondations/2_entrees_territoriales/rhone_amont/15_01_07_livrable_final_SHR_modif_JPB_PK.pdf.

Chapter 4

Boosting resilience through innovative risk governance: the case of Switzerland

This chapter summarises the country case study findings of boosting resilience through innovative risk governance in Switzerland. After providing an overview of the various natural hazards and their relatively high socio-economic impact across Switzerland, the chapter showcases Switzerland's progress and good practices in disaster risk reduction. The chapter illustrates how Switzerland has developed a forward-looking approach to risk management that is firmly centred on the philosophy that successful risk management requires strong whole-of-society engagement and solid stakeholder coordination mechanisms. Despite the exemplary practices in ensuring multi-stakeholder participation in disaster risk management, the chapter found room to further increase risk awareness for current and future risks to enable continued shared risk financing and successful implementation of the well-developed regulations. Finally, the chapter puts forward recommendations to confront future disaster risk prevention challenges, such as maintaining the stock of protective infrastructure, while ensuring sufficient funding for new investments.

Summary

Due to its varied topography and climate Switzerland is exposed to a number of different hazards. Switzerland is surrounded by the Jura Mountains in the north and the Swiss Alps in the south, separated by the Swiss Plateau in the centre. Its climate varies from near Mediterranean to more temperate. As a result, Switzerland is exposed to a variety of gravitational, climate-related and tectonic hazards that differ in source and impacts depending on where the hazard occurs.

The socio-economic costs of disasters in Switzerland are high. Over the last 70 years, Switzerland's population and inhabited land have increased rapidly, resulting in 22% of its population along with 25% of material assets and about 30% of the country's jobs located in flood-prone areas. Damages from floods, landslides and rockfalls alone average some CHF 310 million annually, single hazardous events such as storm *Lothar* in 1999 and the floods of 2005 have caused damages in excess of CHF 2 billion and CHF 3 billion, respectively. Although earthquakes have a much lower occurrence probability, the damages from a major earthquake could cause damage much greater than that expected from the other hazards.

Key Findings

Switzerland has developed a strong whole-of-society approach to risk management. After a long history of exposure to various hazards, Switzerland has developed an exemplary model of risk management that defines and coordinates key roles for all levels of government, as well as public and private insurance companies, other private sector actors and citizens. Switzerland's approach is centred on the philosophy that the state's efforts are only effective if all other actors are contributing to risk management, both in terms of behaviour and investment. As a result, there has been a significant increase in the capacity to cooperate and coordinate strategies and policies across sectors.

Grounded in a long standing risk management tradition, Switzerland has developed a forward-looking, integrated risk management approach to protect citizens. Since 1848, constitutional laws have been developed to create the basis for public investment in infrastructure, including protective infrastructure. Having evolved from a reactive approach to managing risk that focused on measures ex post of disasters, Switzerland's current forward-looking principles of risk management prioritise soft measures that are nature-based over structural protections, as well as a culture of risk in society instead of a sole reliance of the government to manage risks. These principles employ an all-hazard approach to reduce vulnerabilities and ensure society is aware of, accepts and adapts to residual or remaining risks.

While structural measures are implemented by sub-national governments, they are financed in large part by federal contributions. Sustaining the level of financing necessary to continue to increase protection and maintain the large stock of existing protective infrastructure will be a challenge moving forward. Moreover, while the wide-spread use of hazard maps in land-use planning has effectively reduced damages in high-risk zones, more can be done to strengthen regulations in lower-risk areas.

Key recommendations

Strengthen the evidence base on the potential occurrence and costs of disasters

- Enhance understanding of the possible linkages and cascading effects of natural disasters and risks highlighted in the Swiss national risk assessment including pandemics, power outages or nuclear accidents.
- Establish a more systematic approach to disaster loss data collection, especially with regard to socioeconomic impacts, across all cantons, including those where the natural hazard insurance is not organised by public insurance companies.
- Expand the current natural hazards (WSL) database to also include data on the negative socio-economic impact of disasters stemming from metrological and earthquake hazards, and consider including data on indirect damages.

Continue to strengthen risk governance mechanisms across all involved levels

- Ensure that disaster risk management is tailored to the appropriate spatial area, which might require strengthening cross-jurisdictional disaster risk prevention actions and transboundary cooperation in risk management.
- Evaluate the activities of PLANAT and LAINAT more regularly and potentially consider to further opening up their governance structures.

Maintain an integrated, whole-of-society approach to the management of structural and non-structural measures

- Strengthen the maintenance of protective infrastructure, so to ensure the level of protection for which the existing infrastructure was conceived initially. Maintenance investments should ideally not come at the expense of future protective infrastructure needs.
- Efforts to build a central database on the level of maintenance of existing protective infrastructure could be accelerated to enable effective prioritisation of maintenance investments and inform budgeting for maintenance finance needs in the medium term.
- Continue closing the gaps in availability of local hazard and risk assessments to inform disaster risk prevention and mitigation measures needed for new construction projects and older buildings alike, ensuring their harmonisation across municipalities.
- Stronger focus of disaster risk prevention efforts especially in areas of lower hazard level, where more than half of the damages from disasters currently occur.
- Give more attention to seismic hazard assessments and building code enforcement, especially in terms of their potential trigger and cascading impacts. Although

comparatively rare to other hazards, earthquakes can potentially cause significant negative socio-economic impacts.

- Ensure that high levels of risk awareness are maintained and streamlined across hazards. An evaluation of the effectiveness of past and ongoing risk communication campaigns, including those managed by private sector actors such as insurance companies, could help ensure their efficiency in light of changing risk landscapes and channels of communication.
- Evaluate the actual take-up of disaster risk reduction measures across societal actors more systematically to inform future activities that aim at increasing and complementing whole-of-society contributions to disaster risk reduction.

Continue fostering a whole-of-society approach to risk financing

- Improve the picture of the flow of financial contributions by the different actors by centrally and regularly collecting funding information across cantons and different non-governmental actors to better target and prioritise spending and to avoid that expenditure by different actors are undermining each other.
- To meet future disaster risk prevention investment needs, it is important to engage in longer-term financial needs assessments and financial planning to avoid an increase in vulnerability to citizens and assets from the impacts of disasters.

Introduction

Geographically shaped by the Alps in the South and the Swiss Plateau and the Jura in the Northwest, Switzerland has a varied topography and climate. During the last 70 years, Switzerland's population has nearly doubled and increasingly expanded into risk-prone areas. The rise in population was accompanied by an expansion of both industrial and residential areas, about a quarter of which are today located in flood-prone areas. Alongside floods, which account for the biggest part (36%) of damages (covered by insurance companies) observed in the country, Switzerland faces a variety of different hazards, ranging from gravitational and meteorological hazards to tectonic hazards, including earthquakes.

Switzerland has pursued a forward-looking, whole-of-society approach to risk management anchored in a philosophy that the state's effort is only effective if all stakeholders are contributing their share. Due to a long history of solidarity in policy making, Switzerland has an effective system of cooperation and shares the management of risks between all levels of government. The federal government is in charge of guidance and policy setting while local governments lead efforts in providing safety and implementing disaster risk reduction projects, with cantons supporting local levels by providing support and resources for implementation. Moreover, Switzerland includes an inclusive set of public and private actors in its risk governance structure. For example, as a result of a mandatory insurance mechanism, insurance companies play a key role in providing loss compensation, disaster risk prevention and loss mitigation while also placing the onus on citizens to participate in risk management through informing them of their responsibilities and enforcing this when administering pay-outs. Public and private actors are tied together by two coordination platforms that provide strategic and operational support.

This present case study report assesses the progress, achievements and potential challenges for Switzerland's disaster risk prevention system, with a particular emphasis on disaster risk prevention and mitigation, from a decision-making, implementation and financing perspective. The objective of this analysis is to highlight good practices as well as challenges Switzerland may face in fostering its whole-of-society approach to disaster risk prevention and mitigation, where the responsibility for disaster risk prevention and mitigation is shared between both government and non-governmental actors.

This study builds on previous work of the OECD (2014a) that sought to identify effective ways for OECD countries to boost their resilience against extreme disaster events, which informed the OECD Recommendations on the Governance of Critical Risks (OECD, 2014b). In a cross-country comparative study, of which this case study is one selected country, the OECD assessed and compared disaster risk prevention and mitigation systems across a set of OECD countries, based on the framework and recommendations previously developed. The objective of the study was to identify good practices and challenges across case study countries as they attempt to achieve greater resilience through a whole-of-society approach to disaster risk prevention and mitigation. The case study of Switzerland informs the comparative analysis and allows lessons to be shared widely to inform OECD countries' disaster risk prevention policies and practices.

This study analyses whether the institutional roles, responsibilities, financial setup and incentives of Switzerland's core disaster risk prevention institutions and actors are aligned so that each actor's expected contribution to a whole-of-society approach to disaster risk prevention is carried out adequately. Section II provides an overview of Switzerland's hazard landscape and its socio-economic relevance. It includes an assessment of recent significant disasters and the overall trend in socio-economic losses from disasters in Switzerland. Section III provides an overview of the risk governance structure guiding Switzerland's disaster risk prevention and mitigation efforts. Section IV and V assess the management of structural and non-structural disaster risk prevention and mitigation measures as well as current financial frameworks that contribute to fostering a whole-of-society approach to risk management. Section VI provides a final assessment and recommendations.

Switzerland's hazard sources and risk exposure

Section Highlights

- Switzerland is exposed to a range of natural hazards, from Alpine hazards such as avalanches, debris flows, landslides and rock falls to large river floods, storms, earthquakes and heatwaves. Switzerland's population and inhabited land have increased rapidly in the past 50 years resulting in 20% of its population living in flood-prone areas, along with about 30% of the country's jobs and 25% of assets worth an estimated CHF 840 billion.
- Damages from flood, landslides and rock falls alone average some CHF 310 million annually. Highly destructive events such as storm Lothar in 1999 and the floods in 2005 significantly drive damages, respectively causing a total of CHF 2 billion and CHF 3 billion.
- Although earthquakes occur much less frequently, they would be the source of the greatest expected amount of negative socio-economic impacts. A comparable event to the 1356 Basel region earthquake is estimated to cause some CHF 50 to CHF 100 billion in damages today.
- Switzerland gathers information on socio-economic losses in a central database and has embraced a forward-looking, multi-hazard approach to risk management
- Switzerland shows exceptional awareness for future expected changes that could alter natural disaster profiles, which includes climatic changes but also changes in underlying risk factors, such as patterns in socio-economic development and society's risk culture.

Hazard sources

Switzerland is a landlocked country, geographically divided between the high-altitude Alps in the central-south, the Prealps and the relatively flat Swiss Plateau between Lake Geneva and Lake Constance in the northern half and the hilly Jura Mountains in the northwest. Most of its 8 million inhabitants live in the northern half of the country (Figure 4.1). The Swiss Alps range from low to relatively high, and include a large number of mountain peaks that reach beyond 4,000m above sea level. Switzerland's extensive glaciers feed several major European rivers, such as the Rhine, Inn, Ticino and Rhône. Switzerland's Lake Geneva, Lake Constance and Lake Maggiore are some of

Europe's biggest fresh water reservoirs. Its climate is equally varied, from near Mediterranean in the south to more temperate in the rest of the country.

Figure 4.1 Switzerland's topography

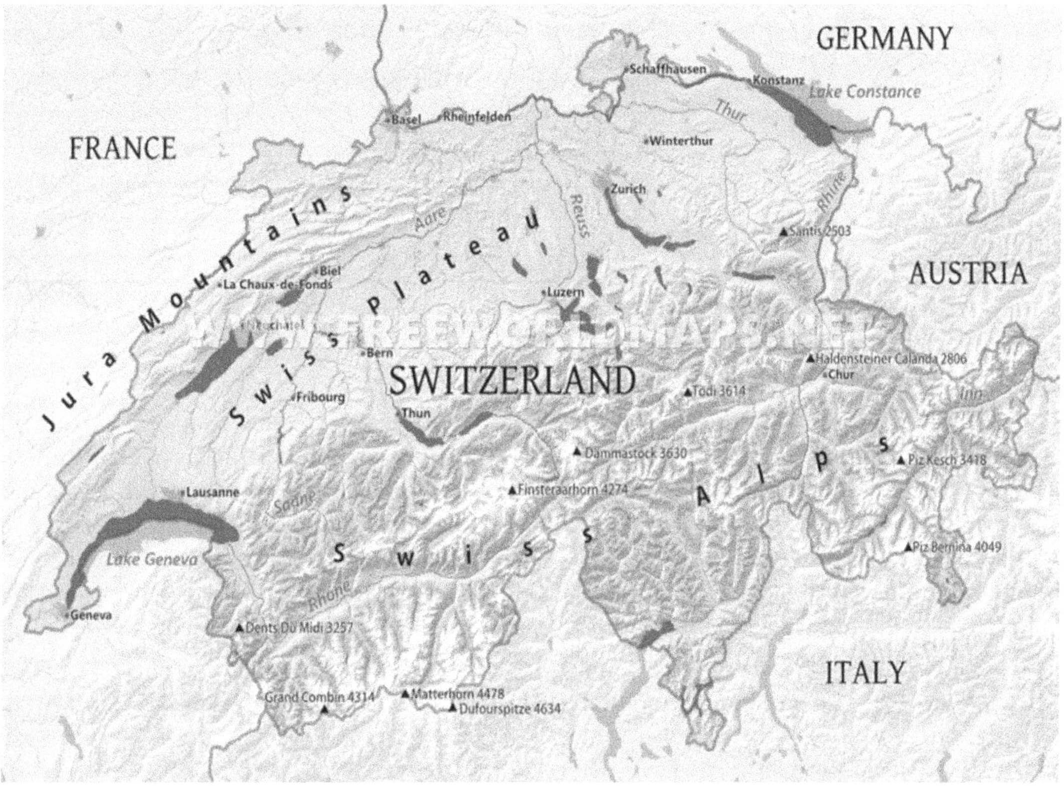

Source: http://www.freeworldmaps.net/europe/switzerland/switzerland-physical-map.jpg

Its distinct topography and regional climatic variations make Switzerland exposed to a number of different hazards, including gravitational and water-related, climate-related, and tectonic hazards (Table 4.1). Hazards related to volcanoes, meteoroids or space weather occur very rarely and are thus not considered prevalent natural hazards in Switzerland.

Switzerland's mountain ranges provide a meteorological divide that impedes natural hazards from spreading across the entire country. This diminishes the likelihood of experiencing a major loss event that affects all of Switzerland.

Switzerland's topography also affects the same source of hazard differently. Floods form from a number of possible causes, including brief heavy bursts of precipitation, long-lasting rainfall, drastic snow melt, or a combination of these processes. In regions with steep hills, the subsequent flood forms primarily as a body of flowing water, which creates mud and debris flows as well as overbank sedimentation. Conversely, ensuing lowland flooding causes rivers, lake and groundwater discharge, which produces damaging large-area flooding, localised flooding, bank erosion or concentrated water run-off.

Table 4.1 Types of natural hazards prevalent in Switzerland

Natural hazard category	Types of natural hazards
Gravitational hazards	• Different types of snow and ice avalanches • Water-related hazards: floods, bank erosions, debris flows, surface water, etc. • Mass movements: rock falls, landslides, permanent or spontaneous slides, etc.
Climate-related and meteorological hazards	• Extreme temperatures (e.g. heatwaves) • Storms, extreme precipitation, hail, freezing rain, snow storms, lightning strikes, wild fires, etc.
Tectonic hazards	• Earthquakes, induced landslides or rock falls, etc.

Source: FOEN (2016b)

Disaster risk exposure

Switzerland has undergone tremendous socio-demographic changes in recent decades. Its total population increased from 4.5 million people in 1946 to over 8 million in 2016. To accommodate this population increase, housing and transport infrastructure grew significantly over the past half-century. Between 1985 and 2009 the built-up area in Switzerland increased by 23.4%. This is not only due to the absolute increase in population numbers, but also due to the increased average share of land that is used by people. To gain land for settlement purposes, agricultural land was given up.

Figure 4.2 Shares of population that live in flood-prone areas across Switzerland

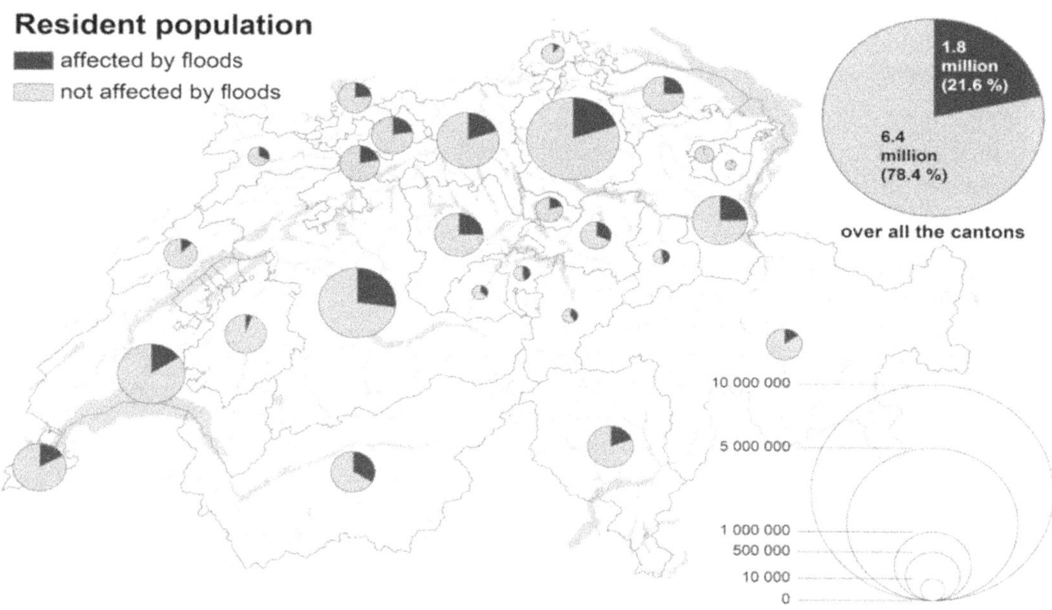

Source: FOEN (2016c) based on Aquaprotect flood zones and population data from the Swiss National Statistical Office

As a consequence, damage potential has increased continuously. Figure 4.2 indicates that around 22% of the Swiss population currently lives in flood-prone areas. Around 25% of material assets are located in flood risk areas, which have an estimated economic value of CHF 840 billion[1]. With about 30% of Switzerland's jobs also located in areas prone to flood risk, a significant part of the country's economic value creation takes place in areas at risk from flooding.

Similar to the increased expansion of land for settlement purposes, the assets that were created have increased Switzerland's exposure to natural hazards significantly. Figure 4.3 shows that the number of insured buildings has increased continuously since 1950. However, their value has grown even more rapidly, which is due to more expensive building materials being used in construction as well as due to the augmentation in the value of the contents of houses and other types of buildings (FOEN, 2016b).

Figure 4.3 Number and insurance value of buildings covered by Public Insurance Companies for Buildings 1950-2014

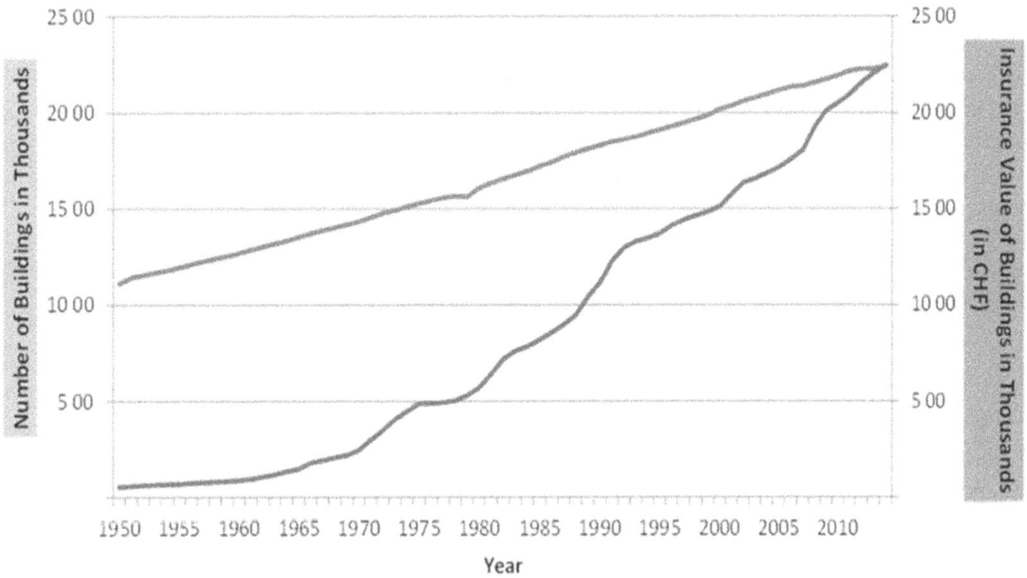

Source: IRV (2016)

Socio-economic impacts of past disasters

Calculating and recording the socio-economic impacts of disasters is useful in many ways. It tracks trends in social and economic losses over time, informing risk managers whether their risk management policies have been effective in reducing risks and decreasing losses over time. It can also support the prioritisation of disaster risk reduction investments by indicating the areas that are most vulnerable to disaster events.

Economic losses can be distinguished by direct and indirect economic losses. Direct economic losses reflect the monetary value of total or partial destruction of physical assets in the affected area. Indirect economic losses reflect the declines in value added as a consequence of direct economic loss and/or human and environmental impacts (UNISDR, 2015).

For certain disasters, the number of fatalities by disaster event has been collected as early as 1812 (Badoux et al., 2016). Systematic recording that includes economic loss accounting did however not start until the 1970's. In 1972 the Federal Institute for Forest, Snow and Landscape Research (WSL) was charged by the Federal Office for the Environment (FOEN) with the task of systematically recording both social and economic disaster losses in a central database. Since 1999, the FOEN has financially supported the WSL to maintain the database[2]. Starting out by systematically collecting data on storm damage in Switzerland since 1972, the WSL now takes damage caused by floods, debris flows, landslides as well as (since 2002) rock falls into account. Damage resulting from other hazards, such as avalanches, snow pressure, earthquake, lightening, hail, windstorm and drought are however not noted in the database. The recording is based on newspaper articles for smaller events and official data from cantons and insurance companies for larger events. Damage records are relatively complete for the hazards listed above, particularly in regards to recorded insurance claims, facilitated by the mandatory natural hazard insurance for buildings and content. In 19 of Switzerland's 26 cantons, public insurance companies keep detailed records of insurance claims of past disaster events. While the records kept are useful and rather comprehensive, they do not come without uncertainties. The information needed to update the database is not always available or complete, as not all damage-causing events are included and as the quality of reporting may differ from event to event. This is particularly relevant when analysing smaller events, whereas major events that dominate yearly losses are rather well accounted for.

Figure 4.4 Damages from floods, debris flows, landslides and rock falls (1973-2015), adjusted for inflation, based on 2015 prices

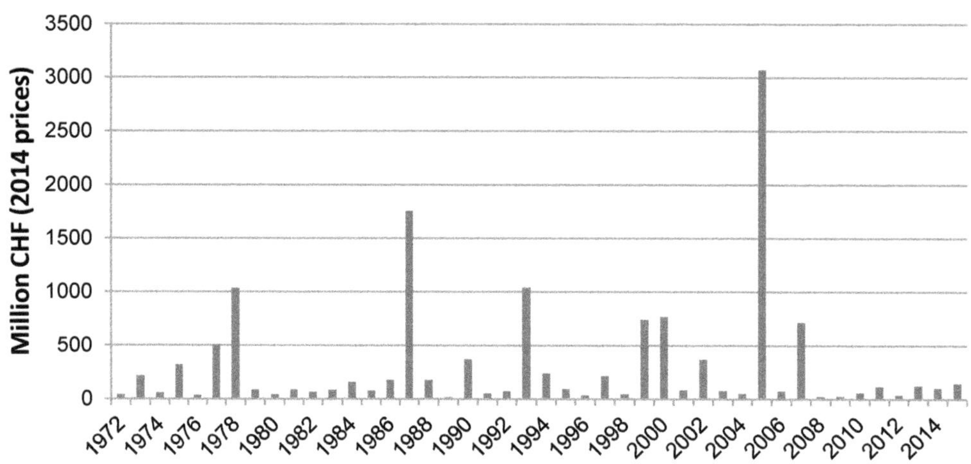

Source: FOEN (2016c), www.bafu.admin.ch/umwelt/indikatoren/08596/08599/index.html?lang=de

In terms of economic losses, a total of nearly CHF 14 billion in economic losses were caused by floods, debris flows, landslides and rock falls in Switzerland between 1972 and 2015. This corresponds to an annual average damage of about CHF 310 million. About half of that was caused by 5 major loss events (Figure 4.4). The floods in August 2005 caused CHF 3 billion in damages alone. They were a result of several days of heavy precipitation in the north side of the Alps causing debris flows, landslides, bank erosions, and large areas of flooding of the low lying valley areas.

Figure 4.5 demonstrates that 36% of damages (those covered by insurance companies) were caused by flood, followed by hail (31%) and storms (27.5%). Direct damages from avalanches, snow, landslides and rock falls have been relatively small, with only about 5.5% of total recorded damages.

Figure 4.5 Average share of damages covered by public insurance companies for buildings, by hazard 1995-2014

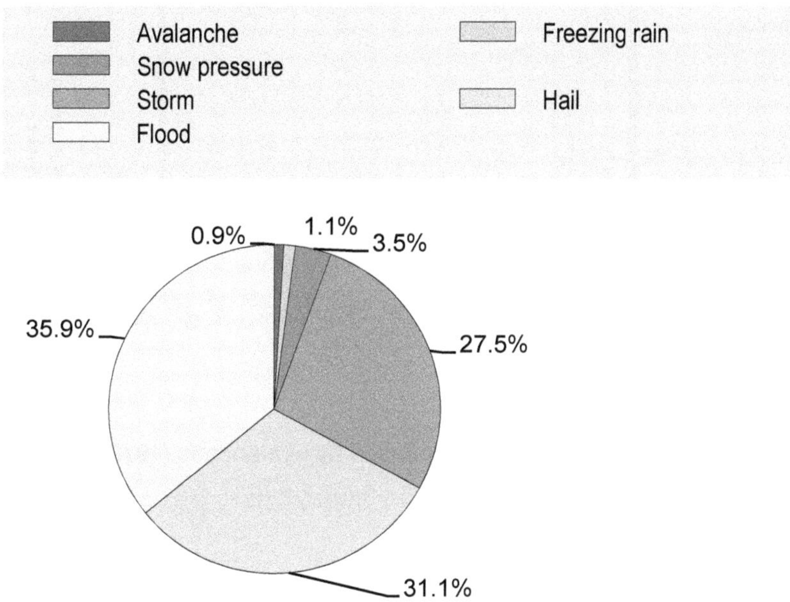

Source: IRV (2010); only based on losses to buildings

Hailstorms, especially in the northern foothills of the Alps and in southern Ticino, can cause considerable damage, such as in the summer of 2009 when hailstorms caused CHF 314 million in direct damage (IRV, 2012a).

In terms of fatalities, heatwaves have caused the highest such number in the recent past. The 2003 heatwave caused nearly 1,000 deaths and most recently, during the summer in 2015, 800 people lost their lives due to extreme heat (BAFU, 2016). Other hazards have caused considerably less, and continuously less, fatalities in the recent past. Floods have caused 52 fatalities between 1972 and 2015, debris flows 21 and landslides 40. Rock falls have caused 16 deaths since recording started in 2002 (Figure 4.6). Fatalities from floods have shown a decreasing trend since the 19th century. Avalanches cause an average of 25 fatalities annually, whereby the large majority is due to recreational activities off the secured slopes (Figure 4.7). For avalanches, the WSL has systematically recorded fatalities since 1936/37 as mandated by the Federal Office for the Environment (FOEN), whereas recording for fatalities from other hazards dates only goes back to the 1970's. Avalanche fatalities are recorded directly by the institute's staff on the basis of the hydrological year (October until September).

Figure 4.6 Fatalities caused by floods, debris flows, landslides and rock falls (1815-2015)

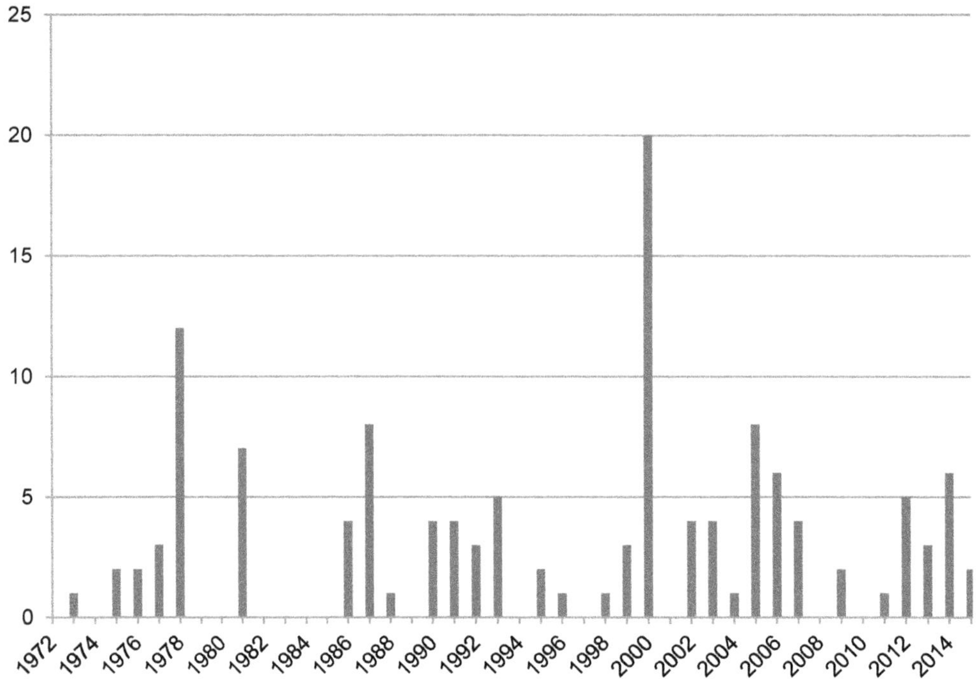

Source: FOEN (2016b)

Figure 4.7 Fatalities caused by avalanches (1972/73 – 2013/14)

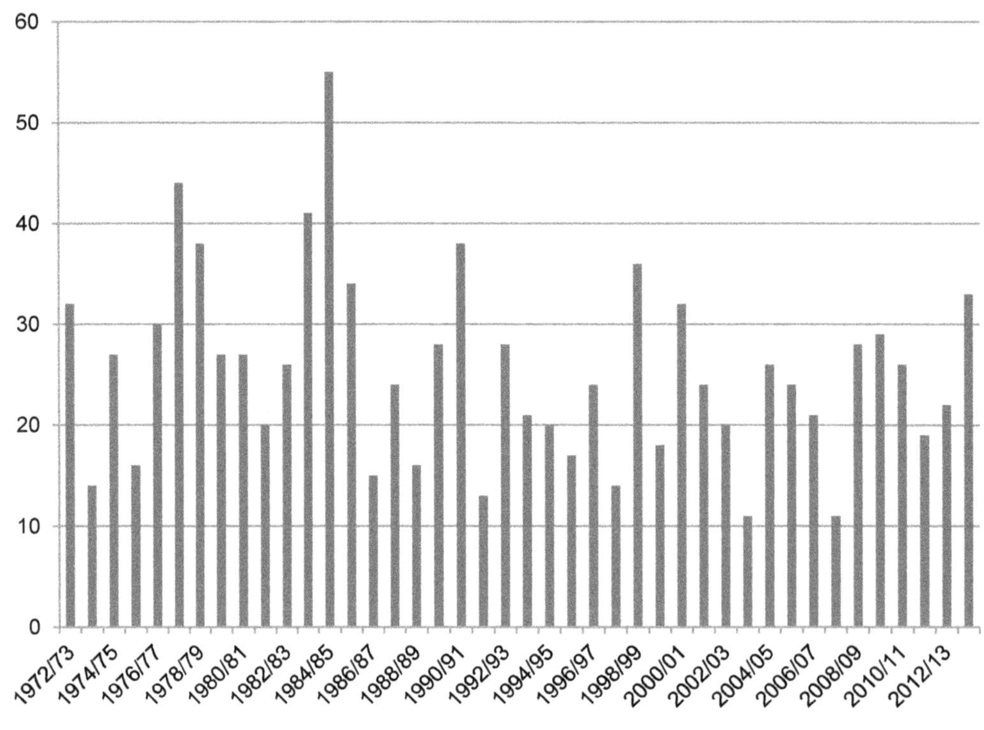

Source: FOEN (2016b)

Major earthquakes have occurred rarely in Switzerland's history, but they could cause a large amount of damage and have caused comparatively high fatality rates in the past. The 1365 earthquake in the Basel region is for example reported to have caused up to 1,500 deaths, though sources vary significantly. Later earthquakes, such as the Unterwalden quake in 1601 and the Stalden-Visp quake in 1855 are reported to have caused major damages (PLANAT, 2004b; SSV, 2010). A comparable earthquake of the Basel region quake in 1356 would for example result in damage of CHF 50 to CHF 100 billion today (SED, 2016). A comparable event in Unterwalden or Visp is estimated to cost up to CHF 21 billion if it occurred today (SSV, 2010). Figure 4.8 shows the regions with the highest earthquake hazard are the Valais, the Basel area and the Canton of Grisons. Large earthquakes could, however, occur anywhere in Switzerland.

Figure 4.8 Earthquakes in and nearby Switzerland.

Shown are the 10 largest events of the last millennium (dark circles, with location and year) as well as all events with magnitude 2 and above between 1975 and 2016 (light circles).

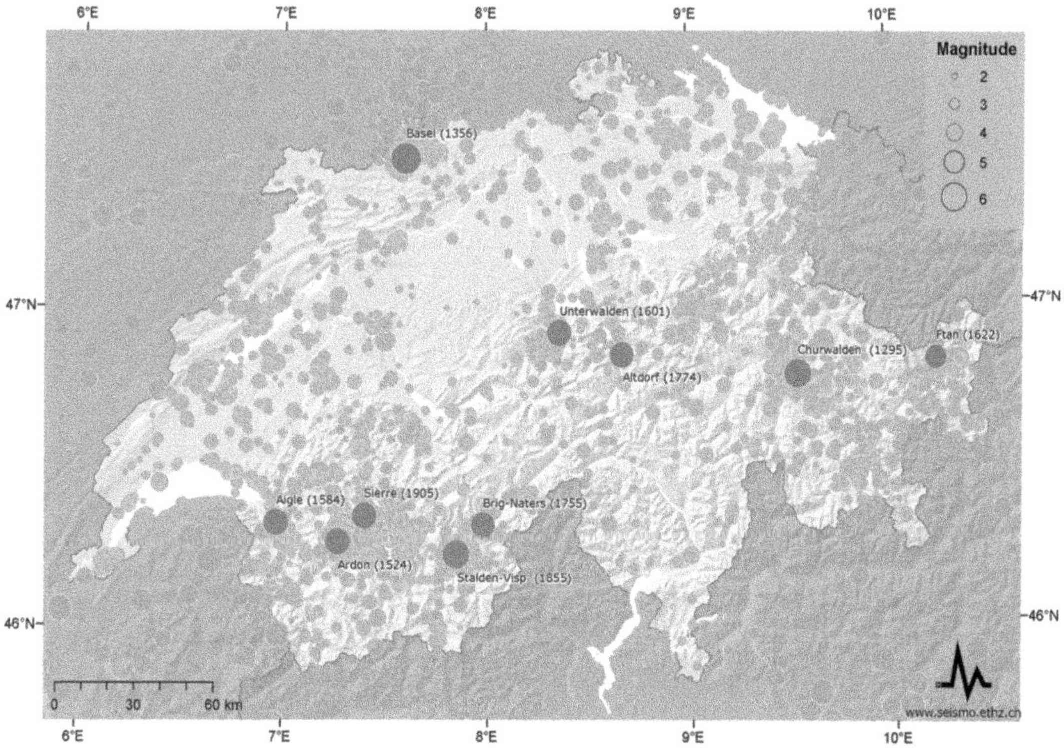

Source: SED (2017), http://www.seismo.ethz.ch/en/knowledge/earthquake-country-switzerland/historical-earthquakes/the-ten-strongest/

Switzerland shows exceptional awareness about the importance of future changes to the exposure to natural hazards. In all its strategies and evaluation of its current systems, the importance of future changes in risk patterns is noted. The natural hazard management strategy elaborated by PLANAT (PLANAT, 2004a) highlights factors that may change future risk exposure, such as mobility, the size of population (Figure 4.9) and settlement areas as well as the increasing value of housing assets. It further highlights the vulnerability arising through inter-connected economies that rely on communication channels. Furthermore, climatic and weather changes are highlighted along with changes in the socio-political sphere. The latter could include changes in the ways through which society deals with risks, based on underlying values, risk perception and readiness to take risks.

Climatic change has increasingly become a focus area. Higher average temperatures and higher glacier melting rates have increased the awareness of climatic change in Swiss society and politics, illustrated for example by the creation of dedicated research bodies, such as the forum for climate and global change (ProClim)[3] (FOEN, 2012a; FOEN, 2016a). The inclusion of climate change aspects in natural hazard modelling has emphasised the importance of planning and preparing for extreme events, as well as climate change as a source of identifying potentially new hazards (FOEN, 2016).

Figure 4.9 Switzerland population projections 2015-2045 (in millions inhabitants)

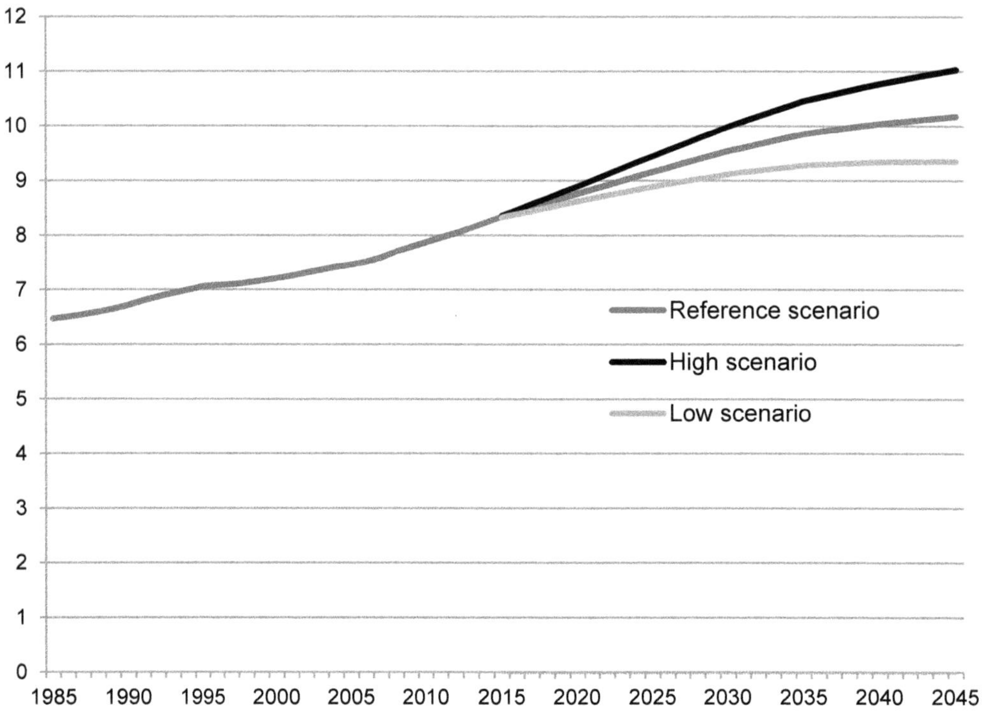

Source: Federal Statistical Office (2016):
http://www.bfs.admin.ch/bfs/portal/de/index/themen/01/03/blank/key/ent_erw.html

In a broader context, natural disasters have to be put in perspective with other risks that the Swiss national risk assessment has highlighted including pandemics, power outages or nuclear accidents (FCOP, 2015). Figure 4.10 shows that other, man-made disasters such as pandemics, power outages or nuclear accidents could cause damages between CHF 100 to 1 000 billion, albeit a much rarer expected return period of 1 500 – 30 000 years.

Figure 4.10 Estimated frequency and damage of major disasters in Switzerland

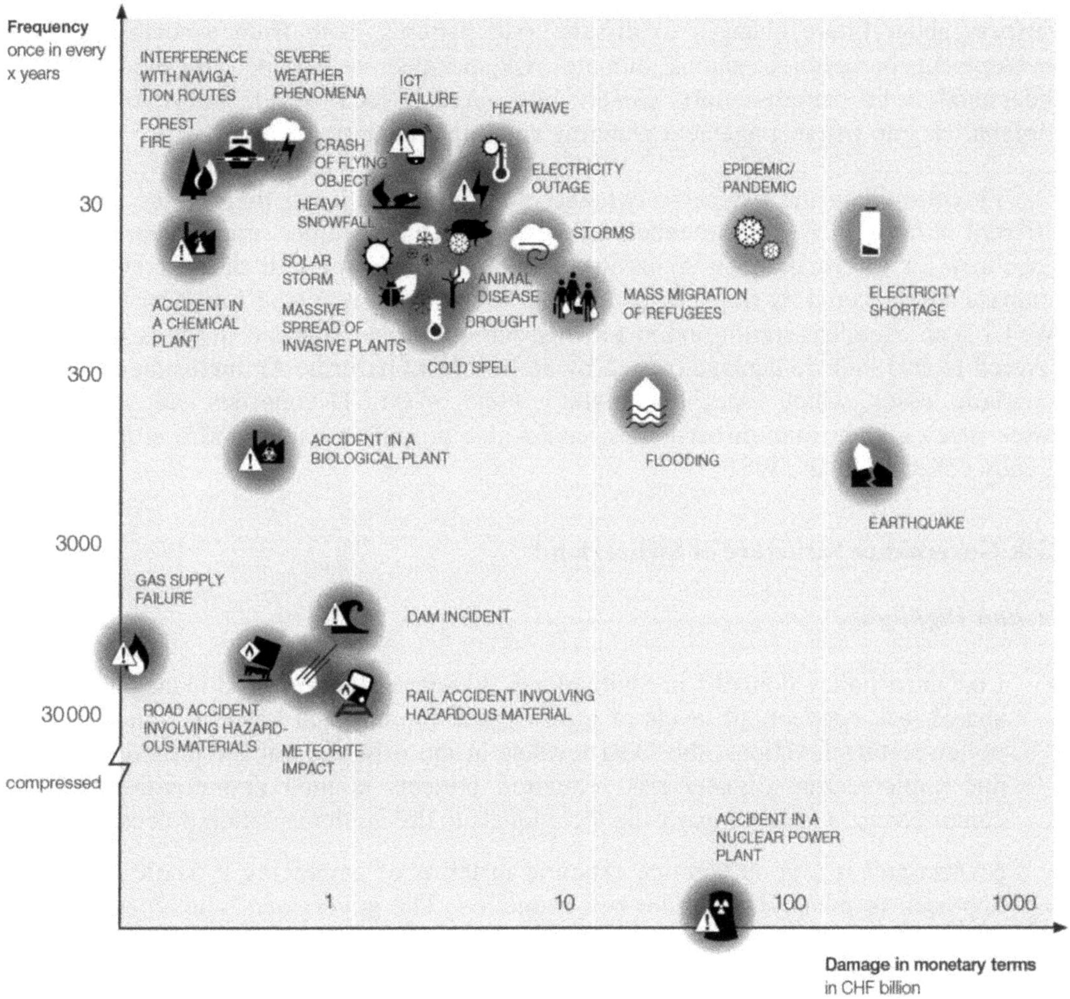

Source: FOCP (2015a), http://www.preventionweb.net/files/submissions/47467_katastrophenundnotlagenschweizreport2015.pdf

Conclusion

Switzerland has taken a forward-looking approach to managing the risks it faces and increasingly puts natural disasters in perspective with other risks and has a high level of awareness and alertness about future changes to disaster risk patterns. Switzerland has also achieved a remarkable level in terms of comprehensiveness and quality in recording disaster events, including their social and economic impacts. Whereas some records, especially for smaller disaster events, rely on newspaper articles, larger event records are based on rigorous disaster evaluations. The most systematic records in terms of economic impact data rely on information gathered through compensation payments to individuals and businesses by public insurance companies for buildings in the event of a disaster. This information has been provided consistently and therefore allows for a relatively good understanding of trends in disaster impacts over time, even though for the time being the duration of records may not yet be long enough to confirm trends. Even though earthquakes occur much less frequently, Switzerland has made an effort to estimate its past economic impacts, which may be used to create future projections of their potential negative socio-economic impact. There seems to be a high level of awareness and alertness about future changes to disaster risk patterns, both from a socio-economic development perspective and a climate risk perspective. Works are underway to understand both patterns more closely and, at the local level, integrate potential implications into risk management planning and implementation.

To consolidate the extensive evidence that is available on the losses caused by different hazards, it is recommended to collect data in a single, multi-hazard national repository for information on social and economic losses of past disaster events. The database administered by the Federal Institute for Forest, Snow and Landscape Research (WSL) is an excellent starting point for this, but could be expanded in terms of hazards covered to also include damage caused by metrological hazards. An inclusion of indirect economic losses, which especially in the context of OECD countries can account for losses much greater than direct losses, could also provide a useful addition to the data already collected by the WSL.

Risk Governance Structure of Switzerland

Section Highlights

- Like most policy domains in Switzerland, disaster risk prevention management is a shared task between all levels of government: the national level has guidance and policy setting functions, the local level is in the drivers' seat for providing safety and implementing disaster risk reduction projects in their communities and the cantos ensure and accompany the local levels in the implementation process.
- Switzerland is a good practice example in terms of embracing a whole-of-society approach to managing disaster risk reduction. The government's interventions are deemed effective only if private actors contribute their share to reducing risks through risk-adapted behaviour and individual disaster risk reduction investments. Insurance companies play a key role in translating, informing and communicating about the expected roles of private sector actors and individuals.
- The Swiss direct democratic governance tradition has positively influenced disaster risk management, emphasising awareness raising and building acceptance for disaster risk reduction investments from the bottom up. Lengthy consultation processes have - more often than not - resulted in more efficient and effective disaster risk reduction investments.
- Multi-stakeholder platforms like PLANAT or LAINAT have provided an effective and inclusive approach to bring actors in disaster risk management together to coordinate their actions. To further ensure their relevance and effectiveness, a regular and independent evaluation could be carried out considering, for example, whether their governance structures (in the case of PLANAT) could be opened up to include civil society stakeholders.
- The large and diverse number of research institutions working on natural disasters (including WSL, ETH, University of Bern, etc.) has contributed to the high quality of disaster risk management practice in Switzerland.

Switzerland is a federal, direct democratic country that has four dominant languages: French in the Western part of the country, German in its centre, Italian in its south and Rhaeto-Romanic in the East. There are three layers of government: national, cantonal (*Kanton*) and local (*Gemeinde*). There are 20 cantons and six half cantons (and 2 324 municipalities) with their own constitution and parliament, judiciary and executive powers (Figure 4.11). The cantons therefore have strong powers compared to sub-national levels in other federally-organised countries. As a consequence, the role of municipalities can differ across cantons, depending on the power that is granted to them by the cantons.

Responsibilities for disaster risk management are equally shared across levels of government. The local municipalities are the first in line, responsible for protecting against hazards that threaten the security of its population. The national government supports this process by providing policy guidance and recommendations, but also by co-financing protective infrastructure investments. The cantonal governments ensure that national level guidance is implemented at the local level and provide support and resources for the implementation process. Solidarity has been viewed as a cornerstone to successful disaster risk prevention management as costs of disasters and disaster risk interventions are unequally distributed across Switzerland.

Figure 4.11 Map of the 26 cantons of Switzerland

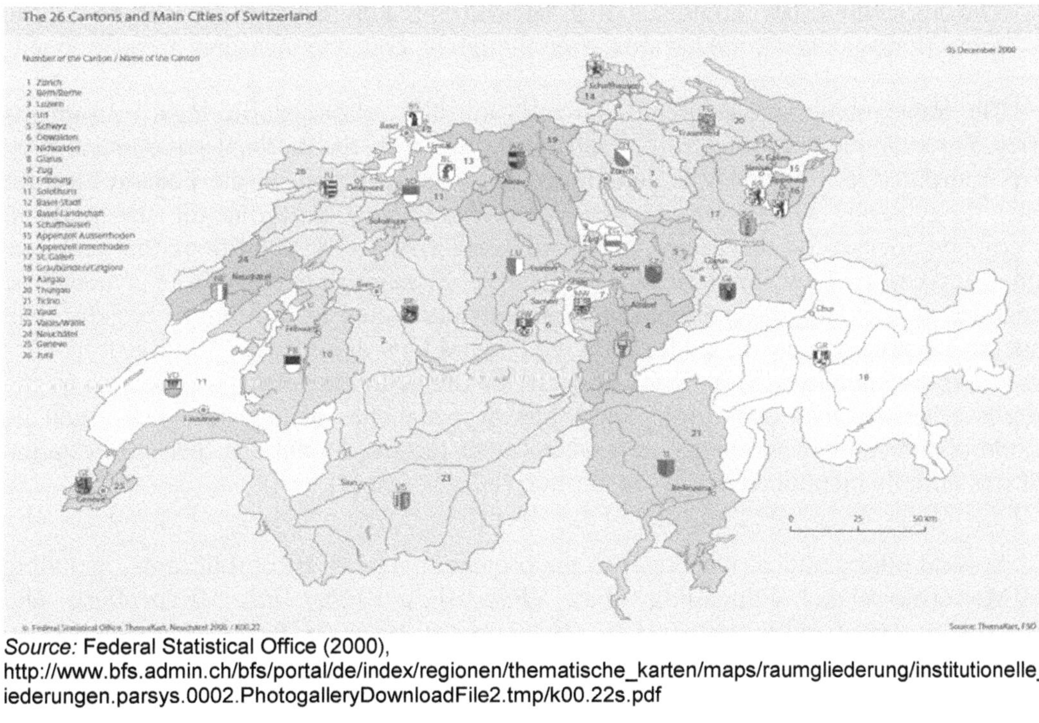

Source: Federal Statistical Office (2000), http://www.bfs.admin.ch/bfs/portal/de/index/regionen/thematische_karten/maps/raumgliederung/institutionelle_gliederungen.parsys.0002.PhotogalleryDownloadFile2.tmp/k00.22s.pdf

In the following sections, the main legal framework instruments as well as the key actors in disaster risk prevention management will be outlined so as to provide an overview of the governance set-up in Switzerland. This understanding is essential for evaluating the effectiveness and efficiency of the different risk management functions in a subsequent step. The following overview will first present the different legal frameworks that guide the government's role and responsibilities in disaster risk management before the different actors and their respective responsibilities are discussed.

Legal instruments

The Swiss national constitution was last revised in 1999. It increased the role of the cantons in public policy making and implementation in general. The national government is thereby obliged to give significant freedom to cantons to decide the way they implement national policies. The management of some natural hazards and related instruments is anchored in the national constitution:

- Water-related hazards: the constitution highlights that the national government has the responsibility to protect people and their assets from water-related hazards.
- Avalanches, landslides or rock falls, but also storm and fire hazards: the constitution can be used as a basis for determining national responsibilities as well, but more indirectly. It obliges the national government to preserve the protective and economic functions of the forests. The constitution thereby only relates this risk management function to maintaining and protecting the forest through afforestation (FOEN, 2011).
- Earthquakes and hail: There are no national responsibilities anchored in the constitution.
- The agriculture law stipulates that agricultural activities can contribute to the protection against natural hazards, even though no concrete measures are mentioned.

The translation of the constitutional rules into the sector-specific legal instruments varies. For example, with regard to water-related hazards, the national government only partly translated its role that was determined in the constitution. In the Federal Law for Water Engineering (*Bundesgesetz über den Wasserbau*) the role for the national government focuses on the determination of some framework conditions that stipulate fundamental rules only. With regard to its role in managing risks from avalanches, landslides or rockfalls, the national government interpreted its role more broadly than what the constitution determines for it. In the Federal Law of Forestry (*Bundesgesetz über den Wald*) the national government can prescribe protection measures in areas where the hazards originate, such as the incipient crack of avalanches or landsides that might lie outside of forest areas and hence necessitate other technical solutions than afforestation that was initially mentioned in the constitution (FOEN, 2016a).

Several other national laws refer to the protection against natural hazards, including the Meteorology and Climatology Law (*Bundesgesetz über die Meteorologie und Klimatologie*), the Civil Protection Law (*Bundesgesetz über den Bevölkerungsschutz und den Zivilschutz*), the water protection act, the nature and patrimony law, the cantonal spatial planning laws, the early warning directive, the emergency management directive, the railway and national roads laws, or the insurance laws. In addition there are cantonal legislations and directives.

Who are the responsible actors

Switzerland is a role model in terms of having developed a whole-of-society approach to disaster risk prevention management. Key roles for disaster risk prevention management are shared by the different government levels, but also by insurance companies, private sector actors and citizens. Switzerland's approach is anchored in the idea that the state's efforts are only effective if all other actors are contributing their share to disaster risk prevention management, both in terms of risk-adapted behaviour, but also in terms of investments in individual self-protection measures. The insurance companies play a key role in translating, informing, and communicating about these expectations to private sector actors and individuals, as well as providing technical and financial support for such investments. Private sector companies play a major role in hazard and risk assessments, in the development of protection schemes and in monitoring and early warning processes. The Natural Hazard Experts Switzerland *(Fachleute Naturgefahren Schweiz*, FAN)[4] is an important association with approximately 450 members from the hazard and disaster risk reduction business (Figure 4.12). Through the publication of reports and the organisation of expert meetings FAN contributes to further advancing Swiss disaster risk prevention efforts and the cooperation of stakeholders from various backgrounds.

Table 4.2 Responsible actors and their tasks in natural hazard management in Switzerland

National & cantonal governments	Municipalities	Insurance companies	Associations	Private sector & citizens
Legal frameworks	Land-use planning & building codes	Providing financial protection of potential damages	Provide the basis for building codes (such as architects or engineers associations)	Natural hazard-based constructions and object-specific protection measures
Public infrastructure, spatial planning and cantonal police	Construction of structural protection measures	Insurance services during disasters	Recommendations and advice	Personal and business preparedness (e.g. emergency plans)
Informing citizens	Safety, law & order	Prevention measures that reduce damage potential		Behaviour during a disaster
Emergency management: preparedness, monitoring, early warning, disaster management	Emergency services	Information and advice (for house owners)		Contributions to hazard and risk assessments, development of protection schemes or in monitoring and early warning

Source: FOEN (2016a)

The following section provides an overview of the role of the most important federal and sub-national actors as well as the one of insurance companies and other coordinating platforms in Switzerland.

Sub-national responsibilities

Given the above-mentioned subsidiarity principle, Switzerland's local municipalities are the first in line for risk management. They are responsible for protecting their citizens against potential threats to their security. Hence, local authorities have a large number of responsibilities in terms of natural hazard management, differing however from one canton to the other. In the Canton of Bern, for example, the municipalities have the following responsibilities (AG NAGEF Bern, 2013):

- Communal land-use planning;
- Building permissions;
- Identifying and assessing prevailing natural hazards in their territory;
- Managing prevailing risks, in terms of reducing them and avoiding exposure to them through local measures;
- Formulating emergency preparedness measures; and,
- Evaluating security measures periodically.

Municipalities are accompanied in this process by cantons that are charged with enforcing laws and providing support for:

- Developing hazard zone maps (quality assurance and approval of hazard maps developed by municipalities);
- Implementing and financing of prevention and mitigation measures, including their operation and maintenance (which includes a periodical survey of the conditions of infrastructures and the approval of maintenance and rehabilitation works);
- Implementing and financing of emergency preparedness measures, especially providing guidance, supervision and technical approval or emergency management plans; and,
- Developing planning measures at the regional scale as well as cantonal emergency management.

The federal level supports municipalities and cantons through:

- Developing legislation and policies;
- Providing recommendations and guidance for the management of natural hazards;
- Providing financial support for the construction of protective infrastructure (including protective forests), whereby the cantons give construction approvals along waterways and assess the needs for installing additional prevention measures;
- Providing financial support for the development of hazard maps;
- Providing financial support for the development and installation of hazard monitoring and early warning systems;
- Providing support for research and education; and,
- Consulting / advice.

In terms of reconstruction and rehabilitation, cantons are in charge of re-establishing and improving the status quo after a disaster event. Direct response functions include the establishment of a minimal level of safety and the re-servicing of important infrastructures. The following reconstruction phase aims at rebuilding buildings, taking due account of future damage potential, infrastructure and the functioning of the economy. Cantons are also asked to engage in systematic lessons-learned activities and to integrate them into long-term planning.

Federal Office for the Environment (FOEN)

The Federal Office for the Environment (FOEN) is part of the Federal Department of the Environment, Transport, Energy and Communications. FOEN's mission is to ensure the sustainable use of natural resources, including soil, water, air and forests. It is also charged with minimising natural hazards, reducing risks to the environment and human health from excessive pollution, conserving biodiversity and representing Switzerland in international environmental policy arenas. Four out of the FOEN's 14 divisions focus on natural hazards related topics, namely the forest, hazard prevention, hydrology and climate change adaptation units.

Based on the legal framework set out in the forestry law and the water engineering law, FOEN is responsible for water-related disasters such as floods and debris flows, landslides, rockfall and avalanches. Storms and forest fires as well as the coordination of the federal earthquake mitigation program also fall under FOEN's responsibility. Climate-related and meteorological hazards, such as heatwaves or cold waves lie in the responsibility of the Federal Office of Meteorology and Climatology.

FOEN is responsible for identifying and assessing risks that fall under its responsibilities. It thus plays a central role in guiding sub-national efforts in those processes and bringing results together at the national level.

FOEN, like other federal offices in Switzerland, is responsible for setting strategic priorities and for co-funding disaster risk reduction measures, but it is the cantons and municipalities that are responsible for actual disaster risk reduction measures. For example, FOEN is guiding efforts on assessing the impacts of climate change on natural hazards in Switzerland, such as a strategy that was issued in 2012 on national climate change adaptation (FOEN 2012a). Moreover, FOEN is providing advice and training for sub-national actors in charge of carrying our disaster risk reduction measures. Finally, FOEN is responsible for monitoring the implementation of disaster risk reduction measures by cantons, ensuring protective measures are in line with the water engineering and environmental laws.

Federal Office for Civil Protection (FOCP)

The Swiss Federal Office for Civil Protection (FOCP) is responsible for the protection of the population in cases of catastrophes and emergencies. Similar to other federal offices, FOCP is subject to the subsidiarity principle that guides Switzerland's administrative set-up. FOCP is responsible for risks that are of national importance (such as increased radioactivity, satellite crashes, dam bursts, epidemics or pandemics, epizootics, and armed conflicts), and for all others it is responsible for providing strategic guidance and working in collaboration with other sub-national levels. For example, FOCP supports the cantons to perform risk analysis and preparedness planning at the cantonal level. It does so by issuing guidelines for risk analysis and preparedness planning (FOCP, 2013).

FOCP is responsible for the national risk analysis for disasters and emergencies in Switzerland (FOCP, 2015b). In addition, it has a coordination function in the implementation of the national critical infrastructure protection strategy issued by the Federal Council in June 2012 (FOCP, 2012). It assists the sector-specific agencies and the operators assessing the risks and fostering resilience of the critical infrastructures. To improve the resilience of critical infrastructures, FOCP encourages and provides guidance for critical infrastructure providers to conduct comprehensive risk analysis or to prepare for outages and failures in the system. FOCP does not provide any subsidies to critical infrastructure providers to implement such activities. As a consequence, it has been difficult to encourage operators to think beyond their individual asset protection to consider wider public safety in their disaster risk prevention and mitigation engagement. To overcome these challenges, FOCP has created an inventory on critical infrastructure objects that identifies highly critical infrastructures and monitors their vulnerabilities (FCOP, 2010).

Federal Office for Spatial Development (ARE)

The Federal Office for Spatial Development (ARE) plays a key role in providing national guidance for a hazard-informed spatial planning approach and determining fundamental rules. ARE views its core function as to develop spatial planning that not only keeps potential damages from natural disasters in the future limited, but aims at reducing it. Damage potential includes assets such as apartment buildings, individual houses or transport infrastructure in hazard-prone areas. The approach anchored in the legal frameworks (such as the water engineering law) also favours the use of spatial planning measures before investments in structural measures are undertaken. Finally, spatial planning also aims at maintaining existing flood retention zones as well as keeping areas unbuilt, where potential protective infrastructure could be built in the future.

ARE closely coordinates its activities with FOEN. In 2005, the two agencies jointly issued a guidance document on hazard-based spatial planning that primarily seeks to inform cantonal authorities in their responsibility to implement hazard-based land-use planning (ARE and FOEN, 2005).

Swiss Seismological Service (SED, Erdbebendienst)

The Swiss Seismological Service (SED) at the Swiss Federal Institute of Technology Zurich (ETHZ) is the federal agency responsible for monitoring earthquakes in Switzerland and its neighbouring countries and for assessing Switzerland's seismic hazard. When an earthquake happens, the SED informs the public, authorities, and the media about the earthquake's location, magnitude, and possible consequences. Earthquake monitoring became legally mandated in 1914, which led to the creation of the SED. In 2009, they released the Earthquake Catalogue of Switzerland (ECOS-09) online. The platform contains historical records of earthquakes from AD 250 until 2008. The records provide information regarding the magnitude, location, depth and other key statistics but not any socio-economic information.

Earthquakes are the hazard that is least present in the risk awareness among Swiss people (see risk communication section).

Swiss Federal Institute for Forest, Snow and Landscape Research (WSL) with the Institute for Snow and Avalanche Research (SLF)

The SLF is an interdisciplinary research and service centre working in the fields of snow, avalanches, permafrost and mountain ecological systems. It forms part of the WSL

– the Swiss Federal Institute for Forest, Snow and Landscape Research. The SLF assesses the avalanche danger in the Swiss Alps and issues daily avalanche bulletins in the winter. The SLF's operational snow-hydrological service continuously analyses the distribution of snow water resources and assists the flood warning service of the FOEN. The work of the WSL has been key to advancing Switzerland's capacity in managing natural hazard based on progress in scientific research. Other institutes, such as the Institute of Geography in Bern, the Universities of Lausanne, Fribourg or Zurich or ETHZ have also contributed to advancing knowledge through natural hazard research.

Federal Office of Meteorology and Climatology (MeteoSwiss)

MeteoSwiss is the national weather and climate service for the Swiss public, for government, industry and science. With its public service, it ensures the basic supply of weather and climate information in Switzerland and thereby makes a substantial contribution to the well-being and the safety of the population. Surface observation systems, weather radars, satellites, radio sounding and other remote sensing instruments monitor the weather. Using the collected data, the weather services of *MeteoSwiss* generate forecasts and warn authorities and the public of imminent severe weather. Furthermore, these data are exploited by other teams of experts who analyse climate change and extreme weather events and develop scenarios for climate development in Switzerland

Federal Roads Office (FEDRO)

As part of the Federal Department of the Environment, Transport, Energy and Communications (DETEC), the Federal Roads Office (FEDRO) is charged with securing sustainable and safe mobility on the country's roads. Its main objective is to guarantee the functionality of Switzerland's motorways and main roads. As such, FEDRO plays an important role in guaranteeing that roads and motorways remain functional or become functional again during and after disasters.

Insurance industry

Switzerland has a mandatory insurance mechanism (for more details see section V). As a consequence, there are a number of insurance actors that play a key role in disaster risk prevention management:

Cantonal Public Insurance Companies for Buildings (Kantonale Gebäudeversicherungen)

The responsibility of the 19 cantonal public insurance companies for buildings (PIBs) is to provide building damage compensation in the event of a catastrophe, or so called elementary damage cover. They cover damages that arise from hail, avalanches, snow pressure, rockfalls, landslides, floods and storms. The cover is included in the fire insurance policy. PIBs have a monopoly status and work on a non-profit basis. In the seven cantons that do not have a PIB, a similar (nationally regulated) cover can be obtained from private insurance providers.

Private insurance companies

Private insurance companies provide the same insurance cover for buildings as the public insurance companies do. The private insurance industry not only covers buildings but also content and business interruption. The insurance cover is based on the respective law (*Aufsichtsverordnung*).

Apart from providing loss compensation, disaster risk prevention and loss mitigation is another role for private and public insurance companies, which have become increasingly important in the framework of an integrated risk management strategy in Switzerland. Insurance companies have become key actors in communicating about risks to private sector actors and citizens. They inform them about their responsibilities such as investments in self-protection, what options there are in investing in self-protection, and financially support such measures.

Other insurance actors include:

- Swiss Insurance Association (*Schweizerischer Versicherungsverband*, SVV): An umbrella organisation representing the private insurance industry, who in turn represents around 80 insurers and re-insurers. With the Swiss Natural Perils Pool (*Schweizerischer Elementarschaden-Pool*), the SVV has established a pooling of private insurance companies that allows better equalizing of risk associated with natural disasters.
- Association of Cantonal Fire Insurance Companies (VKF): An association representing the interests of public insurance companies for buildings and provides services for all prevention-related activities against fire and natural hazards at national and international levels.
- Inter-cantonal Re-insurance Association (*Interkantonaler Rückversicherungsverband*, IRV): A non-profit reinsurance association, which provides reinsurance for fire and natural hazards for public insurance companies for buildings.
- The Federal Financial Market Supervisory Authority (*Eidgenössische Finanzmarktaufsicht,* FINMA): The independent financial market regulator in Switzerland.

National coordinating bodies: PLANAT

The national platform for natural hazards, PLANAT, was founded in 1997 as part of the government structure to improve disaster risk prevention across Switzerland. It brings together representatives from the federal government, cantonal governments, research community, professional associations, private sector and insurance companies to work on three important areas of work to boost disaster risk reduction throughout Switzerland. Its first mission is to engage in strategic priorities in risk management. The second is to introduce and foster a culture of risk that drives the risk management agenda away from averting risks and towards an approach that integrates ecological, social and economic aspects in disaster risk prevention management. Third, PLANAT coordinates disaster risk prevention efforts in Switzerland to avoid duplication and increase synergies between the different actors' activities. It thereby acts as a platform of exchange that gathers and distributes good practices at the national and international level.

To fulfil its role on working on strategic priorities, PLANAT has been charged with developing a comprehensive and interlinked strategy to ensure comparable risk standards throughout Switzerland, with the aim to protect lives, livelihoods and material assets. It issued a major strategy in 2004 (PLANAT, 2004a) that paved the way for thinking of risk management in an integrated manner, also introducing the concept of a culture of risk. A number of consolidated reports on various disaster risk prevention topics followed the initial strategic framework. PLANAT's activities and results present a wealth of information today tailored to different risk management stakeholders across Switzerland.

Since its creation, PLANAT has made major contributions that have ensured that the management of risks remains present in political and public discussions. The composition of PLANAT with members from the different national and sub-national agencies, but also research and insurances as well as the private sector has been important to achieve their significance. To ensure PLANAT's effectiveness and usefulness in contributing to advancing disaster risk prevention management in Switzerland, a regular evaluation of its governance structure and activities could be useful. This could help orientate its activities and ensure relevance in the future as well. The governance structure, for now, is inclusive in terms of the different levels of government and the insurance industry. There could perhaps be room for reflecting upon opening all or some of its activities up to other actors as well, including for example civil society organisations.

National coordinating bodies: LAINAT

The Steering Committee Intervention in Natural Hazards (LAINAT), founded in 2008, brings all federal agencies (FOEN, FOCP, MeteoSuisse, WSL/SLF, ETHZ/SED) in charge of forecasting and warning about natural disasters together in one committee. LAINAT is in charge of informing and preparing for major disasters. It coordinates Federal Council resolutions on the "Optimisation of Warning and Alerting" and manages projects on hazard preparation, warning and altering. Its committee is set up by members from the above-mentioned federal agencies.

LAINAT created an online platform (www.gin.admin.ch) that informs and alerts the authorities about storms, floods, avalanches and earthquakes. This information is provided to the federal, cantonal and local level to facilitate response actions at the appropriate level. LAINAT also operates the website www.naturgefahren.ch, which is aimed at providing alerts regarding natural hazards to the general public (for more information on risk communication in Switzerland see section IV).

Cross-jurisdictional collaboration

Risks are rarely confined to municipal borders and may not halt at cantonal or country borders. Therefore, governance structures should ensure that disaster risk management operates at the adequate scales. Inter-communal collaboration is needed, especially for the development of joint spatial planning strategies for shared river areas and the development of compensation mechanisms between municipalities that pay for protection measures and others that may benefit or have additional costs. Collaboration methods include a range of partnerships, from establishing informal discussion fora and exchanging hazard information, to coordinating land-use planning activities or implementing joint protection measures.

The subsidiarity arrangements in Switzerland should ensure that disaster risk reduction measures are implemented on a functional level. To ensure coordination across administrative borders of cantons, cantonal authorities need to submit their proposals for protective infrastructure investments to the national level (FOEN) when the following occurs (BWG, 2001):

- Protective infrastructures are built along rivers that make up the border between different cantons;
- Protective infrastructure investments by one canton have a potential impact on other cantons;
- Protective infrastructure measures require an environmental performance assessment; or,
- Protective infrastructure coincides with a nationally protected area.

Based on the degree of collaboration across cantons, there are different coordination models, where either both (or several) or just one canton takes the lead in the implementation process. Accordingly, co-financing arrangements are made. In case of differences between the cantons, the federal government acts as a mediator (BWG, 2001).

When a measure is installed upstream, it needs to be proved that it does not worsen the situation further downstream.

The role of international collaboration

Switzerland participates in the Alpine Convention5, an international treaty between eight Alpine countries (Austria, France, Germany, Italy, Liechtenstein, Monaco, Slovenia and Switzerland) and the European Union. The treaty sets out to ensure the protection of the Alps and stresses the high value of sustainable development of the Alpine region. Since 2004, the Alpine Convention includes the Natural Hazards Platform of the Alpine Convention (PLANALP) that contributes to the development of joint approaches to disaster risk reduction and is mandated to implement subsequent measures, including flood (risk) management plans. Switzerland is engaged in the PLANALP through FOEN. Switzerland is also a member of several transboundary river commissions, such as the International Commission for the Protection of the Rhine (ICPR)6 that elaborate basin-level flood risk management plans. Switzerland is engaged in a cross border dialogue on the management of the Rhône that may develop into the creation of a coordinating body administered together with France. On the international level, Switzerland also cooperates with UNISDR, particularly in regards of the implementation of the overarching international frameworks. PLANAT also has a small working group on international affairs and a number of federal offices, including the FOEN, maintain collaborations with neighbouring and overseas countries. Moreover, scientific institutions maintain collaboration with institutions abroad.

Conclusion

This section showed that the governance set-up for disaster risk prevention in Switzerland much reflects its federal set-up, with strong powers devolved to the cantonal level. Switzerland is a good practice example for embracing a whole-of-society approach to disaster risk management. It is considered that government efforts across all levels are only effective if private sector actors and individuals contribute their share in terms of risk adapted behaviour and self-protection investments. Insurance companies have played a key role in establishing a dialogue and informing private actors and citizens about their responsibilities in disaster risk prevention management.

The direct democratic tradition of Switzerland has also shaped disaster risk prevention efforts. Significant protective infrastructure investments are publicly scrutinised through often lengthy consultation processes. Although blockages can occur when only a minority opposes a plan, this process has by large ensured an efficient and effective provision of protective infrastructure that receives the support of its population. Coordination platforms such as PLANAT for strategic risk management issues and LAINAT for operational risk management issues ensure that a potentially fragmented, multi-layered system of actors is coordinated along key strategic priorities. Although these bodies have been effective in establishing a common vision and agenda for disaster risk reduction, their activities could be more regularly evaluated and their governance structures potentially opened up further.

This section's objective was to highlight who the main actors in charge of disaster risk prevention in Switzerland are. This is an important basis to subsequently assess specific disaster risk prevention activities, to ensure that roles and incentives are aligned to carry out disaster risk prevention tasks effectively.

Management of Structural and Non-Structural Disaster Risk Prevention and Mitigation Measures

Section Highlights

- A significant stock of protective infrastructure has been created over the past 100 or more years. Current constraints to funding its maintenance may create significant vulnerabilities and decrease the level of protection they were initially conceived for. Efforts are underway to creating a central database of infrastructure maintenance and rehabilitation needs. This should help prioritise maintenance efforts and inform cross-governmental financial planning
- There has been an important recognition about the need to boost funding for maintaining protective infrastructure. Although central re-allocation of disaster financing towards maintenance is welcome, it should ideally not undermine the long-term investment needs in new protective infrastructure.
- Most of the detailed information on hazard and risk assessments is collected at local and cantonal levels. To effectively manage disaster risk prevention priorities across levels of government, it is important to collate sub-national information centrally to enable the prioritisation of collective disaster risk reduction efforts.
- Switzerland's integration of hazard zone maps into land-use plans is in many ways a good practice example. Although this process has effectively avoided new investments in high-risk zones, it has failed to reduce damages in low-risk zones. A future focus should be on elaborating and finding ways to effectively monitor disaster risk reduction measures that apply to low-risk zones.

- Switzerland is a very good example for implementing a whole-of-society approach to disaster risk prevention management, for example by engaging insurance providers in translating and informing citizens and businesses about expected contributions to disaster risk prevention. Given the substantial investments that have been made in mobilising actors, an evaluation of these measures would be useful to ensure that investments are effective in reaching their objectives.

Introduction

Switzerland's experience with and management of natural disasters underwent significant changes in the past and developed into a modern, forward-looking and holistic risk management system that can serve as an example to many other countries. The Swiss approach to "integrated" risk management considers simultaneous and complementary measures for all phases of the disaster risk management cycle, ranging from preparedness and response measures to recovery (reconstruction) following a hazardous event (Figure 4.12).

Figure 4.12 The cycle of integrated risk management

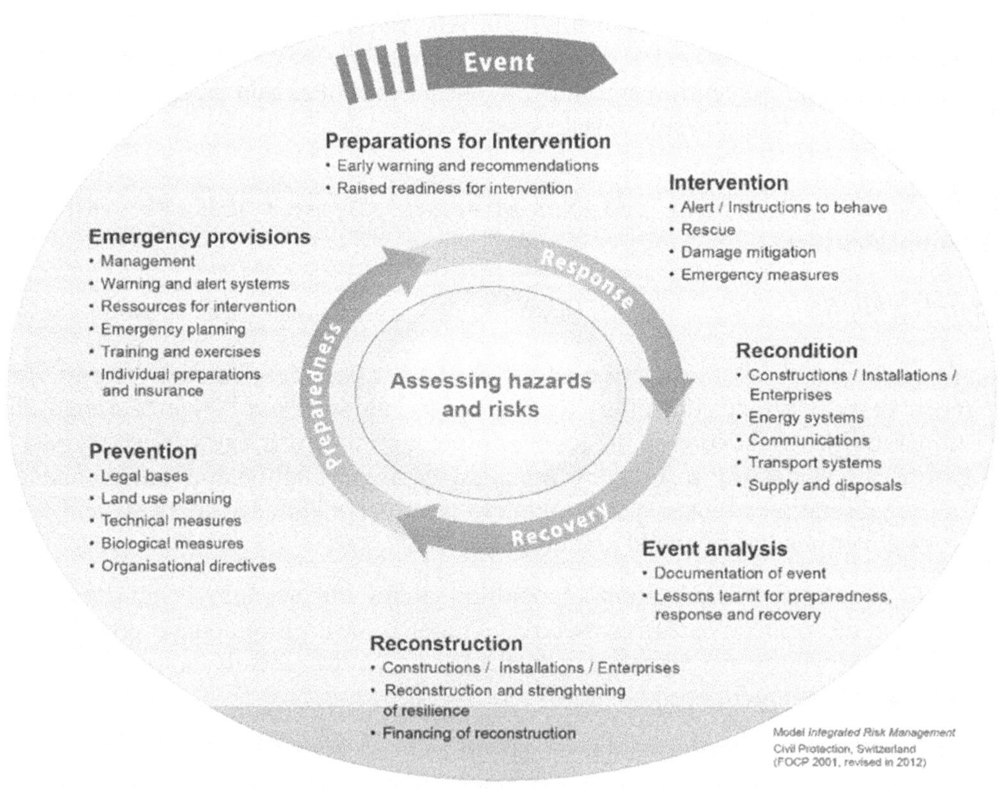

Source: FOCP (2013), http://www.planat.ch/en/specialists/risk-management/what-has-to-be-done/

Experiences with natural disasters and their management date back centuries in Switzerland. Early disaster risk prevention management revolved around individually protecting one's assets. Community engagement and managing risks more collectively started growing in the 18th century, when cantons started to invest in public disaster risk reduction measures. These measures were, at least in the beginning, implemented on the basis of achieving multiple goals and not just disaster risk reduction. For example, buying up (risk exposed) land was done to increase land for agricultural purposes, or the course of rivers was changed so as to decrease the risk of malaria. From the mid-19th century, the central government started to increasingly take on responsibilities to protect against natural hazards. In 1848, a constitutional law was developed to create the basis for investing in public (protective) infrastructure. Subsequently, federal laws were established for the forestry police (1876) and the water police (1877), based on which significant public investments were made for slope stabilisation and to construct protection measures against risks from torrents and rivers. This period was followed by a systematic focus on the protection against snow avalanches.

Most of the early disaster risk prevention measures were implemented as a reaction to the impacts suffered during major natural catastrophes, but recent developments in Switzerland have started to take a forward-looking, integrated approach to managing risks from natural disasters. A strong guiding principle has been developed since then. It prioritises soft measures that are nature-based (such as protective forests) over structural protective measures and creates a culture of risk, rather than a risk management that is reactive to the impacts of past disasters. A culture of risk can help in coping better with uncertainties and enables the uncovering of changes to the current risk profile (FOEN, 2016; BUWAL, BWG, BLW and ARE (2003).

The core of Switzerland's new *Leitbild* is that all measures used to deal with natural hazards are to be combined with one another, embracing the so-called integrated risk management approach, in a way that prevention measures effectively avoid hazards, reduce damage, while ensuring that society knows about and accepts residual or remaining risks.

How are structural measures financed and decided upon?

Target protection levels

Since 2001, Swiss protection goals have been determined by the type of land-use as well as the value of material assets (BWG, 2001; PLANAT, 2014a). The higher the value of the assets, the higher is their target protection level. Figure 4.14 shows the different protection targets by types of land-use and illustrates the correlation between protection level and asset value. Settlement areas, for example, have to be protected against low-probability high-loss disaster events. Industrial plants have to be protected according to their economic and geographic (local, regional or national) significance. A similar distinction is made for determining protection levels for infrastructures. Agricultural land is thereby to be protected the least.

Protection targets have also been adapted based on the experience with past disaster events. For example, in the city of Bern, several recurrent floods of the Aare River, especially those of 1999 (CHF 25 million in damages) and those of 2005 (CHF 60 million in damages) led to an increase in the initial level of targeted protection (Figure 4.14).

Figure 4.13 Protection objectives for different land-use types

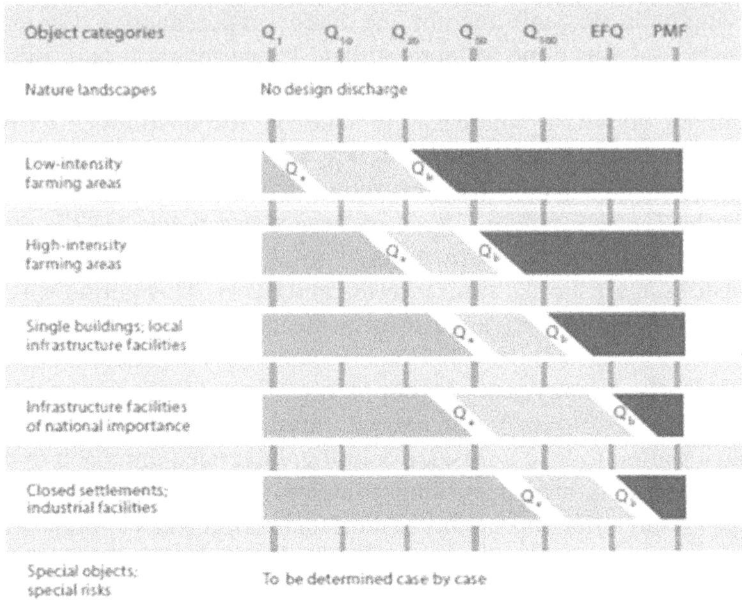

Source: Federal Department of the Environment, Transport, Energy, and Communications (DETEC) (2001), https://www.bafu.admin.ch/dam/bafu/en/.../flood_control_atriversandstreams.pdf

Note: Qa: damage limit; Qb: hazard limit; HQ1 – HQ100: flood return periods; EHQ: extreme flood event; PMF: probable maximum flood; red (right) bar: no protection; beige (middle) bar: limited protection; left (green) bar: complete protection.

Figure 4.14 Discharge rates of the Aare River and adapted target protection levels

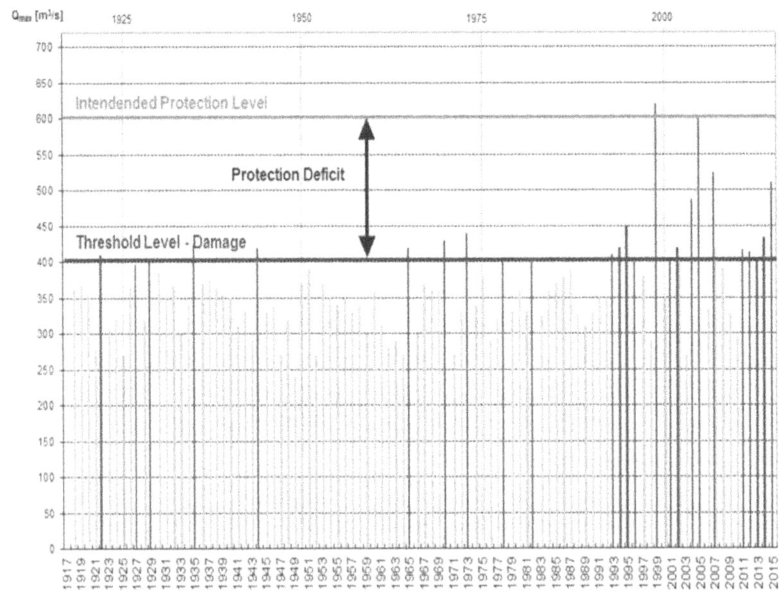

Source: Presentation by Mobilab (Röthlisberger, V. and Künzler, M. (2016) during OECD mission

Implementation process for structural measures

In terms of implementing structural measures, it is the general responsibility of cantons and municipalities to protect citizens and assets from natural hazards. While the operational responsibility is in the hands of cantons, municipalities, infrastructure operators or other public or private authorities can be in charge of constructing protective measures (FOEN, 2016).

Although Switzerland's sub-national levels have the key responsibilities for natural hazard management, the national government finances a large share of structural protective measures. Structural measures implemented by the cantons are supported by the national level in form of four-year, canton-wide program agreements that receive global support as well as project-specific support for exceptionally large investments. The national agency in charge of coordinating these programs is FOEN, who, today, has a good understanding of sub-national finance needs for protective infrastructure investments. However, longer term estimations for funding demands are not available.

The national government finances around 35-45% of the total prevention investment costs. The cost share for cantons is about the same, and the remaining costs are either borne by whoever constructs the measure (e.g. a municipality) or by direct beneficiaries. The national average co-funding share is 35%, but can be as high as 45% if investment projects are especially ecologically friendly. The national level can co-finance structural measures, but is more restricted in compensating or co-financing organisational measures (such as buying up and freeing up land to create flood zones).

Before 2008, central level co-funding for disaster risk prevention also took the relative income level of cantons into consideration for their funding allocations. The equalisation has since been integrated in a national, budget-wide redistribution process so that income levels are no longer considered in the national level disaster risk prevention co-funding mechanisms across cantons; hence all cantons are treated the same way.

Protective measures have to be evaluated against their costs and benefits to receive co-financing by the national level. An instrument called "EconoMe" was developed by FOEN to aid decision makers in prioritising investments (Box 1). Cost-benefit considerations are important, but only part of the considerations when investments are evaluated. FOEN's objective is to plan protective measures in a holistic way, considering safety, social standards and environmental requirements, in addition to cost-benefit ratios. Each protective infrastructure investment should combine organisational and planning measures, restrictions for land-use and emergency planning measures. Finally, large protective infrastructure investments and the management of natural hazards in general, are subject to extensive public consultation processes.

Even though prioritisation tools and evaluations of project options for investing in protective infrastructure are available through national guidance, it is ultimately the cantons that will apply them. Since they receive a programmatic disaster risk reduction allocation from the central level, the question remains how well cantons are prioritising investments and to what extent rigorous evaluations of project objects are subject to sub-national political influence.

Box 4.1 The application of cost-benefit analysis in risk prevention projects

Switzerland has developed a standard Cost-Benefit-Analysis tool called "EconoMe" that supports the calculation of the effectiveness and evaluated the economic efficiency of a structural measure. The platform seeks to answer two central questions in the planning of protective measures against natural hazards:

1. How far can the risk be reduced (effectiveness)?
2. What is the relationship between the disaster risk reduction achieved and the costs of the measure (efficiency)?

The platform aids communal, cantonal and federal authorities in deciding which projects to support and how to subsequently prioritise those projects.

The EconoMe Platform has reached an advanced stage of development and is now used to calculate complex projects, variations of individual measures or combination of measures.

Source: FOEN (n.d.) "EconoMe 4.0" Federal Office for the Environment, Bern, http://www.econome.admin.ch/index.php

Operating and Maintaining Structural Measures

Protective measures implemented by infrastructure operators are often financed 100% by operators. Private insurance companies can co-finance protective measures as well.

The lead agency at the national level, FOEN, is responsible for monitoring that the implementation of structural measures across levels of governments follows the guidelines of the Federal Law for Water Engineering (WBG) and of the Federal Law of Forestry (WaG). Enforcement aids[7] published by FOEN provide additional technical guidance

The large stock of protective infrastructure that has been created over the past decades in Switzerland has to be adequately maintained if it is to provide the level of protection for which it was initially conceived. The same principle also applies to non-structural and "soft" measures, such as emergency plans that have to be practiced on a regular basis, or the maintenance of protection forests.

The water engineering law requires cantons to periodically assess hazard levels, which includes the protection levels of existing structural measures. Cantons have to finance the maintenance of these measures. Maintenance costs for the entire lifetime of the protective infrastructure are included in the cost evaluation conducted at the beginning of a protective measure project, but not necessarily in the actual project financing. In the Canton of Bern, for example, protective infrastructures are surveyed every five years. In the Canton of Bern, maintenance costs are shared between the canton (33%) and the communes (67%).

At present, few central or cantonal repository that provides information about each existing protective infrastructure, the level of maintenance, potential deficiencies or an assessment of the needs for rehabilitation works exist. In some cases, old protective structures fell short in providing the intended protection in part due to unforeseen overload situations. This makes it difficult to provide a clear overview of the functionality of Switzerland's existing protective infrastructure. Existing protective infrastructure is or currently cannot be financially supported by the federal level. In the canton of Bern, such a repository (*Kataster-Geoinfrastruktur*) has already been created and is continuously being updated. Costs for maintaining protective infrastructures are expected to increase in light of the increasing age of many structures. As sub-national funding is expected to be too constraint to meet future maintenance needs, a recent discussion started about whether and how central level funding could be made available to support this task. If this situation prevails, vulnerabilities of current infrastructures could be set to rise in the near- and medium-term.

The Role of the Insurance Sector in Providing Protective Infrastructure

In an attempt to reduce future damage claims, the Public Insurance Companies for Buildings engage actively in supporting or co-financing public protective infrastructure. Insurance companies can provide for the full or partial share of local co-funding requirements for infrastructure investments.

How are non-structural measures managed?

Hazard assessment and mapping and land-use planning

Switzerland developed systematic hazard identification and assessment from early on. Records of hydro-meteorological hazard assessments can be found as early as 1863, where water and discharge levels started to be monitored regularly. Beginning in 1868, information on the channel geometry (cross sections) of the larger Swiss rivers started to be recorded systematically. Since 1979, daily weather reports have been made available. In 1914, an earthquake monitoring system was created. The Swiss Seismological Service (SED) was integrated into the Swiss Federal Institute of Technology (ETHZ) in 1957 (FOEN, 2016a).

As a consequence of the catastrophic "avalanche winter" in 1950/51 that caused 98 fatalities, systematic collection and monitoring of snow data was established, which laid the ground work for today's avalanche forecast system (FOEN, 2016a). WSL is responsible for the avalanche forecasting service.

The SED produces seismic hazard maps for a reference soil at the national level. More than half of the cantons have established so called maps of seismic soil foundation classes or spectral seismic zoning studies to account for the influence of the local soil on the earthquake hazard. This information is taken into account for the design or verification of structures according to the building codes. It has limited implications on zoning plans and do not lead to construction bans (ARE and FOEN, 2005).

At the national level, guidelines to conduct hazard assessments are delivered by the Federal Office for the Environment (FOEN), except for earthquakes. The cantons are responsible for overseeing the development of hazard maps at the local level. The national level finances 50% of the risk assessment and hazard mapping conducted by sub-national levels

Hazard maps in Switzerland provide information about where settlement areas or transport routes are potentially impacted by floods, landslides, rock falls, avalanches, and, to the extent described above, also earthquakes. They provide information about the intensity of a potential hazard as well as the probability of it occurring. Outside of settlement areas, hazard information is provided but in a less detailed manner, which means they do not show information about potential probabilities or intensities of a disaster event[8]. 93% of required hazard maps are currently available (excluding earthquakes). Figure 4.15 shows how rapidly the gap in the availability of flood hazard maps has been closed since 2005.

Figure 4.15 Gaps in the availability of flood hazard maps

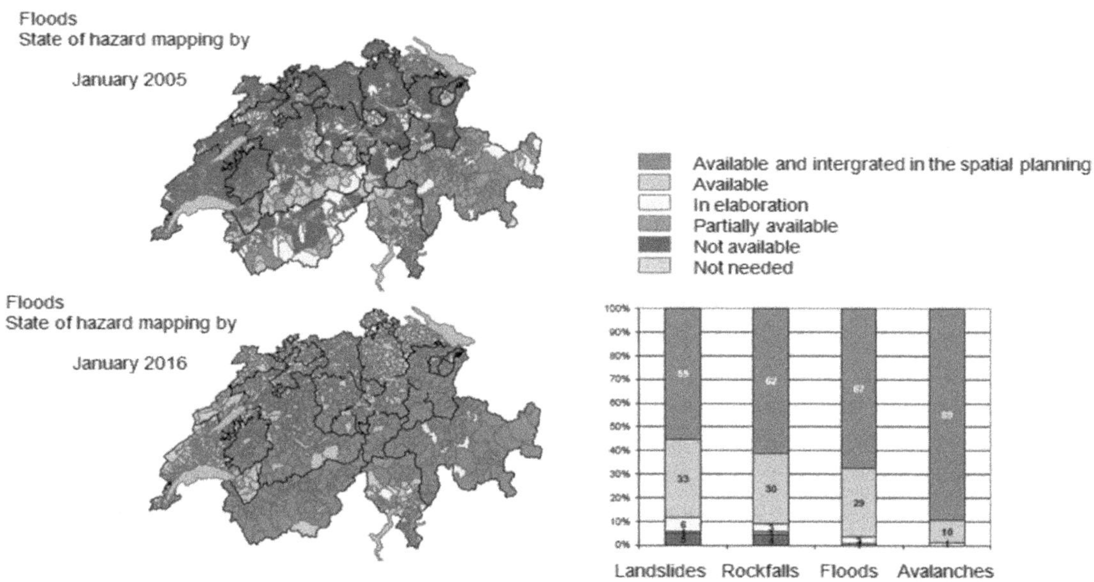

Source: Presentation by BAFU during OECD mission

Hazard maps have to be updated every 10-15 years or after major disaster events. At present, there is no national level aggregated risk map, although Switzerland is currently establishing a national portal that seeks to bring together cantonal geospatial hazard information in a harmonised way[9].

Hazard maps are usually divided into white, yellow/white, yellow, blue and red zones. Sometimes a brown zone is added that identifies land that has to undergo a special hazard assessment before constructions can be permitted.

Hazard maps and their underlying data are not only integrated and used in land-use planning (as will be described below), but they also inform the work of civil protection agencies. The Canton of Bern, for example, started to develop intervention maps that depict the level of threat divided into phases, choosing a colour key to represent and the necessary course of actions that are to be taken in the event of a natural hazard (yellow – observation and preparation / orange – intervention / red – escalation and evacuation). They include, for example, the installation of observers of the flood levels at critical points in municipalities, such as bridges (yellow phase).

Table 4.3 Hazard zones and regulations in Switzerland

Zone (colour)	Regulations
Red hazard zone (significant hazard threat: people in- and outside of buildings are in danger; buildings could be destroyed)	New constructions are forbidden; if land was initially earmarked for constructions it has to be changed to "non-constructible" surface; for changes to existing buildings, the risk is not to be increased; existing buildings must have evacuation plans;
Blue hazard zone (medium hazard threat: people inside buildings are not threatened, but outside they are; damages to buildings (but not full destructions) are possible)	As much as possible, there should be no new constructions; if land was initially earmarked for constructions it should as much as possible be changed to "non-constructible" surface; specific construction regulations apply to new buildings, such as the building of houses' fundaments has to be made of reinforced concrete; if changes are made to existing buildings in this zone, the risk shall not be increased;
Yellow hazard zone (low hazard threat: people are not threatened, but damages to the exterior of buildings and to its interior (if there is a flood) could occur)	Restrictions apply to sensitive buildings, where many people work or live or those that are difficult to evacuate (such as schools or hospitals, railway stations, retirement homes or camping grounds), but also services that are critical during emergency operations (such as fire stations, civil protection services) or buildings where low levels of hazard can cause significant impacts (such as water treatment facilities, switchboard stations, etc.);
Yellow/white hazard zone (residual risk zone: only if extreme events occur could damages occur)	Restrictions apply only to buildings that are important to maintain the level of security to citizens or those that can cause a significant damage potential;
White zone (no risk)	No restrictions.

Source: (AG NAGEF Bern, 2013)

Switzerland's energy sourcing from hydropower and nuclear power has created awareness among authorities about potential cascading impacts. In Switzerland, 56% of electricity is generated by hydropower and 39% from nuclear power. Switzerland shows awareness about the potential cascading impacts of natural hazards, such as earthquakes as a trigger to nuclear accidents and chemical plants, rock falls that can cause a flash flood in dams, oil catastrophes that are triggered by floods, transport accidents as a consequence of snow avalanches (PLANAT, 2004a).

Swiss authorities show increasing awareness that adapted protection against extreme floods with a very low return probability is needed. The EXAR project described in Box 2 above shows that there are research projects underway to better understand such future extreme risks. Switzerland's varied topography and climate make it subject to potentially significant changes in climatic conditions in the future, which will likely have impacts on both the intensity and frequency of future natural disasters. Expected effects could include more extreme weather events, more floods, glacier thawing and its potential impact on the tourism industry.

Box 4.2 EXAR: Evaluating extreme flood risks along the Aare and Rhine Rivers

In 2013 the Swiss Federal Offices for the Environment, Energy, Nuclear Safety Inspectorate as well as Civil Protection launched the EXAR project that aims at establishing a common baseline to evaluate the risk of extreme flood events for infrastructures built close to the rivers Aare and Rhine. In the beginning phase of the project, data were collected and methodologies developed that enable a standard evaluation of extreme flood events along those two rivers, including gauge height, flow velocity, morphological changes of the river and recurrence probabilities. Projections are based on estimated return periods of 10 000 years.

Based on the initial ground work that established the evidence base for modelling extreme flood events of the Aare, in 2016 the Federal Office for the Environment (FOEN) commissioned a study to understand and evaluate interaction scenarios or cascading impacts of extreme flood risk events. These include erosion, landslides, blockages through floating refuse and dyke breaches. The objective of this study is to understand vulnerabilities of infrastructures to extreme flood events.

Source: FOEN (2016d). Beurteilung der Gefährdung durch Extremhochwasser der Aare: Hauptstudie lanciert. [Evaluation of extreme flood hazards along the Aare: Main study launched], Federal Office for the Environment (FOEN), Switzerland, http://www.bafu.admin.ch/dokumentation/medieninformation/00962/index.html?lang=de&msg-id=60609

Integrating hazard assessments in land-use planning

The integration of hazard maps into land-use plans and land-use decisions has been exemplary in Switzerland. Hazard assessments have to be taken into account in land-use planning and mapping. The spatial planning law obliges cantons to identify areas that are potentially threatened by natural hazards. The hazard-informed land-use plan, of which an example is shown in Figure 4.16, constitutes a mandatory regulatory instrument. Local construction permits and construction regulations are adapted to the specific local hazard information. In terms of enforcement, actual application of regulatory prescriptions during construction processes has relied on self-declarations by property owners. Insurance providers can refuse damage compensations if such declarations were falsely made.

In terms of practical implementation, hazard zone maps are overlaid with existing settlement areas that have been identified in land-use plans, whereby potential new construction zones are also considered. The Federal Office for Spatial Planning (ARE), together with FOEN, have been providing trainings and information workshops for cantons and municipalities on how to implement the integration of hazard zones into land-use planning.

Not all communes have integrated their hazard and land-use plans yet, although the gap has been closing. In the Canton of Bern, for example, where the integration of hazard maps into land-use maps has been a mandatory requirement since 10 years, 245 of 352 municipalities have completed this process (AG NAGEF Bern, 2013). Some of the remaining gaps can be explained by planning cycles, for example land-use plans are renewed every eight years. The challenge will be to keep up with the underlying changes in risk patterns, in terms of both, the changes in the hazards, but also the evolution of hazard-exposed populations and assets.

Taking the integration of hazard zones into land-use planning yet a step further, Switzerland has elaborated a national spatial planning concept in 2012 (Schweizerischer Bundesrat, 2012). This was informed by the water protection law (*Gewässerschutzgesetz*) that, in 2011, started to prescribe a minimal space for rivers, which is expected to expand mostly into agricultural land (BUWAL, BWG, BLW and ARE, 2003). The concept, established jointly by the national government, cantonal and municipal authorities, recognises the limits of structural protection measures in disaster risk prevention management, especially given continuously evolving risk patterns. It therefore sets out the objective of creating space for the creation of flood retention zones, as an important complementary disaster risk prevention measure. This needs to be anchored strongly in present land-use decisions (FOEN, 2016).

Even though Switzerland has advanced significantly in integrating hazard information in land-use planning decisions, there are some significant challenges that prevail. The identification of red zones has been effective in prohibiting new building constructions. However, analyses have shown that more than 50% of the insured damage claims are actually being filed in areas that were determined as minor hazard (yellow) zones, where no specific land-use requirement was previously issued, but rather just information about the hazard level provided. This shows that efforts to reduce damages in high risk zones have been highly effective, but that protection or stricter regulations might have been overlooked in low hazard zones. Having recognised this as a challenge, ARE is currently elaborating measures that could be integrated in constructions taking place in low-hazard zones.

Building codes

Since land-use and construction permit decisions are a local responsibility in Switzerland, there are 26 different cantonal laws for building code regulations. Building codes are issued by private architect associations (such as the Swiss Engineers and Architects Association) and cantons adopt them in their legislations. Building code prescriptions for earthquake-proof design were introduced in 1970 that were subsequently made more stringent and more detailed in 1989 and 2003[10]. Critical infrastructure providers have also recognised the need to update their structures to make them resilient against the impacts of potential earthquakes.

Switzerland's building codes mostly correspond to Eurocode 8. Since 2004, there has been a specific pre-standard for the verification of existing buildings regarding earthquakes. This pre-standard will be published as a building code by the end of 2016 and will deal with the verification of the seismic safety of structures in general. The implementation of the seismic safety requirements has significantly improved since 2003 but is not yet systematic enough.

In terms of enforcement, much of the building code implementation relies on private responsibility. Although there are mechanisms, such as through the Public Insurance Companies for Buildings (PIBs), that require the implementation of building codes in order to obtain building insurance (VKF, 2005), public oversight of building code enforcement could be increased.

Resettlement

In general resettlements are a last resort measure and have been executed in only few cases. Examples are an industrial park in Preonzo that had to be relocated due to high risk of landslides and the ice hockey stadium in Ambri-Piotta, as its current location is at high risk of avalanches. The municipality of Weggis on the Lake Lucerne, where the local government decided to evacuate five properties and asked for the removal of the buildings, is the first example, where an owner filed a suit against the resettlement plans. Despite the complaint, both the cantonal court of appeal and the Swiss Federal Tribunal decided in line with the current code of practice of integrated natural hazard risk management and confirmed the evacuation and removal. It is not expected that resettlements will become a widely used disaster risk reduction measure in Switzerland, but they can be an alternative where other protection measures would cause disproportional costs (Heim and Denzler 2016).

Risk Communication

The Swiss risk management agencies have recognised the importance of communicating about natural hazards, risks, uncertainty and the different actions that can be taken to reduce risks. The vision of Switzerland in that regard is that risk management can only be effective if responsible actors and citizens are aware of the risks and actively participate in reducing risks. The core objective of raising risk awareness is to inform citizens about relevant natural hazards and the risks they can pose to them. A key focus of their efforts is to not only raise awareness, but to keep awareness levels up through a continued dialogue on risk and by providing easily accessible information.

Insurance providers have played an important role in risk communication. One of their key objectives is to make sure citizens are informed about what they are expected to do in terms of disaster risk prevention. This includes knowledge about risk-adapted behaviour, but also self-protection measures in terms of construction designs and materials used. To support risk-adapted behaviours, some insurance providers have development automated text messages about bad weather warnings or imminent disasters. Insurance companies have gone a step further still, in providing financial support to boosting the capacity of fire brigades and rescue forces. Among the number of good risk communication practices, a few examples can be mentioned:

- A general information and alert service is provided through the www.natural-hazards.ch platform. Some cantons also have developed a cantonal version of a natural hazards platform, for example, the canton of Bern: www.naturgefahren.sites.be.ch/naturgefahren_sites/de/index.html. Through these platforms, the national government, cantons and municipalities inform and warn the general public about current risks from frosts, snow, heatwaves, floods, avalanches, as well as rain and thunderstorms, slippery roads, forest fires, winds and earthquakes (Figure 4.16). A 5-point scale (0 for no alert to 5 for high alert) is provided that can be broken down to specific places. This platform also provides general and detailed information about which protection measures can be done and what should be done when a disaster occurs. A strong emphasis is put on individual responsibility. A detailed list of situational measures before, during and immediately after the disaster is provided for each of the risks. Finally, the platform provides a full list of past warnings.

Figure 4.16 National hazard information platform

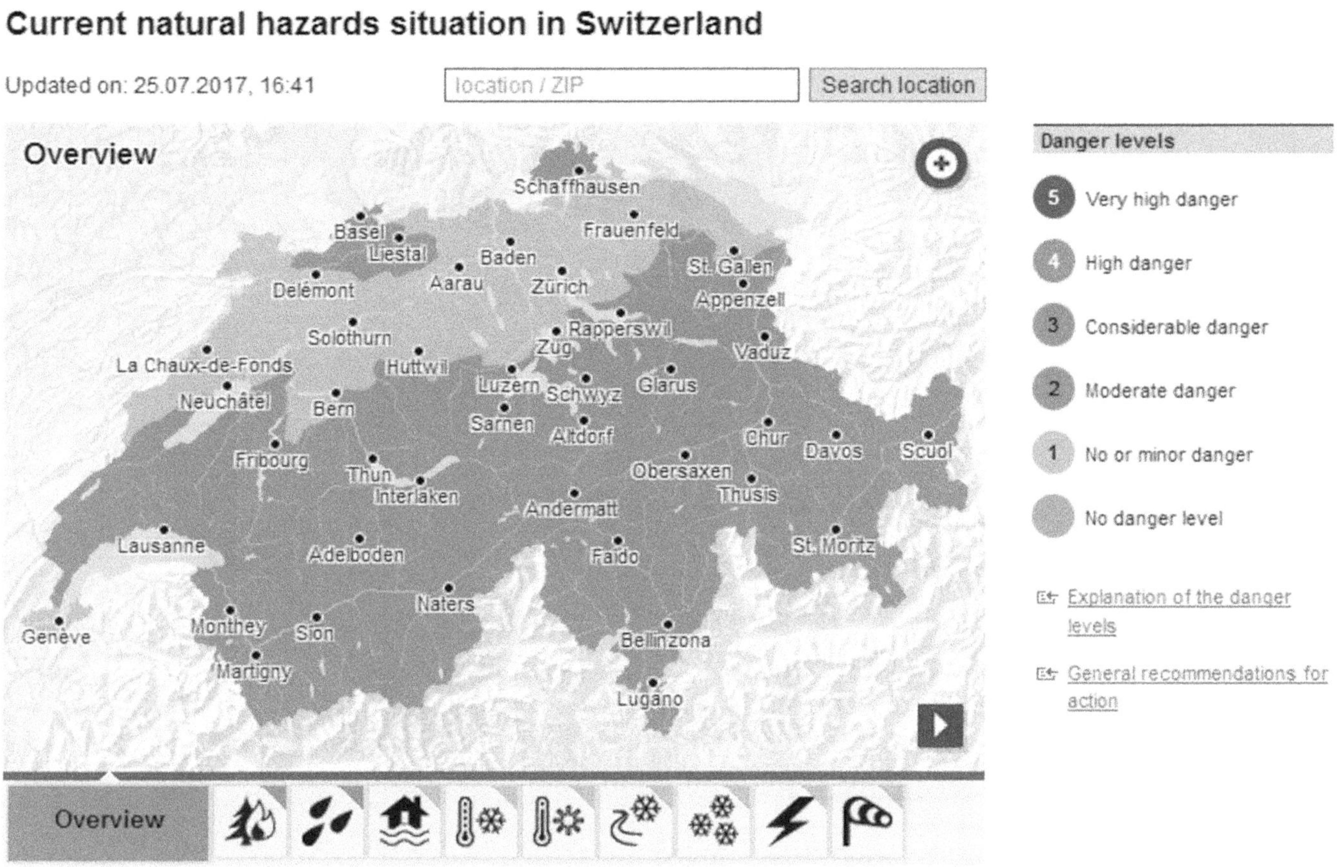

Source: http://www.natural-hazards.ch/home/current-natural-hazards.html

- To assess one's general (rather than immediate) hazard exposure, cantons provide detailed, address-based hazard maps, accessible online. An example is provided in Figure 4.18 for the Canton of Graubünden:

- PLANAT established an initiative entitled "*Risikodialog Naturgefahren*" (www.planat.ch/en/risikodialog/), through which it aims to raise risk awareness among public authorities, cross-governmental levels, citizens, owners and businesses, lay people but also among experts. The platform seeks to inform about what the public authorities can and should do and what other stakeholders can do to increase safety levels. Most importantly, it seeks to inform public authorities, including sub-national governments, about their responsibilities with regard to risk communication. The list of instruments stakeholders should use to inform the wider public about risks and to raise risk awareness include not only hazards and hazard maps, but all activities that public authorities engage in to manage risks (such as risk management strategies, risk-based land-use planning, and so on).

Figure 4.17 Cantonal hazard map for avalanches, water, rock falls and landslide risks (example of Graubünden)

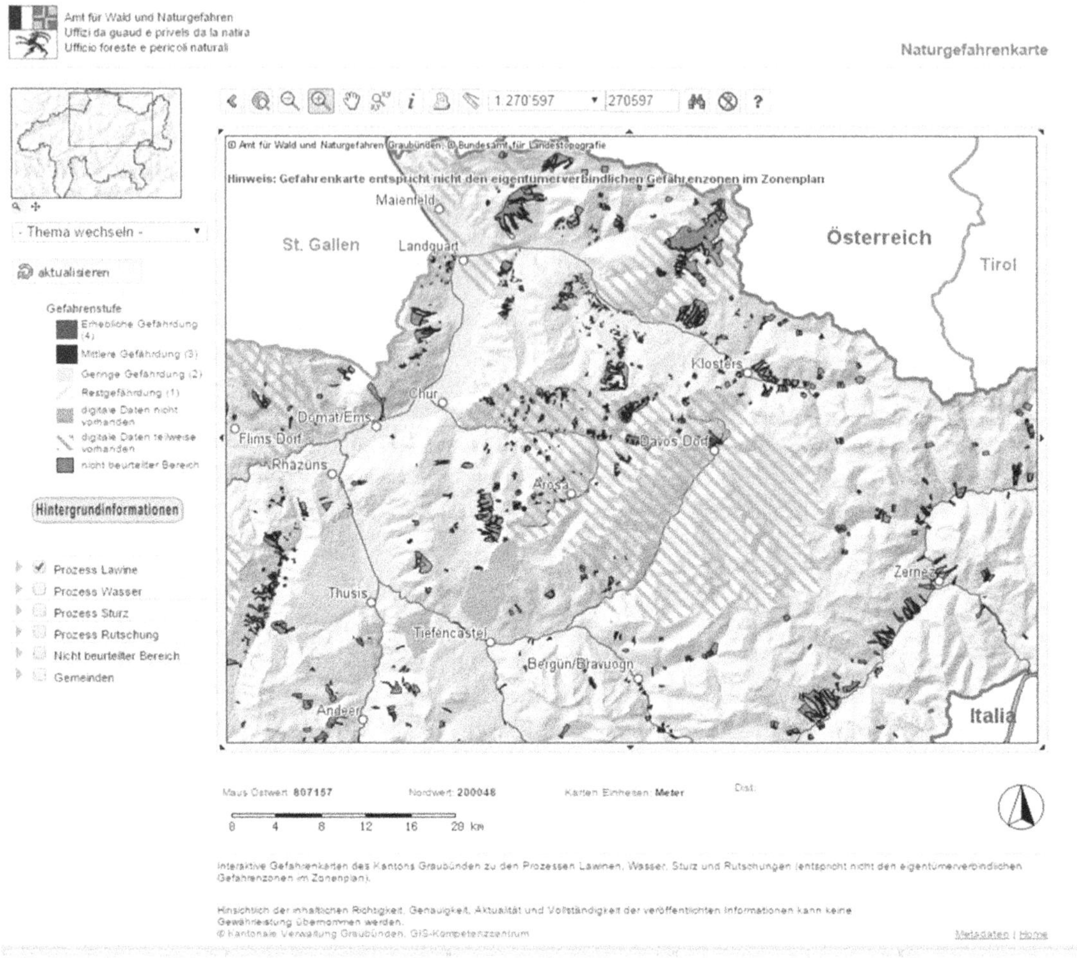

Source: Office for Forest and Natural Hazards (2016), http://map.geo.gr.ch/naturgefahrenkarte/naturgefahrenkarte.phtml

- Switzerland makes sure to integrate risk communication in school curricula. The *Lehrplan 21*"[11] and the "*Plan d'études romand*"[12] seek to introduce children primary school to the origins of natural hazards. The topic is studied again in more depth during high school.

Despite the number of good practices there are some prevailing challenges in risk communication. First, communication regarding earthquake risk is comparatively low. Given that the potential impacts of earthquakes could be greater than those of any other natural hazard, it is important to boost earthquake risk communication efforts. Second, despite all the innovative risk communication approaches and tools, the biggest challenge that remains is to maintain risk awareness levels. Awareness is high after major disaster events, but decreases the more time has passed since then. Especially those citizens that have not personally experienced the impacts of a disaster are not sensitive to the topic. Since Switzerland's direct democratic culture is very much based on citizens' demands, low awareness levels may also negatively impact the public resources allocated towards disaster risk prevention management.

Business continuity planning

Business continuity planning plays a crucial role in the context of critical infrastructure protection. Many enterprises in Switzerland have already established risk management systems including business continuity planning or security management. The primary focus of the application of these management systems usually lies in evaluating and managing the potential economic consequences of disasters for the enterprise. However, there is also a joint responsibility by the operator of the critical infrastructure and the public authority to take potential consequences of a critical infrastructure failure that are of importance for the general public into account. To support the critical infrastructure owners and operators in this endeavour, FOCP has issued a "Guideline for the Protection of Critical Infrastructure"[13] (FOCP 2012). It applies a holistic approach for dealing with relevant hazards and considers all conceivable disaster risk prevention and mitigation measures. In the risk assessment process, natural hazards as well as man-made hazards and technical failures are considered. A broad variety of measures are evaluated, ranging from organizational adjustments to structural-technical provisions. As absolute protection is not possible, nor feasible, proportionality of cost and benefits as well as a continued process of disaster risk prevention and mitigation measures are important. The more likely a risk occurs and the larger its potential damage to the community, the more extensive and comprehensive should the protective and mitigation measures be. The Guideline includes a monitoring and evaluation step in order to evaluate the success of the measures implemented. As the Guideline is non-binding and the FOCP is not a regulatory agency, critical infrastructure operators are not obliged to apply the Guideline. More and more economic associations and specific critical infrastructure owners are however interested in the application of the Guideline.

A whole-of-society approach to disaster risk prevention management

In advocating for a paradigm change, the Swiss risk management strategy of 2004 (PLANAT, 2004a), which is currently being revised, argued that if disaster risk prevention management is to be successful, it needs to be shared by all of society. This includes government, other public authorities, academia, insurers, practitioners as well as private sector actors and citizens.

Individual responsibility in the management of natural hazards has been a key priority in Switzerland. Individuals are expected to contribute to overall safety levels by investing in object-specific safety measures (such as the example provided in Figure 4.18) as well as adapt their behaviour to potential imminent disasters. The public insurance providers and the nation-wide public insurance association play a key role in informing about such individual measures. The insurance association, for example, issues detailed technical guidance notes for engineers, architects and construction companies on the different options to retrofit houses against the impacts of gravitational, climatological or tectonic hazards or to incorporate efficient techniques into new constructions (Egli, 2005).

Figure 4.18 Object-specific protection measure

Source: Jordi, Meier, Staub in Egli (2005), Building Protection against gravitational natural hazards, Guidelines, Union of the cantonal fire insurance agencies Note: adaptation of the house of the roof to its slope to make the avalanche run smoothly over it.

Lessons learned

Systematically assessing major natural disasters and learning lessons for improving risk management have been fostered as part of Switzerland's disaster risk management culture. Many reforms were implemented as a consequence of major disaster events. For example, after the devastating floods in 1987, a paradigm change was introduced recognising the limits of structural protection measures in providing protection against floods. Risk-informed land-use planning based on the development of hazard maps and the determination of different protection levels for different types of land-use came to the fore. Legal frameworks, including the water engineering law and the forestry law were revised and a new risk management strategy developed (BWG and BUWAL, 1991).

Assessing the risk management system after the 2005 floods underlined the importance of preparing for extreme events and reminded Swiss actors at all levels that uncertainties, driven by the potential impacts of climate change, require them to adjust the risk management system throughout its phases. The ex-post evaluations made apparent that many protective measures were built based on old technologies that did not take into account for example the compounding effects of bed loads in rivers. These evaluations identified a need to adapt old protective infrastructure to modern standards, which is a process that could take decades. The lessons learned also emphasised the importance and the need to collaborate and to improve the exchange of information during disaster events. Finally, an extensive analysis of risk awareness was undertaken, based on an historical analysis of media reports as well a survey across Switzerland. The results showed that memories of major disaster events fade quickly with time and those that perceive to be exposed to high levels of risks do not necessarily undertake individual prevention investments (Bezzola and Hegg (2007; 2008a +b).

Box 4.3 Mobiliar Lab for Natural Risks: A Private Public Partnership to bridge the Gap between Science and Application

The Mobiliar Lab was established in 2013 as a joint research initiative of the Swiss Mobiliar Insurance (providing the financial assistance for the initiative) and the Oeschger Centre for Climate Change Research at the University of Bern. The Mobiliar Insurance company has funded risk prevention investments by public authorities over the past 10 years, spending some CHF 32 million. The emphasis has been to provide seed funding to mostly poorer communities (usually around 50% of the community share of prevention measures) for building public protective infrastructure, focusing on river beds. To further support disaster risk reduction efforts, Mobiliar Lab was established to foster progress in high resolution spatial modelling of natural risks to inform the management and insurability of natural risks. The Mobiliar Lab focusses on risks from hail, storm, floods and mass movements in Switzerland.

Among the projects the Mobiliar Lab is working on are:

- Hazard maps of winter storms;
- Developing radar-based hail hazard maps to improve hail warning systems;
- Development of a spatial insurance claim database of Switzerland;
- Development of a country-wide spatial database of buildings and content exposed to and hit by floods;
- Evaluation of 71 flood protection projects to identify improvements in the planning and implementation process and to evaluate the role of insurance involvement; and,
- Beside research, a major goal of the Lab is to bring research findings into practice to improve natural risk management and prevention efforts.

Source: Universität Bern (2016). Mobiliar Lab for Natural Risks University of Bern, Switzerland, http://www.mobiliarlab.unibe.ch/; Presentation by Röthlisberger, V. and Künzler, M (2016)) during OECD mission

Conclusion

Protective infrastructure investments have been a core part of Switzerland's disaster risk prevention measures. A large stock of infrastructure has been created since the early 19th century. Aging infrastructure, much of which has been built in reaction to events rather than in a forward-looking manner, along with sub-national maintenance budget constraints, may contribute to exacerbating vulnerabilities in current infrastructure. Efforts are underway to build a central database to contain information on the level of maintenance and rehabilitation needs of the current infrastructure. This should help prioritise maintenance investments and inform budgeting for term maintenance finance needs in the medium term. Although these developments are encouraging, it is important that maintenance funding is not being made available at the expense of future infrastructure investment needs. When deciding on future infrastructure investments, a forward-looking perspective that takes long-term risk evolution into account is crucial (Suter et al, 2016). This should receive further attention at the local level, but is equally important for cantonal and federal level decisions.

In the past decade, the gaps of locally available hazard and risk assessments as well as their integration into land-use plans for most natural hazards have been closing for new construction projects. Owing to high construction activities prior to the availability of hazard maps, the gaps are closing slower in the case of existing buildings. Efforts to provide information on the effect of local soil on earthquake risks are underway that will inform changes in the development of building codes in different earthquake zones. To improve strategic national level planning, it would be desirable to speed up the compilation and harmonisation of national level risk maps. Although factors that might alter risk patterns in the medium term, such as climate change, have started to being addressed in the risk mapping process, this could perhaps also benefit from being implemented more rapidly so as to allow other risk management actions to adjust swiftly.

Risk communication has been a good example that shows the commitment of Switzerland to a whole-of-society approach to disaster risk prevention management. The role of insurance providers and individual citizens and businesses in reducing risks through behavioural measures and self-protection investments is significant. An evaluation of the actual take-up of disaster risk reduction measures across societal actors could in the future inform activities that aim at increasing whole-of-society contributions to disaster risk reduction.

Risk Management Financing

Section Highlights

- Studies were conducted in the past to collect information about the total value of investments in disaster risk prevention across levels of government and non-governmental actors in Switzerland. This has not been done on a regular and systematic basis. To ensure that public spending in a fragmented context, such as in Switzerland, is effective, it is important to collect figures on investment volumes by all levels of government, and ideally non-governmental actors, on a more regular basis.

- Fluctuations in disaster risk prevention funding across levels of government that are caused by general economic conditions or by the occurrence of major disasters make medium-term planning difficult. In a context of increasing funding needs for maintaining and rehabilitating existing infrastructures, financial planning uncertainty could increase vulnerabilities in aging protective infrastructure.

- The quasi-mandatory insurance system has enabled an extremely high level of household and business resilience against the impacts of disasters. Discussions have been ongoing for preparing the conditions for introducing earthquake risks. Even though insurance companies are actively engaged in fostering risk-prevention measures among their clients, it is important to evaluate the effectiveness of these activities, given the significant disincentivising effects mandatory insurance schemes can have.

Public expenditure for disaster risk prevention and mitigation

Cantons and the federal state share the responsibility for protection measures. Public funding for disaster risk prevention is dependent on financial planning at the federal level, the needs of the cantons and the occurrence of natural disasters. Since funding for disaster risk prevention is provided by several actors and levels of government, the picture of the total investments in natural disaster risk prevention across Switzerland is rather fragmented.

The total allocation for disaster risk prevention at the national level is determined by the needs for investments in disaster risk prevention projects by the cantons as well as on the basis of the 4-year programmatic allocations. There is no longer term planning of financial needs for disaster risk prevention. In recent years, cantonal level funding for disaster risk prevention has reduced, which reduces demand for complementary national funding.

There is no systematic and regular overview of the total budget allocation for disaster risk prevention in Switzerland. PLANAT conducted a study in 2007 where it collected different expenditure figures by different levels of government and non-governmental actors. This exercise revealed that, in 2007, a total of CHF 2.9 billion was spent annually on natural hazard protection in Switzerland. The insurance sector, private companies and households provided CHF 1.7 billion of this amount. Of the remaining CHF 1.2 billion, the national authorities contributed CHF 462 million, the cantons CHF 321 million and the municipalities CHF 393 million, which corresponded to approximately 2% of the federal budget (PLANAT 2014). 30% of the total investments were used for flood risk prevention (PLANAT, 2014).

For 2015, PLANAT conducted a survey of the public funding across levels of government for disaster risk prevention management. It found that, of the total annual amount for risk management, CHF 1.3 billion was spent on prevention, CHF 392 million on emergency interventions and CHF 1.1 billion on rehabilitation.

Figures 4.20 and 4.21 show the evolution of national-level expenditures for floods and other natural hazards. The graphs show that budgets are strongly reactive to the occurrence of significant disaster events. For example, the budget saw a significant increase in terms of funding after the floods in 2005. Before the event, FOEN was not in a position to finance all disaster risk prevention investment requests which is why rigorous application of Cost-Benefit Analysis was necessary to determine priorities. Since the 2005 floods, this process has been reversed and the FOEN has more funding available than requests received. It is expected that in the next years, funding will again become scarce, given an increase in protective infrastructure investments and the potential central level funding requirement for maintenance costs (discussed in section IV).

In combination with the absent systematic and regular overview of the total budget allocation for disaster risk prevention, the federal budget developments indicate that Switzerland's disaster risk prevention system might be in a less proactive position than its responsible actors might like it to be. Variations in the investment budgets for protective infrastructure seem to come from federal level contributions, but also from sub-national level contributions (Figure 4.22).

With regard to flood, landslide, rockfalls and avalanche risk management, the total amount of annual expenditure equals the total estimated average of damages stemming from these hazard sources, which corresponds to about CHF 320 million annually.

Figure 4.19 Expenditure for flood risk management at national level, 1972-2014

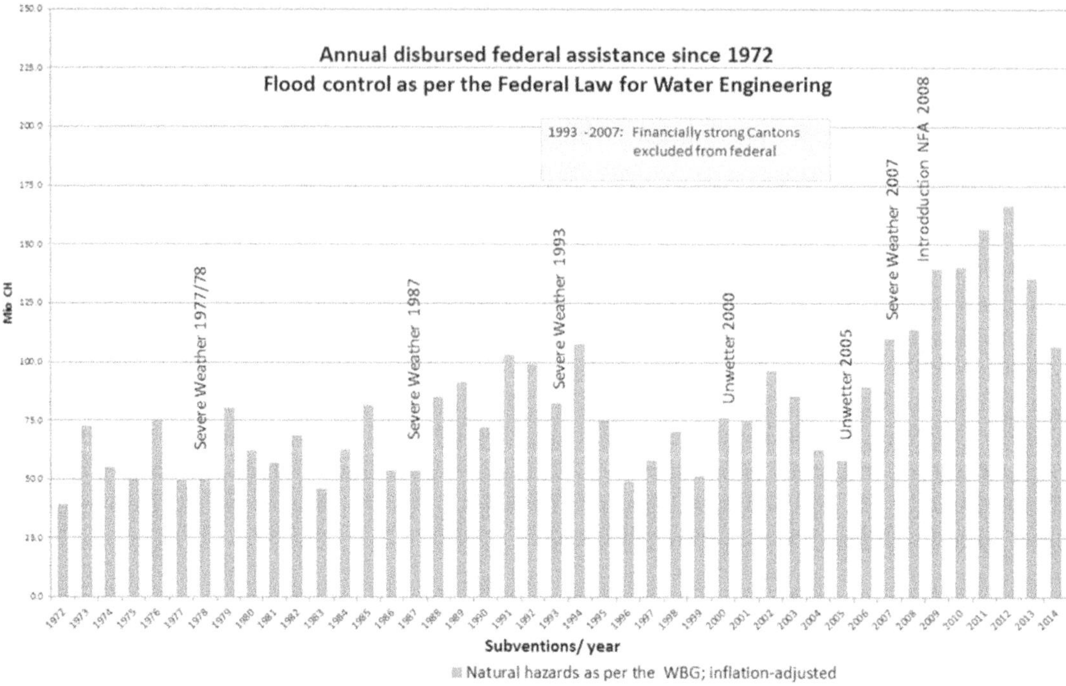

Source: Federal Statistical Office (2016), https://www.bfs.admin.ch/bfs/en/home/statistics.html

Figure 4.20 Expenditure for landslide, rock falls and avalanche risk management at national level, 1972-2014

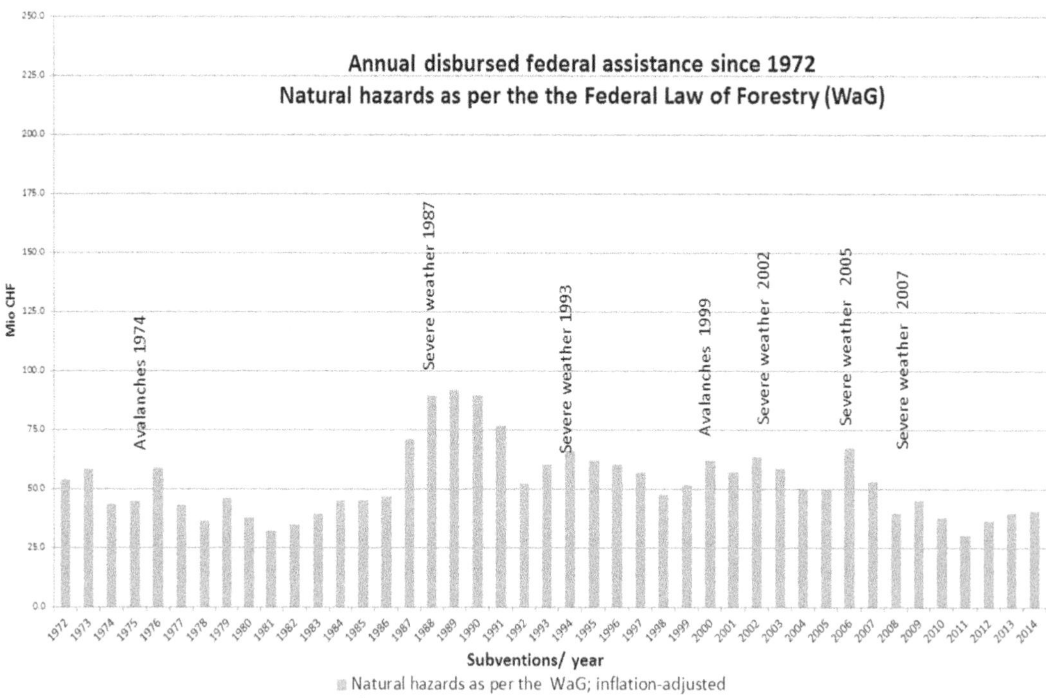

Source: Federal Statistical Office (2016), https://www.bfs.admin.ch/bfs/en/home/statistics.html

Figure 4.21 Investments in Flood Protection, 1970-2012 (Federal contributions versus total investments)

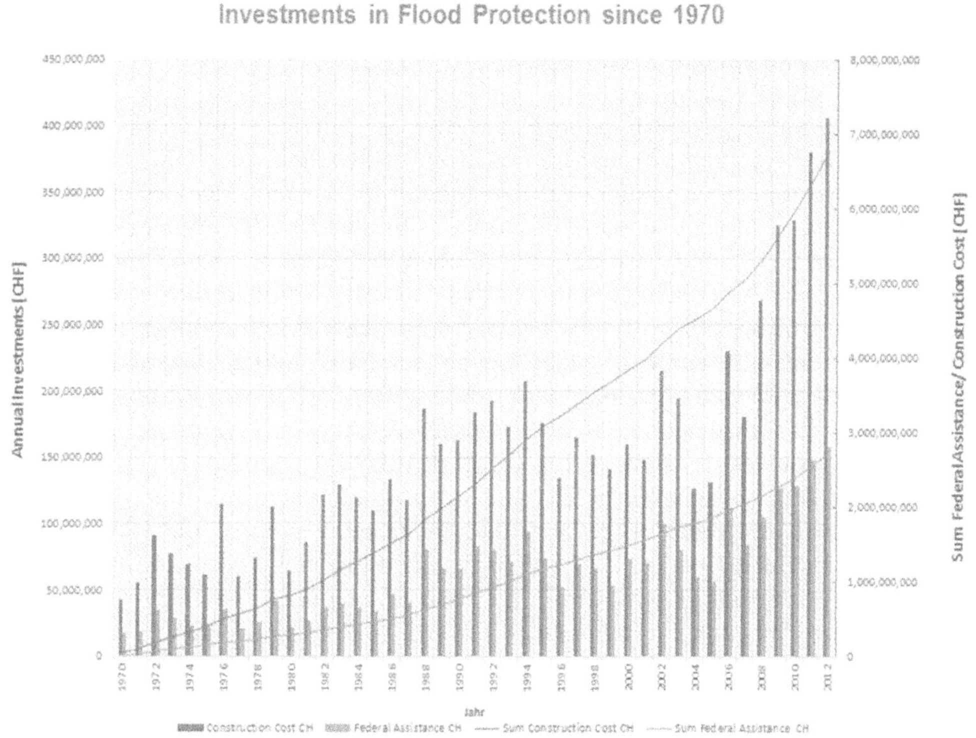

Source: Presentation of PLANAT during OECD mission; FOEN (2016a)

As mentioned in the previous section, central-level funding for structural protective measures is allocated to cantons on a programmatic, 4-years basis. This excludes big investment projects that cost above CHF 5 million, for which separate funding is provided. The basis for programmatic allocation decisions are – among others – the damage potential determined on the basis of the Aquaprotect flood zones[14] and the needs arising from the planning at sub-national level.

Natural Hazard Insurance

Switzerland has nationwide natural hazard insurance for buildings and content, which is linked to fire insurance. Cover is provided for damages arising from floods, storms, hail, avalanches, snow pressure and rockfall or landslides.

In 19 cantons, building insurance is provided by cantonal monopoly insurers (PIBs), which are public, non-profit companies. In the remaining seven cantons (Geneva, Uri, Schwyz, Ticino, Appenzell Innerrhoden, Valais and Obwalden) natural hazard insurance for buildings is provided by private insurance companies. Insurance must be provided for all buildings in a canton, regardless of their risk exposure, but premium rates can be adjusted, if they face high risk exposure (e.g. in one of the cantons: glasshouses and buildings with an extraordinarily bad loss experience may face premium rates of 40 per mill instead of 0.4 per mill of the sum insured) (OECD, 2016). The PIBs cover 80% of the insured assets.

Coverage for building insurance is similar across the country and premium tariffs are affordable. In all but four cantons (Geneva, Tessin, Valais and Appenzell Innerrhoden) building insurance is mandatory. The total value of building damages has to be compensated. Deductibles can vary between 10% and 15% of damage, with a minimum of CHF 200 and a maximum of CHF 2000).

Content insurance against natural hazards is provided by private insurance companies across the country, except for Vaud and Nidwalden where this is provided by the PIBs. The extent of the content cover is regulated and is similar across the country. In contrast to building insurance, content insurance is limited by policyholder and by event. Content insurance is voluntary throughout the country, except for Vaud and Nidwalden. The Swiss Insurance Association estimates that 90% of all households have household insurance, which means that property owners very likely have building insurance and renters have household insurance. Many businesses have natural hazard insurance for their inventory as well as for business interruption. The PIBs formed a non-profit, inter-cantonal reinsurance association (*Interkantonaler Rückversicherungsverband,* IRV) in 1910. The IRV provides reinsurance for 18 of 19 PIBs for fire and natural hazards (the canton of Bern left the association in 2014). Losses accumulated over one year are added together for calculating reinsurance pay-outs. In its own interest, the IRV is strongly engaged in loss prevention as well. The PIBs founded their own prevention fund in 2004 (IRV, 2016) to support those activities in the field of long-term risk research projects. In addition, private insurance companies formed the Swiss Natural Perils Pool (*Schweizerischer Elementarschaden-Pool*) to better equalize the risk associated with natural disasters and to enable affordable flat premiums for all policy holders[15].

Finally, Switzerland created the *"fondssuisse",* a fund for natural hazard damages that cannot be insured, formerly called the Swiss elementary damage fund (*Schweizerischer Elementarschädenfonds*)[16]. Created in 1901, it was founded by the Swiss society for public utility (*Schweizerische Gemeinnützige Gesellschaft,* SGG). It is funded by taxes and insurance premiums. The fund provides support for damages from natural hazards that were not predictable or insurable. The payments from the fund are voluntary and no one can claim a right for pay-out. The pay-outs are dependent on the financial situation of the persons suffering the damage (deductions are made for persons having an income above CHF 100,000). 60% of the damages are usually compensated, which often gets complemented by cantonal funds.

Switzerland's insurance system is strongly rooted in solidarity and has in the past demonstrated that its objective of achieving resilience in citizens and businesses against natural disasters has been efficiently achieved. Swiss insurance authorities are conscious of the potential moral hazard risk that arises when insured clients rely on insurance pay-outs instead of investing in disaster risk reduction efforts prior to a disaster. Therefore, insurance companies have been actively engaged in not only informing citizens about their individual responsibility (in terms of adapting their behaviour in the event of a disaster, and in terms of investing in self-protection measures), but enforcing it when providing eventual pay-outs for damage compensation. For example, if expected disaster risk reduction measures were not installed, the insurance company would decrease the pay-out amounts. It is important to systematically evaluate the effectiveness of these measures to understand whether moral hazard is being successfully avoided.

Mandatory earthquake insurance currently does not exist, except for the canton of Zurich, although private insurers supply earthquake covers for interested clients. Cover is provided by the PIBs in 17 out of 26 cantons if an intensity of VII on the European Macro-seismic Scale or higher is reached. As earthquake is an excluded peril, the cover granted by the PIB is technically neither insurance nor an indemnification, but rather a voluntary contribution. This is done through the Swiss Pool for Earthquake coverage (*Schweizerischer Pool für Erdbebendeckung*), managed by the IRV. No additional premium is paid by policy holders. The Pool has a maximum of CHF 2 billion of pay out, plus another 2 billion in case of further earthquakes following the first. If losses exceed this amount, percent deductions will be applied to all claims. The deductible amounts to 10% of the insured value, with a minimum of CHF 50 000.

A proposal for nationwide mandatory earthquake insurance with a capacity of CHF 20 billon has been worked out by the federal government (under the lead of the Federal Department of Finance, EFD) and the insurance industry between 2013 and 2014. This proposal could be implemented in two ways, either through an agreement between all cantonal governments (concordat) or through a constitutional modification. To date, neither solution could be implemented as 6 of the 26 cantons are against the introduction of a mandatory insurance and the majority of the parliament is against a constitutional modification. Further discussions are currently being held to try to convince all cantonal governments to adhere to the idea of a concordat. In the meantime, it has been recognised that an organisation should be created to assess the damage after an event and distribute the financial aids to the building owners. Such an organisation would be needed with or without a mandatory insurance. Work in this direction involving FOEN and the insurance industry started in 2016.

Conclusion

Switzerland has invested significant amounts of resources in protecting their citizens and the economy against the negative impacts of natural disasters. Guided by solidarity, all levels of government as well as non-governmental actors have contributed to reducing risks stemming from natural disasters. However, in despite of these contributions – or perhaps because of them – there exists an incomplete picture of the financial contributions by the different actors. Without an understanding of the total regular contributions by all actors, the steering of disaster risk prevention management towards priority projects is difficult and may render protective infrastructure investments less effective. It is important to compile this information across cantons and different non-governmental actors to better target and prioritise spending, to make sure that expenditures by different actors are not undermining each other and to provide more transparency and accountability.

A clearer picture of the total available resources is even more important in the future. With changing climatic conditions and other risk factors evolving in the future, Swiss authorities expect investment needs for protective measures will increase. At the same time, it is becoming increasingly clear that maintenance and rehabilitation needs for the large existing stock of aging infrastructure are set to increase too. To meet future disaster risk prevention investment needs, it is important to engage in longer-term financial needs assessments and financial planning to avoid an increase in vulnerability to citizens and assets from the impacts of disasters.

Finally, Switzerland is a best practice example in terms of achieving near-universal coverage against natural disasters through mandatory insurance. Swiss citizens and businesses enjoy affordable access to full coverage of eventual natural disaster damages, except for earthquake risks are currently under debate for inclusion. Insurance companies and Swiss authorities are very aware of the potential moral hazard risk that arises if insured households or businesses refrain from investing in self-protection measures to reduce eventual damages. In light of this, active campaigns have been launched to inform clients of their disaster risk reduction obligations. Insurance companies may also reduce or refuse damage compensation payments in case expected disaster risk reduction measures were not implemented. It is important to evaluate the effectiveness of past and ongoing campaigns to reduce the risk of moral hazard so as to improve the efficiency of natural disaster insurance in the future.

Assessment and Recommendations

Switzerland is a landlocked country, geographically marked by the Alps in the South and the Swiss Plateau and the Jura in the Northwest, where the majority of the population is concentrated. The topographical differences between the three geographical areas and regional climatic variations leave the country exposed to a variety of different hazards, ranging from gravitational and water-related hazards over meteorological hazards to tectonic hazards.

Over the last seventy years, Switzerland's population almost doubled and housing and infrastructure grew accordingly. The increase in building stock and land used for infrastructure and industrial activities went hand in hand with an increase in infrastructure and building stock at risk, with for example 25% of assets and 22% of the population as well as 30% of jobs located in flood risk areas.

Switzerland has recognised the need to address the risk it faces and has embraced a modern and forward-looking whole-of-society approach to managing disaster risk reduction. Different levels of government, as well as insurance companies, private sector actors and citizens share the responsibility for disaster risk reduction management. Swiss disaster risk management has a long tradition, with first cantonal investments dating back to the 18th century and the first legal basis passed in 1848. In contrast to the original measures, Switzerland today prioritises nature-based protective measures and a culture of risk in society, taking a forward-looking rather than a reactive approach to managing disaster risks.

Identification and monitoring of current and future risks

Switzerland has taken a forward-looking approach to managing the risks it faces and increasingly puts natural disasters in perspective with other risks, including pandemics and nuclear accidents. Systematically assessing major natural disasters and learning lessons for improving risk management has been fostered as part of Switzerland's disaster risk management culture. As a consequence the level of awareness and alertness about future changes to disaster risk patterns, both from a socio-economic development perspective and a climate risk perspective, is high. The natural hazard management strategy highlights factors that may change future risk exposure, addresses expected increases in vulnerability linked to economic interconnectivity and takes changes in climate and weather into account. Works are underway to understand the underlying socioeconomic and climatic patterns more closely and to integrate potential implications into local risk management planning and implementation. Well-established channels of risk communication at the national and cantonal level and by insurance providers help informing citizens and authorities about the risks they face.

Switzerland has achieved a remarkable level in terms of comprehensiveness and quality in recording losses caused by disaster events. Since the 1970s social and economic disaster losses from storms, floods, debris flows, landslides and (since 2002) rockfalls are systematically registered in a central data repository administered by the Federal Institute for Forest, Snow and Landscape Research (WSL). Data currently is obtained from three main sources: newspaper articles, official data from cantons and data shared by the insurance industry. While it is a good practice to bring different actors on board of the data collection efforts, data may not always be equally complete or of the same quality. To address this, it could be useful to establish a more systematic approach to data collection across all cantons, including those where the natural hazard insurance is not organised by public insurance companies. It equally could be useful to expand the current database to also include damage caused by hazards currently not accounted for, such as metrological hazards. As indirect economic losses account for a significant share of total disaster losses, collecting data on them could provide a useful addition to the data already collected by the WSL.

Legal and institutional frameworks for disaster risk prevention management

Owing to Switzerland's long experience in addressing disaster risks, capacity for risk management is high. The strong legal and institutional risk management framework and the country's whole-of-society approach illustrate this.

The national level takes a steering role in defining the overall direction of risk management, underpinned by various sector-specific federal legal instruments and anchored in the Swiss constitution. At the federal level, the task of addressing different aspects of disaster risk reduction is shared between a range of actors, with FOEN in the lead of storm-, forest fire,- and water-related hazards, MeteoSwiss responsible for climate-related and meteorological hazards and FOCP in charge of the other risks of national importance. As a federal state, the responsibility for risk management is not only shared between various ministries, but also across levels of government. Cantons take the lead in enforcing national policies and supporting their implementation, while local municipalities actually turn policies into action.

Owing to the nature of Switzerland's federal system, local and cantonal responsibilities are not always the same, allowing for possible reinforcements of the system through a more streamlined division of responsibilities. As risks rarely take municipal or cantonal borders into account and may even cross national borders, governance structures also need to ensure that disaster risk management operates at the adequate scales. Inter-communal collaboration is crucial and should be further encouraged and streamlined across the country, especially as regards developing joint spatial planning strategies for shared river areas and for sharing the cost of protection measures across all communities that may benefit from the investment. International cooperation with neighbouring communities and stakeholders across Switzerland's borders, for example in flood risk management along transboundary rivers should be part of these efforts.

By creating national coordination platforms such as PLANAT for strategic risk management issues and LAINAT for operational risk management issues Switzerland has addressed some of the potential shortcomings of a fragmented governance system. While PLANAT is a key example for the Swiss whole-of-society approach to risk management, LAINAT is a platform on the federal level, bridging gaps between the various government actors involved in operational risk management. Although these bodies have been effective in establishing a common vision and agenda for disaster risk reduction, their activities could be more regularly evaluated and their governance structures potentially opened up further and strengthened further.

Switzerland is a good practice example for embracing a whole-of-society approach to disaster risk management. It is recognised that government efforts cannot be effective if private sector actors and individuals do not contribute their share in terms of risk adapted behaviour and self-protection investments. Insurance companies have played a key role in establishing a dialogue and informing private actors and citizens about their responsibilities in disaster risk prevention management.

Managing structural and non-structural measures to foster disaster risk prevention

Switzerland has a long and solid experience with natural disasters and their management. Over the last thirty years, the management of natural disasters underwent significant changes and developed into a modern, forward-looking risk management system that can serve as an example to many other countries. While structural measures for a long time have constituted the core of Switzerland's disaster risk prevention management, the last years have seen an increased use of non-structural measures along with a strong preference for "soft", nature-based measures.

Rather than fostering a reactive approach to disaster risk management, Switzerland has opted for an increasingly forward-looking system that integrates ecological, social and economic aspects in disaster risk prevention management and expects all actors of society to do their share for effective protection against natural hazards.

An exemplary whole-of-society responsibility for boosting resilience

Switzerland is an exemplary case of a country embracing a strong whole-of-society approach to risk management. The responsibility for risk management is shared across all relevant actors of society, from national and cantonal governments and municipalities over insurance companies, private sector actors to citizens and researchers. The approach is based on the philosophy that a state's efforts are only effective if all other actors are contributing to risk management, both in terms of behaviour and investment.

Along with public measures, individual responsibility in the management of natural hazards has been a key priority in Switzerland. Individuals and businesses are expected to contribute to overall safety levels by investing in object-specific safety measures, adapt their behaviour to potential imminent disasters and in the case of businesses evaluate and manage the potential economic consequences of disasters. As a result, there has been a significant increase in the capacity to cooperate and coordinate strategies and policies across sectors, but some challenges exist. Much of the implementation of building codes and of low hazard (yellow) regulations for example relies on private responsibility and requires high citizen awareness and private investments. Although insurance companies may reduce or refuse damage compensation payments if disaster risk reduction measures were not adequately implemented, there is a certain moral hazard risk. In the absence of strict public enforcement, this could potentially have negative impacts on overall private protection levels, as is observed in the case of yellow level hazards, which account for half of filed insured damage claims. Another challenge lies in the circumstance that individuals have to carry a significant part of the financial burden of individual disaster risk prevention measures. Financial rewards for preventive measures can help increase the likelihood of individuals implementing all disaster risk reduction measures recommended for their property, including those that are not mandatory.

The national platform for natural hazards, PLANAT, takes a key role in bringing together representatives from the federal government, cantonal governments, research community, professional associations, private sector and insurance companies to work on three important areas of work to boost disaster risk reduction throughout Switzerland. Especially the role of insurance providers and individual citizens and businesses in reducing risks through behavioural measures and self-protection investments is significant. An evaluation of the actual take-up of disaster risk reduction measures across societal actors could in the future inform activities that aim at increasing whole-of-society contributions to disaster risk reduction.

The whole-of-society approach also benefited from Switzerland's direct democratic governance tradition that has positively influenced disaster risk management by emphasising awareness and building acceptance for disaster risk reduction investments from the bottom up. Lengthy consultation processes have - more often than not - resulted in more efficient and effective disaster risk reduction investments.

A large stock of protective infrastructure protecting Switzerland

Protective infrastructure investments have been a core part of Switzerland's disaster risk prevention measures. Cantons and municipalities share the responsibility to protect citizens and assets from natural hazards, but the financing and construction of protective measures is distributed between the national government, cantons, municipalities, infrastructure operators or other public or private authorities.

A large stock of infrastructure has been created since the early 19th century, much of which is aging and has been built in response to disasters rather than in a forward-looking manner that takes long-term risk evolution into account. Aging infrastructure, along with sub-national maintenance budget constraints, may however contribute to exacerbating vulnerabilities in current infrastructure. Maintaining the existing stock of infrastructure is crucial, but challenging, especially in the absence of information on the status of maintenance and protection capacity. Efforts to build a central database on the level of maintenance of existing protective infrastructure are underway and show that Switzerland recognises this shortcoming. Once available the platform can help uncover possible gaps early on to prioritise maintenance investments and inform budgeting for maintenance finance needs in the medium term. It is however important that maintenance funding is not being made available at the expense of future infrastructure investment needs where no prior structural protection exists. It is also crucial that decisions for the construction of new protective infrastructure continue to embrace a forward-looking perspective that takes long-term risk evolution into account. This especially applies to local-level decisions, but is equally valid for cantonal and federal level decisions.

An increasing importance of non-structural disaster risk prevention measures

Systematically assessing major natural disasters and learning lessons for improving risk management has been fostered as part of Switzerland's disaster risk management culture. Since the late 1980's a paradigm change towards a greater use of non-structural risk management has been observed. Non-structural measures range from hazard mapping and land-use planning to risk communication and are important and cost-effective complements to structural protection measures.

Risk-informed land-use planning based on up-to-date hazard maps and the determination of protection levels for different types of land-use are key instruments to manage the risk exposure of people and assets. Although Switzerland has embraced this, some challenges remain. The gaps of locally available hazard and risk assessments have been closing rapidly for new construction projects, but are closing slower for older buildings. The integration of hazard and land-use plans has also not always been of the same pace across all municipalities and levels of government. In some cases, hazard information in land-use decisions appear to not have been adequately integrated yet or have not unlocked their full potential yet. Minor hazard (yellow) zones for example account for half of filed insured damage claims. It is recommended to speed up the process addressing this and to raise awareness for the need to respect regulations even in low hazard zones.

To further improve risk planning, it would also be desirable to speed up the integration of hazard and land-use plans, as well as the compilation and harmonisation of national level risk maps. Factors expected to influence risk patterns in the medium term, such as climate change, could perhaps also benefit from being implemented more rapidly into the risk mapping process to enable a swift adjustment of other risk management actions.

Even though earthquakes are assumed to be the hazard with the greatest expected amount of negative socio-economic impacts, only about half of the cantons have established maps of seismic soil foundation classes or spectral seismic zoning studies to account for the influence of the local soil on the earthquake hazard. The maps have only limited implications on zoning plans and do not lead to construction bans, which could lead to significant damage in case of an earthquake. It would be recommended to provide more attention to seismic hazard when designing hazard maps.

Risk communication, organized at the national level through LAINAT and PLANAT initiatives and accompanied by the efforts of insurance providers and cantonal governments, has been a good example that shows the commitment of Switzerland to a whole-of-society approach to risk management. Despite the many innovative risk communication approaches, it remains challenging to maintain high risk awareness levels. Awareness is high after major disaster events, but decreases the more time has passed. For citizens that have not personally experienced the impacts of a disaster the awareness may often be even less persistent. Communication efforts are also not equally high across all hazards and appear especially low for low reoccurrence high impact disasters. Earthquakes, which despite their potentially substantial impact do not feature high in Switzerland's risk communication efforts, are a key example for this. Since Switzerland's direct democratic culture is strongly based on citizens' demands, citizens' awareness level can significantly influence the amount of public resources allocated towards disaster risk prevention management. High awareness across hazards is also a critical factor in ensuring that everyone – including citizens and the private sector - fulfils their responsibilities. It is important to evaluate the effectiveness of past and ongoing campaigns to ensure their efficiency in light of changing channels of communication.

Shared risk financing across all levels of government and society

Switzerland has invested significant amounts of resources in protecting their citizens and the economy against the negative impacts of natural disasters. Guided by the principle of solidarity, all levels of government as well as non-governmental actors and citizens have contributed to reducing risks stemming from natural disasters. Along with the public and private sector, individual citizens are expected to contribute to overall safety levels by investing in safety measures for their properties. However, in despite of these contributions – or perhaps because of them – picture of the flow of financial contributions by the different actors is not complete. Reviews on the total budget allocation for disaster risk prevention are not done on a regular or systematic basis and even the picture on public funding flows is rather fragmented, making the steering of funding towards priority projects difficult. In light of the parallel absence of vast information on the status of maintenance and protection capacity of existing structural measures, the risk that investment decisions are not made strategically enough is substantial and effectiveness of public funding may be compromised. It is recommended to centrally and regularly collect funding information across cantons and different non-governmental actors to better target and prioritise spending and to avoid that expenditure by different actors are undermining each other. Collecting funding information in a central and regular manner also enhances transparency and accountability.

A clearer picture of the total available resources is even more important in the future. With changing climatic conditions and other risk factors evolving in the future, Swiss authorities expect higher investment needs for protective measures in the future. At the same time, it is becoming increasingly clear that maintenance and rehabilitation needs for the large existing stock of aging infrastructure are set to increase too. To meet future disaster risk prevention investment needs, it is important to engage in longer-term financial needs assessments and financial planning to avoid an increase in vulnerability to citizens and assets from the impacts of disasters.

Switzerland is a best practice example in terms of achieving near-universal coverage against natural disasters. Swiss citizens and businesses enjoy affordable access to full coverage of possible damages caused by the majority of natural hazard events. Insurance companies and Swiss authorities are very aware of the potential moral hazard risk that arises if insured households or businesses refrain from investing in self-protection measures to reduce eventual damages. In light of this, active campaigns have been launched to inform clients of their disaster risk reduction obligations. Insurance companies may also reduce or refuse damage compensation payments in case expected disaster risk reduction measures were not implemented. It is important to evaluate the effectiveness of past and ongoing campaigns to reduce the risk of moral hazard so as to improve the efficiency of natural disaster insurance in the future.

Notes

[1] http://www.bafu.admin.ch/umwelt/indikatoren/08596/08599/index.html?lang=en

[2] http://www.wsl.ch/fe/gebirgshydrologie/HEX/projekte/schadendatenbank/index_EN

[3] www.proclim.ch

[4] www.fan-info.ch

[5] http://www.alpconv.org/en/convention/default.html

[6] http://www.iksr.org/en/international-cooperation/about-us/index.html

[7] http://www.bafu.admin.ch/naturgefahren/14187/index.html?lang=en; http://www.bafu.admin.ch/naturgefahren/14186/14809/15591/index.html?lang=fr

[8] http://www.FOEN.admin.ch/naturgefahren/14186/14801/15746/index.html?lang=de

[9] https://www.geodienste.ch/

[10] *Tragwerksnormen des Schweizerischen Ingenieur- und Architektenverein (SIA)* (Norms for supporting structures of the Swiss Society of Engineers and Architects (SIA))

[11] http://v-ef.lehrplan.ch/index.php?code=b|6|4|1

[12] https://www.plandetudes.ch/shs_31#16914

[13] http://www.babs.admin.ch/en/aufgabenbabs/ski.html

[14] The Aquaprotect project, completed in 2008, is a joint venture by Swiss Re and FOEN to define flood hazard zones across Switzerland. Cantons without hazard maps covering the whole of their territory can use Aquaprotect to provide indications about the dangers of floods outside areas covered by hazard maps. The Aquaprotect, however, cannot replace hazard maps (FOEN, 2016c).

[15] http://www.svv.ch/en/consumer-info/non-life-insurance/swiss-natural-perils-pool

[16] https://www.fondssuisse.ch/de/fondssuisse

Bibliography

AG NAGEF Bern (2013), *Achtung, Naturgefahr! Verantwortung des Kantons und der Gemeinden im Umgang mit Naturgefahren* [Attention, Natural Hazard! Responsibility of the Canton and the Communities in Dealing with Natural Hazards], *Arbeitsgruppe Naturgefahren des Kantons Bern* [Working Group on Natural Hazards for the Canton of Bern], Bern, http://www.vol.be.ch/vol/de/index/direktion/ueber-die-direktion/publikationen.assetref/dam/documents/VOL/Naturgefahren/de/Achtung_Naturgefahr_deutsch.pdf

ARE and FOEN (2005), *Recommendation: Spatial Planning and Natural Hazards,* Federal Office for Spatial Planning and Federal Office for the Environment, Bern, www.bafu.admin.ch/publikationen/publikation/00806/index.html?lang=en

Badoux, A., N. Andres, F. Techel and C. Hegg (2016), "Natural Hazard fatalities in Switzerland from 1946 to 2015", *Natural Hazards and Earth System Sciences*, (forthcoming) doi:10.5194/nhess-2016-232

Bezzola, G.R. and C. Hegg (eds.) (2007), "*Ereignisanalyse Hochwasser 2005, Teil 1 – Prozesse, Schäden und erste Einordnung*" [Event Analysis: The Floods of 2005, Part 1 – Processes, Damage and First Classifications], Federal Office for the Environment (FOEN) and Swiss Federal Institute for Forest, Snow and Landscape Research (WSL), Bern, www.bafu.admin.ch/publikationen/publikation/00044/index.html?lang=de

Bezzola, G.R. and C. Hegg (eds.) (2008a), "*Ereignisanalyse Hochwasser 2005, Teil 2 – Analyse von Prozessen, Maßnahmen und Gefahrengrundlagen*" [Event Analysis: The Floods of 2005, Part 2 – Analysis of Processes, Measures and Risk Fundamentals], Federal Office for the Environment (FOEN) and Swiss Federal Institute for Forest, Snow and Landscape Research (WSL), Bern, www.bafu.admin.ch/publikationen/publikation/00100/ index.html?lang=de

Bezzola, G.R. and C. Hegg (eds.) (2008b), "The Floods of 2005 in Switzerland: Synthesis Report on the Event Analysis", Federal Office for the Environment (FOEN), Bern, www.bafu.admin.ch/publikationen/publikation/00819/index.html?lang=en.

BUWAL, BWG, BLW and ARE (2003), Guiding principles for Swiss watercourses. Promoting sustainable watercourse management, Federal Office for the Environment, Forests and Landscape, Federal Office for Water and Geology, Federal Office for Agriculture and Federal Office for Spatial Development, Bern, http://www.sib.admin.ch/fileadmin/_migrated/content_uploads/DIV-2703-E.pdf.

BWG (2001), Flood control at rivers and streams, Federal Office for Water and Geology, Bern, https://www.bafu.admin.ch/dam/bafu/en/.../flood_control_atriversandstreams.pdf.

BWG and BUWAL (1991), *Ursachenanalyse der Hochwasser 1987: Ergebnisse der Untersuchungen* [Cause Analysis of the Floods of 1987: Results of the Tests], Federal Office for Water and Geology and Federal Office for the Environment, Forests and Landscape, Bern, www.bafu.admin.ch/publikationen/publikation/00210/index.html? lang=de.

Denzler, L. (2016), *Rückbau wird zur Option.* [Deconstruction becomes an option], TEC21 12–13/2016, Zürich, pp. 35-36 https://www.espazium.ch/uploads/56eaec4aceeef.pdf

Egli, Th. (2005). *Wegleitung Objektschutz gegen gravitative Naturgefahren*, [Instructions for Physical Protection against Natural Hazards], Vereinigung Kantonaler Feuerversicherungen [Association of Cantonal Fire Insurers, VKF], Bern.

FCOP (2010), *Methode zur Erstellung des SKI Inventars. Programm zum Schutz Kritischer Infrastrukturen* [Method for the Creation of a SKI Inventory: Programme for the Protection of Critical Infrastructure]. Federal Office for Civil Protection, Bern. http://www.babs.admin.ch/content/babs-internet/de/aufgabenbabs/ski/kritisch/_jcr_content/contentPar/tabs/items/downloads/tabPar/downloadlist/downloadItems/211_1461243168279.download/methodeskiinventarde.pdf

Federal Statistical Office (2000), *"Die 26 Katone und Hauptorte der Schweiz"* [The 26 Cantons and Major Destinations in Switzerland], Federal Statistical Office, Neuchâtel, www.bfs.admin.ch/bfs/portal/de/index/regionen/thematische_karten/maps/raumgliederung/institutionelle_gliederungen.parsys.0002.PhotogalleryDownloadFile2.tmp/k00.22s.pdf

Federal Statistical Office (2016), "*Zukünftige Bevölkerungsentwicklung – Daten, Indikatoren - Schweiz Szenarien*" [Future Population Trends – Data, Indicators – Switzerland Scenarios], Federal Statistical Office, Neuchâtel, www.bfs.admin.ch/bfs/portal/de/ index/themen/01/03/blank/key/ent_erw.html

FOCP (2003), *Katarisk - Katastrophen und Notlagen in der Schweiz: eine Risikobeurteilung aus der Sicht des Bevölkerungsschutzes* [Disaster Risk – Catastrophes and Emergencies in Switzerland: Risk Assessment from a Civil Protection Point of View], Bern. http://www.babs.admin.ch/content/babs-internet/de/aufgabenbabs/gefaehrdrisiken/studienberichte/_jcr_content/contentPar/accordion/accordionItems/katarisk_eine_risiko/accordionPar/downloadlist_114077779/downloadItems/26_1461854500770.download/ragrinfoprintde.pdf

FOCP (2012), *Nationale Strategie zum Schutz kritischer Infrastrukturen* [National Strategy for the Protection of Critical Infrastructure], Federal Office for Civil Protection, Bern, www.admin.ch/opc/de/federal-gazette/2012/7715.pdf.

FOCP (2013), *Leitfaden KATAPLAN: Kantonale Gefährdungsanalyse und Vorsorge* [Guide KATAPLAN: Cantonal Hazard Analysis and Prevention], Federal Office for Civil Protection, Bern, www.babs.admin.ch/content/babs-internet/de/publikationen-und-service/downloads/

FOCP (2015), Welche Risiken gefährden die Schweiz? Katastrophen und Notlagen Schweiz 2015 [*What risks does Switzerland face? Disasters and Emergencies in Switzerland 2015]*, Federal Office for Civil Protection, Bern, http://www.preventionweb.net/files/submissions/47467_katastrophenundnotlagenschweizreport2015.pdf

FOCP (n.d.), *KATARISK – Katastrophen und Notlagen in der Schweiz. Eine Risikobeurteilung aus der Sicht des Bevölkerungsschutzes* [Disasters and Emergencies in Switzerland. A Risk Assessment from the Perspective of Civil Protection], Federal Office for Civil Protection, Bern, www.babs.admin.ch/content/babs-internet/de/aufgabenbabs/gefaehrdrisiken/studienberichte/_jcr_content/contentPar/accordion/accordionItems/katarisk_eine_risiko/accordionPar/downloadlist/downloadItems/4_1461852642742.download/zusammenprintde.pdf.

FOEN (2011), *Rechtliche Verankerung des integralen Risikomanagements beim Schutz vor Naturgefahren: Rechtsgutachten* [Legal Anchouring of Integrated Risk Management in Protecting Against Natural Hazards: Legal Opinion], Federal Office for the Environment, Bern, www.bafu.admin.ch/publikationen/publikation/01619/index.html?lang=de

FOEN (2012a), Adaptation to Climate Change in Switzerland: Goals, Challenges and Fields of Action – First Part of the Federal Council's Strategy, 2 March 2012, Federal Office for the Environment, Bern, www.bafu.admin.ch/publikationen/publikation/01673/ index.html?lang=en

FOEN (2012b), *Aufgabenteilung zwischen Versicherungen und der öffentlichen Hand im Bereich Naturgefahren. Zusammenfassender Bericht* [Tasks between Insurance Companies and the Public Sector in the Field of Natural Hazards: Summary Report], Federal Office for the Environment, Bern.

FOEN (2016a), *Umgang mit Naturgefahren in der Schweiz: Bericht des Bundesrats in Erfüllung des Postulats 12.4271 Darbellay am 14.12.2012* [Natural Hazards in Switzerland: Report of the Federal Council in Response to the Postulate 12.4271 of 14 December 2012], Federal Office for the Environment, Bern, http://www.bafu.admin.ch/naturgefahren/14144/16640/index.html?lang=de&download=NHzLpZeg7t,lnp6I0NTU042l2Z6ln1acy4Zn4Z2qZpnO2Yuq2Z6gpJCHe3x7gmym162epYbg2c_JjKbNoKSn6A--

FOEN (2016b), *Indikator Naturgefahren: Todesfälle durch Hochwasser, Murgänge, Rutschungen, Sturzprozesse und Lawinen* [Indicator Natural Hazards: Fatalities caused by floods, debris flows, landslides, fall processes and avalanches], Federal Office for the Environment (FOEN), Switzerland, *https://www.bafu.admin.ch/bafu/de/home/ themen/thema-*

naturgefahren/naturgefahren--daten--indikatoren-und-karten/ naturgefahren--indikatoren/indikator-naturgefahren.pt.html/aHR0cHM6Ly93d3cuaW5kaWthdG9yZW4uYWRtaW4uY2gvUHVibG/ljL0FlbURldGFpbD9pbmQ9R0UwMTQmbG5nPWRl.html

FOEN (2016c), "Aquaprotect," Federal Office for the Environment (FOEN), Switzerland, www.bafu.admin.ch/naturgefahren/14186/14801/16598/index.html?lang=de

FOEN (2016d), *Beurteilung der Gefährdung durch Extremhochwasser der Aare: Hauptstudie lanciert*. [Evaluation of extreme flood hazards along the Aare: Main study launched], Federal Office for the Environment (FOEN), Switzerland, http://www.bafu.admin.ch/dokumentation/medieninformation/00962/index.html?lang=de&msg-id=60609

FOEN (2016e), "EconoMe 4.0," Federal Office for the Environment, Bern, www.econome.admin.ch/index.php

FOEN (2016f), *Programmvereinbarungen und Einzelprojekte im Bereich Naturgefahren* [Programme Conventions and individual projects in the domain of natural hazards], Federal Office for the Environment, Bern, http://www.bafu.admin.ch/naturgefahren/ 14186/14809/15590/index.html?lang=de

FOEN (2016g), *Hitze und Trockenheit im Sommer 2015. Auswirkungen auf Mensch und Umwelt* [Heat and Drought in Summer 2015. Consequences for People and the Environment], Federal Office for the Environment, Bern, https://www.bafu.admin.ch/bafu/de/home/themen/klima/publikationen-studien/publikationen/Hitze-und-Trockenheit-im-Sommer-2015.html.

Heim, R. (2016), *Risikokarten. Gefahren erkannt – und die Risiken?* [Risk Maps. Recognizing Dangers – and the Risk?], TEC21 12–13/2016, Zürich, pp. 26-29, https://www.espazium.ch/uploads/56eaec4aceeef.pdf.

Heim, R. and L. Denzler (2016), *Naturgefahren in der Schweiz. Mehr als ein Fünftel der Bauzonen sind gefährdet.* [Natural Hazards in Switzerland. More than a fifth of Construction Areas are at Risk], TEC21 12–13/2016, Zürich, pp. 30-34, https://www.espazium.ch/uploads/56eaec4aceeef.pdf.

Hilker, N., Badoux, A. and Hegg, C. (2009), “The Swiss flood and landslide damage database 1972–2007.”, Natural Hazards Earth Systems Science, Vol. 9, pp. 913–925, doi:10.5194/nhess-9-913-2009

IRV (2008), *Ereignisanalyse Hochwasser 8./9. August 2007* [Incident Analysis Floods August 8/9 2007]. Inter-Cantonal Re-Insurance Association, Bern. irv.ch/getmedia/d029b45e-09aa-4fdc-909a-4d3018dcb118/Hochwasser-2007_d.pdf.aspx

IRV (2010), *Analyse langfristiger Gebäudeschadendaten. Auswertung des Datenbestandes der Schadenstatistik VKF* [Analysis of Long-Term Structural Damage Data: Evaluation of VKF's Stock of Damage Data]. Inter-Cantonal Re-Insurance Association, Bern, irv.ch/getmedia/dc580f6c-5cb3-4606-82cf-cdfd586a74d6/Bericht-SchadenstatDaten_2011-12-27_V1-1.pdf.aspx.

IRV (2012a), *Ereignisanalyse Hagel 2009. Untersuchung der Hagelunwetter vom 26. Mai und 23. Juli 2009* [Incident Analysis Hail 2009. A Study of the May 26 and July 23 2009 Hailstorms]. Inter-Cantonal Re-Insurance Association, Bern. irv.ch/kgvonline/ media/IRV/Downloads/Ereignisanalyse-Hagel-Website_2012-03-23_V1-3d.pdf

IRV (2012b), *Ereignisanalyse Hagel 2011. Untersuchung des Hagelunwetters vom 12. / 13. Juli 2011 im Kanton Aargau* [Incident Analysis Hail 2011. A Study of the July 12/ 13 2011 Hailstorms in Aargau]. Inter-Cantonal Re-Insurance Association, Bern. irv.ch/getmedia/8007ce65-e40a-48d2-961f-0cd5c0d2f0c6/VKF_Brosch_Hagel_2011__DT_GzDb.pdf.aspx

IRV (2013), *Außergewöhnliche Schadenereignisse 2013* [Exceptional Damage Events 2013. Inter-Cantonal Re-Insurance Association, Bern. irv.ch/kgvonline/ media/IRV/ Ereignisse/Elementar/Ereignisse-2013d_2013-06-25_V0-0.pdf?ext=.pdf

IRV (2016), *Die Rückversicherung des IRV* [The Reinsurance IRV, Inter-Cantonal Re-Insurance Association], Bern. irv.ch/getmedia/f317969e-1939-4182-95cd-720b5c18333e/ Ruckversicherung_d.pdf.aspx

OECD (2014a), Boosting Resilience through Innovative Risk Governance, OECD Publishing, Paris, http://dx.doi.org/10.1787/9789264209114-en.

OECD (2014b), Recommendation of the Council on the Governance of Critical Risks, OECD Publishing, Paris.

OECD (2016), Financial Management of Flood Risk, OECD Publishing, Paris

PLANAT (2004a), *Sicherheit vor Naturgefahren. Vision und Strategie* [Protection against Natural Hazards: Vision and Strategy], National Platform for Natural Hazards, Biel, www.planat.ch/fileadmin/PLANAT/planat_pdf/alle_2012/2001-2005/PLANAT_2004_-_Sicherheit_vor_Naturgefahren.pdf.

PLANAT (2004b), *Strategie Naturgefahren Schweiz. Synthesebericht* [Protection against Natural Hazards: Synthesis Report], National Platform for Natural Hazards, Biel, www.planat.ch/fileadmin/PLANAT/planat_pdf/alle_2012/2001-2005/Ammann__Schneider_2004_-_Strategie_Naturgefahren_Schweiz.pdf.

PLANAT (2014), *Security Level for Natural Hazards: Strategy Protection against Natural Hazards*, National Platform for Natural Hazards, Biel, www.planat.ch/ fileadmin/PLANAT/planat_pdf/alle_2012/2011-2015/PLANAT_2014__Security_ Level_for_Natural_Hazards.pdf.

PLANAT (2016), The cycle of integrated risk management, National Platform for Natural Hazards, Biel, http://www.planat.ch/en/specialists/risk-management/what-has-to-be-done/

Röthlisberger, V. and Künzler, M (2016), "Mobiliar Lab for Natural Risks: Bridging the Gap between Science and Application," Presentation during OECD mission to Bern, 18 April 2016, Bern.

Schweizerischer Bundesrat (2012), *Raumkonzept Schweiz: Überarbeitete Fassung* [Spatial Concept for Switzerland: Revised Version], Schweizerischer Bundesrat, Bern, www.are.admin.ch/themen/raumplanung/00228/00274/index.html?lang=de.

SED (2016), *Earthquake risk in Switzerland,* Swiss Seismological Service, Bern, http://www.seismo.ethz.ch/en/knowledge/seismic-hazard-switzerland/

SSV (2010), *Die flächendeckende Erdbebenversicherung* [The comprehensive earthquake insurance]. Swiss Insurance Association SSV, Chur.

Suter, H. et al. (2016), *Was macht Hochwasserschutzprojekte erfolgreich? Eine Evaluation von Projektablauf und Risiko basierend auf den Perspektiven Schweizer Gemeinden.* [What makes a successful flood control project? – An evaluation of project procedure and risk based on the perspectives of Swiss communes.], INTERPRAEVENT 2016 – Conference Proceedings, Bern, pp. 159-167, http://interpraevent2016.ch/assets/editor/files/IP16_CP_digital.pdf

UNISDR (2015), "Concept note on Methodology to estimate direct economic losses from hazardous events to measure the achievement of target C of the Sendai Framework for Disaster Risk Reduction: A Technical Review", the United Nations Office for Disaster Risk Reduction (UNISDR), Geneva, www.preventionweb.net/documents/framework/Concept%20Paper%20-%20Direct%20Economic%20Loss%20Indicator%20methodology%2011%20November%202015.pdf

Universität Bern (2016), Mobiliar Lab for Natural Risks University of Bern, Switzerland, http://www.mobiliarlab.unibe.ch/

VKF (2005), *Wegleitung: Objektschutz gegen gravitative Naturgefharen* [Guidelines: Object Protection against Gravitational Natural Hazards], Association of Cantonal Fire Insurance Companies, Bern, http://www.vkf.ch/getmedia/cbc3e6c2-077c-4c66-bbab-d767c0e408f8/Wegleitung_Objektschutz_gegen_gravitative_Naturgefahren_D_V0-0.pdf.aspx.

WFCP (2016), "Switzerland: Cover system," World Forum of Catastrophe Programmes, www.wfcatprogrammes.com/c/document_library/get_file?folderId=14392&name=DLFE-2417.pdf

Annexes

Annex 1 List of Stakeholders met in the studied countries

Austria	France	Switzerland
Federal Ministry for Transport, Innovation and Technology (BMVIT)	Chamber of Agriculture of the Vaucluse	Canton of Bern - Office of Public Works, Transportation and Energy - Roads and Highways Authority
Federal Ministry of Agriculture, Forestry, Environment and Water Management (BMLFUW): Federal Water Engineering Administration (BWV)	Departmental directory for Territories and the Sea (DDTM) n°13 – Bouches du Rhone department: Natural hazards unit	Federal Office for Civil Protection (FOCP)
Federal Ministry of Agriculture, Forestry, Environment and Water Management (BMLFUW): Austrian Service for Torrent and Avalanche Control (WLV)	European Center for Flood risk prevention (CEPRI):	Federal Office for Environment (FOEN)
Federal Ministry of Agriculture, Forestry, Environment and Water Management (BMLFUW): Federal Forestry Service	French Insurance Association : Natural Risk Mission (MRN)	Federal Office for Spatial Development (ARE)
Federal Ministry of the Interior (BMI): International Civil Protection and Disaster Relief Affairs Department	French national railway company (SNCF): Defence Unit	Federal Roads Office
Federal Ministry of the Interior (BMI): National Crisis and Disaster Protection Management (SKKM)	General Secretariat for Regional Affairs (Prefecture)	Intercantonal RelInsurance Association (IRV)
Ministry of Defence and Sports (BMLVS)	Haut Rhone union (SHR)	Mobiliar Insurance
Ministry of Finance (BMF)	Joint Flood Commission	Mobiliar Lab for Natural Risks - University of Bern
Austrian Railway Services (OEBB)	Lyon Metropole (great Lyon)	Platform for Natural Hazards Management (PLANAT)
Austrian Insurance Association (VVO)	Ministry of Ecology, Sustainable Development and Energy, Directorate General for Risk Prevention: – Meteorological Risk Unit – Electric Energy, Great Dams and Hydraulic Technical Service – Flash Floods Plan Mission	Swiss Federal Institute for Forest, Snow and Landscape Research (WSL)

	– Territorial action unit	
Austrian Economic Research Institute (WIFO)	National Center for Scientific Research (CNRS)	
University of Natural Resources and Life Sciences (BOKU)	Regional council Provence-Alpes-Côte d'Azur (PACA): Major Natural Hazards Service	
The Austrian Conference of Spatial Planning (OEROK)	Regional Directorate for Environment, Land Management and Housing – Rhône Alpes (DREAL)	
Regional Torrent and Avalanche Control Service, Salzburg	Rhône National Company (CNR): Concession et heritage unit	
Austrian Association of Municipalities	SYMADREM, France Dikes association	
Mayor of the the municipality of Wald im Pinzgau	Syndicat Intercommunal du Bassin de l'Yzeron (SAGYRC)	
Government of the province of Salzburg, including Water Management and Flood Protection Service, Forestry Service and Deputy Governor	The Central Reinsurance Fund (CCR) – Natural Catastrophes in France – Actuarial Management - State-guaranteed	
Cooperatives for Protecting Waters	Transport of Electricity Network (RTE)	
	Urban community (*Établissement public de coopération intercommunale*, EPCI) Porte de Dromardeche	

Annex 2 Country Questionnaire

0. Statistics

We would be grateful if you could share any relevant disaster statistics you may have, including historical records of (but not limited to):

- Disaster events
- Socio-economic losses and damages of disaster events (public and private)
- Vulnerability information (population and assets at risk, and similar)
- Public expenditure for disaster risk management
- Public expenditure for disaster risk prevention and mitigation (ideally for different measures and activities)
- Potential evaluation studies of disaster risk prevention and mitigation activities
- Lessons learnt reports of past disasters

1 General institutional arrangements for disaster risk prevention and mitigation

1.Please share with us any relevant policy documents and strategies that set out the types of responsibilities you have in the management of disaster risk prevention and mitigation in Austria/ France/ Switzerland. Please also specify what types of risks these responsibilities cover.

2.Who are other key actors in different ministries, agencies and at different governmental levels, as well as the non-governmental sector, in charge of preventing and mitigating risks?

3.Is there a national coordinating body for disaster risk prevention and mitigation across different ministries and levels of government? *If so, please describe its role and functioning briefly.*

2 Disaster Risk Prevention and Mitigation Policies and Practice

4.What have been the priorities for disaster risk prevention and mitigation over the past years and what have they been influenced and determined by? What are the objectives for future disaster risk prevention and mitigation?

2.a Structural Measures

5. What types of structural measures is your organisation responsible for (e.g. structural measures to prevent avalanches (e.g. avalanche barriers), landslides (e.g. protective forests), rockfalls (e.g. steel nets), etc.)?

6. Is this responsibility shared with other organisations and/or other levels of government? If so, how is coordination and communication ensured? Have you encountered any challenges in coordination with other government entities e.g. overlapping responsibilities?

7. What is your approximate annual budget for structural measures? How has it evolved over the past years and what are the expectations for the future?

8. How is available funding at the national level allocated across the *Cantons*?

9. Who decides on structural measures? What is the decision-making process? What are your assumptions regarding return-periods and likelihood estimations underlying your structural measures?

Please name all actors involved in this process.

10. How are priorities set for implementing structural measures? Are evaluation tools used such as Cost-Benefit, Cost-Effectiveness or Multi-Criteria Analysis? *Please describe the application of such tools and their experienced advantages or disadvantages.*

11. How is cross-governmental corporation in the implementation and financing of structural measures assured? *(This includes sharing arrangements between national and sub-national governments, but also sharing arrangements among local communities.)*

12. Are other non-governmental organisations (including the private sector) participating in the financing of structural measures? If yes, please indicate how much they contribute on average.

13. Who is responsible for carrying out and for financing operation (if applicable) and **maintenance** of structural measures? How well are existing measures maintained?

14. Is proper maintenance of structural measures monitored? If yes, how and by whom?

15. What are the existing financial models for financing operations (if applicable) and maintenance in Austria/ France/ Switzerland? Are there cross-governmental (between national and sub-national or among different sub-national entities) financial arrangements? Are other, non-governmental actors, implicated in financing maintenance? What are the challenges?

16. Are there any innovative practices that you could highlight in the implementation and financing, or maintenance of structural measures?

2.b Non-Structural Measures

Hazard mapping and spatial/land use planning

17. Can you describe the processes for risk/hazard assessments (*Gefahrenzonenplanung*) in Austria/ France/ Switzerland, highlighting your role vis-à-vis others? Do you carry hazard assessments out for all of Austria/ France/ Switzerland? Is this assessment responsibility shared with sub-national organisations? If yes, who are they and how is this responsibility shared? *If a relevant document describes this best feel free to simply attach this as an answer.*

18. To our knowledge these assessments are used to develop risk/hazard maps. Are these maps accessible for the public? Are they accessible online? Can users - through this tool - determine their individual hazard and/ or risk exposure? Presuming that the availability of such information has improved over time, did this change the prevention investments among local stakeholders (e.g. citizens, private enterprises, etc.)?

19. How often are these risk/hazard assessments updated? Is the regularity sufficient to keep up with the pace of the development of exposure?

20. Do you include other actors (e.g. private sector, citizens, other non-governmental organisations, etc.) in the risk/hazard assessment process, if yes why and how? For example, public consultation after a first draft of the assessment is published, where actors can raise their concerns and provide feedback. *Please describe how this process is managed and what values or challenges this has brought to the process.*

21. What measures are in place to ensure the impartiality of experts conducting hazard analyses?

22. How is the formulation of land use policies linked to the above hazard assessment exercise and lessons learnt from previous disasters? Please describe the roles and responsibilities of institutions responsible for designing and implementing land use policies designed to reduce disaster damages in Austria/ France/ Switzerland?

23. To what extent is risk information integrated in land-use policies? For example, is construction forbidden on highly exposed land parcels? Can construction occur if specific mitigation measures are put in place? What are the challenges in integrating risk information in land use planning?

24. What are the enforcement mechanisms to ensure risk/hazard informed land use policies? Who is liable in the event of a disaster, if risk/hazard-based land use restrictions have been ignored? Have there been cases of malfeasance among responsible persons in terms of not using the results of risk analyses to inform land use policy or to grant building permits?

25. Please describe possible recent evolutions in land use policy in Austria/ France/ Switzerland related to disaster risk reduction? Have past disasters influenced policy changes and if so, how? Have previous disasters facilitated the implementation of planned policy changes before?

Building codes

26. Is hazard information/results of hazard assessment work translated into building codes and if yes how? If not, why not?

27. What are the mechanisms for enforcing building codes in Austria/ France/ Switzerland (e.g. inspections)? Is there a difference in treatment of public and private buildings? What measures are taken to shelter responsible organisations/inspectors from undue influence?

Risk communication / raising awareness

28. What are your organisation's role and responsibilities with regard to risk communication? Is this responsibility shared with other governmental levels at *cantonal* or local level? If so, how?

29. What are the purposes of risk communication of your activities? *Check all that apply.*

☐ Raise public awareness about hazards and risks
☐ Enhance knowledge about risks through education and training
☐ Enhance knowledge about what the recipient can do to self-protect against risks
☐ Encourage protective behaviour
☐ Promote the acceptance of risk management measures
☐ Inform on how to behave during hazardous events
☐ Warn of and trigger actions in response to imminent and current events
☐ Reassure the audience, improve relationships (build trust, cooperation, networks)
☐ Enable mutual dialogue and understanding
☐ Involve actors in decision making
☐ Other, *please specify* ___________________________

30. Are other actors involved in framing the communication process? If so, who and how? If so, has this contributed to an increase in the awareness level? *Please provide examples, if possible.*

Investments in disaster risk prevention and mitigation from private actors

31. What is the level of engagement by citizens and companies in investing in their individual protection against natural hazards?

32. What have been the measures to encourage self-protection? Has this changed recently and if so, how?

33. Has risk communication contributed to increased levels of stakeholders' protection? Has there been an evaluation of the effectiveness of risk communication in achieving this aim?

Business continuity planning and implementation

34. Are there policy tools in place to encourage business continuity planning (such as tax incentives, subsidies, regulations, awareness raising, etc)? If yes, have many businesses taken advantage of such policy tools.

Other non-structural prevention measures

35. Are there other non-structural prevention measures your organisation is responsible for that have not been mentioned in the above? Please describe.

3 Financial Arrangements *ex ante* and *ex post* of disasters

36. In case of a publicly declared disaster, is there public financial compensation or relief for damages offered to i) citizens; ii) enterprises; iii) public bodies (for public infrastructure reconstruction)? Please describe your organisation's role and responsibilities in such programmes?

37. If compensation is available, what are the exact arrangements? Is everyone compensated? At 100 percent of their losses? How long does the compensation process normally take?

38. Are there private (or semi-private) insurance schemes available for individual households or enterprises to protect themselves in the event of a disaster? If yes, are there public policies to encourage the purchase of insurance among individual households and

businesses? Is risk information shared with insurers? If this is not available, what are the reasons for its non-existence?

39. On average, or for a specific disaster event in the past, what share of reconstruction cost is paid by individual households or enterprises?

40. What role have supra-national funding arrangements (such as the European Solidarity Fund) played during past disasters, and in comparison to financial arrangements within Austria/ France/ Switzerland?

41. What have been the challenges in ensuring sufficient levels of financing for disaster risk prevention and mitigation activities?

4 Feedback and Organisational Change

42. Please describe your organisation's role and responsibilities with regard to feedback and organisational change to learn lessons from past disasters?

43. Are there past examples where experience has led to organisational or legislative change?

ORGANISATION FOR ECONOMIC CO-OPERATION AND DEVELOPMENT

The OECD is a unique forum where governments work together to address the economic, social and environmental challenges of globalisation. The OECD is also at the forefront of efforts to understand and to help governments respond to new developments and concerns, such as corporate governance, the information economy and the challenges of an ageing population. The Organisation provides a setting where governments can compare policy experiences, seek answers to common problems, identify good practice and work to co-ordinate domestic and international policies.

The OECD member countries are: Australia, Austria, Belgium, Canada, Chile, the Czech Republic, Denmark, Estonia, Finland, France, Germany, Greece, Hungary, Iceland, Ireland, Israel, Italy, Japan, Korea, Latvia, Luxembourg, Mexico, the Netherlands, New Zealand, Norway, Poland, Portugal, the Slovak Republic, Slovenia, Spain, Sweden, Switzerland, Turkey, the United Kingdom and the United States. The European Union takes part in the work of the OECD.

OECD Publishing disseminates widely the results of the Organisation's statistics gathering and research on economic, social and environmental issues, as well as the conventions, guidelines and standards agreed by its members.

OECD PUBLISHING, 2, rue André-Pascal, 75775 PARIS CEDEX 16
(42 2017 43 1 P) ISBN 978-92-64-28136-3 – 2017

www.ingramcontent.com/pod-product-compliance
Ingram Content Group UK Ltd.
Pitfield, Milton Keynes, MK11 3LW, UK
UKHW051459290926
15471UKWH00008B/1307

9 789264 28136